The Complete Homebrew Beer Book

The Complete Homebrew Beer Book

200 easy recipes
from ales & lagers to extreme
beers & international favorites

George Hummel

Robert
ROSE

For complete cataloguing information, see page 448.

Disclaimer
The recipes in this book have been carefully tested by our kitchen and our tasters.
To the best of our knowledge, they are safe and nutritious for ordinary use and users.
For those people with food or other allergies, or who have special food requirements
or health issues, please read the suggested contents of each recipe carefully and
determine whether or not they may create a problem for you. All recipes are used at
the risk of the consumer.

We cannot be responsible for any hazards, loss or damage that may occur as a
result of any recipe use.

For those with special needs, allergies, requirements or health problems, in the
event of any doubt, please contact your medical adviser prior to the use of any recipe.

Design and Production: Kevin Cockburn/PageWave Graphics Inc.
Editor: Susan Girvan
Copyeditor: James Gladstone
Indexer: Elaine Melnick
Illustrations: Kveta/Three in a Box
Cover Photography: Colin Erricson
Associate Photographer: Matt Johannsson
Prop Styling: Charlene Erricson

We acknowledge the financial support of the Government of Canada through
the Book Publishing Industry Development Program (BPIDP) for our
publishing activities.

Published by Robert Rose Inc.
120 Eglinton Avenue East, Suite 800, Toronto, Ontario, Canada M4P 1E2
Tel: (416) 322-6552 Fax: (416) 322-6936
www.robertrose.ca

Printed and bound in Canada

1 2 3 4 5 6 7 8 9 TCP 19 18 17 16 15 14 13 12 11

Contents

Part 1

Homebrewing for Beginners

Why would you make your own beer? Because it is a fun and rewarding hobby, as well as a great way to save some cash on an essential household commodity. Unlike home winemaking, you'll be making a beverage that is generally preferred fresh. Also unlike home winemaking, which relies on the quality of the grapes available, beer is process-driven. The quality of your beer depends on your skills as a brewer. As a bonus, you can vary your product to suit your taste by modifying the ingredients or adjusting the process. Whatever the result, if you like it, that's what counts. Welcome to the world of homebrewing!

The goal of this book is to get you brewing great beers as quickly as possible. To that end, Part 1 of this book is a crash course on basic ingredients and equipment—brewing gear—with a quick overview of the process from preparation, brewing and fermentation to bottling and conditioning. Then it's on to some simple recipes for ales to get you started.

Once you've mastered brewing basics, more details are provided at the beginning of Part 2 to help you refine your skills before you plunge into recipes for an exciting variety of beer styles.

What Ingredients Do You Need?

Beer is basically composed of four ingredients:

- water
- malt
- hops
- yeast

Each of these ingredients deserves your attention because each one has a profound effect on the taste of your beer. The ingredients are assembled during the initial brewing process—boiling the first three ingredients together and then leaving them to ferment with the fourth.

Water of Life

Over the years, various large commercial brewers have sung the praises of their water. (As one pioneering craft brewer pointed out, "If you were skimping on the malt and hops, you'd talk about the water, too!") Bottom line: whether it's commercial or homebrewed beer, water quality has a big influence on taste.

As a beginner brewer, ask yourself two questions about your tap water: Is it drinkable? Is it chlorinated? Logically, if you don't drink your tap water, don't use it to make beer! And, if your water is chlorinated and you wish to use it rather than purchasing water for brewing, you either have to filter it or you need to dechlorinate it. Otherwise, your beer will have a slightly medicinal taste, particularly if the water has been treated with chloramines, a longer-lasting water disinfectant.

Charcoal filters remove most of the chlorine or chloramines in water without affecting the minerals that make beer tasty, so you could run your brewing water through a charcoal filter. However, it would then be best to pre-boil the filtered water to eliminate any microbes. Bring the water to a rolling boil and boil it for one minute before proceeding with your brewing session.

If you decide to dechlorinate the water instead, follow the instructions for dechlorinating found on page 20. (You could do this before brew day and store the water in the refrigerator so you concentrate on brewing on the big day.) If you choose to buy bottled water for brewing instead, use bottled spring water. Never use distilled water because it lacks minerals.

As you become a more experienced brewer, you may want to consider other water-related issues such as mineral content (hardness or softness) and pH levels. But initially, particularly because you're using malt extracts, those are the concerns of the manufacturer of the malt extract, not yours—the manufacturers have compensated for these water-related factors.

For the recipes in this book, you need about 5.5 US gallons (21 L) of brewing water to make each 5 US gallon (19 L) batch of beer, and it's best to prepare (or purchase) it all at once. By the end of brew day, you will use most or all of the brewing water. "By the end of brew day" means that you do not need to work with the full amount of brewing water as you begin the brewing process on the stove. The recipes suggest you build your brew by starting with 3 US gallons (11 L) in the brew kettle and add the remaining brewing water before you begin the fermentation process.

Why build your brew using less than the full amount of brewing water? One US gallon (3.8 L) weighs 8.35 lbs (3.8 kg). As you brew, you work with a kettle of boiling water and several pounds (or kilograms) of additives. The lesser weight is easier to work with. (Bear in mind that you need enough water to dissolve the additives. Three US gallons (11 L)

Gallons: US vs Imperial

The recipes in this book show volume measures in US gallons (or fluid ounces) and their metric equivalents of liters or milliliters. A US gallon is smaller than an Imperial gallon. It is less than 4 liters (3.785 L), while an Imperial gallon is more than 4 liters (4.546 L). Do not use Imperial gallon measures for the recipes in this book. If you do, you will dilute your batch of beer by adding about 16% more water than is called for.

is the recommended minimum shown in all of the recipes.) Once you move the brew to the primary fermenter, add the rest of the brewing water.

Malt Extract and Other Sugars: How Sweet It Is

For beginners, malt extract is the backbone of your beer. It provides most of the sugars that are converted to alcohol by the yeast during fermentation. Malt extract also provides body, color, sweetness and enticing flavors and aromas such as caramel and toast. When you move on to recipes in Parts 2 and 3, you work with malted grains as well as malt extracts. They, too, supply body, color, flavor and aroma.

Other sugars, such as honey, molasses, raw cane sugars and rice syrup, are often added to the brew kettle as additional fermentables. There is one other important sugar: the priming sugar added just prior to bottling. This carbonates the beer while it ages in the bottle. The bottling process outlined in this book (page 31) calls for dextrose (corn sugar or brewing sugar).

Choosing Malt Extracts

Malt extracts come in two forms: syrup and powder. When a recipe calls for malt extract, use the syrup form. When a recipe calls for dry malt extract (DME), use the powdered form. The difference between these products is 20% water. You can easily substitute a DME for a syrup by using 20% less than the amount of syrup called for in the recipe. Conversely, you can switch a syrup for a DME by using 20% more than the amount of DME called for.

Some recipes simply specify the type of malt extract to use (for example, extra-light, light, amber, wheat or dark), but other recipes suggest a country of origin (for example, UK) or a specific brand (for example, Alexander's Sun Country). Malt extracts from a specified country of origin have certain characteristics that contribute to the particular brew. The brands of each country of origin or type have subtle differences. Your choice of malt extract affects the taste of your beer and should be recorded so you can establish which malt extracts contribute to the beers you enjoy.

If the brand of malt extract specified in the recipe is not available, substitute one that is a similar type. For example, some recipes specify Alexander's Sun Country Pale Malt Extract. That brand is particularly suited to those recipes, but if it is not available, substitute any brand of extra-light malt extract. If you can only find US or Coopers extra-light to make your English ale, it's not the end of the world.

Let's Go to the Hops

Hops are the bitter flowers of the hop plant that are added to beer for bitterness, flavor and aroma, although they also have preservative properties. The bitterness comes from the alpha acids in hops. The flavor and aroma properties are found in the oils in hops. These oils break down over time, so hops should be stored in the refrigerator to preserve them before use.

Hops are available in leaf, plug and pellet form. I recommend beginners use pellets because they are the easiest form of hops to work with and their oils break down the most slowly.

Hops are added at different stages in the brewing (boiling) process: bittering hops are added at the beginning; hops used for flavor are added partway through the boil; aroma hops are usually added at the end. Hops may also be added during fermentation, in a process known as "dry hopping." Each recipe specifies which hops to use, how much and when they should be added, but you can experiment with different varieties and amounts to suit your taste.

Bittering Hops

Bittering hops provide balance to the sweetness of the malt and other sugars in your brew. Bittering hops are added right after the malt extract has completely dissolved and your brew reaches a rolling boil, because the release of the alpha acids happens during the course of the full boil period (one hour).

Two things determine the degree of bitterness in beer: the actual quantity of bittering hops used and what is known as their alpha acid percentage, which is expressed as a percentage of the weight of the hops. The alpha acid percentage should be shown on the hop product's package.

Beer recipes call for bittering hops in alpha acid units (AAUs), which are a combination of weight and alpha acid percentage. The actual weight in ounces (grams) of bittering hops you use, usually for a 5 US gallon (19 L) batch, is determined by dividing the alpha acid percentage on the product's package into the number of AAUs called for in the recipe. The result tells you how many ounces (grams) of the product to use. For example: if the recipe calls for 10 AAUs of the bittering hops and your hops have an alpha acid of 10%, you would use 1 oz (28 g) of the hops ($^{10}/_{10}$). However, if your hops have an alpha acid of 5%, you would use 2 oz (56 g) of the hops ($^{10}/_5$).

Note that recipes in other sources may refer to Homebrew Bittering Units (HBUs). These are identical to AAUs.

Leave Some Things to the Professionals

You may see recipes that refer to IBUs or International Bittering Units. There are enough homebrew recipes on the market using AAUs or HBUs to ensure you can make great beer without tangling with IBUs.

Flavor and Aroma Hops

Flavor and aroma hops add flavorful and aromatic floral properties to beer thanks to the oils in the hops. These properties range from sweet and floral to piney, citrusy, woody or even somewhat skunky. These hops are simply measured by weight.

Yeastie Boys

Yeast is a type of fungus that lives on sugar and reproduces by cell division. As the yeast takes in sugars (such as maltose), it produces by-products that include carbon dioxide and alcohol. Thus, yeast is the workhorse of your home brewery. Just as bread would not be bread without the magic of yeast, your beer will not be beer without yeast to ferment its sugars into alcohol. This precious microorganism should be stored in the refrigerator until brew day to preserve its properties. The step of adding the yeast prior to fermentation is called "pitching the yeast."

There are two main categories of yeast: ale and lager. Ale yeast works at the top of the liquid in the primary fermenting bucket and works best at room temperatures; lager yeast works closer to the bottom of the primary fermenting bucket at cooler temperatures. In addition, there are two forms of yeast: dry and liquid. The dry form is the easiest to use. Dry yeast is simply scattered over the top of the wort after it has been transferred to the primary fermenter and stirred in. The ale recipes that follow this introductory text call for the dry form of yeast. The dry yeasts recommended in the recipes are produced by Fermentis, Danstar and Lalvin.

When you graduate to intermediate brewing techniques and the recipes in Parts 2 and 3, you are instructed (and encouraged) to use the liquid form of yeast. (That said, almost all recipes also have a dry yeast equivalent listed.) Using liquid yeast requires some advance preparation, but you will likely find that it produces a better-tasting brew. Liquid yeasts recommended in the recipes are made by Wyeast and White Labs. Both dry and liquid yeasts come in many, many strains. The strain or strains of yeast required for a particular brew are specified in each recipe.

Yeast produces sediment that is filtered out as the brew moves from one fermenter to another and into bottles, although some sediment remains and settles at the bottom of each bottle. You decant your beer off of this sediment as you pour it into

Brewing to Suit Your Tastes

As you build your experience as a brewer, start to adjust the bittering, flavor and aroma hops up or down to suit your taste. For each batch of each recipe, record what hops you used (and how much), how you rated the taste of the beer in terms of sweetness or bitterness and how you would like it to taste if you think it should change. Note each refinement until you get a batch of beer from that recipe that tastes exactly the way you want it to.

The Fart Factor

Some folks are "a little sensitive to the yeast" in bottle-conditioned beer. It's true that the yeast may create gastric disturbances with particularly offensive results. Usually, after you've enjoyed the beers for a few sessions, your system becomes used to the yeast. In the meantime, Beano® or a similar product may help. (Stepping into the other room won't hurt either.)

your glass. This is known as bottle-conditioned beer, and it is a living healthful drink.

Also Starring...

There are other ingredients you can add to your beer:

- **Irish moss:** a clarifying agent made from seaweed that helps eliminate cloudiness in the beer. Almost all recipes in this book include Irish moss.
- **yeast nutrient:** a vitamin pill for your yeast that helps it do its work. Most recipes in this book include yeast nutrient.
- **campden tablets:** If your water is treated with chloramines and is not filtered, you need to dechlorinate it with potassium metabisulfite (also known as campden tablets). (see page 20)

Equipping Your Home Brewery

In order to boil and ferment your ingredients into a fabulous homebrew, you need some brewing gear. That said, you don't need an extensive collection. Most items can be obtained from a homebrew supply store. Others may come from a kitchen supply store or may already live in your well-stocked home. Many of the items you need are sold as a "homebrew equipment kit." It is usually much more economical to buy a kit than it is to buy the components separately when you're starting out.

Brewing Gear and Supplies

Different stages of the homebrewing process require different gear, plus a few basic supplies beyond beer ingredients. The gear and supplies you need are listed in the Brewing Gear and Supplies table that follows.

Since proper cleaning and sanitizing are key to great-tasting beer, cleaning and sanitation supplies are listed first in the Brewing Gear and Supplies table, under the heading Preparation. Other stages that require brewing gear and supplies are brewing, fermentation and bottling. These stages are shown as separate headings in the table.

The Brewing Gear and Supplies table distinguishes between the essentials and the items that are optional but handy to have. A mini-glossary follows the Brewing Gear and Supplies table to describe the purpose of the more obscure items listed in the table (these items are marked by * in the table). The items usually found in a standard homebrew kit are highlighted in **bold** in the table.

Brewing Gear and Supplies

ESSENTIAL	OPTIONAL (BUT VERY HELPFUL)
Preparation	
• cleaner: either B-Brite™ or PBW™ from the homebrew store or Oxi-clean™ (Never use soap or detergent. Many contain perfumes, and they don't rinse off well enough.)	
• sanitizer (Use unscented household bleach or a no-rinse, commercial sanitizing product from the homebrew store.)	
Brewing	
• 5 to 8 US gal (19 to 30 L) brew kettle with a lid (This can be a stock pot made of stainless steel or enamel-coated steel—it must not be aluminum because aluminum could give your brew a metallic taste.)	• wort chiller* (for quick cooling of wort before yeast addition)
• large spoon of steel or food-grade plastic (Use a wooden spoon only if it is solely for brewing use. Do not use a wooden spoon post-boil because it is almost impossible to sanitize.)	
• thermometer: either a floating dairy or an instant-read probe that covers the temperature range from freezing to boiling	
• large plastic funnel with a straining screen	
• kitchen timer	
• kitchen or postage scale for weighing the ingredients	
• measuring cups	
Fermentation	
• **airlock**	
• **blow-off hose***	
• **6.5 to 7 US gal (25 to 27 L) primary fermenter** (This is usually a food-grade plastic pail but can also be a glass carboy; it should have a tight-fitting lid that has a drilled hole. You can also use this as your bottling bucket if it has a faucet.)	• press-apply adhesive thermometer strips for the fermenter; once mounted, the thermometer is permanently in place (recommended)

ESSENTIAL	OPTIONAL (BUT VERY HELPFUL)

Fermentation (continued)

ESSENTIAL	OPTIONAL (BUT VERY HELPFUL)
• **5 US gal (19 L) glass carboy** (to use as a secondary fermenter)	• carboy cleaning brush • carboy handle or hauler (Note: Don't rely on a carboy handle alone to support the weight of a full carboy. Hold it from below as well. To make the job easier, fit the carboy into a square plastic milk crate. The crate provides a way to lift it and protects the bottom.)
• **hydrometer*, with sample tube or jar** • turkey baster (dedicated to brewing) for taking samples	• The Thief (a handy device that simplifies taking samples and hydrometer readings)
• **racking cane***	• auto-siphon for ease in siphoning
• **rubber stopper**, drilled (to fit bucket lid or carboy)	
• **siphon hose**, clear, with a shut-off clamp, at least 5 ft (1.5 m)	• wort aerator*

Bottling

ESSENTIAL	OPTIONAL (BUT VERY HELPFUL)
• **6.5 to 7 US gal (24.6 to 26.5 L) bottling bucket, with a faucet** (This could double as your primary fermenter if you keep the faucet closed.)	• bottle draining tree
• 48 to 50 12-US fl oz (355 mL) or 24 to 26 22-US fl oz (650 mL) bottles, amber, long-necked, non-twist off, either recycled or new (You can also use old-style "swing top" bottles that have gaskets instead of caps. If using swing tops, remove gaskets and sanitize separately. Replace any that are old or cracked.)	• beer bottle brush • jet bottle washer • Avinator to pump sanitizer into bottles
• **bottler filler**	
• **bottle caps**	
• **bottle capper***	

Miscellaneous

ESSENTIAL	OPTIONAL (BUT VERY HELPFUL)
• brewing journal/notebook*	

Some of the items in the table may be unfamiliar. Here is what you need to know about the * items:

Blow-off hose: You may need this piece of gear during fermentation if the fermentation is so active that the brew starts to back up into the airlock. If you're brewing stronger beers or wheat beers, you may need it during the first day or two. In these cases, replace the airlock with the blow-off hose by inserting the hose into the hole in the stopper and submerging the other end of the hose in a small container— about 1 US quart (1 L) size—half-filled with sanitizing solution. The hose carries the excess foam into the container. Change the liquid in the container at least once daily or as it becomes fouled, or it could contaminate the beer. Once the blow-off subsides, re-install the airlock.

Bottle capper: This is a crimping tool used to put the flat caps on the bottles and seal your beer after bottling.

Brewing Journal: This is for your brewing notes, and putting the notes in a simple spiral-bound notebook is just fine. (Yes, throughout the brewing process, you are encouraged to make notes.) Every time you brew, keep a record of the process. At the beginning, you may note observations that you may later come to recognize as a normal part of the brewing process. Keeping detailed notes during your early batches helps you develop your understanding of the process. That said, there is basic information you should note in your journal every time you brew:
- recipe name, batch number and style of beer
- date brewed, date moved into secondary fermenter and date bottled
- size of batch (all recipes provided here make about 5 US gallons (19 L))
- malt extracts (type, brand, weight and time added)
- hops (type, alpha acid for bittering addition, weight and time added)
- any kettle sugars or other additives (type, weight and time added)
- yeast (type, brand/format)
- priming sugar (amount and type)
- Note any observations you make during the brewing, fermenting and conditioning processes. Notes on times and temperatures are helpful.
- Note any problems in the brewing process or steps that you would do differently next time.

- Most important, make tasting notes and date them so you track how the flavors unfold.

Hydrometer: The hydrometer helps you determine when fermentation is finished, and the brew is ready for bottling. It also helps you determine how strong your beer is. The hydrometer is the one item that intimidates beginner brewers because they're unlikely to have used anything like it before. Once you understand the purpose of the hydrometer, its use is straightforward.

A hydrometer measures the density (or specific gravity) of a liquid. Density is an expression of weight and volume. If you weigh one US gallon (3.8 L) of water, it weighs 8.35 lbs (3.8 kg) at 60°F (15.6°C). If you then add, for example, 6.6 lbs (3 kg) of fermentables to that water, the resulting wort immediately weighs more. However, when the yeast turns the fermentables into alcohol (which is less dense than water) and carbon dioxide (which is released), the density of the wort drops. This is the change you want to measure with your hydrometer as fermentation proceeds.

When you brew, you use the hydrometer to measure the specific gravity after the boil but before fermentation begins, and again (and again) during fermentation, until that process is finished. (For specific instructions on using the hydrometer, see page 26.)

Once fermentation has finished, the specific gravity reading stabilizes and should be the same for subsequent readings. Therefore, if you're not sure fermentation has finished, take specific gravity measurements for a few more days.

Each recipe in this book gives an estimated original gravity, so you have a benchmark reference.

Racking cane: "Racking" means moving your brew from one container to another, for example, from brew kettle to primary fermenter, from primary fermenter to secondary fermenter, from secondary fermenter to tertiary fermenter or bottling bucket.

The goal of racking is not just to move the brew. A second goal is to move the brew while leaving behind the sediment in the first container. A third goal of racking is to move the brew without adding oxygen (with one exception, noted in the description of the wort aerator on page 18), bacteria, wild yeast or other contaminants that could be floating in the air or resting on any surfaces with which the brew comes in contact.

Racking the brew is done primarily with the siphon hose. The racking cane is a device—usually made of plastic or sometimes stainless steel or copper—that attaches to one end of the siphon hose. It is basically a tube bent at an angle of roughly 100° with a small cup on it. The racking cane rests close to the bottom of the first container without disturbing the sediment lying there and picks up the liquid during racking (siphoning). The small cup sits on top of the sediment.

Wort aerator: First, what is "wort"? Wort is the term used for the liquid in the brew kettle once it's no longer just water and before it's beer. As hinted at in the comments about the racking cane, at one point in the brewing process, oxygen is welcomed. The boiling process releases a lot of the oxygen from the wort, and yeast needs oxygen for reproduction. Therefore, just this one time, when the wort is moving from the brew kettle to the primary fermenter, it needs added oxygen. The simplest ways to add oxygen are (1) stir the wort in the primary fermenter vigorously with a sanitized spoon or a sanitized whisk and (2) let the wort splash as it comes out of the siphon hose into the primary fermenter.

As you build your store of brewing gear, you may want to add a wort aerator. It fits onto the end of the siphon hose that goes into the primary fermenter and causes the wort to spray and splash as it goes into the bucket.

Wort chiller: A wort chiller is a handy heat-exchanger device used to rapidly drop the temperature of the wort to one that's suitable to activate yeast. There are two common styles of wort chiller: immersion and counter-flow.

An immersion chiller is a copper coil that is placed into the kettle. Cold water runs through it and out through a drain hose.

A counter-flow chiller has two circuits for liquid: one for the hot wort, encased by one for cold water. They run in opposite directions, hence the name counter-flow.

The immersion chiller is less expensive to buy or easier to build. It's also easier to clean, sanitize and use. It is, however, less efficient than the counter-flow chiller. Chillers come with easy-to-follow instructions.

Obtaining Your Brewing Gear and Supplies

Locate a quality homebrew supply retailer in your area for your purchases of brew gear and supplies. An added advantage to having a local retailer is that you can see, touch, smell and taste the brewing supplies you're getting. For example, you can sniff a particular hop variety, and, if it isn't to your liking, you can choose a different one on the spot. If you use a mail-order source for your brew gear and supplies, pick one that is only one or two shipping zones away to minimize expense and turnaround time on your orders. Also, it is best to buy mail order from brick-and-mortar shops rather than Internet-only retailers because they likely have more hands-on experience dealing with homebrewers. They also tend to be more reliable.

A local shop can also get you in touch with a local homebrew club, which is a valuable resource for any homebrewer. Both the shop and the club are great ways to learn how to troubleshoot and tweak your homebrew. If you lack a local shop and want to explore clubs in your area, contact and join the American Homebrewer's Association (www.beertown.org). Yes! They cover Canada, too.

Setting Up Your Work Space

For brewing
- You need a stove, a counter and a sink close at hand.
- You need a place to do your sanitizing and to lay out your sanitized gear.
- You need a place close to the stove that's clear for when you move your brew kettle on and off the stove.
- If you're not using a wort chiller, then you also need a big sink or laundry tub that holds enough cold water and ice to surround your brew kettle and cool its contents quickly.

Brewing involves large quantities of boiling, sticky liquid— sometimes on the move—so children and pets should be out of the way. And because it involves times when you need to move quickly, make sure there's no clutter on the floor or in your path.

For fermentation
- You need a spot where your fermenter can sit undisturbed (and out of the light, if it's not opaque) at the temperature specified in the recipe.
- You need to be able to easily access your fermenter to regularly check on fermentation progress, action in the air lock and the temperature.
- You need to choose a spot that accommodates moving the fermenter—often back to the brewing site—when racking is required.

Brew Day Basics

The following is a detailed look at the process described in the recipes.

For a typical brew day, plan on an afternoon's work to allow for set-up, brewing and clean-up. Your beer then ferments for seven to ten days. During that time you transfer the wort from the primary to the secondary fermenter. You spend another afternoon bottling your beer. The ales in the recipes that follow bottle-condition for three to six weeks. Then you enjoy the freshest beer that you ever had in your life!

Setting Up to Brew

- Assemble your brew kettle, measuring tools and spoons.
- Have the primary fermenter and fermentation gear at hand, along with your sanitation supplies, so you can sanitize the fermentation gear and fermenter while the brew is boiling.
- Use the scale or measuring cup to measure out the ingredients for use during the brewing session.
- Put your brewing water into the kettle.

Preparing Brewing Water from Municipal Tap Water

You can use filtered water or purchase spring water to use as your brewing water, but most North American homebrewers start with unfiltered municipal tap water, which is chlorinated. This water must be treated to remove the chlorine or chloramines to avoid any medicinal taste in your finished beer. All of the tap water you use in your brew must be treated.

Work With Less Water

As suggested earlier, at the beginning of your homebrew career, work with about 3 US gallons (11 L) of brewing water during the brewing process. Add the rest of your brewing water after the brew is transferred to the primary fermenter. (The remainder of the brewing water is often referred to as the "top-off" water.)

As you become more accustomed to how the ingredients react during the process—including the possibility that your brew will boil over—and you become more accustomed to handling and moving the brew kettle around, you may decide to work with the full amount during brewing. The recipes all specify starting with 3 US gallons (11 L) in the brew kettle, but working with the full amount is fine.

How to treat chlorinated water

- Put as much water as you can handle into your brew kettle on the stove.
- Dissolve $\frac{1}{8}$ tsp (0.5 mL) of potassium metabisulfite or one campden tablet in the water and bring it to a boil.

- When the water comes to a rolling boil, turn off the heat, and leave it to dechlorinate for 15 minutes.
- If you're preparing all of the water (or just the 2 US gallons (7.5 L) top-off portion of the water) before brew day, let the water cool to room temperature and transfer it into sanitized, sealable plastic jugs.
- Seal the jugs and refrigerate them until brew day. If you're using the water the same day, there is no need to cool and store the water.

Beginning the Brew
- Bring the brewing water to a boil.
- Remove the kettle from the burner, and add the malt extract, stirring vigorously to ensure it doesn't settle on the bottom of the kettle (where it could scorch and caramelize); stir until it dissolves completely. The mixture is now known as "sweet wort."

Managing the Boil
- Return the kettle to the stove, and bring the wort back to a boil. Just before the wort begins to boil, creamy foam (resembling beer head) begins to form. This is the "hot break," and it is critical that you not let this foam seal the top of the boiling wort. (If it does, it acts like a lid, heat builds up and the wort boils over. This is very messy.)
- Use your spoon to keep moving the hot break to one side of the kettle and keep the boil rolling, uncovered.
- As the wort boils, reduce the heat until you reach the lowest temperature setting that maintains a rolling boil, uncovered. (You may want to note this temperature setting in your brewing journal for future reference.)
- Stir in the bittering hops. Set the timer for 45 minutes, but keep an eye on the kettle to ensure the boil remains steady and manageable. (The complete boil is 60 minutes, with later additions going in for the final 15 minutes.)

Sanitizing the Fermentation Gear
Once the wort comes off the boil, everything it comes into contact with must be sanitized—this holds right up to the bottling session. Therefore, while the wort is on a steady boil for that 45 minutes, sanitize your primary fermenting gear.

Preventing Boil-overs

One potential pitfall confronting all home brewers is that the boil can get out of control very quickly. Be aware of how long it takes to reduce the heat under your brew kettle—electric stove elements cool much more slowly than elements on gas burners do.

Simply turning down the heat won't stop a boil-over that's building, even with a gas stove. You'll also need to have some ice cubes or a mister full of ice water at the ready to instantly lower the temperature of the wort. As soon as you suspect you're losing the battle with the hot break—the level of the wort is rising fast—toss in some ice cubes to lower the temperature in the kettle or mist the foam vigorously. Then turn down the heat. Keep moving the foam out of the way and keep lowering the heat until the wort can boil without foam sealing over the top.

How to sanitize

- Fill your primary fermenter bucket with water, as near to the top as possible without spilling over when the other gear is added.
- Add 2 US fl oz (60 mL) of unscented household bleach or use homebrew sanitizer according to the directions on the package.
- Add the following pieces of equipment to the fermenter bucket: airlock, stopper, racking cane, siphon hose, wort aerator (if you're using one), hydrometer, turkey baster and sample tube (or Thief), funnel, straining screen, floating thermometer and fermenter lid. (If you're using an instant-read thermometer, only sanitize the part that is in contact with the beer.) Flush sanitizer through the tubes to ensure that their interiors are sanitized. Leave these items to soak for 30 minutes if you're using bleach, or, if you're using commercial sanitizer, follow the instructions on the package. (Don't forget to check on your brew on the stove periodically.)
- As items are soaking, use a clean paper towel to wipe sanitizer on the parts of the bucket and lid that have not been immersed in the sanitizer.

Since the goal is to sanitize any items that will contact the beer after the boil, be cautious—sanitizing items that don't need to be sanitized is better than missing something that will contaminate your beer.

Rest assured that there are no known pathogens that grow in beer. You're not going to get sick. The concern here is that you will make a beer with "off" flavors. Contamination falls into two categories: either a slight off flavor that you can live with, even though it's not your best effort, or an intense off flavor that you can't drink!

Preparing the Cooling Bath or Wort Chiller

If you plan to use a sink or tub full of ice and salted water (a cooling bath) to cool your wort, get that ready during the boil. Also have an additional bag of ice on hand in case you need it. Or, get out the wort chiller, if that's what you're using instead of a cooling bath. Re-read the wort chiller instructions carefully.

Test the Cooling Bath

Test the cooling bath before your brewing session in order to establish how much water needs to be in there.

- Place the brew kettle full of water in the tub, and fill the tub with ice and water.

- Remove the full kettle.
- Note the level of water you actually need when the kettle is in there and displacing water. The cooling bath water should not go over the lid of the kettle, which would allow it to seep into the brew. The cooling bath water should only come up the sides of your brew kettle to within a couple of inches of the top or a couple of inches higher than the contents of the kettle.

Adding the Later Additions
- When the timer goes off at the end of 45 minutes, turn off the heat, move the kettle to a cool burner and add any late extract additions, flavor hops, kettle sugars, Irish moss or yeast nutrient called for in the recipe.
- Once you're sure these items have been thoroughly combined and perhaps dissolved, return the wort to the heat and boil for the final 15 minutes.
- After 15 minutes have elapsed, stir in the aroma hops (if called for in the recipe), cover the pot and remove it from the heat.

Cooling the Brew
At the end of the boil, the temperature of your brew must be brought down to a point that enables the yeast to get to work (less than 75°F/24°C). It's best to do this as quickly as possible, because once the temperature drops below about 160°F (71°C)—pasteurization temperature—bacteria and wild yeast are eager to move into your carefully prepared wort and start multiplying and contaminating your beer.

How to cool the wort
- Immerse the covered pot in your prepared cooling bath or use a wort chiller.
- If you use a cooling bath, stir the cooling bath occasionally to disburse the warming water that is close to the kettle.
- Add ice to the bath as the water warms.
- Monitor the temperature of the wort with a sanitized thermometer. (It is possible to get the wort too cool for the yeast, so remove it from the cooling bath when it's at 75°F (24°C) or just below.)

Preparing for Fermentation
- While the wort chills, clean your brewing spoon and sanitize it.
- When the wort is cooled, move the kettle from the cooling bath to a counter.

> ### Brewer's Tip
> Using salt water is more efficient than using fresh water because salt water has a lower freezing point, so you can use colder water. Depending on the size of your cooling bath, add $\frac{1}{2}$ to 1 cup (125 to 250 mL) of salt to the water in the bath.

- Use the sanitized spoon to stir the wort in one direction for about five minutes. Then cover it, and let it rest for 10 to 15 minutes. This is called the "whirlpool" in a commercial brewery. It causes the hops and trub (solids) to form a cone at the bottom of the kettle. The cone makes it easier for you to transfer the wort to the primary fermenter while leaving most of the sediment behind when you rack the beer.

Racking Your Brew

- Remove the items that were soaking in the fermenting bucket, resting the smaller items on the inside of the sanitized lid.
- Place the remaining items on a larger, sanitized surface.
- Drain the sanitizer out of the primary fermenter.
- Place the primary fermenter on the floor or on another surface that is lower than the brew kettle on the counter.
- Assemble the sanitized siphon hose and racking cane. If you purchased a wort aerator (and sanitized it), put it on the other end of the hose (the one that goes into the fermenter). (If you start the siphon with your mouth, insert the wort aerator after removing the mouthpiece.)
- Once the hose is assembled, siphon as much clear wort as possible into the primary fermenter. Place the end of the siphoning hose high in the primary fermenter to allow the wort to splash and take on air as it is transferred. (Keep the racking cane at the side of the kettle during siphoning to avoid sucking up the cone of trub in the center.)
- When the clear wort is drained, remove the racking cane and hose, and put the lid on the primary fermenter.
- Position your sanitized funnel and straining screen over the hole in the lid of the primary fermenter.
- Pick up the kettle and pour the trub (which contains the remaining green mud of leftover wort and spent hops) through the straining screen on the funnel. More wort will drain into the fermenter.
- Rinse the trub in the straining screen with hot brewing water (to release more sugars); don't let the trub get into the fermenter—simply rinse it with about a quart (liter) of brewing water that will drain into the fermenter.
- Add your remaining brewing water (the top-off water) until you have about 5.5 US gal (21 L) of wort in the primary fermenter.

Brewer's Tip

This is the only time in the brewing process when it's good to aerate (oxygenate) your wort. After this move to the primary fermenter, air is the enemy! Subsequent transfers should be made with minimal splashing to avoid taking in air.

The Art of Siphoning

Siphoning is all about gravity. The container holding the liquid being siphoned must be higher than the container into which the liquid is being siphoned. Practice siphoning with water to make sure you have mastered the technique before you siphon your beer.

Once the two containers are in place, and the siphon and racking cane have been assembled, there are a couple of ways to start the siphon.

1. Fill the sanitized racking cane and siphon hose assembly with water. Then place the racking cane in the wort in the upper container and the end of the siphon hose in the empty lower container to start the flow. OR
2. Place the racking cane in the wort in the upper container and, using a mouthpiece, suck on the hose to prime the siphon. Put the mouthpiece in your mouth and suck on the hose to start the flow. Then, use the hose clamp to stop the flow temporarily, remove the mouthpiece (attach wort aerator, if using) and lower the siphon hose into the lower container. (To make a mouthpiece, use a piece from a thinner hose that has an outer diameter equal to the inner diameter of the siphon hose such as a small section cut from the blow-off hose. Insert one end of the smaller tube inside the end of the larger tube.)

If, after practicing the first two methods, you're still not comfortable with the process of starting the siphon, invest in an auto siphon. It is a racking cane with a pump built around it. Place the mechanism halfway into the upper container. Pump once or twice to prime the pump and then gently place the racking tip on the bottom of the container. The unit comes with complete instructions. Remember that it also needs sanitizing.

Taking the First Readings

Check the temperature of the wort.

- Use your sanitized thermometer to check the temperature of the wort. Or, read the temperature on the adhesive strip thermometer on the outside of your fermenter. The temperature should be below 75°F (24°C). If the wort is still too warm, you need to cool the primary fermenter in a cooling bath; if the temperature is too cool (below 60°F/16°C), you need to warm it up with a warm water bath or a heating pad.

Take a reading of the specific gravity.

- Use the hydrometer to take a reading of the specific gravity (original gravity or OG) and record the reading in your brewing journal. This is the reference point for judging the completion of fermentation later in the process.

Density Readings of Brewing Liquids

If you float your hydrometer in a sample of plain water at 60°F (15.6°C), it will indicate that the water has a specific gravity of 1.000. When you add, for example, 6.6 lbs (3 kg) of malt extract to the water, the density will increase to around 1.040 or 1.045. As you add more ingredients, the density will continue to increase. Each recipe indicates an estimated Original Gravity for the batch as a guide.

Taking a Hydrometer Reading

- Always withdraw a sample of the brew to take a hydrometer reading. Take the reading in either a sample tube or jar (or in the Thief, if you've invested in one).
- Use a sanitized siphon hose or turkey baster, or the sanitized Thief, to get a big enough sample to fill three-quarters of the sample tube and float the hydrometer.
- You read the hydrometer where it breaks the surface of the sample. Usually, to keep the instrument easy to read, only the last two numbers of the gravity are shown. When you read past 1.000, the first number you'll see is 10; that means the density is 1.010; the next is 20 (1.020) and so on.
- Note the original gravity reading in your brewing journal and use the same technique to take later readings.
- Do not return the sample to the rest of your brew unless you were using a sanitized Thief.

Pitching the Yeast and Sealing the Fermenter

- Pitching the yeast: For dry yeast, simply open the packet and sprinkle the contents on the surface of the wort.
- Stir the brew vigorously with the re-sanitized spoon until the yeast is thoroughly combined.
- Sealing the fermenter: Put the lid on the primary fermenter.
- Fill the airlock with boiled water or sanitizer and put it in the stopper.
- Put the airlock and the stopper into the hole in the lid. Press down on the lid; if bubbles move through the airlock, the seal is good. If bubbles do not move through the airlock, check and retest the seal until they do.
- An improperly sealed fermenter results in an increased risk of contamination.

Primary Fermentation

- Move the sealed fermenter to a place that is in the range of 60–72°F (16–22°C) or as specified in the recipe.
- Protect the brew from light (which will oxidize your beer). A plastic bucket for primary fermentation provides sufficient protection from light. If you are using a glass carboy for primary fermentation, you must place it in a

dark place or cover the carboy completely with an opaque material to keep out the light.

- After 12 hours, if there are no bubbles coming through the airlock, open the fermenter to see if the fermenting process has begun. If you see foam (kräusen) on the top of the beer, fermentation has begun. If there is no kräusen and there are no bubbles coming through the airlock, stir the brew with a sanitized spoon. Check the temperature of the brew and warm or cool it as necessary. If there is still no sign of life after 24 hours, re-pitch the yeast.
- Once you've confirmed the start of fermentation, reseal the fermenter and allow the yeast to work undisturbed for the next few days.
- During primary fermentation, check the thermometer on the outside of the fermenter to confirm that the temperature remains below 75°F (24°C). Fermentation generates a bit of heat, and you may discover— particularly when brewing stronger beers—that the temperature of the beer during the first few days is warmer than the air around it. If this occurs, move the fermenter to a cooler location or use a water or ice bath for primary fermentation to keep the yeast comfortable.

Primary fermentation takes as little as a day or two, or as long as four or five days (even longer when you move into lagered and strong beers). Each recipe tells you about how long to expect primary fermentation to take, but your eyes tell you exactly how long it's taking. Fermentation is subtly affected by conditions at your particular home brewery, so take notes each day or each time you check so you can get a sense of how your very local facility works with different brews.

Primary fermentation is characterized by the rise, peak and eventual fall of the kräusen. The kräusen indicates that the yeast is at work and its fall indicates when the yeast has finished converting most of the sugars to alcohol and carbon dioxide. When the kräusen has peaked and begun to fall, or if you've missed that point, and the marks on the inside of the primary fermenter show that the level has already fallen, it is time to rack the beer to the secondary fermenter.

Secondary Fermentation

- Sanitize the secondary fermenter, the racking cane and the siphon hose (remember, you're not aerating this time). The move to the secondary fermenter leaves behind the nasty looking residue that has been settling in the bottom of the primary fermenter.

Brewer's Tip

It is most important to maintain a proper temperature during the first three or four days of primary fermentation—that is when most of the beer's flavor profile is created, courtesy of the yeast.

Brewer's Tip

If the brew is not visibly active and you want to check on the level of the kräusen without opening your opaque primary fermenter, put a bright light on one side of the fermenter and look through the fermenter from the other side. You should be able to see the "high water" mark made by the kräusen. As an alternative, you could briefly remove the airlock and peek through the hole in the lid to find out what's happening with a minimum of disturbance.

Troubleshooting During Primary Fermentation

My Original Gravity reading is not the same as the one cited in the recipe.
There could be a couple of explanations for this.

1. Often, when topping off your beer with cold water, the heavier part of the liquid (the wort) settles to the bottom of the fermenter. Give the brew a good stir and take another sample.
2. Hydrometers are typically calibrated at 60°F (16°C), and your reading will be off by .003 to .005 for every 10°F (12°C) the wort temperature is above that benchmark. Avoid having to do the math to compensate for the temperature difference by cooling the sample (not the wort itself) down to 60°F (16°C). If numbers are still off, check the accuracy of the hydrometer with 60°F (16°C) water. It should read 1.000. If that reading is off by a few degrees, note the discrepancy and take that into account in future calculations. If the reading is way off, replace the hydrometer.

   Remember to recheck the device periodically. If the discrepancy varies, the glue that holds the paper with the numbers on it has failed. Replace the hydrometer. Only once in my many years in the homebrew business have I seen defective malt extract as the problem when the OG was way off. The problem was obvious, however, because the product was watery.

It's 24 hours after racking, and fermentation has not started.
If there is no sign of action after 12 hours, move the fermenter to a warmer spot and aerate it vigorously with a sanitized spoon or whisk. If, after ensuring the temperature of the fermenter is suitable for fermentation (below 75°F/24°C) and/or stirring the batch (with a sanitized spoon) to aerate it some more, there is still no action after 24 hours, it's time to re-pitch the yeast.

   Prepare the specified yeast according to the package directions, open the fermenter and sprinkle or pour in the yeast; stir vigorously (with a sanitized spoon) to distribute the yeast and aerate the brew. Reseal the fermenter with lid, stopper and airlock.

Fermentation is so active that the foam is getting into the airlock.
This is when you use the blow-off hose. Replace the airlock with the sanitized blow-off hose by inserting the hose into the hole in the stopper and submerging the other end of the hose in a 1 US quart (1 L) container half-filled with sanitizing solution. The excess foam should travel through the hose into the container. Change the liquid in the container at least daily or as it becomes fouled, it could contaminate the beer. Once the action in the container subsides, reinstall the airlock.

The fermenter is getting too warm.
As mentioned, most ales want to ferment between 60 and 75°F (16 to 24°C). The recipe you use indicates the preferred temperature range.

If you need to lower the temperature of the brew during primary fermentation, try the following tactics. (You can also use these tactics during secondary fermentation and conditioning.)

- Use a water or ice bath. Place your fermenter pail in a tub of cold water. That should provide a 5 to 10 degree drop in temperature.
- Wrap the fermenter in a towel and allow it to wick water out of a tub of cold water and surround the fermenter with chilling water. A small fan blowing on the towel aids further evaporation and cooling.
- Take some old plastic soda bottles, fill them three-quarters full of water and freeze them. Place a couple of the bottles in a water bath. Rotate in fresh frozen bottles as the ice melts.

The consequences of the brew getting too warm range from slight off-flavors to ruined, depending on the beer and the temperature. This can't be fixed, so it's best to keep an eye on the temperature. Most beers do just fine at room temperature, but for warm-weather brewing, consider brewing Belgian-style beers that enjoy higher temperature fermentation.

The fermenter is too cool.
Conversely, as the cool weather approaches, that cool basement floor that kept your beer happy all summer may become too cold for ale-yeast fermentation. Fermentation may be sluggish or stop altogether. Be sure you're fermenting above 60°F (16°C). You may need to move your fermenter to a warmer part of your home. Or consider brewing a cold-fermenting lager beer. (You can also use these tactics during secondary fermentation.)

The beer is covered with nasty looking stuff!
As your beer ferments, a foam called kräusen forms on the beer. It can look a little nasty. If you sneak a peek and you see that the beer is covered with an unpleasant looking foam flecked with green (spent hops) and brown (tannin from the malt) bits—don't panic! If there is kräusen on the beer, all is well—the yeast is hard at work.

The beer is not covered with nasty looking stuff!
If you sneak a peek after a day and you don't see that the beer is covered with kräusen, FIRST check for a scummy ring an inch or two (two to five centimeters) above the surface that would indicate that the kräusen has risen and fallen. (This means the primary ferment has finished.) If there is no ring, move the fermenter to a warmer spot and stir vigorously with a sanitized spoon or whisk. If that doesn't get fermentation started by the next day, re-pitch a fresh packet of yeast into the beer and hope for the best. (Re-pitching yeast is the kind of thing you should note in your brewing journal.) If there is an off-flavor in the beer at the end of your labors, the lag in starting fermentation is likely the culprit.

There's a scummy green-brown ring above the surface of the beer.
If you've seen no activity and you open the fermenter to see this ring, the beer has most likely fermented. Take a reading with your hydrometer to check for a drop in the specific gravity, if you're not sure. Either it fermented out when you weren't looking, or your fermenter wasn't completely sealed.

- Rack the beer into your secondary fermenter (usually a glass carboy) by putting the end of the hose on the bottom of the secondary fermenter to minimize aeration during the transfer. The beer should flow steadily and gently, instead of spraying and splashing as it did the first time.
- Gently rest the tip of the racking cane on the sediment in the bottom of the primary fermenter, trying not to disturb it. If a bit of sediment makes its way over during the transfer, don't worry, since you rack the beer again at the end of fermentation.
- If your secondary fermenter is not filled to the base of its neck, add brewing water to complete the volume.
- Fill the airlock with sanitizer or boiled water and put the stopper and airlock into the opening of the carboy.
- Cover the glass carboy to protect it from light, which can oxidize the hops and give the beer a cardboard-like or skunky flavor. The beer finishes fermenting in the carboy over the next few days, and it clarifies and begins to mellow.

Secondary Fermenting for Advanced Brewers

- Adding fruit and flavor: In your more advanced brewing sessions, you may add ingredients, such as fruit or flavors, when the beer is transferred to the secondary fermenter. This technique will be explained in Part 3.
- Dry hopping: You may add hops when activity in the secondary fermenter has slowed. When hops are added at this stage (known as dry hopping), allow another week or two for the beer to clear. Sometimes when pellet hops are added, your beer may foam for a little while. No, it didn't start to re-ferment; it's just acting as a nucleation point for dissolved CO_2 in the beer. Use a blow-off hose briefly, if needed.

Completing Fermentation

Again, the recipe gives you a rough idea of how long it takes to finish fermentation, but the proof is in your observations. When the bubbling in the air lock occurs less than once every 90 seconds, the fermentation is slowing down. As described in the previous section, this is the time when advanced brewers add a few more ingredients. For beginners, it's simply time to take more hydrometer readings. While the final gravity readings should be two-thirds to three-quarters of the original gravity reading (recorded in your brewing journal), the fact that the hydrometer readings are unchanged over the course of several days is what tells you that the beer has finished fermenting and is ready for bottling. (If the readings are still changing, wait until they are stable.)

You do not need to rush to bottle the beer. It can sit for up to four weeks before bottling without harm, as long as the airlock doesn't dry out. (A dry airlock sets your brew up for the disaster of contamination.) Beers sitting longer than three months should be re-yeasted with a fresh packet of yeast at bottling time.

Preparing the Bottles

- Assemble enough bottles for your batch of beer: 48 to 50 12-US fl oz (355 mL) or 24 to 26 22-US fl oz (650 mL) bottles or a combination of the two sizes or other sizes that can accommodate your batch of beer, with sufficient caps. (It's a good idea to have a few more bottles on hand than you think you need in case of mishaps or more than two cases of wort.)
- If you've purchased new bottles, sanitize them. If you're reusing bottles, clean them thoroughly. (Your best bet is to clean them thoroughly as soon as they've been emptied. This saves a lot of scrubbing and grumbling when you're ready to bottle a new batch.)
- Rinse (or scrub) and de-label bottles that you're reusing. Soak them in a sink full of hot water with 2 US fl oz (60 mL) unscented household bleach per 5 US gallons (19 L), or homebrew cleanser OR non-detergent ammonia to loosen the label glue. (CAUTION: Never mix bleach and ammonia together when doing anything, anywhere! The combination can result in toxic gases and/or explosions.)
- Use vinegar to help remove labels that do not come off easily. By far the best product for getting labels off is B-Brite™ (Beer Brite), which is available from most homebrew suppliers. If high-gloss or foiled stock labels were used, slice up the labels with a razor knife prior to soaking; it makes them a little less difficult to remove. (Because it can be difficult to remove labels, most homebrewers don't label their own beer, except when it's for gifts or a special occasion.)

Racking, Priming and Bottling

Once your beer has finished secondary fermentation, it's on to the next milestone in the process: Bottling Day!

- Once again, you will be racking the brew—this time into the sanitized bottling bucket. To do this, the secondary fermenter

Brewer's Tip

Re-yeasting a batch that has sat with stable hydrometer readings for more than three months should be done with a package of the same yeast used during fermentation. Simply hydrate dry yeast or prepare the yeast according to the package instructions and gently stir it into the batch after racking it into the bottling bucket.

must be higher than the bottling bucket; if you have to move the secondary fermenter, let the remaining sediment settle for a few hours while you're getting your equipment ready.

- Sanitize the bottles and caps, as well as the racking cane, siphon hose, bottle filler and bottling bucket. Once again, use commercial sanitizer according to the package directions or use unscented household bleach—2 US fl oz (60 mL) to 5 US gallons (19 L) of water and soak for 30 minutes.

- You could use the bottling bucket to hold the sanitizer for the smaller items inside the bucket, and then run sanitizer through the siphon hose, bottle filler and bottling faucet.

- Line the bottle case with paper towels or newspaper, and allow the bottles to drain upside down in their case. (A bottle tree is an alternative for drying the bottles.)

- When the bottles are ready to be filled (and you're ready to fill them), place them somewhere lower than the bottling bucket, in a tray or sink that can catch any overflow during the filling process.

- Rack the beer from the secondary fermenter into the bottling bucket. Make sure you close the faucet of the bottling bucket before you start. (Everyone makes that mistake at least once!) As before, your goal is to transfer the beer with a minimum of aeration, so have the end of the siphon hose on the bottom of the bottling bucket. If your batch is less than 5 US gallons (19 L), add brewing water to take it up to that volume.

- As the beer transfers to the bottling bucket, bring one cup (250 mL) of water to a boil in a small saucepan. Dissolve 5 oz (140 g) of dextrose in the water and heat it until it boils again. Allow the liquid, now known as priming solution, to cool.

- Once the transfer to the bottling bucket is complete, pour the priming solution into the beer and give the brew a gentle stir with the racking cane. At this point, the beer is flat—there are no bubbles. If you taste the beer at this point, it tastes a little thin, and the flavors may be a little rough because they haven't matured. Don't jump to any conclusions about your brewing skills based on those flavors. The priming sugar causes the beer to re-ferment after bottling. This in-bottle fermentation is what carbonates the beer and completes flavor development.

- After stirring in the priming solution, attach the siphon hose to the faucet on the bottling bucket and put the bottle filler on the opposite end of the hose. If your bottling bucket does not have a faucet, just use the sanitized racking cane, siphon hose and bottle filler to transfer the beer into the bottles.

- Again, the bottling bucket needs to be higher than the bottles for siphoning to work. I like to place my bucket on a small stool on the kitchen counter, next to the kitchen sink, which is filled with bottles. A friend likes to place his bottling bucket on the counter and the bottles on the open door of the dishwasher below.
- Fill each bottle to the very top; when you remove the bottle filler it leaves about 1 to 1.5 in (2.5 to 3.8 cm) of space, which is just what you're looking for.
- Loosely place a bottle cap on top of each bottle and proceed until all are filled. Then take each bottle and crimp the cap in place with the capper.

Conditioning Your Beer

- Allow the beer to condition (sit) with the bottles in an upright position to allow sediment to settle in the bottom. Again, keep it in the dark.
- Check the conditioning after three or four weeks by holding a bottle up to the light. If you can see the tan sediment of yeast on the bottom of the bottle, then the beer is beginning to carbonate.
- Stronger beers (those with a higher original gravity) take longer to carbonate, and beer stored at cooler temperatures also take longer to carbonate (but will have a smoother flavor). Ales should be stored at a temperature of at least 60°F (15.5°C) and not more than 75°F (24°C).
- If early samples indicate that carbonation is light, don't panic—it picks up a bit as the beer continues to condition. The flavor of the beer evolves as the brew conditions. Flavors of early samples that are a little strong should mellow as the beer conditions. (As the beer conditions, if it begins to become over-carbonated, refrigerate the remainder of the batch.)
- Judgment of the flavor is subjective, but, generally speaking, pale ales are best enjoyed fresh—that is, within three to four weeks of bottling. Porters and stouts may only knock your socks off with flavor after three months of conditioning. Strong Belgian ales might want six to nine months to really taste perfect. Keep notes in your journal so you'll have a clue about what to expect the next time around. Never be too quick to judge a beer unless you think it's been contaminated. It's often a question of time.

Brewer's Tip

Having a helper can make the bottling process go a whole lot faster. If one person fills the bottles while the other caps them, you can bottle a batch in no time.

Storing Your Beer

Once the beer has fully conditioned, that is, it's reached a point of flavor and carbonation that you enjoy, store it at room temperature or in the refrigerator for a longer shelf life. The warmer the storage temperature, the more quickly the beer will oxidize and develop a cardboard-like or skunky flavor.

The shelf life of beer varies. Stronger beers and hoppy beers have a longer shelf life than weaker beers. The beauty of this hobby is the enjoyment of really fresh beer. Normal strength beer at cellar temperatures should have a shelf life of three to six months. It lasts longer if it is refrigerated.

Sometimes, as beer is stored, a contamination issue can emerge. If the beer picked up a bug during your brewing process, it might not be noticeable at first. As the beer conditions, however, it could rear its ugly little head. The best advice is, if, after a couple of months, the flavor seems to be going downhill, put the remaining beer in the fridge and drink it as soon as possible. Or use it in that chili or stew recipe that calls for a bottle or two of brew!

Pouring and Enjoying Your Brew

You may think this is the one part of the process that you fully understand, and you're likely right. But, having paid your dues making your own beer, take some steps to really reap the rewards. Set aside a little "me time." Chill one down. Serving temperature is very important when enjoying a beer. Large commercial brewers promote the notion of serving beer at tongue-numbing temperatures, almost near freezing. There's a reason for that: if you allowed the beer to warm a little, you could actually taste it and it may be just a little disappointing.

The fine beer that you make should be served at a proper temperature. Lagers and wheat beers should be served at 40 to 45°F (4.5 to 7°C); ales should be served at 50 to 55°F (10 to 13°C). If an ale has been in the refrigerator, allow its temperature to come up a bit before serving it.

People may tell you, "My grandpa was in England after WWII, and they serve their beer warm there!" This is hardly the case. The British serve their ales at cellar temperature. You wouldn't walk into a 55°F (13°C) house and say, "It's warm in here!" An ale really opens up at this temperature.

Pop open a beer. Gently pour it in one continuous motion into a glass. Keep an eye on the neck of the bottle. As you near the bottom, you'll see the yeast sediment moving toward the neck. Stop pouring before it comes out. If you're using large bottles, pour it into glasses all at once, or decant the beer into a pitcher. You'll leave maybe a sip or two of beer behind. Should some sediment find its way into your glass, it's rich in B vitamins and good for you. In fact, Bavarian Hefeweizens are served "mit hefe" (with the yeast). In that case, roll the bottle between your hands before serving, and pour the yeast into the glass with the beer to cherish it as a health tonic.

Enhancing Your Brewing Talents

In the name of building your skills as a brewmaster, do your homework: drink as much beer as you can. Research is important!

If you've led a sheltered beer life, you'll probably want to try commercial examples of unusual beers before you brew up a couple cases for the house. When you try any new beer, take notes. It's just as important to note what you like about a beer as it is to note what you don't like. Don't just push a beer away saying, "I don't like it!" Think about it. What don't you like? Is it too bitter or too sweet? Too thick or too thin?

In addition, try a few examples of a style—for example Belgian or Bock or a fruit beer—because there can be some variation among brewers. It's also possible with niche beers to pick up an example that is past its prime. Needless to say, it isn't fair to base your impressions on a style of beer that isn't as the brewer intended.

Remember that seasonality applies to beer enjoyment. If you have just finished cutting the lawn, you might enjoy a cream ale or a wheat beer. If you have just finished shoveling several feet of snow off the walk, a more robust beer like a barley wine or an Imperial stout will ward off the winter chill. Therefore, plan seasonality into your brewing. Think about when you want to drink a type of beer and work your way backward to figure out the time that's best to brew the beer.

As a rule of thumb, brew your summer ales in spring; strong winter beers and fall beers should be brewed in the summer (along with beers made with fresh fruit—see Part 3); normal winter beers are brewed in the fall; and then, herald the coming of spring with those beers brewed at the end of a long winter such as stouts and maibocks. (Check the recipe sections for examples of all of these styles.) With a little planning you'll enjoy the right beer in the right season.

Also remember that there's a big difference between saying, "This beer is bad." and "This beer is not to my taste."

Learn to appreciate the difference between what you don't like and what is not well made. Just because you don't like opera, doesn't mean it isn't great art!

Don't be afraid to try new flavors. The late, great beer writer Michael Jackson used to complain about people who'd say, "I don't like dark beer."

"Which ones have you tried?" he would ask them. When they'd reply "None," because, as they said, they didn't like dark beer, he'd dispense a sound tongue lashing, ending with, "Why don't you go try a few, and then get back to me?"

Don't be the pouting kid with the Brussels sprouts at the dinner table! Give new styles a try; you might find something that you like.

I always like to tell the story of a keg of my spiced Belgian Grand Cru. It arrived at a party of friends that was a mixed group of beer lovers and consumers of mainstream swill and their unenthusiastic partners. Many of the significant others of the swill drinkers became enamored of the spicy elixir.

They said, "I don't usually like beer [i.e., the stuff their husbands drink], but this is really good!" People without exposure to good, fresh beer often discover that it's boring mainstream beer that they don't care for. A beer with flavor may be a different story.

Also remember, as with food, the more flavors that go into something, the fewer people it appeals to. But the folks who like the result really like it. Flavor creates passion. So be passionate about your beer.

If you're fond of a particular kind of beer, do a little espionage. Check the packages, flyers, websites and reviews of the beer. Often you'll be able to glean enough information about its ingredients to help you to make the correct choices for your homebrewed version. For example, if you discover that your favorite pale ale gets its citrusy aroma from Cascade hops, then you'll want Cascade hops in your pale ale. Or, you may find out the brewers of your favorite beer use particular grains or strains of yeast. Conversely, if you don't like that character in a beer, then avoid the ingredients that make it the way it is. All this information helps you decide what to use in your brew.

You've had the crash course introduction. Now, let's make some beer! The first four recipes are relatively simple, but they've been laid out in more detail than you will need once you progress in your brewing career. The next few recipes are only slightly more complex. Once you've got the basics down, in Part 2, you'll be able to learn more of the refinements and get a lot more creative.

Brew Day Process Summary

The following tips and techniques have been condensed from the detailed look at the brew day process found on pages 20 to 36.

❶ Preparing Chlorinated Water for Brewing

Municipal tap water must be dechlorinated before it's used for brewing. If you prepare the water before brew day, store it in the refrigerator in sanitized, sealed containers.

6 US gal	municipal tap water	23 L
⅛ tsp	potassium metabisulfite (1 campden tablet) per kettle-full of water	0.5 mL

1. Fill brew kettle with half or all of the water needed.
2. Add potassium metabisulfite to water, stirring to dissolve it.
3. Bring water to a rolling boil; turn off heat.
4. Allow water to rest for 15 minutes as it dechlorinates.

If you know that your water has been treated with chlorine rather than chloramines, you can bring the water to a boil and boil it vigorously for 15 minutes to remove the chlorine. Chloramines are not broken down by boiling.

❷ Preventing Boil-overs

Have a bowl of ice cubes or a mister full of chilled or ice water on hand. (This water does not need to be dechlorinated brewing water.)

1. Move the foam to the side of the boil as it builds.
2. If the foam seals the boil and the wort level starts rising, toss in some ice cubes or mist the foam diligently (and keep moving it to the side).
3. Once the level has stopped rising, turn the heat down. Lower the temperature *in* the kettle before lowering the temperature *under* the kettle.

❸ Sanitizing Fermentation Gear (and Everything Else)

Sanitize all gear and containers used in primary and secondary fermentation and bottling just prior to the relevant stage in the process.

1. Place items such as the airlock, stopper, racking cane, siphon hose, mouthpiece (if using), aerator (if using), hydrometer, turkey baster or Thief, funnel with straining screen, floating thermometer, bottler filler and bottle caps (when bottling) and fermenter lid into primary fermenter or bottling bucket. Fill the container with water. If sanitizing a glass carboy, fill it with water.
2. Add 2 US fl oz (60 mL) unscented household bleach to the water in the container and let sit for 30 minutes. (If using homebrew sanitizer, use it according to the package instructions.)
3. Run sanitizer through anything the brew will pass through: siphon tube, racking cane, mouthpiece, bottle filler or faucet (when bottling). Wipe sanitizer on parts that cannot be immersed.

4. Drain sanitizer out of the container. Place sanitized gear on a sanitized counter until ready to use.

5. Keep a small amount of sanitizer available to re-sanitize items such as spoons that are used during the brewing process.

④ Using the Hydrometer

Always withdraw a sample of the brew and take the reading in either a sample tube or jar or in the Thief.

1. Sanitize turkey baster for withdrawing the sample or sanitize the Thief, which can both withdraw the sample and float the hydrometer. If using the turkey baster, you also need a sample tube or jar large enough to float the hydrometer.

2. Withdraw a wort sample big enough to fill three-quarters of the sample tube and float the hydrometer.

3. Place the hydrometer in the sample and read it where it breaks the surface. Only the last two numbers of the gravity are shown. When you read past 1.000, the first number you'll see is 10; that means the density is 1.010; the next is 20 (1.020) and so on.

4. Record the gravity reading in your brewing journal and use the same technique to take later readings. Do not return the sample to the rest of your brew unless you used a sanitized Thief.

⑤ Preparing and Using the Cooling Bath

If you're cooling your brew with the ice-and-saltwater bath, prepare it while the boil is on and the fermentation gear is soaking in sanitizer.

1. Fill the tub with enough water to surround your kettle at or above the level of the beer inside it when the kettle is in the tub (in other words, allow for displacement of the water).

2. Add ½ to 1 cup (125 to 250 mL) of salt and stir to dissolve.

3. Add ice to bring the temperature of the salt water down.

4. At the end of the boil, remove the kettle from the stove, cover it and put it in the saltwater bath, ensuring that the salt water doesn't get into the brew.

5. Add ice to the bath, and keep the warm water around the kettle on the move to assist in cooling.

6. After 20 minutes, check the wort temperature with the sanitized thermometer. The temperature goal is around 75°F (24°C) or as per yeast instructions. Ideally, you should bring the temperature down within 30 to 45 minutes. At that point, the beer can be prepared for racking into the fermenter.

⑥ Racking Tips

Racking (transferring) the beer from one container to another is all about siphoning, which is all about gravity. The container holding the liquid being siphoned must be higher than the container into which the liquid is being siphoned.

Key points to remember:

- sanitize all gear and containers
- when racking the beer into the primary fermenter, aerate the wort

- when racking the beer into the secondary fermenter or the bottling bucket, *avoid* aerating the wort
- when racking the beer at any time, leave behind as much sediment as possible

❼ Fermentation Tips (also see pages 28 to 29)

Both primary and secondary fermentation work best when:
- the bucket or carboy is sealed properly (A proper seal includes a tight-fitting lid, a stopper and a properly installed airlock.)
- the beer in the bucket or carboy is protected from light to avoid oxidation (use an opaque plastic bucket as your primary fermenter; when using a glass carboy, put it in a dark place or cover it completely with an opaque blanket)
- the bucket or carboy is in the proper ambient temperature (for the ale recipes in Part 1, the proper temperature is below 75°F (24°C))

Check for bubbles: At the start of fermentation, check for bubbles coming through the airlock; this tells you fermentation has begun. If you don't see bubbles within 12 hours of starting fermentation, check the temperature and take a look inside. If the temperature is within the range and no air bubbles are coming through the air lock, stir the brew vigorously with a sanitized spoon to add more air. If there is still no action 24 hours after brew day, pitch a new packet of yeast. (Reseal the fermenter and double check the seal each time you check your brew.)

Monitor temperature: Monitor the fermenter's temperature periodically during the fermentation period. If things get too cool, fermentation could stop; move the fermenter to a warmer place. If it gets too warm, cool things down with a water bath or by wrapping the fermenter in a cold, wet towel.

❽ Racking, Priming, Bottling and Conditioning

Once the hydrometer readings confirm that fermentation is complete, your brew is ready to bottle. This step adds some sugar to carbonate the beer as it conditions in the bottle.

1 cup	brewing water	250 mL
5 oz	dextrose (corn sugar) for priming	140 g

1. Clean and sanitize the bottles using your standard sanitizing procedure. Sanitize caps, racking cane, siphon hose, spoon, bottle filler and bottling bucket. Run sanitizer through bottling faucet.

2. In a small saucepan, bring brewing water to a boil. Add dextrose. Return mixture to a boil and stir to dissolve dextrose. Remove from heat and cover. Cool to room temperature.

3. Gently rack the beer into the bottling bucket, leaving sediment behind and being careful not to aerate. Gently add priming solution. Using a sanitized spoon, stir the beer gently to ensure even distribution of priming solution.

4. Using bottling faucet or siphon and bottle filler, fill bottles to top; 1 to 1.5 in (2.5 to 3.8 cm) of space remains when filler is removed. Cap bottles securely.

5. Store bottles upright in cool, dark place to allow for carbonation and settling of sediment.

6. After 3 to 4 weeks, hold a bottle to the light to check that sediment is settling. Unless otherwise indicated in the recipe, sample some brew! Note the date, flavor and level of carbonation each time you sample to compare as it ages.

The recipes on the following pages are for ales. You will follow a standard brewing process using malt extract syrups and dry yeast for each of them. The variation is in the ingredients and when you add them.

Ales for Absolute Beginners

Irish (Red) Amber

This is the classic pub ale from the Emerald Isle. It's an easy drinking, copper-colored ale. It's neither too bitter nor cloyingly sweet. Smithwick's and Murphy's Amber are the most widely available commercial examples of the style.

Estimated Original Gravity: 1.047

Equipment

- **brew kettle**
- **fermentation gear (page 14)**

If you are a first-time brewer, read pages 8 to 36 thoroughly before you begin. Consult the summaries on pages 37 to 39 for details on preparing chlorinated water for brewing, preventing boil-overs, sanitizing fermentation gear, using the hydrometer, preparing and using the cooling bath, racking, checking fermentation, and priming, bottling and conditioning your beer.

5.5 US gal	brewing water (page 37)	21 L

Malt Extracts

4 lbs	UK amber malt extract syrup (such as Mountmellick Irish Unhopped Amber or other UK malt)	1.8 kg
1 lb	any UK brand amber dry malt extract	450 g

Bittering Hops

6 to 7 AAUs	UK hops (such as Bramling Cross, East Kent Golding, Fuggle or other)	6 to 7 AAUs

Aroma Hops

1 oz	UK hops (such as Bramling Cross, East Kent Golding, Fuggle or other), divided in half	28 g

Later Additions

1 lb	Demerara sugar (or turbinado or unrefined brown cane sugar)	450 g
1 tsp	Irish moss	5 mL
1 tsp	yeast nutrient	5 mL

Yeast

1 pack	Fermentis S-04 or Danstar Nottingham ale yeast	1 pack

1. In a brew kettle, bring at least 3 US gal (11 L) brewing water to a boil. Remove from the heat, add both malt extracts and stir until dissolved completely. Do not allow the extracts to settle and scorch.
2. Return kettle to the burner and increase the heat until the liquid (wort) begins to boil. Using a spoon, clear any foam to one side. Do *not* allow it to seal the boil. Reduce the heat until a rolling boil can be maintained without foam buildup.
3. Add the bittering hops, stirring to combine. Boil for 45 minutes, uncovered. Monitor to prevent boiling over.
4. Meanwhile, prepare the fermentation gear (see page 37) and cooling bath (see page 38) or wort chiller.
5. After 45 minutes, remove the kettle from the heat and add half of the aroma hops, the sugar, Irish moss and yeast nutrient. Stir to ensure that the sugar and nutrient are dissolved. Return the kettle to the burner and bring back to a rolling boil. Boil for 15 minutes; add the remainder of the aroma hops, turn off the heat and cover.

6. To cool the brew, place the covered kettle in the prepared cooling tub or use a wort chiller according to directions. Cool to yeast-pitching temperature, 75°F (24°C), within 30 to 45 minutes.

7. While the wort is cooling, clean and sanitize the brewing spoon. When the wort has cooled, move the kettle to a counter and stir wort briskly in one direction for about 5 minutes. After stirring, cover and let rest for 10 to 15 minutes; the hops and trub should form a cone in the bottom of the kettle.

8. Using a racking cane and siphon, rack as much wort as possible into the sanitized primary fermenter. Using the sanitized funnel and straining screen, strain the rest of the wort into the fermenter. Top off with brewing water to bring the volume to around 5.5 US gal (21 L). Aerate well by stirring vigorously with a sanitized spoon. Using the hydrometer (see page 38), take a reading of the specific gravity and record it in your brewing journal.

9. Sprinkle the yeast over the surface; vigorously stir with a sanitized spoon, distributing it well throughout the liquid. Seal the fermenter with lid, stopper and airlock. Keep the fermenter at room temperature (68 to 72°F/20 to 22°C) during primary fermentation (which typically lasts 1 to 4 days after fermentation begins), in a dark place or under a lightproof cover if using a glass carboy.

10. When the kräusen (brownish foam on top of the wort) has peaked and begun to fall (you'll see a ring around the inside of the bucket), rack the beer into the secondary fermenter gently to avoid aerating it, leaving most of the sediment behind. Seal and keep at room temperature, covered or in a dark place, to allow fermentation to continue.

11. Once the bubbling in the airlock has slowed, confirm completion of fermentation by using the hydrometer to take final gravity readings. (Hydrometer readings should be the same for several days in a row.)

12. Prime, bottle and condition the beer (see page 39).

Brewer's Tips

I recommend the 4 lbs/1.8 kg can of Mountmellick Irish Unhopped Amber malt extract, if available. If not, any UK malt extract will work. If using a 3.3 lbs/1.5 kg can of malt syrup, increase the dry malt extract by .8 lb/363 g.

Instead of removing the kettle from the heat, use a medium saucepan to scoop out some of the wort (about 6 cups/1.5 L) and add the later additions to the wort in the saucepan. Stir until the sugar and nutrient are dissolved and return to the wort in the kettle. Stir to disperse.

During the first 12 hours, check that fermentation has begun, and continue occasional aeration with a sanitized spoon if it has not. If fermentation has not begun within 24 hours, re-pitch the yeast and aerate.

American Amber

Although similar to the Irish Amber, this brew has more malt character and body and a lot more hops. For a sweeter, maltier brew, use the lower end of the recommended AAUs; for a more bitter approach, use the higher number. The Briess and Northwestern extracts are the same product packaged by different companies.

Estimated Original Gravity: 1.053

Equipment

- **brew kettle**
- **fermentation gear (page 14)**

If you are a first-time brewer, read pages 8 to 36 thoroughly before you begin. Consult the summaries on pages 37 to 39 for details on preparing chlorinated water for brewing, preventing boil-overs, sanitizing fermentation gear, using the hydrometer, preparing and using the cooling bath, racking, checking fermentation, and priming, bottling and conditioning your beer.

5.5 US gal	brewing water (page 37)	21 L

Malt Extract

6.6 lbs	amber malt extract (such as Briess, Coopers, Northwestern or any brand), divided in half	3 kg

Bittering Hops

8 to 10 AAUs	high-alpha American hops (such as Amarillo, Centennial, Chinook or Columbus)	8 to 10 AAUs

Later Additions

1 tsp	Irish moss	5 mL
1 tsp	yeast nutrient	5 mL

Aroma Hops

2 oz	American aroma hops (such as Ahtanum, Amarillo, Cascade or Willamette)	56 g

Yeast

1 pack	Fermentis S-05 American ale (or any clean-fermenting ale yeast)	1 pack

1. In a brew kettle, bring at least 3 US gal (11 L) brewing water to a boil. Remove from the heat, add half the malt extract and stir until dissolved completely. Do not allow the extract to settle and scorch.

2. Return kettle to the burner and increase the heat until the liquid (wort) begins to boil. Using a spoon, clear any foam to one side. Do *not* allow it to seal the boil. Reduce the heat until a rolling boil can be maintained without foam buildup.

3. Add the bittering hops, stirring to combine. Boil for 45 minutes, uncovered. Monitor to prevent boiling over.

4. Meanwhile, prepare the fermentation gear (see page 37) and cooling bath (see page 38) or wort chiller.

5. After 45 minutes, remove the kettle from the heat and add remaining half of the malt extract, Irish moss and yeast nutrient. Stir to ensure that the extract and nutrient are dissolved. Return the kettle to the burner and bring back to a rolling boil. Boil for 15 minutes; stir in the aroma hops, turn off the heat and cover.

6. To cool the brew, place the covered kettle in the prepared cooling tub or use a wort chiller according to directions. Cool to yeast-pitching temperature, 75°F (24°C), within 30 to 45 minutes.

7. While the wort is cooling, clean and sanitize the brewing spoon. When the wort has cooled, move the kettle to a counter and stir wort briskly in one direction for about 5 minutes. After stirring, cover and let rest for 10 to 15 minutes; the hops and trub should form a cone in the bottom of the kettle.

8. Using a racking cane and siphon, rack as much wort as possible into the sanitized primary fermenter. Using the sanitized funnel, strain the rest of the wort into the fermenter. Top off with brewing water to bring the volume to around 5.5 US gal (21 L). Using the hydrometer (see page 38), take a reading of the specific gravity and record it in your brewing journal. Aerate well by stirring vigorously with a sanitized spoon.

9. Sprinkle the yeast over the surface; vigorously stir with a sanitized spoon, distributing it well throughout the liquid. Seal the fermenter with lid, stopper and airlock. Keep the fermenter at room temperature (68 to 72°F/20 to 22°C) during primary fermentation (which typically lasts 1 to 4 days after fermentation begins), in a dark place or under a lightproof cover if using a glass carboy.

10. When the kräusen (brownish foam on top of the wort) has peaked and begun to fall (you'll see a ring around the inside of the bucket), rack the beer into the secondary fermenter gently to avoid aerating it, leaving most of the sediment behind. Seal and keep at room temperature, covered or in a dark place, to allow fermentation to continue.

11. Once the bubbling in the airlock has slowed, confirm completion of fermentation by using the hydrometer to take final gravity readings. (Hydrometer readings should be the same for several days in a row.)

12. Prime, bottle and condition the beer (see page 39).

Brewer's Tips

Instead of removing the kettle from the heat, use a medium saucepan to scoop out some of the wort (about 6 cups/1.5 L) and add the later additions to the wort in the saucepan. Stir until the extract and nutrient are dissolved and return to the wort in the kettle. Stir to disperse.

During the first 12 hours, check that fermentation has begun, and continue occasional aeration with a sanitized spoon if it has not. If fermentation has not begun within 24 hours, re-pitch the yeast and aerate.

British Brown Ale

Brown ales are one of the easiest first-time brews. Classic examples from across the pond are Samuel Smith's Nut Brown Ale and Newcastle Brown. The Sammy's is a robust version; the Newkie is lighter-bodied. The brew in this recipe should be in the middle. This is a great beer to quaff on an autumn's eve.

Estimated Original Gravity: 1.048

Equipment

- brew kettle
- fermentation gear (page 14)

If you are a first-time brewer, read pages 8 to 36 thoroughly before you begin. Consult the summaries on pages 37 to 39 for details on preparing chlorinated water for brewing, preventing boil-overs, sanitizing fermentation gear, using the hydrometer, preparing and using the cooling bath, racking, checking fermentation, and priming, bottling and conditioning your beer.

5.5 US gal	brewing water (page 37)	21 L

Malt Extracts

3.3 lbs	UK dark	1.5 kg
3.3 lbs	UK amber (later addition)	1.5 kg

Bittering Hops

6 to 8 AAUs	UK hops (such as Challenger, First Gold, Northern Brewer, Pilgrim or Target)	6 to 8 AAUs

Later Additions

8 oz.	Demerara sugar (or turbinado or other raw cane sugar)	224 g
1 tsp	Irish moss	5 mL
1 tsp	yeast nutrient	5 mL

Aroma Hops

0.5 oz	UK hops (such as Bramling Cross, Fuggle or East Kent Golding)	14 g

Yeast

1 pack	Fermentis S-33 or Danstar Windsor ale yeast	1 pack

1. In a brew kettle, bring at least 3 US gal (11 L) brewing water to a boil. Remove from the heat, add the dark malt extract only and stir until dissolved completely. Do not allow the extract to settle and scorch.

2. Return kettle to the burner and increase the heat until the liquid (wort) begins to boil. Using a spoon, clear any foam to one side. Do *not* allow it to seal the boil. Reduce the heat until a rolling boil can be maintained without foam buildup.

3. Add the bittering hops, stirring to combine. Boil for 45 minutes, uncovered. Monitor to prevent boiling over.

4. Meanwhile, prepare the fermentation gear (see page 37) and cooling bath (see page 38) or wort chiller.

5. After 45 minutes, remove the kettle from the heat and add amber malt extract, sugar, Irish moss and yeast nutrient. Stir to ensure that the extract, sugar and nutrient are dissolved. Return the kettle to the burner and bring back to a rolling boil. Boil for 15 minutes; stir in the aroma hops, turn off the heat and cover.

6. To cool the brew, place the covered kettle in the prepared cooling tub or use a wort chiller according to directions. Cool to yeast-pitching temperature, 75°F (24°C), within 30 to 45 minutes.

7. While the wort is cooling, clean and sanitize the brewing spoon. When the wort has cooled, move the kettle to a counter and stir wort briskly in one direction for about 5 minutes. After stirring, cover and let rest for 10 to 15 minutes; the hops and trub should form a cone in the bottom of the kettle.

8. Using a racking cane and siphon, rack as much wort as possible into the sanitized primary fermenter. Using the sanitized funnel and straining screen, strain the rest of the wort into the fermenter. Top off with brewing water to bring the volume to around 5.5 US gal (21 L). Using the hydrometer (see page 38), take a reading of the specific gravity and record it in your brewing journal. Aerate well by stirring vigorously with a sanitized spoon.

9. Sprinkle the yeast over the surface; vigorously stir with a sanitized spoon, distributing it well throughout the liquid. Seal the fermenter with lid, stopper and airlock. Keep the fermenter at room temperature (68 to 72°F/20 to 22°C) during primary fermentation (which typically lasts 1 to 4 days after fermentation begins), in a dark place or under a lightproof cover if using a glass carboy.

10. When the kräusen (brownish foam on top of the wort) has peaked and begun to fall (you'll see a ring around the inside of the bucket), rack the beer into the secondary fermenter gently to avoid aerating it, leaving most of the sediment behind. Seal and keep at room temperature, covered or in a dark place, to allow fermentation to continue.

11. Once the bubbling in the airlock has slowed, confirm completion of fermentation by using the hydrometer to take final gravity readings. (Hydrometer readings should be the same for several days in a row.)

12. Prime, bottle and condition the beer (see page 39).

Brewer's Tips

Instead of removing the kettle from the heat, use a medium saucepan to scoop out some of the wort (about 6 cups/1.5 L) and add the later additions to the wort in the saucepan. Stir until the extract, sugar and nutrient are dissolved and return to the wort in the kettle. Stir to disperse.

During the first 12 hours, check that fermentation has begun, and continue occasional aeration with a sanitized spoon if it has not. If fermentation has not begun within 24 hours, re-pitch the yeast and aerate.

This is a beer style that was actually invented by homebrewers. Hobby brewers began to produce beers that were fuller-bodied and much more aggressively hopped than the classic examples of Brown Ale from the British Isles. Commercial examples were Pete's Wicked Ale and Brooklyn Brown Ale. This is a beer that is particularly enjoyable when fresh.

Estimated Original Gravity: 1.045

Equipment

- **brew kettle**
- **fermentation gear (page 14)**

If you are a first-time brewer, read pages 8 to 36 thoroughly before you begin. Consult the summaries on pages 37 to 39 for details on preparing chlorinated water for brewing, preventing boil-overs, sanitizing fermentation gear, using the hydrometer, preparing and using the cooling bath, racking, checking fermentation, and priming, bottling and conditioning your beer.

American (Texas) Brown

5.5 US gal	brewing water (page 37)	21 L

Malt Extracts

3.3 lbs	amber (such as Briess, Coopers, Northwestern or any brand)	1.5 kg
3.3 lbs	dark (such as Briess, Coopers, Northwestern or any brand) (later addition)	1.5 kg

Bittering Hops

8 to 10 AAUs	high-alpha American hops (such as Amarillo, Centennial, Chinook or Columbus)	8 to 10 AAUs

Later Additions

1 tsp	Irish moss	5 mL
1 tsp	yeast nutrient	5 mL

Aroma Hops

1.5 oz	citrusy American hops (such as Ahtanum, Amarillo or Cascade)	42 g

Yeast

1 pack	Fermentis S-05 American ale (or any clean-fermenting ale yeast)	1 pack

1. In a brew kettle, bring at least 3 US gal (11 L) brewing water to a boil. Remove from the heat, add amber malt extract only and stir until dissolved completely. Do not allow the extract to settle and scorch.

2. Return kettle to the burner and increase the heat until the liquid (wort) begins to boil. Using a spoon, clear any foam to one side. Do *not* allow it to seal the boil. Reduce the heat until a rolling boil can be maintained without foam buildup.

3. Add the bittering hops, stirring to combine. Boil for 45 minutes, uncovered. Monitor to prevent boiling over.

4. Meanwhile, prepare the fermentation gear (see page 37) and cooling bath (see page 38) or wort chiller.

5. After 45 minutes, remove the kettle from the heat and add dark malt extract, Irish moss and yeast nutrient. Stir to ensure that the extract and nutrient are dissolved. Return the kettle to the burner and bring back to a rolling boil. Boil for 15 minutes; stir in the aroma hops, turn off the heat and cover.

6. To cool the brew, place the covered kettle in the prepared cooling tub or use a wort chiller according to directions. Cool to yeast-pitching temperature, 75°F (24°C), within 30 to 45 minutes.

7. While the wort is cooling, clean and sanitize the brewing spoon. When the wort has cooled, move the kettle to a counter and stir wort briskly in one direction for about 5 minutes. After stirring, cover and let rest for 10 to 15 minutes; the hops and trub should form a cone in the bottom of the kettle.

8. Using a racking cane and siphon, rack as much wort as possible into the sanitized primary fermenter. Using the sanitized funnel and straining screen, strain the rest of the wort into the fermenter. Top off with brewing water to bring the volume to around 5.5 US gal (21 L). Using the hydrometer (see page 38), take a reading of the specific gravity and record it in your brewing journal. Aerate well by stirring vigorously with a sanitized spoon.

9. Sprinkle the yeast over the surface; vigorously stir with a sanitized spoon, distributing it well throughout the liquid. Seal the fermenter with lid, stopper and airlock. Keep the fermenter at room temperature (68 to 72°F/20 to 22°C) during primary fermentation (which typically lasts 1 to 4 days after fermentation begins), in a dark place or under a lightproof cover if using a glass carboy.

10. When the kräusen (brownish foam on top of the wort) has peaked and begun to fall (you'll see a ring around the inside of the bucket), rack the beer into the secondary fermenter gently to avoid aerating it, leaving most of the sediment behind. Seal and keep at room temperature, covered or in a dark place, to allow fermentation to continue.

11. Once the bubbling in the airlock has slowed, confirm completion of fermentation by using the hydrometer to take final gravity readings. (Hydrometer readings should be the same for several days in a row.)

12. Prime, bottle and condition the beer (see page 39).

Brewer's Tips

Instead of removing the kettle from the heat, use a medium saucepan to scoop out some of the wort (about 6 cups/1.5 L) and add the later additions to the wort in the saucepan. Stir until the extract and nutrient are dissolved and return to the wort in the kettle. Stir to disperse.

During the first 12 hours, check that fermentation has begun, and continue occasional aeration with a sanitized spoon if it has not. If fermentation has not begun within 24 hours, re-pitch the yeast and aerate.

When brewing became a commercial enterprise and hops became more prevalent, hop roasting temperatures became more precise and British Pale Ale was born. Before this, beers were brown or black—thus, a copper-colored ale was pale. In this age of fizzy yellow lagers, some consumers are mystified. "It looks kind of dark to me," they think. The archetype for the style is Bass, but fine examples are produced all over England and North America.

Estimated Original Gravity: 1.048

Equipment

- **brew kettle**
- **fermentation gear (page 14)**

If you are a first-time brewer, read pages 8 to 36 thoroughly before you begin. Consult the summaries on pages 37 to 39 for details on preparing chlorinated water for brewing, preventing boil-overs, sanitizing fermentation gear, using the hydrometer, preparing and using the cooling bath, racking, checking fermentation, and priming, bottling and conditioning your beer.

British Pale Ale (Special Bitter)

5.5 US gal	brewing water (page 37)	21 L
Malt Extract		
6.6 lbs	UK light, divided in half	2.72 kg
Bittering Hops		
10 to 12 AAUs	UK hops (such as Challenger, First Gold, Northern Brewer, Pilgrim or Target)	10 to 12 AAUs
Later Additions		
1 tsp	Irish moss	5 mL
1 tsp	yeast nutrient	5 mL
Aroma Hops		
1.5 oz	UK hops (such as Bramling Cross, Fuggle or East Kent Golding)	42 g
Yeast		
1 pack	Fermentis S-04 or Danstar Nottingham ale yeast	1 pack

1. In a brew kettle, bring at least 3 US gal (11 L) brewing water to a boil. Remove from the heat, add half the malt extract and stir until dissolved completely. Do not allow the extract to settle and scorch.
2. Return kettle to the burner and increase the heat until the liquid (wort) begins to boil. Using a spoon, clear any foam to one side. Do *not* allow it to seal the boil. Reduce the heat until a rolling boil can be maintained without foam buildup.
3. Add the bittering hops, stirring to combine. Boil for 45 minutes, uncovered. Monitor to prevent boiling over.
4. Meanwhile, prepare the fermentation gear (see page 37) and cooling bath (see page 38) or wort chiller.
5. After 45 minutes, remove the kettle from the heat and add remaining half of malt extract, Irish moss and yeast nutrient. Stir to ensure that the extract and nutrient are dissolved. Return the kettle to the burner and bring back to a rolling boil. Boil for 15 minutes; stir in the aroma hops, turn off the heat and cover.
6. To cool the brew, place the covered kettle in the prepared cooling tub or use a wort chiller according to directions. Cool to yeast-pitching temperature, 75°F (24°C), within 30 to 45 minutes.

7. While the wort is cooling, clean and sanitize the brewing spoon. When the wort has cooled, move the kettle to a counter and stir wort briskly in one direction for about 5 minutes. After stirring, cover and let rest for 10 to 15 minutes; the hops and trub should form a cone in the bottom of the kettle.

8. Using a racking cane and siphon, rack as much wort as possible into the sanitized primary fermenter. Using the sanitized funnel and straining screen, strain the rest of the wort into the fermenter. Top off with brewing water to bring the volume to around 5.5 US gal (21 L). Using the hydrometer (see page 38), take a reading of the specific gravity and record it in your brewing journal. Aerate well by stirring vigorously with a sanitized spoon.

9. Sprinkle the yeast over the surface; vigorously stir with a sanitized spoon, distributing it well throughout the liquid. Seal the fermenter with lid, stopper and airlock. Keep the fermenter at room temperature (68 to 72°F/20 to 22°C) during primary fermentation (which typically lasts 1 to 4 days after fermentation begins), in a dark place or under a lightproof cover if using a glass carboy.

10. When the kräusen (brownish foam on top of the wort) has peaked and begun to fall (you'll see a ring around the inside of the bucket), rack the beer into the secondary fermenter gently to avoid aerating it, leaving most of the sediment behind. Seal and keep at room temperature, covered or in a dark place, to allow fermentation to continue.

11. Once the bubbling in the airlock has slowed, confirm completion of fermentation by using the hydrometer to take final gravity readings. (Hydrometer readings should be the same for several days in a row.)

12. Prime, bottle and condition the beer (see page 39).

Variation

ESB or Strong Bitter: Follow the recipe for Pale Ale, but add 1.5 lbs (680 g) Demerara sugar. Estimated Original Gravity: 1.048

Brewer's Tips

Instead of removing the kettle from the heat, use a medium saucepan to scoop out some of the wort (about 6 cups/1.5 L) and add the later additions to the wort in the saucepan. Stir until the extract and nutrient are dissolved and return to the wort in the kettle. Stir to disperse.

During the first 12 hours, check that fermentation has begun, and continue occasional aeration with a sanitized spoon if it has not. If fermentation has not begun within 24 hours, re-pitch the yeast and aerate.

Ordinary Bitter

In the UK, a low-alcohol pale ale served from a cask is called Bitter. The term comes from a time when beers were unhopped. When hops came into use, beers that contained them were more bitter than those that did not. British brewers usually produce three strengths: Ordinary Bitter (shortened to just Bitter); Special Bitter, a little bit stronger and would be a cask version of the British Pale Ale recipe provided; and Strong Bitter (for example, Fuller's "Extra Special" aka ESB).

Estimated Original Gravity: 1.043

Equipment

- **brew kettle**
- **fermentation gear (page 14)**

If you are a first-time brewer, read pages 8 to 36 thoroughly before you begin. Consult the summaries on pages 37 to 39 for details on preparing chlorinated water for brewing, preventing boil-overs, sanitizing fermentation gear, using the hydrometer, preparing and using the cooling bath, racking, checking fermentation, and priming, bottling and conditioning your beer.

5.5 US gal	brewing water (page 37)	21 L

Malt Extracts

1 lb	UK light dry	450 g
4 lbs	UK light syrup (later addition)	1.8 kg

Bittering Hops

6 to 7 AAUs	UK hops (such as Bramling Cross, East Kent Golding, Fuggle or other)	6 to 7 AAUs

Flavor and Aroma Hops

1 oz	UK hops (such as Bramling Cross, East Kent Golding, Fuggle or other), divided in half	28 g

Later Additions

8 oz	Demerara sugar (or turbinado or raw brown cane sugar)	224 g
1 tsp	Irish moss	5 mL
1 tsp	yeast nutrient	5 mL

Yeast

1 pack	Fermentis S-04 or Danstar Nottingham ale yeast	1 pack

1. In a brew kettle, bring at least 3 US gal (11 L) brewing water to a boil. Remove from the heat, add the light dry malt extract only and stir until dissolved completely. Do not allow the extract to settle and scorch.

2. Return kettle to the burner and increase the heat until the liquid (wort) begins to boil. Using a spoon, clear any foam to one side. Do *not* allow it to seal the boil. Reduce the heat until a rolling boil can be maintained without foam buildup.

3. Add the bittering hops, stirring to combine. Boil for 45 minutes, uncovered. Monitor to prevent boiling over.

4. Meanwhile, prepare the fermentation gear (see page 37) and cooling bath (see page 38) or wort chiller.

5. After 45 minutes, remove the kettle from the heat and add light malt extract syrup, half the aroma hops, sugar, Irish moss and yeast nutrient. Stir to ensure that the extract, sugar and nutrient are dissolved. Return the kettle to the burner and bring back to a rolling boil. Boil for 15 minutes; stir in the remainder of the aroma hops, turn off the heat and cover.

6. To cool the brew, place the covered kettle in the prepared cooling tub or use a wort chiller according to directions. Cool to yeast-pitching temperature, 75°F (24°C), within 30 to 45 minutes.

7. While the wort is cooling, clean and sanitize the brewing spoon. When the wort has cooled, move the kettle to a counter and stir wort briskly in one direction for about 5 minutes. After stirring, cover and let rest for 10 to 15 minutes; the hops and trub should form a cone in the bottom of the kettle.

8. Using a racking cane and siphon, rack as much wort as possible into the sanitized primary fermenter. Using the sanitized funnel and straining screen, strain the rest of the wort into the fermenter. Top off with brewing water to bring the volume to around 5.5 US gal (21 L). Using the hydrometer (see page 38), take a reading of the specific gravity and record it in your brewing journal. Aerate well by stirring vigorously with a sanitized spoon.

9. Sprinkle the yeast over the surface; vigorously stir with a sanitized spoon, distributing it well throughout the liquid. Seal the fermenter with lid, stopper and airlock. Keep the fermenter at room temperature (68 to 72°F/20 to 22°C) during primary fermentation (which typically lasts 1 to 4 days after fermentation begins), in a dark place or under a lightproof cover if using a glass carboy.

10. When the kräusen (brownish foam on top of the wort) has peaked and begun to fall (you'll see a ring around the inside of the bucket), rack the beer into the secondary fermenter gently to avoid aerating it, leaving most of the sediment behind. Seal and keep at room temperature, covered or in a dark place, to allow fermentation to continue.

11. Once the bubbling in the airlock has slowed, confirm completion of fermentation by using the hydrometer to take final gravity readings. (Hydrometer readings should be the same for several days in a row.)

12. Prime, bottle and condition the beer (see page 39).

Brewer's Tips

Instead of removing the kettle from the heat, use a medium saucepan to scoop out some of the wort (about 6 cups/1.5 L) and add the later additions to the wort in the saucepan. Stir until the extract, sugar and nutrient are dissolved and return to the wort in the kettle. Stir to disperse.

During the first 12 hours, check that fermentation has begun, and continue occasional aeration with a sanitized spoon if it has not. If fermentation has not begun within 24 hours, re-pitch the yeast and aerate.

This is another style that was pioneered by American homebrewers and transferred to the craft-brewing movement. Hoppier than their counterparts from across the pond, this pale ale showcases the citrus and pine flavors of the hop varieties from the Pacific Northwest.

Estimated Original Gravity: 1.046

Equipment

- **brew kettle**
- **fermentation gear (page 14)**

If you are a first-time brewer, read pages 8 to 36 thoroughly before you begin. Consult the summaries on pages 37 to 39 for details on preparing chlorinated water for brewing, preventing boil-overs, sanitizing fermentation gear, using the hydrometer, preparing and using the cooling bath, racking, checking fermentation, and priming, bottling and conditioning your beer.

American Pale Ale (APA)

5.5 US gal	brewing water (page 37)	21 L

Malt Extracts

3.3 lbs	amber (such as Briess, Coopers, Northwestern or any brand)	1.5 kg
3.3 lbs	light (or gold) (such as Briess, Coopers, Northwestern or any brand) (later addition)	1.5 kg

Bittering Hops

12 to 14 AAUs	high-alpha American hops (such as Amarillo, Centennial, Chinook or Columbus)	12 to 14 AAUs

Later Additions

1 tsp	Irish moss	5 mL
1 tsp	yeast nutrient	5 mL

Aroma Hops

2 oz	citrusy American hops (such as Ahtanum, Amarillo or Cascade)	56 g

Yeast

1 pack	Fermentis S-05 American ale (or any clean-fermenting ale yeast)	1 pack

1. In a brew kettle, bring at least 3 US gal (11 L) brewing water to a boil. Remove from the heat, add the amber malt extract only and stir until dissolved completely. Do not allow the extract to settle and scorch.

2. Return kettle to the burner and increase the heat until the liquid (wort) begins to boil. Using a spoon, clear any foam to one side. Do *not* allow it to seal the boil. Reduce the heat until a rolling boil can be maintained without foam buildup.

3. Add the bittering hops, stirring to combine. Boil for 45 minutes, uncovered. Monitor to prevent boiling over.

4. Meanwhile, prepare the fermentation gear (see page 37) and cooling bath (see page 38) or wort chiller.

5. After 45 minutes, remove the kettle from the heat and add light malt extract, Irish moss and yeast nutrient. Stir to ensure that the extract and nutrient are dissolved. Return the kettle to the burner and bring back to a rolling boil. Boil for 15 minutes; stir in the aroma hops, turn off the heat and cover.

6. To cool the brew, place the covered kettle in the prepared cooling tub or use a wort chiller according to directions. Cool to yeast-pitching temperature, 75°F (24°C), within 30 to 45 minutes.

7. While the wort is cooling, clean and sanitize the brewing spoon. When the wort has cooled, move the kettle to a counter and stir wort briskly in one direction for about 5 minutes. After stirring, cover and let rest for 10 to 15 minutes; the hops and trub should form a cone in the bottom of the kettle.

8. Using a racking cane and siphon, rack as much wort as possible into the sanitized primary fermenter. Using the sanitized funnel and straining screen, strain the rest of the wort into the fermenter. Top off with brewing water to bring the volume to around 5.5 US gal (21 L). Using the hydrometer (see page 38), take a reading of the specific gravity and record it in your brewing journal. Aerate well by stirring vigorously with a sanitized spoon.

9. Sprinkle the yeast over the surface; vigorously stir with a sanitized spoon, distributing it well throughout the liquid. Seal the fermenter with lid, stopper and airlock. Keep the fermenter at room temperature (68 to 72°F/20 to 22°C) during primary fermentation (which typically lasts 1 to 4 days after fermentation begins), in a dark place or under a lightproof cover if using a glass carboy.

10. When the kräusen (brownish foam on top of the wort) has peaked and begun to fall (you'll see a ring around the inside of the bucket), rack the beer into the secondary fermenter gently to avoid aerating it, leaving most of the sediment behind. Seal and keep at room temperature, covered or in a dark place, to allow fermentation to continue.

11. Once the bubbling in the airlock has slowed, confirm completion of fermentation by using the hydrometer to take final gravity readings. (Hydrometer readings should be the same for several days in a row.)

12. Prime, bottle and condition the beer (see page 39).

Brewer's Tips

Instead of removing the kettle from the heat, use a medium saucepan to scoop out some of the wort (about 6 cups/1.5 L) and add the later additions to the wort in the saucepan. Stir until the extract and nutrient are dissolved and add to the wort in the kettle. Stir to disperse.

During the first 12 hours, check that fermentation has begun, and continue occasional aeration with a sanitized spoon if it has not. If fermentation has not begun within 24 hours, re-pitch the yeast and aerate.

India Pale Ale (IPA)

In the glory days of the British Empire, those in India thirsted for ales from home. Since India was too hot to produce ales, beer was exported from home. But the ales created in England suffered during the long trip, so a new brew was born. Both alcohol and hops act as natural preservatives, so both were increased and the casks conditioned in the cool hold of the ship on the way to satisfying the thirst in the colonies.

Most of the IPAs available today are brewed in the American style, which, like the standard Pale Ale cousins, are hoppier and feature Pacific Northwest hop varieties. For a more traditional English approach, check out the UK IPA recipe in the next section of the book. Feel free to tone the hops up or down as your taste dictates. For a darker color, use some or all amber extract; to go paler, switch to extra light.

Estimated Original Gravity: 1.068

Equipment

- brew kettle
- fermentation gear (page 14)

5.5 US gal	brewing water (page 37)	21 L

Malt Extracts

1 lb	light dry malt extract (DME)	450 g
6.6 lbs	light or gold syrup (such as Briess, Coopers, Northwestern or any brand) (later addition)	3 kg

Bittering Hops

15 to 25 AAUs	super high-alpha hops (such as Chinook, Columbus, Summit, Tomahawk or Warrior)	15 to 25 AAUs

Later Additions

1 lb	turbinado (or other raw sugar)	450 g
1 tsp	Irish moss	5 mL
1 tsp	yeast nutrient	5 mL

Aroma and Dry Hops

4 oz	citrusy American hops (such as Ahtanum, Amarillo, or Cascade), divided in half	112 g

Yeast

1 pack	Fermentis S-05 American ale (or any clean-fermenting ale yeast)	1 pack

1. In brew kettle, bring at least 3 US gal (11 L) brewing water to a boil. Remove from heat, add light dry malt extract only and stir until dissolved completely.
2. Return kettle to burner and increase heat until liquid (wort) begins to boil. Using a spoon, clear any foam to one side. Do *not* allow it to seal the boil. Reduce heat until a rolling boil can be maintained without foam buildup.
3. Add the bittering hops, stirring to combine. Boil for 45 minutes, uncovered. Monitor to prevent boiling over.
4. Meanwhile, prepare the fermentation gear (see page 37) and cooling bath (see page 38) or wort chiller.
5. After 45 minutes, remove the kettle from the heat and add light malt extract syrup, sugar, Irish moss and yeast nutrient. Stir to ensure that the extract, sugar and nutrient are dissolved. Return the kettle to the burner and bring back to a rolling boil. Boil for 15 minutes; stir in half of the aroma hops (2 oz/56 g), turn off the heat and cover.
6. To cool the brew, place the covered kettle in the prepared cooling tub or use a wort chiller according to directions. Cool to yeast-pitching temperature, 75°F (24°C), within 30 to 45 minutes.

7. While wort is cooling, clean and sanitize brewing spoon. When wort has cooled, move kettle to a counter and stir wort briskly in one direction for about 5 minutes. Cover and let rest for 10 to 15 minutes; hops and trub should form a cone in the bottom of the kettle.

8. Using a racking cane and siphon, rack as much wort as possible into the sanitized primary fermenter. Using the sanitized funnel and straining screen, strain the rest of the wort into the fermenter. Top off with brewing water to bring the volume to around 5.5 US gal (21 L). Using the hydrometer (see page 38), take a reading of the specific gravity and record it in your brewing journal. Aerate well by stirring vigorously with a sanitized spoon.

9. Sprinkle the yeast over the surface; vigorously stir with a sanitized spoon, distributing it well throughout the liquid. Seal the fermenter with lid, stopper and airlock. Keep the fermenter at room temperature (68 to 72°F/20 to 22°C) during primary fermentation (which typically lasts 1 to 4 days after fermentation begins), in a dark place or under a lightproof cover if using a glass carboy.

10. When kräusen (brownish foam on top of the wort) has peaked and begun to fall (you'll see a ring around the inside of the bucket), rack the beer into the secondary fermenter gently to avoid aerating it, leaving most of the sediment behind. Seal and keep at room temperature, covered or in a dark place.

11. Once the bubbling in the airlock has slowed, gently add the remaining hops (2 oz/56 g). Seal and leave for another 2 weeks. Confirm completion of fermentation by using the hydrometer to take final gravity readings. (Hydrometer readings should be the same for several days in a row.)

12. Prime, bottle and condition the beer (see page 39).

Brewer's Tips

Instead of removing the kettle from the heat, use a medium saucepan to scoop out some of the wort (about 6 cups/1.5 L) and add the later additions to the wort in the saucepan. Stir until the extract, sugar and nutrient are dissolved and return to the wort in the kettle. Stir to disperse.

During the first 12 hours, check that fermentation has begun, and continue occasional aeration with a sanitized spoon if it has not. If fermentation has not begun within 24 hours, re-pitch the yeast and aerate.

Dry Hopping

IPA brewers shipping beer to India dosed the casks with hops prior to shipping. This dry hopping was done to take advantage of the preservative character of the hops, but it was soon discovered that, because the hops weren't boiled, they contributed an intense hop aroma to the beer.

If the beer you love has a hoppy floral aroma, you'll want to experiment with dry hopping. It is best to add dry hops to the secondary fermenter when activity has slowed. Allow another week or two for the beer to clear. Sometimes when pellet hops are added, your beer will foam for a little while. No, it didn't start to re-ferment; it's just acting as a nucleation point for dissolved CO_2 in the beer. Use a blow-off hose briefly, if needed.

Fest Bier

The beers of the German Oktoberfest are popular in autumn. Traditionally an amber lager beer, for beginners we'll brew it as a traditional amber-style ale. In this case, the malt extract brands specified are really the best choices for this beer. They are made from 100% Munich malt. If not available, you could settle for an amber malt. This beer is a little big for the style, but I like it that way!

Estimated Original Gravity: 1.061

Equipment

- **brew kettle**
- **fermentation gear (page 14)**

If you are a first-time brewer, read pages 8 to 36 thoroughly before you begin. Consult the summaries on pages 37 to 39 for details on preparing chlorinated water for brewing, preventing boil-overs, sanitizing fermentation gear, using the hydrometer, preparing and using the cooling bath, racking, checking fermentation, and priming, bottling and conditioning your beer.

5.5 US gal	brewing water (page 37)	21 L

Malt Extract

8.8 lbs	Weyermann Munich Amber syrup or Briess Munich Amber	4 kg

Bittering Hops

8 to 10 AAUs	Perle, Northern Brewer or Saphir	8 to 10 AAUs

Later Additions

1 tsp	Irish moss	5 mL
1 tsp	yeast nutrient	5 mL

Aroma and Dry Hops

1 oz	Noble European hops (such as Hallertau, Saaz, Spalt or Tettnang), divided in half	28 g

Yeast

1 pack	Fermentis S-05 American ale (or any clean-fermenting ale yeast or cold-fermenting lager yeast)	1 pack

1. In a brew kettle, bring at least 3 US gal (11 L) brewing water to a boil. Remove from the heat, add the malt extract and stir until dissolved completely. Do not allow the extract to settle and scorch.

2. Return kettle to the burner and increase the heat until the liquid (wort) begins to boil. Using a spoon, clear any foam to one side. Do *not* allow it to seal the boil. Reduce the heat until a rolling boil can be maintained without foam buildup.

3. Add the bittering hops, stirring to combine. Boil for 45 minutes, uncovered. Monitor to prevent boiling over.

4. Meanwhile, prepare the fermentation gear (see page 37) and cooling bath (see page 38) or wort chiller.

5. After 45 minutes, remove the kettle from the heat. Add the Irish moss and yeast nutrient and stir to combine. Return the kettle to the burner and bring back to a rolling boil. Boil for 15 minutes; stir in half the aroma hops, turn off the heat and cover.

6. To cool the brew, place the covered kettle in the prepared cooling tub or use a wort chiller according to directions. Cool to yeast-pitching temperature, 75°F (24°C), within 30 to 45 minutes.

7. While the wort is cooling, clean and sanitize the brewing spoon. When the wort has cooled, move the kettle to a counter and stir wort briskly in one direction for about 5 minutes. After stirring, cover and let rest for 10 to 15 minutes; the hops and trub should form a cone in the bottom of the kettle.

8. Using a racking cane and siphon, rack as much wort as possible into the sanitized primary fermenter. Using the sanitized funnel and straining screen, strain the rest of the wort into the fermenter. Top off with brewing water to bring the volume to around 5.5 US gal (21 L). Using the hydrometer (see page 38), take a reading of the specific gravity and record it in your brewing journal. Aerate well by stirring vigorously with a sanitized spoon.

9. Sprinkle the yeast over the surface; vigorously stir with a sanitized spoon, distributing it well throughout the liquid. Seal the fermenter with lid, stopper and airlock. Keep the fermenter at room temperature (68 to 72°F/20 to 22°C) during primary fermentation (which typically lasts 5 to 7 days after fermentation begins), in a dark place or under a lightproof cover if using a glass carboy.

10. When the kräusen (brownish foam on top of the wort) has peaked and begun to fall (you'll see a ring around the inside of the bucket), rack the beer into the secondary fermenter gently to avoid aerating it, leaving most of the sediment behind. Seal and keep at room temperature, covered or in a dark place to allow fermentation to continue.

11. Once the bubbling in the airlock has slowed, gently add remaining hops, reseal and leave for about 2 more weeks. Confirm completion of fermentation by using the hydrometer to take final gravity readings. (Hydrometer readings should be the same for several days in a row.)

12. Prime, bottle and condition the beer (see page 39).

Brewer's Tips

During the first 12 hours, check that fermentation has begun, and continue occasional aeration with a sanitized spoon if it has not. If fermentation has not begun within 24 hours, re-pitch the yeast and aerate.

If active fermentation backs up into the airlock, replace airlock with blow-off hose (see page 16). Change water as needed; re-install airlock when fermentation settles down.

Ale or Lager?

The difference between ale and lager is determined by yeast, temperature and time. Lager yeasts ferment at colder temperatures than ale yeasts. This means you must ferment lagers in a refrigerator if you're not brewing during cold weather.

To brew a lager, select a lager yeast such as Fermentis S-23. Store your primary fermenter at room temperature until fermentation begins, then refrigerate (or otherwise chill) it to a temperature between 46 and 55°F (8 and 13°C.) After 7 days, rack to a secondary fermenter and drop the temperature to 35 to 45°F (2 to 7° C). Expect the ferment to continue for another 4 to 6 weeks. If you're not sure it's ready for bottling, wait!

Store bottled beer in the refrigerator or other cold storage for 3 to 4 weeks before sampling.

Colonial Porter

When colonists found their way to the New World, they thirsted for the beers of home. (One of the reasons cited for landing the Mayflower at Plymouth Rock in Massachusetts was a shortage of beer.) None other than George Washington was noted for his love of porter. This one, spiked with molasses, is typical of the Colonial style.

Estimated Original Gravity: 1.077

Equipment

- **brew kettle**
- **fermentation gear (page 14)**

If you are a first-time brewer, read pages 8 to 36 thoroughly before you begin. Consult the summaries on pages 37 to 39 for details on preparing chlorinated water for brewing, preventing boil-overs, sanitizing fermentation gear, using the hydrometer, preparing and using the cooling bath, racking, checking fermentation, and priming, bottling and conditioning your beer.

5.5 US gal	brewing water (page 37)	21 L

Malt Extract

8 lbs	UK dark	3.6 kg

Bittering Hops

8 to 10 AAUs	UK-style hops (such as Challenger, First Gold, Pilgrim or Target)	8 to 10 AAUs

Later Additions

8 oz	blackstrap molasses	224 g
1 tsp	Irish moss	5 mL
1 tsp	yeast nutrient	5 mL

Aroma Hops

1.5 oz	UK hops (such as Bramling Cross, Fuggle or East Kent Golding)	42 g

Yeast

1 pack	Fermentis S-04 or Danstar Nottingham ale yeast	1 pack

1. In a brew kettle, bring at least 3 US gal (11 L) brewing water to a boil. Remove from the heat, add the dark malt extract and stir until dissolved completely. Do not allow the extract to settle and scorch.
2. Return kettle to the burner and increase the heat until the liquid (wort) begins to boil. Using a spoon, clear any foam to one side. Do *not* allow it to seal the boil. Reduce the heat until a rolling boil can be maintained without foam buildup.
3. Add the bittering hops, stirring to combine. Boil for 45 minutes, uncovered. Monitor to prevent boiling over.
4. Meanwhile, prepare the fermentation gear (see page 37) and cooling bath (see page 38) or wort chiller.
5. After 45 minutes, remove the kettle from the heat and add molasses, Irish moss and yeast nutrient. Stir to combine and dissolve molasses and yeast nutrient. Return the kettle to the burner and bring back to a rolling boil. Boil for 15 minutes; stir in the aroma hops, turn off the heat and cover.
6. To cool the brew, place the covered kettle in the prepared cooling tub or use a wort chiller according to directions. Cool to yeast-pitching temperature, 75°F (24°C), within 30 to 45 minutes.

7. While the wort is cooling, clean and sanitize the brewing spoon. When the wort has cooled, move the kettle to a counter and stir wort briskly in one direction for about 5 minutes. After stirring, cover and let rest for 10 to 15 minutes; the hops and trub should form a cone in the bottom of the kettle.

8. Using a racking cane and siphon, rack as much wort as possible into the sanitized primary fermenter. Using the sanitized funnel and straining screen, strain the rest of the wort into the fermenter. Top off with brewing water to bring the volume to around 5.5 US gal (21 L). Using the hydrometer (see page 38), take a reading of the specific gravity and record it in your brewing journal. Aerate well by stirring vigorously with a sanitized spoon.

9. Sprinkle the yeast over the surface; vigorously stir with a sanitized spoon, distributing it well throughout the liquid. Seal the fermenter with lid, stopper and airlock. Keep the fermenter at room temperature (68 to 72°F/20 to 22°C) during primary fermentation (which typically lasts 5 to 7 days after fermentation begins), in a dark place or under a lightproof cover if using a glass carboy.

10. When the kräusen (brownish foam on top of the wort) has peaked and begun to fall (you'll see a ring around the inside of the bucket), rack the beer into the secondary fermenter gently to avoid aerating it, leaving most of the sediment behind. Seal and keep at room temperature, covered or in a dark place, to allow fermentation to continue.

11. Once the bubbling in the airlock has slowed, confirm completion of fermentation by using the hydrometer to take final gravity readings. (Hydrometer readings should be the same for several days in a row.)

12. Prime, bottle and condition the beer (see page 39).

Brewer's Tips

Instead of removing the kettle from the heat, use a medium saucepan to scoop out some of the wort (about 6 cups/1.5 L) and add the later additions to the wort in the saucepan. Stir until the molasses and nutrient are dissolved and return to the wort in the kettle. Stir to disperse.

During the first 12 hours, check that fermentation has begun, and continue occasional aeration with a sanitized spoon if it has not. If fermentation has not begun within 24 hours, re-pitch the yeast and aerate.

If active fermentation backs up into the airlock, replace airlock with blow-off hose (see page 16). Change water as needed; re-install airlock when fermentation settles down.

Old or Stock Ale

Stock ales were the stronger ales of the early British brewer. Due to extended aging in wood, they were reputed to have a slightly sour, lactic character that we've eliminated in this modern version of the classic style. This is a nice, warming tipple to share on a winter's eve. Expect a longer ferment when brewing stronger beers.

**Estimated Original
Gravity: 1.064**

Equipment

brew kettle
- **fermentation gear
(page 14)**

If you are a first-time brewer, read pages 8 to 36 thoroughly before you begin. Consult the summaries on pages 37 to 39 for details on preparing chlorinated water for brewing, preventing boil-overs, sanitizing fermentation gear, using the hydrometer, preparing and using the cooling bath, racking, checking fermentation, and priming, bottling and conditioning your beer.

This recipe is slightly more challenging than the earlier ones. Try this one after one or two batches of the early recipes.

5.5 US gal	brewing water (page 37)	21 L

Malt Extract

8 lbs	UK light	3.6 kg

Bittering Hops

6 to 7 AAUs	UK hops (such as Bramling Cross, East Kent Golding, Fuggle or other)	6 to 7 AAUs

Later Additions

2 lbs	amber, Barbados or baking molasses	900 g
1 tsp	Irish moss	5 mL
1 tsp	yeast nutrient	5 mL

Aroma Hops

.5 oz	UK hops (such as Bramling Cross, East Kent Golding or Fuggle)	14 g

Yeast

1 pack	Fermentis S-04 or Danstar Nottingham ale yeast	1 pack

1. In a brew kettle, bring at least 3 US gal (11 L) brewing water to a boil. Remove from the heat, add the malt extract and stir until dissolved completely. Do not allow the extract to settle and scorch.
2. Return kettle to the burner and increase the heat until the liquid (wort) begins to boil. Using a spoon, clear any foam to one side. Do *not* allow it to seal the boil. Reduce the heat until a rolling boil can be maintained without foam buildup.
3. Add the bittering hops, stirring to combine. Boil for 45 minutes, uncovered. Monitor to prevent boiling over.
4. Meanwhile, prepare the fermentation gear (see page 37) and cooling bath (see page 38) or wort chiller.
5. After 45 minutes, remove the kettle from the heat and add molasses, Irish moss and yeast nutrient. Stir to combine and dissolve molasses and yeast nutrient. Return the kettle to the burner and bring back to a rolling boil. Boil for 15 minutes; stir in the aroma hops, turn off the heat and cover.
6. To cool the brew, place the covered kettle in the prepared cooling tub or use a wort chiller according to directions. Cool to yeast-pitching temperature, 75°F (24°C), within 30 to 45 minutes.

7. While the wort is cooling, clean and sanitize the brewing spoon. When the wort has cooled, move the kettle to a counter and stir wort briskly in one direction for about 5 minutes. After stirring, cover and let rest for 10 to 15 minutes; the hops and trub should form a cone in the bottom of the kettle.

8. Using a racking cane and siphon, rack as much wort as possible into the sanitized primary fermenter. Using the sanitized funnel and straining screen, strain the rest of the wort into the fermenter. Top off with brewing water to bring the volume to around 5.5 US gal (21 L). Using the hydrometer (see page 38), take a reading of the specific gravity and record it in your brewing journal. Aerate well by stirring vigorously with a sanitized spoon.

9. Sprinkle the yeast over the surface; vigorously stir with a sanitized spoon, distributing it well throughout the liquid. Seal the fermenter with lid, stopper and airlock. Keep the fermenter at room temperature (68 to 72°F/20 to 22°C) during primary fermentation (which typically lasts 5 to 7 days after fermentation begins), in a dark place or under a lightproof cover if using a glass carboy.

10. When the kräusen (brownish foam on top of the wort) has peaked and begun to fall (you'll see a ring around the inside of the bucket), rack the beer into the secondary fermenter gently to avoid aerating it, leaving most of the sediment behind. Seal and keep at room temperature, covered or in a dark place, to allow fermentation to continue for 10 days to two weeks.

11. Once the bubbling in the airlock has slowed, confirm completion of fermentation by using the hydrometer to take final gravity readings. (Hydrometer readings should be the same for several days in a row.)

12. Prime, bottle and condition the beer (see page 39).

Variation

Christmas Spice Ale: This is often the beer style that is served with mulling spices for a Winter Solstice beer. While there is a more complex recipe later in the book, if you want an easy version now, add two or three of your favorite spiced herbal tea bags during the last 15 minutes of the boil. (Use herbal tea, not black or green tea!) These beers make for great holiday gifts. Estimated Original Gravity: 1.064

Brewer's Tips

During the first 12 hours, check that fermentation has begun, and continue occasional aeration with a sanitized spoon if it has not. If fermentation has not begun within 24 hours, re-pitch the yeast and aerate.

If active fermentation backs up into the airlock, replace airlock with blow-off hose (see page 16). Change water as needed; re-install airlock when fermentation settles down.

California Blonde

Hoppy blonde ales are favorite summertime quaffs in West Coast brewpubs. There's something about that bite of the hop that makes you want to take another sip. If you want a less citrusy, more floral finish to the beer, use Liberty, Mt. Hood, Tradition or Vanguard hops for the aroma hops rather than the ones specified here.

The Alexander's extracts are widely distributed and work best for the recipes that call for it. If not available, substitute the lightest extra-light extract you can find.

Estimated Original Gravity: 1.059

Equipment

- **brew kettle**
- **fermentation gear (page 14)**

If you are a first-time brewer, read pages 8 to 36 thoroughly before you begin. Consult the summaries on pages 37 to 39 for details on preparing chlorinated water for brewing, preventing boil-overs, sanitizing fermentation gear, using the hydrometer, preparing and using the cooling bath, racking, checking fermentation, and priming, bottling and conditioning your beer.

5.5 US gal	brewing water (page 37)	21 L

Malt Extract

8 lbs	Alexander's Sun Country Pale Malt Extract, divided in half	3.6 kg

Bittering Hops

12 to 14 AAUs	high-alpha American hops (such as Amarillo, Centennial, Chinook or Columbus)	12 to 14 AAUs

Later Additions

1 tsp	Irish moss	5 mL
1 tsp	yeast nutrient	5 mL

Aroma Hops

2 oz	citrusy American hops (such as Ahtanum, Amarillo, Cascade or Williamette)	56 g

Yeast

1 pack	Fermentis S-05 American ale (if not available, select any clean-fermenting ale yeast)	1 pack

1. In a brew kettle, bring at least 3 US gal (11 L) brewing water to a boil. Remove from the heat, add half of the malt extract and stir until dissolved completely. Do not allow the extract to settle and scorch.

2. Return kettle to the burner and increase the heat until the liquid (wort) begins to boil. Using a spoon, clear any foam to one side. Do *not* allow it to seal the boil. Reduce the heat until a rolling boil can be maintained without foam buildup.

3. Add the bittering hops, stirring to combine. Boil for 45 minutes, uncovered. Monitor to prevent boiling over.

4. Meanwhile, prepare the fermentation gear (see page 37) and cooling bath (see page 38) or wort chiller.

5. After 45 minutes, remove the kettle from the heat and add remaining half of malt extract, Irish moss and yeast nutrient. Stir to combine and dissolve yeast nutrient. Return the kettle to the burner and bring back to a rolling boil. Boil for 15 minutes; stir in the aroma hops, turn off the heat and cover.

6. To cool the brew, place the covered kettle in the prepared cooling tub or use a wort chiller according to directions. Cool to yeast-pitching temperature, 75°F (24°C), within 30 to 45 minutes.

7. While the wort is cooling, clean and sanitize the brewing spoon. When the wort has cooled, move the kettle to a counter and stir wort briskly in one direction for about 5 minutes. After stirring, cover and let rest for 10 to 15 minutes; the hops and trub should form a cone in the bottom of the kettle.

8. Using a racking cane and siphon, rack as much wort as possible into the sanitized primary fermenter. Using the sanitized funnel and straining screen, strain the rest of the wort into the fermenter. Top off with brewing water to bring the volume to around 5.5 US gal (21 L). Using the hydrometer (see page 38), take a reading of the specific gravity and record it in your brewing journal. Aerate well by stirring vigorously with a sanitized spoon.

9. Sprinkle the yeast over the surface; vigorously stir with a sanitized spoon, distributing it well throughout the liquid. Seal the fermenter with lid, stopper and airlock. Keep the fermenter at room temperature (68 to 72°F/20 to 22°C) during primary fermentation (which typically lasts 1 to 4 days after fermentation begins), in a dark place or under a lightproof cover if using a glass carboy.

10. When the kräusen (brownish foam on top of the wort) has peaked and begun to fall (you'll see a ring around the inside of the bucket), rack the beer into the secondary fermenter gently to avoid aerating it, leaving most of the sediment behind. Seal and keep at room temperature, covered or in a dark place, to allow fermentation to continue.

11. Once the bubbling in the airlock has slowed, confirm completion of fermentation by using the hydrometer to take final gravity readings. (Hydrometer readings should be the same for several days in a row.)

12. Prime, bottle and condition the beer (see page 39).

Brewer's Tips

Instead of removing the kettle from the heat, use a medium saucepan to scoop out some of the wort (about 6 cups/1.5 L) and add the later additions to the wort in the saucepan. Stir until the extract and nutrient are dissolved and return to the wort in the kettle. Stir to disperse.

During the first 12 hours, check that fermentation has begun, and continue occasional aeration with a sanitized spoon if it has not. If fermentation has not begun within 24 hours, re-pitch the yeast and aerate.

Bavarian Hefeweizen

A great beer for summer enjoyment is a Bavarian Hefeweizen, the traditional German wheat beer. The beer is light and spritzy and has a nice spicy character from the yeast. In some taverns, it is served with a slice of lemon. The elimination of the Irish moss makes a traditional, hazy wheat beer. Feel free to include it if you'd like a clearer brew.

If you are not using the extract brands mentioned, be sure you use a 50/50 to 60/40 blend. If using 100% wheat, use 50% wheat and 50% extra-light extract, using the extra-light for the later addition.

Estimated Original Gravity: 1.048

Equipment

- **brew kettle**
- **fermentation gear (page 14)**

If you are a first-time brewer, read pages 8 to 36 thoroughly before you begin. Consult the summaries on pages 37 to 39 for details on preparing chlorinated water for brewing, preventing boil-overs, sanitizing fermentation gear, using the hydrometer, preparing and using the cooling bath, racking, checking fermentation, and priming, bottling and conditioning your beer.

5.5 US gal	brewing water (page 37)	21 L

Malt Extract

6.6 lbs	Cooper's or Munton's wheat malt extract, divided in half	3 kg

Bittering Hops

3 to 4 AAUs	European hops (such as Hallertau, Tettnang, Saaz or Spalt)	3 to 4 AAUs

Later Additions

1 tsp	yeast nutrient	5 mL

Aroma Hops

.5 oz	European hops (such as Hallertau, Tettnang, Saaz or Spalt)	14 g

Yeast

1 pack	Fermentis WB-06 or any other wheat-beer specific yeast	1 pack

1. In a brew kettle, bring at least 3 US gal (11 L) brewing water to a boil. Remove from the heat, add half the malt extract and stir until dissolved completely. Do not allow the extract to settle and scorch.

2. Return kettle to the burner and increase the heat until the liquid (wort) begins to boil. Using a spoon, clear any foam to one side. Do *not* allow it to seal the boil. Reduce the heat until a rolling boil can be maintained without foam buildup.

3. Add the bittering hops, stirring to combine. Boil for 45 minutes, uncovered. Monitor to prevent boiling over.

4. Meanwhile, prepare the fermentation gear (see page 37) and cooling bath (see page 38) or wort chiller.

5. After 45 minutes, remove the kettle from the heat and add remaining half of malt extract and yeast nutrient. Stir to combine and dissolve yeast nutrient. Return the kettle to the burner and bring back to a rolling boil. Boil for 15 minutes; stir in the aroma hops, turn off the heat and cover.

6. To cool the brew, place the covered kettle in the prepared cooling tub or use a wort chiller according to directions. Cool to yeast-pitching temperature, 75°F (24°C), within 30 to 45 minutes.

7. While the wort is cooling, clean and sanitize the brewing spoon. When the wort has cooled, move the kettle to a counter and stir wort briskly in one direction for about 5 minutes. After stirring, cover and let rest for 10 to 15 minutes; the hops and trub should form a cone in the bottom of the kettle.

8. Using a racking cane and siphon, rack as much wort as possible into the sanitized primary fermenter. Using the sanitized funnel and straining screen, strain the rest of the wort into the fermenter. Top off with brewing water to bring the volume to around 5.5 US gal (21 L). Using the hydrometer (see page 38), take a reading of the specific gravity and record it in your brewing journal. Aerate well by stirring vigorously with a sanitized spoon.

9. Sprinkle the yeast over the surface; vigorously stir with a sanitized spoon, distributing it well throughout the liquid. Seal the fermenter with lid, stopper and airlock. Keep the fermenter at room temperature (68 to 72°F/20 to 22°C) during primary fermentation (which typically lasts 1 to 4 days after fermentation begins), in a dark place or under a lightproof cover if using a glass carboy.

10. When the kräusen (brownish foam on top of the wort) has peaked and begun to fall (you'll see a ring around the inside of the bucket), rack the beer into the secondary fermenter gently to avoid aerating it, leaving most of the sediment behind. Seal and keep at room temperature, covered or in a dark place, to allow fermentation to continue.

11. Once the bubbling in the airlock has slowed, confirm completion of fermentation by using the hydrometer to take final gravity readings. (Hydrometer readings should be the same for several days in a row.)

12. Prime, bottle and condition the beer (see page 39).

Variations

Belgian Wit: If you like the Belgian-style white ales made by Hoegaarden, Allagash or Blue Moon, eliminate the aroma hops and add 1 oz (28 g) Bitter Orange Peel and 1 oz (28 g) coriander seed, lightly crushed and tied in a cheesecloth bag during the last 15 minutes of the boil. Switch the yeast to Fermentis T-58. Estimated OG: 1.048

American Wheat: Many brewpubs in North America make a light wheat ale as their entry level beer. To brew in this style, switch to a light American hop variety and change the yeast to Fermentis S-05. Estimated OG: 1.048

Brewer's Tips

Instead of removing the kettle from the heat, use a medium saucepan to scoop out some of the wort (about 6 cups/1.5 L) and add the later additions to the wort in the saucepan. Stir until the extract and nutrient are dissolved and return to the wort in the kettle. Stir to disperse.

During the first 12 hours, check that fermentation has begun, and continue occasional aeration with a sanitized spoon if it has not. If fermentation has not begun within 24 hours, re-pitch the yeast and aerate.

For all your friends who ask, "Yeah, but can you make regular beer?" here's a conventional, light-yellow beer. These beers are actually the hardest kind to produce because it is especially important that you not caramelize the sugars in your wort. This is another case where the best possible extract for this beer is the brand specified. If it's not available, substitute any brand of extra-light malt extract.

The rice syrup and malto-dextrin powder give the beer a nice creamy character.

Estimated Original Gravity: 1.050

Equipment

- **brew kettle**
- **fermentation gear (page 14)**

This recipe is slightly more challenging than the earlier ones. Try this one after one or two batches of the early recipes.

Cream Ale (Canadian Ale)

5.5 US gal	brewing water (page 37)	21 L

Malt Extract

5.4 lbs	Alexander's Sun Country Pale malt extract, divided 1.4:4 lbs (700 g:1.8 kg)	2.5 kg

Bittering Hops

4 to 6 AAUs	hops with alpha acid below 6%	4 to 6 AAUs

Later Additions

1 lb	rice syrup	450 g
8 oz	malto-dextrin powder	224 g
1 tsp	Irish moss	5 mL
1 tsp	yeast nutrient	5 mL

Aroma Hops

.5 oz	hops with alpha acid below 4%	14 g

Yeast

1 pack	Fermentis S-05 American ale yeast	1 pack

1. In a brew kettle, bring at least 3 US gal (11 L) brewing water to a boil. Remove from the heat, add 1.4 lbs (700 g) malt extract and stir until dissolved completely. Do not allow the extract to settle and scorch.

2. Return kettle to the burner and increase the heat until the liquid (wort) begins to boil. Using a spoon, clear any foam to one side. Do not allow it to seal the boil. Reduce the heat until a rolling boil can be maintained without foam buildup.

3. Add the bittering hops, stirring to combine. Boil for 45 minutes, uncovered. Monitor to prevent boiling over.

4. Meanwhile, prepare the fermentation gear (see page 37) and cooling bath (see page 38) or wort chiller.

5. After 45 minutes, remove the kettle from the heat and add remaining 4 lbs (1.8 kg) of malt extract, rice syrup, malto-dextrin powder, Irish moss and yeast nutrient. Stir to combine and dissolve powder and yeast nutrient. Return the kettle to the burner and bring back to a rolling boil. Boil for 15 minutes; stir in the aroma hops, turn off the heat and cover.

6. To cool the brew, place the covered kettle in the prepared cooling tub or use a wort chiller according to directions. Cool to yeast-pitching temperature, 75°F (24°C), within 30 to 45 minutes.

7. While wort is cooling, clean and sanitize brewing spoon. When wort has cooled, move the kettle to a counter and stir wort briskly in one direction for about 5 minutes. After stirring, cover and let rest for 10 to 15 minutes; hops and trub should form a cone in the bottom.

8. Using a racking cane and siphon, rack as much wort as possible into the sanitized primary fermenter. Using the sanitized funnel and straining screen, strain the rest of the wort into the fermenter. Top off with brewing water to bring the volume to around 5.5 US gal (21 L). Using the hydrometer (see page 38), take a reading of the specific gravity and record it in your brewing journal. Aerate well by stirring vigorously with a sanitized spoon.

9. Sprinkle the yeast over the surface; vigorously stir with a sanitized spoon, distributing it well throughout the liquid. Seal the fermenter with lid, stopper and airlock. Keep the fermenter at room temperature (68 to 72°F/20 to 22°C) during primary fermentation (which typically lasts 1 to 4 days after fermentation begins), in a dark place or under a lightproof cover if using a glass carboy.

10. When the kräusen has peaked and begun to fall (you'll see a ring around the inside of the bucket), rack the beer into the secondary fermenter gently to avoid aerating it, leaving most of the sediment behind. Seal and keep at room temperature, covered or in a dark place, to allow fermentation to continue.

11. Once the bubbling in the airlock has slowed, confirm completion of fermentation by using the hydrometer to take final gravity readings. (Hydrometer readings should be the same for several days in a row.)

12. Prime, bottle and condition the beer (see page 39).

Variations

Dry Cream Ale: To brew a drier, cheaper version of this ale, substitute dextrose for the rice syrup and eliminate the malto-dextrin powder.

Light Lager: To brew a light lager, follow this recipe but switch to a lager yeast such as Fermentis S-23. Follow the lagering directions with the Fest Bier recipe (see page 59). Estimated Original Gravity: 1.050

Honey Cream Ale: To brew a Honey Cream Ale, add 1 lb (450 g) of a light-colored honey as an additional kettle sugar when you add the rice syrup at the end of the 45-minute boil. Estimated Original Gravity: 1.050

Brewer's Tips

Instead of removing the kettle from the heat, use a medium saucepan to scoop out some of the wort (about 6 cups/1.5 L) and add the later additions to the wort in the saucepan. Stir until the extract, syrup, powder and nutrient are dissolved and return to the wort in the kettle. Stir to disperse.

During the first 12 hours, check that fermentation has begun, and continue occasional aeration with a sanitized spoon if it has not. If fermentation has not begun within 24 hours, re-pitch the yeast and aerate.

Ale-sner

A friend of mine once started up a brewpub in the summertime. Needing a light, pilsner-like beer for hot weather quaffing, he didn't have the time to do a lager beer. The solution? Make an ale that tastes like a Pils.

Estimated Original Gravity: 1.048

Equipment

- **brew kettle**
- **fermentation gear (page 14)**

If you are a first-time brewer, read pages 8 to 36 thoroughly before you begin. Consult the summaries on pages 37 to 39 for details on preparing chlorinated water for brewing, preventing boil-overs, sanitizing fermentation gear, using the hydrometer, preparing and using the cooling bath, racking, checking fermentation, and priming, bottling and conditioning your beer.

This recipe is slightly more challenging than the earlier ones. Try this one after one or two batches of the early recipes.

5.5 US gal	brewing water (page 37)	21 L

Malt Extract

6.6 lbs	extra-light, divided in half	3 kg

Bittering Hops

8 to 10 AAUs	Perle, Premiant or Northern Brewer hops	8 to 10 AAUs

Later Additions

8 oz	malto-dextrin powder	224 g
1 tsp	Irish moss	5 mL
1 tsp	yeast nutrient	5 mL

Aroma and Dry Hops

3 oz	Saaz (Czech) or Hallertau, Spalt or Tettnang (German) hops, divided in half	85 g

Yeast

1 pack	Fermentis S-05	1 pack

1. In a brew kettle, bring at least 3 US gal (11 L) brewing water to a boil. Remove from the heat, add half of the malt extract and stir until dissolved completely. Do not allow the extract to settle and scorch.

2. Return kettle to the burner and increase the heat until the liquid (wort) begins to boil. Using a spoon, clear any foam to one side. Do *not* allow it to seal the boil. Reduce the heat until a rolling boil can be maintained without foam buildup.

3. Add the bittering hops, stirring to combine. Boil for 45 minutes, uncovered. Monitor to prevent boiling over.

4. Meanwhile, prepare the fermentation gear (see page 37) and cooling bath (see page 38) or wort chiller.

5. After 45 minutes, remove the kettle from the heat and add remaining half malt extract, malto-dextrin powder, Irish moss and yeast nutrient. Stir to combine and dissolve powder and yeast nutrient. Stir to ensure that the extract, sugars and nutrient are dissolved. Return the kettle to the burner and bring back to a rolling boil. Boil for 15 minutes; stir in half of the hops, turn off the heat and cover.

6. To cool the brew, place the covered kettle in the prepared cooling tub or use a wort chiller according to directions. Cool to yeast-pitching temperature, 75°F (24°C), within 30 to 45 minutes.

7. While the wort is cooling, clean and sanitize the brewing spoon. When the wort has cooled, move the kettle to a counter and stir wort briskly in one direction for about 5 minutes. After stirring, cover and let rest for 10 to 15 minutes; the hops and trub should form a cone in the bottom of the kettle.

8. Using a sanitized racking cane and siphon, rack as much wort as possible into the sanitized primary fermenter. Using the sanitized funnel and straining screen, strain the rest of the wort into the fermenter. Top off with brewing water to bring the volume to around 5.5 US gal (21 L). Using the hydrometer (see page 38), take a reading of the specific gravity and record it in your brewing journal. Aerate well by stirring vigorously with a sanitized spoon.

9. Sprinkle the yeast over the surface; vigorously stir with a sanitized spoon, distributing it well throughout the liquid. Seal the fermenter with lid, stopper and airlock. Keep the fermenter at room temperature (68 to 72°F/20 to 22°C) during primary fermentation (which typically lasts 1 to 4 days after fermentation begins), in a dark place or under a lightproof cover if using a glass carboy.

10. When the kräusen (brownish foam on top of the wort) has peaked and begun to fall (you'll see a ring around the inside of the bucket), rack the beer into the secondary fermenter gently to avoid aerating it, leaving most of the sediment behind. Seal and keep at room temperature, covered or in a dark place, to allow fermentation to continue.

11. Once the bubbling in the airlock has slowed, gently add the remaining hops, reseal and leave for about 2 more weeks. Confirm completion of fermentation by using the hydrometer to take final gravity readings. (Hydrometer readings should be the same for several days in a row.)

12. Prime, bottle and condition the beer (see page 39).

Brewer's Tips

During the first 12 hours, check that fermentation has begun, and continue occasional aeration with a sanitized spoon if it has not. If fermentation has not begun within 24 hours, re-pitch the yeast and aerate.

For a true lagered version, see the note on lagering on page 59.

Part 2

Taking Your Brewing Skills to the Next Level

Now that you have brewed a few batches of beer, you should be ready to refine your technique and become more adventurous with the styles of beer you brew and the ingredients you use.

Upgrading Your Brewing Ingredients

For the absolute beginner brewing recipes in Part 1, the ingredients were basic and often chosen based on ease of use—malt extract, hop pellets and dry yeast. Now that you're more familiar with your brewing gear and the brewing process, you can start to work with malted grains as well as malt extracts and liquid yeasts. You may also wish to experiment with leaf hops.

Working with Malted Grains

Most beers are brewed from malted barley or wheat grains, and the recipes here are no exception. In the recipes in the next two parts of the book, other malted grains, such as wheat and occasionally rye and oats, are sometimes added to the mix or "grain bill," as it is called by brewers. Barley or wheat grains, and any additional grains, add complexity to the flavor of your beer. These malted grains are the backbone of your beer, but what exactly are they? While you likely know what barley and the other grains are, other than a malted milk shake or a candy reference, you won't often hear the term "malted" used outside the context of beer.

Turning Grains into Malted Grains

Grains are the seeds of the grasses we eat. When a seed hits the ground and is exposed to heat and moisture, germination occurs and a new plant begins to grow. During germination, enzymes in the seed spring into action and begin to convert starches in the seed into sugars it can use to grow into a plant. Until the seed develops a root structure and is able to draw nutrients from the soil, it is these starches that the seed feeds on. If the process is allowed to continue, the seed becomes a plant, grows and matures and eventually produces more seeds.

The maltster interrupts this process; he has his own agenda. He soaks and germinates the grains under controlled conditions and then dries them in a kiln at a relatively low temperature to stop the germination process while enzymes and starches are still available. Light-colored malted grains

Degrees Lovibond

The color of the beer that results from brewing with the various roasts of malted grains is rated in "degrees Lovibond," based on a scale developed by British brewer Joseph William Lovibond. This rating indicates the color that the malt contributes to your beer. Pale and Pilsner base malts might read around +/- 2 to 3 degrees Lovibond. Light-toasted malts like Munich and Vienna range from +/- 6 to 10. Crystal and other toasted malts run from 10 to 150. Dark roasted malts could be from 300 to 500. You can tweak the color of your beer, knowing that the higher the degrees Lovibond, the darker the resulting beer. If you want your pale ale to be paler, experiment with lighter toasted malts. If you want your brown ale to be darker, use a higher Lovibond malt.

such as pale ale malt, Pilsner and malted wheat are the result, and these malted grains (or their malt extract equivalent) provide the bulk of the fermentable sugars for the beer. The maltster may toast or roast some of the grains at higher temperatures to produce malts with fewer available enzymes but more flavor; malted grains such as Vienna, Munich and brown are the result. Specialty malted grains such as crystal and caramel malts have been wet before heating. All their starches are converted to sugar during heating; they give flavor, aroma and different colors to the beer but do not contribute fermentable sugars.

Preparing and Steeping Malted Grains

The malted grains are handed over to either the commercial brewer or the malt extract manufacturer. Whether the product is beer or malt extract, the grains are cracked, which simply breaks the tough outer case of the seed. The cracked grains are mixed with hot brewing water and mashed, putting the enzymes back to work breaking down the remaining starches into sugar.

The grains are rinsed in a process called sparging, and the rinse water (which contains more sugars) creates sweet wort. The grains are discarded.

The brewer uses this liquid to begin the process of brewing beer. The maker of malt extract evaporates the water off the liquid to make malt extract. If 80% of the water is removed, malt extract syrup is produced. If all the water is removed, the result is dry malt extract (DME).

Why Choose Malted Grains?

In the recipes in Part 1, the beers were made with malt extract. But malt extract is to beer what commercially made chicken stock is to homemade chicken noodle soup. Just as you would use commercial chicken stock instead of rendering a chicken in a pot to make the soup stock for your first soup, your brewing process is streamlined and simplified by the use of malt extract.

To extend the chicken soup analogy, your first batches of beer, made entirely from malt extract, were akin to opening a can labeled "chicken noodle soup" and heating it. You can create a more robust and complex, "from scratch" chicken soup flavor by adding fresh chicken, vegetables and noodles to commercially made chicken stock. Although you didn't go through the effort of making homemade stock, the latter approach tastes a lot more like it was made from scratch than a canned soup.

Similarly, in the recipes that follow, you begin to incorporate malted grains, rather than just malt extract, into the brewing process. This brings a whole new level of flavor to your beer. As there are many different kinds of malted grains, you can bring many different flavors and colors to your brew by tweaking your use of different grains.

The recipes call for coarsely cracked malted grains that are placed in a grain bag. This bag is steeped in the brewing water at around 150 to 160°F (65 to 71°C) and rinsed with brewing water before it is discarded. Making this "grain tea" or sweet wort is an early step in the intermediate brewing process, and it will change the depth of flavor in your beer.

The chart that follows shows the types of malted grains available for brewing and their countries of origin.

Consult the chart any time you need to change an unobtainable specified malted grain for one that is available, or if you simply wish to experiment with grains in your brew.

Malted Grains for Homebrewing

	North American	UK	Germany	Belgium/France
Base Malt 1^+ to 3^+ Lovibond; used to make malt extracts	• 2-row • 6-row • pale • Pilsner or Pilsen • rye • wheat	• lager • maris otter • mild • oat • pale • wheat	• dark wheat • light wheat • pale • Pilsner or Pilsen • rye	• pale • Pilsner or Pilsen • wheat
Light Crystal 1^+ to 20 Lovibond; used for caramel flavor, sweetness and color	• Carapils® • Carastan® • crystal/caramel malts (10 to 20 Lovibond)	• caramel	• Carafoam® • Carahelles®	• Carapils®
Light Toasted 6 to 20 Lovibond; used as base malt or specialty grains used for color and toasted flavor	• Munich • Vienna		• Abbey™ • Carabelge® • Munich I & II • Vienna	• Munich • Vienna
Medium Crystal 20^1 to 65 Lovibond	• caramel Vienne • Caravienne® • crystal/caramel (20 to 40 Lovibond)	• crystal (40 to 60 Lovibond)	• Caramunich® I, II & III • Caravienne®	• Caramunich® I, II & III • Caravienne®
Medium Toasted 20^+ to 75^+/- Lovibond	• aromatic • honey • victory	• amber • brown	• Caraamber® • Carared® • Melanoidin®	• aromatic • biscuit
Dark Crystal 65^+ to 150 Lovibond	• crystal (60 to 120^+ Lovibond)	• crystal (150 Lovibond)	• Caraaroma® • Caraboheme®	• Special B
Dark Roasted up to 700 Lovibond	• black patent • chocolate	• black patent • chocolate	• Carafa® I, II & III (dehusked version preferred)	• black • chocolate
Specialty Malts and Unmalted Grains Lovibond varies; use varies	• cherry wood • roast unmalted barley • smoked	• peat smoked • roast unmalted barley	• acidulated • caramel wheat & rye; chocolate wheat & rye • rauchmalt (smoked) • roast unmalted barley	
Flaked Grains used to enhance body of beer	• barley • corn • oat • rice • wheat	• barley • oat		

Working With Leaf Hops

Hops remain the spice of beer, although some recipes contain additional flavorings. The bitter flowers of the female plant (the hops) are added to beer to give bitter flavors and spicy floral aromas that offset the sweetness of the malt. Hops also have preservative properties.

Early beers were not hopped; instead, they were flavored with various medicinal and bitter herbs. This blend was called gruit (rhymes with fruit). Hops came originally from Asia and were brought westward to Europe. They weren't used widely in beer until around the 13th century. Today, herbalists still use hop cones to make mild sedatives. It is this soporific quality that adds to the enjoyment of beer.

All of the recipes in this book assume you will be using hop pellets for bittering, aroma or flavor hops or for dry hopping, although leaf or plug hops are available. As you become more sophisticated in your brewing, you may wish to try working with leaf hops.

Leaf hops have slightly different properties, so when bittering the beer with leaf hops, use 1 AAU more. For the aroma hops, add the same weight of leaf hops but add them five minutes before the end of the boil rather than at the end of the boil.

For ease of use, you can put leaf hops in a hop bag (nylon or cheesecloth). There is less mess with the trub if the hops are contained in a bag. And if you're using leaf hops for dry hopping during fermentation, boil the bag to sanitize it before filling it with hops.

The charts that follow list the varieties of hops by country of origin, showing alpha acid ratings, flavor and aroma attributes, possible substitutions and uses. Consult these charts any time you wish to change an unobtainable specified hop for one that is available, or if you simply wish to experiment with the hops in your brew. Consider the following guidelines:

- Lower alpha acid hops tend to be used for aroma and flavor.
- Hops over 10% are generally for bittering, although any hops can be used for aroma.
- Mid-range alpha acid hops (6 to 10%) are more flexible and can be used at any point in a brew.
- There are some traditional brews that use a single hop such as a Czech Pilsner brewed with Saaz hops.

As a homebrewer, using the hops in the mid- and low-alpha acid range is recommended. If you are using the higher alpha acid hops for bittering, you may find that fine flavor control is difficult. All of the hops listed are available in pellet form.

American Hop Varieties	Alpha Acid Rating	Flavor/ Aroma Attributes	Substitutes	Use
Ahtanum	5.7 to 6.3%	used for its citrusy aromatic properties and moderate bittering	Cascade, Amarillo	• American pale ales • light lagers
Amarillo	8 to 11%	notes of tangerine aroma; medium to high bitterness	Cascade, Centennial; possibly Chinook or Ahtanum	• American ales • IPA
Brewer's Gold	8 to 10%	blackcurrant, fruity, spicy	Bullion (difficult to find)	• ale • Pilsners • lambic
Cascade	4.5 to 7.0%	flowery and citrusy; can have a grapefruit note	Centennial, Amarillo; to a lesser extent, Columbus	• American-style ales, especially pale ale • barley wines • IPA • porter • Witbier
Centennial	9.5 to 11.5%	medium intensity with floral and citrus tones	Cascade, possibly Columbus or Chinook; analytically, a blend of 70% Cascade and 30% Columbus gives similar profile	• all American ale styles • American wheat beers
Chinook	12.0 to 14.0%	medium intensity; spicy, piney, distinctive grapefruit	Nugget, Columbus, Northern Brewer, Target; possibly Centennial	• American-style pale ale • barley wine • IPA • lager (bittering hop) • porter • stout
Cluster	5.5 to 8.5%	floral and spicy	Galena; possibly US Northern Brewer	• ale (aroma) • lager (bittering) • stout

American Hop Varieties	Alpha Acid Rating	Flavor/ Aroma Attributes	Substitutes	Use
Columbus	14 to 16%	pungent	Nugget, Chinook, Target, Northern Brewer; possibly Centennial	• American IPA • American pale ale • barley wine • lager (bittering) • stout
Crystal	3.5 to 5.5%	mild; spicy and flowery	Mt Hood, Hersbrucker, French Strisselspalt, Liberty, Hallertau	• alt • Belgian-style ales • ESB • Kölsch • lager • Pilsner
Fuggle	4.0 to 5.5%	mild; woody and fruity	UK Fuggle, Willamette, Styrian Golding, US Tettnang	• any English-style beer or American ale • lambic
Galena	12 to 14%	citrusy	Nugget	• most English-style and American ales
Glacier	5.5%	excellent, pleasant hoppiness	Willamette, US Fuggle, US Tettnang, Styrian Golding	• bitter • English-style pale ale • ESB • pale ale • porter • stout
Golding	4.0 to 5.0%	mild, delicate classic English-type	UK Kent Golding, UK Progress; possibly the Fuggle family	• all English-style beers, especially all bitters and pale ale • barley wine • Belgian-style ales
Hallertau	3.5 to 5.5%	very mild, slightly flowery and somewhat spicy	Liberty, German Hallertau, German Tradition	• Belgian-style ales • bock • Kölsch • lager • Munich Helles • Pilsner • wheat

American Hop Varieties	Alpha Acid Rating	Flavor/ Aroma Attributes	Substitutes	Use
Horizon	11 to 13%	floral, spicy	Magnum	• all ales and lagers
Liberty	3.0 to 5.0%	mild with a slightly spicy character	US or German Hallertau, German Tradition, Mt Hood; possibly German Spalt	• American wheat • bock • Kölsch • lager • Pilsner
Magnum	12 to 14%	no real distinct aroma character, so is viewed favorably as a clean bittering hop	German Magnum; possibly Horizon	• good bittering hop for all ales and lagers
Millenium	15.5%	mild; herbal, similar to nugget	Nugget, Columbus	• ales • barley wine • stout
Mt Hood	5.0 to 8.0%	mild; somewhat pungent	Crystal, French Strisselspalt, German Hersbrucker	• alt • American wheat • bock • lager • Munich Helles • Pilsner
Newport	13.5 to 17%	mild	Galena, Nugget, Fuggle, Magnum, Brewer's Gold	• hoppy American ales
Northern Brewer	8 to 10%	medium-strong	German Northern Brewer, Chinook	• all English-styles, especially porter • American ales • Kölsch • Munich Helles
Nugget	12-14%	herbal	Galena, Magnum, Columbus, Target	• ales • barley wine • stout
Perle	7 to 9.5%	floral and slightly spicy	German Perle, German and US Northern Brewer	• alt • barley wine • Kölsch • lager • pale ale • porter • stout • weizen

American Hop Varieties	Alpha Acid Rating	Flavor/ Aroma Attributes	Substitutes	Use
Saaz	3.0 to 4.5%	very mild; spicy and earthy	Czech Saaz, Polish Lublin, Sterling	• American wheat • Belgian-style ales • bitter • lager • Pilsner
Santiam	5 to 7%	floral, slightly spicy	German Tettnang, German Spalt, German Spalter, German Select	• American ales • Belgian trippel and other Belgian-styles • bock • Kölsch • lager • Munich Helles • Pilsner
Simcoe™	12 to 14%	unique; pine-like aroma	unknown (try blending Chinook and Amarillo)	• American ales
Sterling	6 to 9%	herbal, spicy with a hint of floral and citrus	Czech Saaz	• ales and Belgian-style ales • Pilsner and other lagers
Tettnang	4.0 to 5.0%	slightly spicy	German Select, German Spalt, Santiam	• American ales • American wheat • bitter • lager • Pilsner
Vanguard	5.5% - 6%	similar to Hallertau	Hallertau, German Hersbrucker, Mt Hood, Liberty	• Belgian-style ales • bock • Kölsch • lager • Munich Helles • Pilsner • wheat
Warrior™	15 to 17%	very mild	Nugget, Columbus	• IPA • pale ale
Willamette	4.0 to 6.0%	mild and pleasant, slightly spicy	US Fuggle, US Tettnang, Styrian Golding	• all English-style ales • American pale and brown ales

British Hop Varieties	Alpha Acid Rating	Flavor/ Aroma Attributes	Substitutes	Use
Bramling Cross	4 to 6%	spicy	Fuggle, Golding; Sovereign	• English-style ales
Challenger	6.5 to 8.5%	mild to moderate; quite spicy	US or German Perle, Northern Brewer	• barley wine • bitter • brown ales • English-style ales • ESB • porter • stout
First Gold	6.5 to 8.5%	a little like Golding; spicy	UK Kent Golding; possibly Crystal	• ale • ESB
Fuggle	4 to 5.5%	mild, pleasant and hoppy	US Fuggle, Willamette, Styrian Golding	• all English-style ales • ESB • bitter • lager • lambic
Kent Golding	4 to 5.5%	gentle, fragrant and pleasant	US Golding, Whitbread Golding, UK Progress	• Belgian-style ales • English-style ales
Northdown	7.5 to 9.5%	mild, pleasant and delicate hop aroma	UK Challenger, Northern Brewer, Pilgrim	• all ales • porter
Progress	5 to 7%	moderately strong; good aroma	UK Kent Golding, Fuggle, Pilgrim	• ale • bitter • ESB • Porter
Target	9.5 to 12.5%	pleasant English hop aroma; quite intense	Fuggle, Willamette	• all ales and lagers

European Hop Varieties	Alpha Acid Rating	Flavor/ Aroma Attributes	Substitutes	Use
Czech Saaz	3 to 4.5%	very mild with pleasant hoppy notes	US Saaz, Polish Lublin, US Sterling	• Belgian-style ales • lagers • Pilsner

European Hop Varieties	Alpha Acid Rating	Flavor/Aroma Attributes	Substitutes	Use
French Strisselspalt	3 to 5%	medium intensity; pleasant and hoppy	Mt Hood, Crystal, German Hersbrucker	• lager • Pilsner • wheat
GR Brewer's Gold	5.5 to 6.5%	black currant, fruity, spicy	UK Northdown, Northern Brewer, Galena, Bullion, Brewer's Gold	• ale • heavier German-style lagers • lambic
GR Hallertau	3.5 to 5.5%	mild and pleasant	Liberty, German Tradition, Ultra	• Belgian-style ales • bock • Kölsch • lager • Munich Helles • Pilsner • weizen • wheat
GR Hersbrucker	3 to 5.5%	mild to semi-strong; pleasant and hoppy	Mt Hood, French Strisselspalt	• Belgian-style ales • bock • Kölsch • lager • Munich Helles • Pilsner • weizen • wheat
GR Magnum	12 to 14%	no real distinct aroma character, so it is viewed favorably as a clean bittering hop	Columbus, Nugget	• ales • lagers • Pilsner types • stout • This hop is typically used as the base bitterness in lager beers and many ales
GR Northern Brewer	7 to 10%	medium-strong with some wild American tones	Chinook, US Northern Brewer, German Brewer's Gold	• bitter • English pale ale • ESB • lager • lambic • Munich Helles • porter

European Hop Varieties	Alpha Acid Rating	Flavor/ Aroma Attributes	Substitutes	Use
GR Perle	6 to 8%	moderately intense; good and hoppy	US Perle, Northern Brewer	• ale • alt • Kölsch • lager • Munich Helles • pale ale • Pilsner • porter • stout • weizen
GR Select	4 to 6%	very fine Spalt type aroma	US Saaz, US Tettnang, German Spalt, German Tettnang, German Hersbrucker	• lager • This hop is used in any beer where noble aroma is wanted (e.g., Pilsner).
GR Spalt	4 to 5%	mild and pleasant; slightly spicy	US Saaz, US Tettnang, German Spalt, German Select	• alt • bock • Kölsch • lager • Munich Helles • Pilsner
GR Tettnang	3.5 to 5.5%	mild and pleasant, slightly spicy	German Spalt, German Select, US Tettnang, US Saaz, German Hersbrucker	• ale • alt • Kölsch • lager • lambic • Munich Helles • Pilsner • weizen
GR Tradition	5 to 7%	very fine; similar to German Hallertau	Liberty, German Hallertau	• bock • lager • Pilsner • weizen • wheat
Styrian Golding	4.5 to 6%	delicate; slightly spicy	US Fuggle, Willamette, UK Fuggle	• Belgian-style ales • English-style ales • ESB • lager • Pilsner

Working with Liquid Yeast

Until the invention of the microscope, the function of yeast and how it worked to make beer was a mystery. We now know that yeast lives to eat malt sugar and turn it into alcohol and carbon dioxide.

There are two main types of yeast for brewing purposes. As noted earlier, top-fermenting yeast (ale yeast) works at the top of the fermenting vessel in the cellar-to-room temperature range. Bottom-fermenting yeast (lager yeast) toils in the bottom of the fermenter in colder temperatures. (Lager yeast was isolated in the northern European climate where ale yeasts would languish during the winter months, and, prior to the invention of refrigeration, lagers were only produced during cold-weather seasons.)

Within the two main categories, there are many different strains of yeast. Each strain is suited to a particular style of beer. As you become familiar with the various yeasts, you can select the strains that make your beer taste the way you like. Use your brewing journal to track which strains of yeast you chose and how the beer tastes as a result.

To simplify the brewing process in the recipes in Part 1 of the book, only dry yeast strains were specified. As an intermediate brewer, you can start to work with the liquid yeast cultures available from your homebrew supplier. These yeasts open up a new brewing universe to you. Each of the recipes in this part of the book suggests yeasts in both liquid form (from Wyeast or White Labs) and dry form (from Fermentis, Danstar or Lalvin). Go for the liquid yeasts if possible.

Preparing the yeast is the first step in the recipes in this part of the book, even though the yeast is pitched at the same stage in the brewing session as in recipes from Part 1. Like the rest of the brewing process, once you become accustomed to the liquid yeast process, it is just another easy step. Complete instructions on how to prepare the yeast are provided on the yeast package, but plan on preparing the liquid yeast three to five hours (or as specified on the package) before you begin the brewing session so it is ready at the appropriate time. (This is why yeast appears first on the ingredient lists of these intermediate-level recipes.)

Liquid yeasts cost a bit more than dry yeasts; however, with advance planning, you can re-pitch (reuse) a liquid yeast for up to six batches of beer, making it a less expensive yeast in the long run.

Depending on the manufacturer, you either need to activate the yeast pack according to the package instructions (often called a "smack pack") or make a yeast starter.

Making a Yeast Starter

A starter is simply a mini batch of beer that is used to start the reproduction of the yeast. Giving the yeast a head start enables it to divide to produce more yeast cells before it goes into the beer for fermentation. Note that a number of recipes suggest that you either use two packs of yeast or one pack of yeast in a starter. This is because yeast in a starter has many more yeast cells than yeast straight from the package. Using a starter requires more advance planning—the starter itself requires at least 24 hours to develop.

Yeast starter is a mixture of yeast, brewing water, dry malt extract and yeast nutrient.

1 pack	specified yeast	1 pack
32 US fl oz	brewing water	950 mL
3.5 oz	DME	98 g
½ tsp	yeast nutrient	3 mL

1. Activate yeast according to package instructions.
2. In a small saucepan, bring the brewing water to a boil. Stir in the DME and nutrient; boil for 20 minutes.
3. Remove from heat and cool to 70°F (21°C).
4. Pour cooled brewing water into a sealable, sanitized jar with a lid or a bottle that can be fitted with a stopper and airlock. Cover loosely and shake well.
5. Add yeast culture and let jar sit, loosely covered to allow gas to escape (if not using stopper and airlock), at room temperature (below 75°F/24°C) for at least 24 hours. If not using yeast culture immediately, it can be refrigerated for up to one week. Bring the yeast to fermentation temperature before pitching.

Re-pitching Liquid Yeast

You can reuse liquid yeasts if you plan a cycle of beers that use the same strain. To do this successfully, run the cycle from lighter, weaker beers to darker, stronger beers. For example, you may work with a liquid English ale yeast. You could start the cycle with an ordinary bitter, then move on to a pale ale or ESB, followed by a brown ale, porter, stout or old ale and finish the cycle with a barley wine or Imperial stout.

How to collect yeast for re-pitching:
- Before you collect yeast for re-pitching, rack the current brew into the secondary fermenter and set up the beer for secondary fermentation.

- Collect about 1 US quart (1 L) of the slurry (sludge) left in the bottom of the primary fermenter.
- Put the slurry into a sanitized jar with a lid or a bottle that can be fitted with a stopper and airlock, seal it and store it in the refrigerator. (The slurry will settle out into a layer of beer on top of a layer of tan yeast on top of a layer of trub.)
- If not using an airlock, "burp" the jar daily by cracking the lid to allow any built-up pressure to escape.
- *Within one week,* brew the next batch of beer.
- At the beginning of the next brewing session, remove the sealed jar of slurry from the refrigerator and allow the contents to warm to room temperature.
- When it comes time to pitch the yeast, open the jar and pour out as much of the top layer of beer as you can.
- Pour the tan yeast layer into the new batch of beer in the primary fermenter. (Most of the bottom trub layer sticks to the bottom of the jar; leave it there.)
- Repeat the yeast collection process at the end of primary fermentation.
- Do not re-pitch a yeast more than five or six times.
- Never re-pitch yeast from a contaminated batch.

Brewing a True Lager

The recipes for Mexican lagers on pages 98 and 99 are the first for true lager beers. Lagers require cold fermentation, which means either refrigerating your fermenter or brewing during cold-weather months.

Pitch the yeast and keep the fermenter at room temperature until fermentation begins. Then drop the temperature to the 46 to 55°F (8 to 13°C) range for one week. You will then rack the beer to the secondary fermenter and keep it at 35 to 45°F (2 to 7°C) for four weeks. Bottle and store the beer in the refrigerator for three to four weeks. If a cold ferment is not possible, brew like an ale using a neutral yeast such as those used in American, German, Kölsch or European ales. See Ale-sner (page 70) for method.

Young lagers often give off a sulphur smell. Don't panic. Just give the beer some time.

The beer recipes in Part 2 are separated by country of origin, beginning with North America, then the United Kingdom, Belgium, Germany, the Czech Republic and the Baltic region. The recipes end with a reprise of the recipes for ales from Part 1, recreated with liquid yeasts and grains. Recipes from modern craft brewing, which transcend geographical borders and are sorted by type, await you in Part 3.

Brewer's Tip

To learn more about the various styles of beer that can be brewed, check out the Beer Judge Certification Program (BJCP) at www.bjcp.org.

Brew Day Process Summary

The following tips and techniques have been condensed from the detailed look at the brew day process found on pages 20 to 36.

❶ Preparing Chlorinated Water for Brewing

Municipal tap water must be dechlorinated before it's used for brewing. If you prepare the water before brew day, store it in the refrigerator in sanitized, sealed containers.

6 US gal	municipal tap water	23 L
⅛ tsp	potassium metabisulfite (1 campden tablet) per kettle-full of water	0.5 mL

1. Fill brew kettle with half or all of the water needed.
2. Add potassium metabisulfite to water, stirring to dissolve it.
3. Bring water to a rolling boil; turn off heat.
4. Allow water to rest for 15 minutes as it dechlorinates.

If you know that your water has been treated with chlorine rather than chloramines, you can bring the water to a boil and boil it vigorously for 15 minutes to remove the chlorine. Chloramines are not broken down by boiling.

❷ Preparing a Yeast Starter

Starter requires at least 24 hours to develop.

1 pack	specified yeast	1 pack
32 US fl oz	brewing water	950 mL
3.5 oz	DME	99 g
½ tsp	yeast nutrient	3 mL

1. Activate yeast according to package instructions.
2. In a small saucepan, bring the brewing water to a boil. Stir in the DME and nutrient; boil for 20 minutes.
3. Remove from heat and cool to 70°F (21°C).
4. Pour cooled brewing water into a sealable, sanitized jar with lid or bottle with stopper and airlock. Cover loosely and shake well.
5. Add yeast culture and let jar sit, loosely covered to allow gas to escape, at room temperature (below 75°F/24°C) for at least 24 hours. If not using yeast culture immediately, it can be refrigerated for up to one week. Bring yeast to fermentation temperature before pitching.

How to collect yeast for re-pitching:
- Rack the current brew into the secondary fermenter and set up for secondary fermentation.
- Collect about 1 US quart (1 L) of slurry from bottom of the primary fermenter.
- Put the slurry into a sanitized jar with lid or bottle with stopper and airlock, seal and store in refrigerator.

- If not using airlock, "burp" the jar daily.
- Within one week, brew the next batch of beer.
- At the beginning of the next brewing session, remove the sealed jar of slurry from refrigerator and allow to warm to room temperature.
- To pitch yeast, open jar and pour as much of top layer of beer as you can down the drain.
- Pour tan yeast layer into new batch of beer in primary fermenter. (Leave trub layer in bottom of the jar.)
- Repeat yeast collection process at end of primary fermentation.
- Do not re-pitch a yeast more than five or six times.
- Never re-pitch yeast from a contaminated batch.

❸ Sanitizing Fermentation Gear (and Everything Else)

Sanitize all gear and containers used in primary and secondary fermentation and bottling just prior to the relevant stage in the process.

1. Place items such as the airlock, stopper, racking cane, siphon hose, mouthpiece (if using), aerator (if using), hydrometer, turkey baster or Thief, funnel with straining screen, floating thermometer, bottler filler and bottle caps (when bottling) and fermenter lid into primary fermenter or bottling bucket. Fill the container with water. If sanitizing a glass carboy, fill it with water.
2. Add 2 US fl oz (60 mL) unscented household bleach to the water in the container and let sit for 30 minutes. (If using homebrew sanitizer, use it according to the package instructions.)
3. Run sanitizer through anything the brew will pass through: siphon tube, racking cane, mouthpiece, bottle filler or faucet (when bottling). Wipe sanitizer on parts that cannot be immersed.
4. Drain sanitizer out of the container. Place sanitized gear on a sanitized counter until ready to use.
5. Keep a small amount of sanitizer available to re-sanitize items such as spoons that are used during the brewing process.

❹ Using the Hydrometer

Always withdraw a sample of the brew and take the reading in either a sample tube or jar or in the Thief.

1. Sanitize turkey baster for withdrawing the sample or sanitize the Thief, which can both withdraw the sample and float the hydrometer. If using the turkey baster, you also need a sample tube or jar large enough to float the hydrometer.
2. Withdraw a wort sample big enough to fill three-quarters of the sample tube and float the hydrometer.
3. Place the hydrometer in the sample and read it where it breaks the surface. Only the last two numbers of the gravity are shown. When you read past 1.000, the first number you'll see is 10; that means the density is 1.010; the next is 20 (1.020) and so on.
4. Record the gravity reading in your brewing journal and use the same technique to take later readings. Do not return the sample to the rest of your brew unless you used a sanitized Thief.

❺ Preparing and Using the Cooling Bath

If you're cooling your brew with the ice-and-saltwater bath, prepare it while the boil is on and the fermentation gear is soaking in sanitizer.

1. Fill the tub with enough water to surround your kettle at or above the level of the beer inside it when the kettle is in the tub (in other words, allow for displacement of the water).

2. Add ½ to 1 cup (125 to 250 mL) of salt and stir to dissolve.

3. Add ice to bring the temperature of the salt water down.

4. At the end of the boil, remove the kettle from the stove, cover it and put it in the saltwater bath, ensuring that the salt water doesn't get into the brew.

5. Add ice to the bath, and keep the warm water around the kettle on the move to assist in cooling.

6. After 20 minutes, check the wort temperature with the sanitized thermometer. The temperature goal is around 75°F (24°C) or as per yeast instructions. Ideally, you should bring the temperature down within 30 to 45 minutes. At that point, the beer can be prepared for racking into the fermenter.

❻ Racking, Priming, Bottling and Conditioning

Once the hydrometer readings confirm that fermentation is complete, your brew is ready to bottle. This step adds some sugar to carbonate the beer as it conditions in the bottle.

1 cup	brewing water	250 mL
5 oz	dextrose (corn sugar) for priming	140 g

1. Clean and sanitize the bottles using your standard sanitizing procedure. Sanitize caps, racking cane, siphon hose, spoon, bottle filler and bottling bucket. Run sanitizer through bottling faucet.

2. In a small saucepan, bring brewing water to a boil. Add dextrose. Return mixture to a boil and stir to dissolve dextrose. Remove from heat and cover. Cool to room temperature.

3. Gently rack the beer into the bottling bucket, leaving sediment behind and being careful not to aerate. Gently add priming solution. Using a sanitized spoon, stir the beer gently to ensure even distribution of priming solution.

4. Using bottling faucet or siphon and bottle filler, fill bottles to top; 1 to 1.5 in (2.5 to 3.8 cm) of space remains when filler is removed. Cap bottles securely.

5. Store bottles upright in cool, dark place to allow for carbonation and settling of sediment.

6. After 3 to 4 weeks, hold a bottle to the light to check that sediment is settling. Unless otherwise indicated in the recipe, sample some brew! Note the date, flavor and level of carbonation each time you sample to compare as it ages.

The beers that have dominated the craft beer scene in North America are about hops more often than not. In the 1960s, North American wines were feeble attempts to emulate European wines. North American wines became interesting when winemakers developed their own style and stopped trying to make wine that tasted like it came from somewhere else. Similarly, North American beers became interesting when brewers stopped trying to make a boring rendition of a northern European lager (the least exciting Euro beer).

The distinctive hops that are grown in the Pacific Northwest have become the cornerstone of North American craft beers with their flavors and aromas in the forefront. If that's not your cup of tea, use Perle hops for bittering all recipes and bitter on the low end (or below it if your taste dictates). For aroma hops, use Liberty, Mt Hood or Willamette. Alternately, check out the more moderately hopped beers from the UK and Europe. Needless to say there are a few recipes in this section that aren't hop bombs, but if a recipe contains more than 2 oz (56 g) of hops, you can consider it hoppy.

North American Brews

California Common (Steam-style)

Most beer styles available in the Americas are variations of classic European beer styles. Very few beer styles, other than South American corn-based Chichas, show evidence that they were created in the New World. This one, however, born in the days of the California Gold Rush, is truly a beverage with its roots in North America.

By the 1970s, this style was produced by only one brewery — Anchor.

Estimated Original Gravity: 1.053

Equipment

- **brew kettle**
- **fermentation gear (page 14)**

As you build your brewing skills, switching to liquid yeast products (from Wyeast or White Labs) will give you a brew that is more complex than the ones made with the dry yeast (from Fermentis or Danstar) in the Absolute Beginner recipes. See page 86 for more information about liquid yeasts.

Yeast

1 pack	Wyeast 2112 or White Labs WLP810 or Fermentis S-23	1 pack

Grains

8 oz	Special Roast malt (or any other toasted malt 25 to 50 Lovibond)	224 g
1 lb	crystal or caramel malt (30 to 60 Lovibond)	450 g
5.5 US gal	brewing water (page 89)	21 L

Malt Extract

6.6 lbs	light or gold (such as Briess, Coopers, Northwestern or any brand), divided in half	3 kg

Bittering Hops

10 to 12 AAUs	Northern Brewer, Perle or Centennial	10 to 12 AAUs

Later Additions

1 tsp	Irish moss	5 mL
1 tsp	yeast nutrient	5 mL

Aroma Hops

1.5 oz	Cascade or Northern Brewer	42 g

1. Prepare the liquid yeast in advance, according to the package directions (if using).
2. Coarsely crack the malt grains and place them in a cheesecloth or nylon grain bag.
3. In a brew kettle, bring at least 3 US gal (11 L) brewing water to steeping temperature (150 to 160°F/65 to 71°C). Turn off the heat, add the grain bag, cover and steep for 30 minutes. (If the temperature drops below steeping temperature, turn the element back on briefly to bring it back up.) Remove grain bag and discard.
4. Increase heat and bring grain tea to a boil. Remove from heat, add half the malt extract and stir until dissolved.
5. Return kettle to burner and increase heat until wort begins to boil. Using a spoon, clear foam to one side. Reduce heat until a rolling boil is maintained without foam buildup.
6. Add the bittering hops, stirring to combine. Boil for 45 minutes, uncovered. Monitor to prevent boiling over.
7. Meanwhile, prepare fermentation gear and cooling bath or wort chiller.

8. After 45 minutes, remove the kettle from the heat and add the remaining half of the extract, Irish moss and yeast nutrient. Stir to ensure that the extract and nutrient are dissolved. Return the kettle to the burner and bring back to a rolling boil. Boil for 15 minutes, then stir in the aroma hops, turn off the heat and cover.

9. To cool the brew, place the covered kettle in the prepared cooling tub or use a wort chiller according to the manufacturer's directions. Cool to the desired temperature, 75°F (24°C), within 30 to 45 minutes.

10. While the wort is cooling, clean and sanitize the brewing spoon. When the wort has cooled, move the kettle to a counter and stir the wort briskly in one direction for about 5 minutes. After stirring, cover and let rest for 10 to 15 minutes as the hops and trub form a cone.

11. Using a racking cane and siphon, rack as much wort as possible into the sanitized primary fermenter. Using the sanitized funnel and straining screen, strain the rest of the wort into the fermenter. Top off with brewing water to bring the volume to around 5.5 US gal (21 L). Using the hydrometer, take a reading of the specific gravity and record it in your brewing journal.

12. Add yeast; vigorously stir it with a sanitized spoon to distribute it throughout the wort. Seal the fermenter with lid, stopper and airlock. Keep the fermenter at cool room temperature (50 to 60°F/10 to 15°C). (Keep it in a dark place or under a lightproof cover if using a glass carboy.)

13. Gently rack the beer into the secondary fermenter to avoid aerating it, leaving as much of the sediment behind as possible. Seal and keep at cool room temperature (50 to 60°F/10 to 15°C), covered or in a dark place, to allow fermentation to continue for about 2 weeks.

14. Once the bubbling in the airlock has slowed, confirm completion of fermentation by using the hydrometer to take final gravity readings. (Hydrometer readings should be the same for several days in a row.)

15. Prime and bottle the beer (see page 91). Store it at a cool room temperature (around 60°F/15°C or slightly higher) for 1 week or until carbonated; then move beer to the refrigerator for 3 to 4 weeks.

Brewer's Tips

No special equipment is required to crack the grains. Place them in a gallon-sized, sealable plastic bag (so there's room for them to move but they can't escape) and use the malt can or a heavy rolling pin to lightly crush them. The goal is to crack the outer shells and break them apart lightly, not to make flour. Cracked grains should have a coarse texture. Alternatively, your homebrew supplier can crack them for you. Just don't use a food processor to pulse them.

If you want to get all the possible goodness out of your grain after the steeping process, sparge the grain. To sparge, place the grain bag in a colander or strainer and gently rinse the bag over the kettle with about 1 US qt (1 L) of 170°F (77°C) brewing water before discarding the bag. Don't wring the bag out; wringing it out will release harsh tannins.

West Coast Amber Ale

This is another style that is born of North American craft brewers. Originally there was some consumer resistance to beers that were labelled "ale" so often brewers began calling their copper ales "amber beer." As these beers evolved into a bona fide style, they became maltier than pale ales. They still showcase the flavor and aromatics of the hops rather than a strong bitterness.

Estimated Original Gravity: 1.056

Equipment

- **brew kettle**
- **fermentation gear (page 14)**

As you build your brewing skills, switching to liquid yeast products (from Wyeast or White Labs) will give you a brew that is more complex than the ones made with the dry yeast (from Fermentis or Danstar) in the Absolute Beginner recipes. See page 86 for more information about liquid yeasts.

Yeast

1 pack	Wyeast 1056 or 1272, White Labs WLP001 or 051 or Fermentis S-05	1 pack

Grains

1 lb	Melanoidin® malt or other toasted malt (25 to 40 Lovibond)	450 g
1 lb	crystal or caramel malt (40 to 60 Lovibond)	450 g
1 oz	any dark-roasted malt such as chocolate, black patent, Carafa® or Roast Barley	28 g
5.5 US gal	brewing water (page 89)	21 L

Malt Extract

6.6 lbs	light or gold (such as Briess, Coopers or Northwestern or any brand), divided in half	3 kg

Bittering Hops

8 to 10 AAUs	any medium-alpha acid	8 to 10 AAUs

Later Additions

1 tsp	Irish moss	5 mL
1 tsp	yeast nutrient	5 mL

Aroma Hops

1.5 oz	Cascade, Liberty, Mt Hood or Willamette	42 g

1. Prepare the liquid yeast in advance, according to the package directions (if using).
2. Coarsely crack the malt grains and place them in a cheesecloth or nylon grain bag.
3. In a brew kettle, bring at least 3 US gal (11 L) brewing water to steeping temperature (150 to 160°F/65 to 71°C). Turn off the heat, add the grain bag, cover and steep for 30 minutes. (If the temperature drops below steeping temperature, turn the element back on briefly to bring it back up.) Remove grain bag and discard.
4. Increase the heat and bring grain tea to a boil. Remove from heat, add half of the malt extract and stir until dissolved completely.
5. Return kettle to the burner and increase the heat until the wort begins to boil. Using a spoon, clear any foam to one side. Reduce heat until a rolling boil can be maintained without foam buildup.
6. Add the bittering hops, stirring to combine. Boil for 45 minutes, uncovered. Monitor to prevent boiling over.

7. Meanwhile, prepare fermentation gear and cooling bath or wort chiller.

8. After 45 minutes, remove the kettle from the heat and add the remaining half of the malt extract, Irish moss and yeast nutrient. Stir to ensure that the extract and nutrient are dissolved. Return the kettle to the burner and bring back to a rolling boil. Boil for 15 minutes, then stir in the aroma hops, turn off the heat and cover.

9. To cool the brew, place the covered kettle in the prepared cooling tub or use a wort chiller according to the manufacturer's directions. Cool to the desired temperature, 75°F (24°C), within 30 to 45 minutes.

10. While the wort is cooling, clean and sanitize the brewing spoon. When the wort has cooled, move the kettle to a counter and stir the wort briskly in one direction for about 5 minutes. After stirring, cover and let rest for 10 to 15 minutes as the hops and trub form a cone.

11. Using a racking cane and siphon, rack as much wort as possible into the sanitized primary fermenter. Using the sanitized funnel and straining screen, strain the rest of the wort into the fermenter. Top off with brewing water to bring the volume to around 5.5 US gal (21 L). Using the hydrometer, take a reading of the specific gravity and record it in your brewing journal.

12. Add the yeast; vigorously stir it with a sanitized spoon to distribute it throughout the wort. Seal the fermenter with lid, stopper and airlock. Keep the fermenter at room temperature (68 to 72°F/20 to 22°C) during primary fermentation (which typically lasts 1 to 4 days after fermentation begins). (Keep in a dark place or under a lightproof cover if using a glass carboy.)

13. After 1 to 4 days or when the kräusen has fallen, gently rack the beer into the secondary fermenter to avoid aerating it, leaving as much of the sediment behind as possible. Seal and keep at room temperature, covered or in a dark place, to allow fermentation to continue.

14. Once the bubbling in the airlock has slowed, confirm completion of fermentation by using the hydrometer to take final gravity readings. (Hydrometer readings should be the same for several days in a row.)

15. Prime and bottle the beer (see page 91) and condition it for 3 to 4 weeks.

Brewer's Tips

No special equipment is required to crack the grains. Place them in a gallon-sized, sealable plastic bag (so there's room for them to move but they can't escape) and use the malt can or a heavy rolling pin to lightly crush them. The goal is to crack the outer shells and break them apart lightly, not to make flour. Cracked grains should have a coarse texture. Alternatively, your homebrew supplier can crack them for you. Just don't use a food processor to pulse them.

If you want to get all the possible goodness out of your grain after the steeping process, sparge the grain. To sparge, place the grain bag in a colander or strainer and gently rinse the bag over the kettle with about 1 US qt (1 L) of 170°F (77°C) brewing water before discarding the bag. Don't wring the bag out; wringing it out will release harsh tannins.

These recipes are from south of the American border. Often the beers of Mexico are associated with fizzy yellow lagers typically served with a wedge of lime shoved down the neck. This was not a taste decision, but rather an idea from outdoor Mexican beach bars. The lime wedge keeps the bugs out of the bottle! No limes will be needed for these tasty Mexican brews. The amber is a classic Vienna-style lager. The dark brew is an Oscura beer; these were usually produced for the winter holidays.

Estimated Original Gravity: 1.059

Equipment

- **brew kettle**
- **fermentation gear (page 14)**

As you build your brewing skills, switching to liquid yeast products (from Wyeast or White Labs) will give you a brew that is more complex than the ones made with the dry yeast (from Fermentis or Danstar) in the Absolute Beginner recipes. See page 86 for more information about liquid yeasts.

Amber Mexican Lager

Yeast

2 packs	Wyeast 2206 or White Labs WLP940 or 920 (or 1 pack in starter) or Fermentis S-23	2 packs

Grains

1 lb	Vienna Malt	450 g
8 oz	Melanoidin® malt or other toasted malt (25 to 40 Lovibond)	224 g
8 oz	crystal or caramel malt (40 to 60 Lovibond)	224 g
5.5 US gal	brewing water (page 89)	21 L

Malt Extract

5.4 lbs	Alexander's Sun Country Pale Malt Extract or any brand of extra-light	2.5 kg

Bittering Hops

3 to 5 AAUs	Tettnang, Spalt or Hallertau	3 to 5 AAUs

Later Additions

1 lb	rice syrup	450 g
1 tsp	Irish moss	5 mL
1 tsp	yeast nutrient	5 mL

Aroma Hops

.5 oz	Tettnang, Spalt or Hallertau	14 g

1. Prepare the liquid yeast in advance, according to the package directions (if using).
2. Coarsely crack the malt grains and place them in a cheesecloth or nylon grain bag.
3. In a brew kettle, bring at least 3 US gal (11 L) brewing water to steeping temperature (150 to 160°F/65 to 71°C). Turn off the heat, add the grain bag, cover and steep for 30 minutes. (If the temperature drops below steeping temperature, turn the element back on briefly to bring it back up.) Remove grain bag and discard.
4. Increase the heat and bring grain tea to a boil. Remove from heat, add the malt extract and stir until dissolved completely.
5. Return kettle to the burner and increase the heat until the wort begins to boil. Using a spoon, clear any foam to one side. Reduce the heat until a rolling boil can be maintained without foam buildup.
6. Add the bittering hops, stirring to combine. Boil for 45 minutes, uncovered. Monitor to prevent boiling over.

7. Meanwhile, prepare fermentation gear and cooling bath or wort chiller.

8. After 45 minutes, remove the kettle from the heat and add rice syrup, Irish moss and yeast nutrient. Stir to ensure that sugar and nutrient are dissolved. Return the kettle to the burner and bring back to a rolling boil. Boil for 15 minutes, then stir in the aroma hops, turn off the heat and cover.

9. To cool the brew, place the covered kettle in the prepared cooling tub or use a wort chiller according to the manufacturer's directions. Cool to the desired temperature, 75°F (24°C), within 30 to 45 minutes.

10. While the wort is cooling, clean and sanitize the brewing spoon. When the wort has cooled, move the kettle to a counter and stir it briskly in one direction for about 5 minutes. After stirring, cover and let rest for 10 to 15 minutes as the hops and trub form a cone.

11. Using a racking cane and siphon, rack as much wort as possible into the sanitized primary fermenter. Using the sanitized funnel and straining screen, strain the rest of the wort into the fermenter. Top off with brewing water to bring the volume to around 5.5 US gal (21 L). Using the hydrometer, take a reading of the specific gravity and record it in your brewing journal.

12. Add the yeast; vigorously stir it with a sanitized spoon to distribute it throughout the wort. Seal the fermenter with lid, stopper and airlock. Keep the fermenter at room temperature (68 to 72°F/20 to 22°C) until fermentation begins (bubbles will be moving through the airlock). (Keep it in a dark place or under a lightproof cover if using a glass carboy.) Once fermentation begins, drop the temperature to 46 to 55°F (8 to 13°C) for one week of primary fermentation.

13. Gently rack the beer into the secondary fermenter to avoid aerating it, leaving as much of the sediment behind as possible. Seal and drop the temperature to 35 to 45°F (2 to 7°C); keep it at that temperature, covered or in a dark place, to allow fermentation to continue for 4 weeks.

14. Once the bubbling in the airlock has slowed, confirm completion of fermentation by using the hydrometer to take final gravity readings. (Hydrometer readings should be the same for several days in a row.)

15. Prime and bottle the beer (see page 91). Condition it in the refrigerator for 3 to 4 weeks.

Variations

Vienna Lager: When large commercial breweries were set up in Mexico, Vienna was the brewing center of Europe. Their copper-colored lager beers were all the rage. In an effort to be cutting-edge, fledgling Mexican brewers imported their equipment and brewers from Austria.

As tastes changed in Europe, darker, malty Vienna lagers were replaced with the hoppy golden lagers of Pilsen in what is now the Czech Republic. As a quirk of modern brewing, Vienna lager is produced in Mexico, but no longer in Vienna. To modify this recipe to produce a true Vienna lager, replace the rice syrup with 1.4 lbs (640 g) Alexander's Sun Country Pale or any extra-light malt extract. (Estimated) Original Gravity: 1.058

Dark Mexican Lager: To brew a dark Mexican lager in the Oscura style, follow the Amber Mexican Lager recipe and add 4 oz (112 g) dehusked Carafe II™ or chocolate malt to the grain bill.

American Wheat Ale

Estimated Original Gravity: 1.056

Equipment

- **brew kettle**
- **fermentation gear (page 14)**

As you build your brewing skills, switching to liquid yeast products (from Wyeast or White Labs) will give you a brew that is more complex than the ones made with the dry yeast (from Fermentis or Danstar) in the Absolute Beginner recipes. See page 86 for more information about liquid yeasts.

Yeast

1 pack	Wyeast 1010 or White Labs WLP 320 or Fermentis S-05	1 pack

Grains

1 lb	Carafoam®, Carapils® or dextrin malt	450 g
1 lb	wheat malt	450 g
5.5 US gal	brewing water (page 89)	21 L

Malt Extract

6.6 lbs	any brand wheat or weizen, divided in half	3 kg

Bittering Hops

4 to 6 AAUs	Liberty, Mt Hood or Vanguard	4 to 6 AAUs

Later Additions

1 tsp	yeast nutrient	5 mL

Aroma Hops

1.5 oz	Liberty, Mt Hood or Vanguard	42 g

1. Prepare the liquid yeast in advance, according to the package directions (if using).
2. Coarsely crack the malt grains and place them in a cheesecloth or nylon grain bag.
3. In a brew kettle, bring at least 3 US gal (11 L) brewing water to steeping temperature (150 to 160°F/65 to 71°C). Turn off the heat, add the grain bag, cover and steep for 30 minutes. (If the temperature drops below steeping temperature, turn the element back on briefly to bring it back up.) Remove grain bag and discard.
4. Increase the heat and bring grain tea to a boil. Remove from heat, add half of the malt extract and stir until dissolved completely.
5. Return kettle to the burner and increase the heat until the wort begins to boil. Using a spoon, clear any foam to one side. Reduce heat until a rolling boil can be maintained without foam buildup.
6. Add the bittering hops, stirring to combine. Boil for 45 minutes, uncovered. Monitor to prevent boiling over.
7. Meanwhile, prepare fermentation gear and cooling bath or wort chiller.

8. After 45 minutes, remove the kettle from the heat and add the remaining half of the malt extract and the yeast nutrient. Stir to ensure that the extract and nutrient have dissolved. Return the kettle to the burner and bring back to a rolling boil. Boil for 15 minutes, then stir in the aroma hops, turn off the heat and cover.

9. To cool the brew, place the covered kettle in the prepared cooling tub or use a wort chiller according to the manufacturer's directions. Cool to the desired temperature, 75°F (24°C), within 30 to 45 minutes.

10. While the wort is cooling, clean and sanitize the brewing spoon. When the wort has cooled, move the kettle to a counter and stir the wort briskly in one direction for about 5 minutes. After stirring, cover and let rest for 10 to 15 minutes as the hops and trub form a cone.

11. Using a racking cane and siphon, rack as much wort as possible into the sanitized primary fermenter. Using the sanitized funnel and straining screen, strain the rest of the wort into the fermenter. Top off with brewing water to bring the volume to around 5.5 US gal (21 L). Using the hydrometer, take a reading of the specific gravity and record it in your brewing journal.

12. Add the yeast; vigorously stir it with a sanitized spoon to distribute it throughout the wort. Seal the fermenter with lid, stopper and airlock. Keep the fermenter at room temperature (68 to 72°F/20 to 22°C) during primary fermentation (which typically lasts 1 to 4 days after fermentation begins). (Keep in a dark place or under a lightproof cover if using a glass carboy.)

13. After 1 to 4 days or when the kräusen has fallen, gently rack the beer into the secondary fermenter to avoid aerating it, leaving as much of the sediment behind as possible. Seal and keep at room temperature, covered or in a dark place, to allow fermentation to continue.

14. Once the bubbling in the airlock has slowed, confirm completion of fermentation by using the hydrometer to take final gravity readings. (Hydrometer readings should be the same for several days in a row.)

15. Prime and bottle the beer (see page 91) and condition it for 3 to 4 weeks.

Brewer's Tips

No special equipment is required to crack the grains. Place them in a gallon-sized, sealable plastic bag (so there's room for them to move but they can't escape) and use the malt can or a heavy rolling pin to lightly crush them. The goal is to crack the outer shells and break them apart lightly, not to make flour. Cracked grains should have a coarse texture. Alternatively, your homebrew supplier can crack them for you. Just don't use a food processor to pulse them.

If you want to get all the possible goodness out of your grain after the steeping process, sparge the grain. To sparge, place the grain bag in a colander or strainer and gently rinse the bag over the kettle with about 1 US qt (1 L) of 170°F (77°C) brewing water before discarding the bag. Don't wring the bag out; wringing it out will release harsh tannins.

Hopfen Weiss

This is another style invented by ingenious modern brewers. When Brooklyn Brewing Co.'s Garrett Oliver was invited to co-brew with the prestigious Schneider brewery in Germany, he decided to marry several classic styles together. If you take a classic Bavarian wheat beer and combine it with a Czech Pils and add a dash of IPA, you have Hopfen Weiss—a very refreshing warm weather quaffer.

Estimated Original Gravity: 1.076

Equipment

- **brew kettle**
- **fermentation gear (page 14)**

Beers with an Estimated Original Gravity higher than 1.065 require a longer time in both primary and secondary fermentation. Primary fermentation will take 7 to 10 days, and secondary fermentation will take about 2 weeks longer than weaker brews.

Yeast

1 pack	Wyeast 3056 or White Labs WLP380 or Fermentis WB-06	1 pack

Grains

1 lb	Carafoam®, Carapils® or dextrin malt	450 g
1 lb	Pilsner malt	450 g
1 lb	light wheat malt	450 g
5.5 US gal	brewing water (page 89)	21 L

Malt Extract

8 lbs	Alexander's Sun Country Wheat Malt Extract or any brand wheat extract, divided in half	3.6 kg

Bittering Hops

10 to 12 AAUs	Perle or Northern Brewer	10 to 12 AAUs

Later Additions

1 tsp	Irish moss	5 mL
1 tsp	yeast nutrient	5 mL

Aroma and Dry Hops

3 oz	Hallertau, Tettnang or Saaz, divided in half (reserve half for dry hopping)	85 g

1. Prepare the liquid yeast in advance, according to the package directions (if using).
2. Coarsely crack the malt grains and place them in a cheesecloth or nylon grain bag.
3. In a brew kettle, bring at least 3 US gal (11 L) brewing water to steeping temperature (150 to 160°F/65 to 71°C). Turn off the heat, add the grain bag, cover and steep for 30 minutes. (If the temperature drops below steeping temperature, turn the element back on briefly to bring it back up.) Remove grain bag and discard.
4. Increase the heat and bring grain tea to a boil. Remove from heat, add half of the malt extract and stir until dissolved completely.
5. Return kettle to the burner and increase the heat until the wort begins to boil. Using a spoon, clear any foam to one side. Reduce heat until a rolling boil can be maintained without foam buildup.
6. Add the bittering hops, stirring to combine. Boil for 45 minutes, uncovered. Monitor to prevent boiling over.

7. Meanwhile, prepare fermentation gear and cooling bath or wort chiller.

8. After 45 minutes, remove the kettle from the heat and add the remaining half of the malt extract, Irish moss and yeast nutrient. Stir to ensure that the extract and nutrient are dissolved. Return the kettle to the burner and bring back to a rolling boil. Boil for 15 minutes, then stir in half of the aroma hops, turn off the heat and cover.

9. To cool the brew, place the covered kettle in the prepared cooling tub or use a wort chiller according to the manufacturer's directions. Cool to the desired temperature, 75°F (24°C), within 30 to 45 minutes.

10. While the wort is cooling, clean and sanitize the brewing spoon. When the wort has cooled, move the kettle to a counter and stir the wort briskly in one direction for about 5 minutes. After stirring, cover and let rest for 10 to 15 minutes as the hops and trub form a cone.

11. Using a racking cane and siphon, rack as much wort as possible into the sanitized primary fermenter. Using the sanitized funnel and straining screen, strain the rest of the wort into the fermenter. Top off with brewing water to bring the volume to around 5.5 US gal (21 L). Using the hydrometer, take a reading of the specific gravity and record it in your brewing journal.

12. Add the yeast; vigorously stir it with a sanitized spoon to distribute it throughout the wort. Seal the fermenter with lid, stopper and airlock. Keep the fermenter at room temperature (68 to 72°F/20 to 22°C) during primary fermentation (which typically lasts 7 to 10 days after fermentation begins). (Keep in a dark place or under a lightproof cover if using a glass carboy.)

13. After 7 to 10 days or when the kräusen has fallen, gently rack the beer into the secondary fermenter to avoid aerating it, leaving as much of the sediment behind as possible. Seal and keep at room temperature, covered or in a dark place, to allow fermentation to continue.

14. Once the bubbling in the airlock has slowed, gently add the remainder of the hops, reseal and leave it for about 2 more weeks. Confirm completion of fermentation by using the hydrometer to take final gravity readings. (Hydrometer readings should be the same for several days in a row.)

15. Prime and bottle the beer (see page 91) and condition it for 3 to 4 weeks.

Brewer's Tips

No special equipment is required to crack the grains. Place them in a gallon-sized, sealable plastic bag (so there's room for them to move but they can't escape) and use the malt can or a heavy rolling pin to lightly crush them. The goal is to crack the outer shells and break them apart lightly, not to make flour. Cracked grains should have a coarse texture. Alternatively, your homebrew supplier can crack them for you. Just don't use a food processor to pulse them.

If you want to get all the possible goodness out of your grain after the steeping process, sparge the grain. To sparge, place the grain bag in a colander or strainer and gently rinse the bag over the kettle with about 1 US qt (1 L) of 170°F (77°C) brewing water before discarding the bag. Don't wring the bag out; wringing it out will release harsh tannins.

Maple Porter

This is a brew born of necessity in colonial times. Beer drinkers were faced with a dwindling supply of malt and a good amount of maple syrup, so the solution was obvious… brew a beer with maple syrup!

Estimated Original Gravity: 1.078

Equipment

- **brew kettle**
- **fermentation gear (page 14)**

Beers with an estimated original gravity higher than 1.065 require a longer time in both primary and secondary fermentation. Primary fermentation will take 7 to 10 days, and secondary fermentation will take about 2 weeks longer than weaker brews.

Yeast

1 pack	Wyeast 1187 or White Labs WLP006 or Fermentis S-33	1 pack

Grains

1 lb	brown or other dark-toasted malt (50 to 70 Lovibond)	450 g
1 lb	Caraaroma® or other dark crystal malt (100 to 150 Lovibond)	450 g
8 oz	dehusked Carafa I® malt	224 g
5.5 US gal	brewing water (page 89)	21 L

Malt Extract

6.6 lbs	any brand light	3 kg

Bittering Hops

6 AAUs	any medium-alpha acid	6 AAUs

Later Additions

1 lb	amber maple syrup	450 g
1 tsp	Irish moss	5 mL
1 tsp	yeast nutrient	5 mL

Aroma Hops

None

1. Prepare the liquid yeast in advance, according to the package directions (if using).
2. Coarsely crack the malt grains and place them in a cheesecloth or nylon grain bag.
3. In a brew kettle, bring at least 3 US gal (11 L) brewing water to steeping temperature (150 to 160°F/65 to 71°C). Turn off the heat, add the grain bag, cover and steep for 30 minutes. (If the temperature drops below steeping temperature, turn the element back on briefly to bring it back up.) Remove grain bag and discard.
4. Increase the heat and bring grain tea to a boil. Remove from heat, add the malt extract and stir until dissolved completely.
5. Return kettle to the burner and increase the heat until the wort begins to boil. Using a spoon, clear any foam to one side. Reduce heat until a rolling boil can be maintained without foam buildup.

6. Add the bittering hops, stirring to combine. Boil for 45 minutes, uncovered. Monitor to prevent boiling over.

7. Meanwhile, prepare fermentation gear and cooling bath or wort chiller.

8. After 45 minutes, remove the kettle from the heat and add maple syrup, Irish moss and yeast nutrient. Stir to ensure that the syrup and nutrient are dissolved. Return the kettle to the burner and bring back to a rolling boil. Boil for 15 minutes, turn off the heat and cover.

9. To cool the brew, place the covered kettle in the prepared cooling tub or use a wort chiller according to the manufacturer's directions. Cool to the desired temperature, 75°F (24°C), within 30 to 45 minutes.

10. While the wort is cooling, clean and sanitize the brewing spoon. When the wort has cooled, move the kettle to a counter and stir the wort briskly in one direction for about 5 minutes. After stirring, cover and let rest for 10 to 15 minutes as the hops and trub form a cone.

11. Using a racking cane and siphon, rack as much wort as possible into the sanitized primary fermenter. Using the sanitized funnel and straining screen, strain the rest of the wort into the fermenter. Top off with brewing water to bring the volume to around 5.5 US gal (21 L). Using the hydrometer, take a reading of the specific gravity and record it in your brewing journal.

12. Add the yeast; vigorously stir it with a sanitized spoon to distribute it throughout the wort. Seal the fermenter with lid, stopper and airlock. Keep the fermenter at room temperature (68 to 72°F/20 to 22°C) during primary fermentation (which typically lasts 7 to 10 days after fermentation begins). (Keep in a dark place or under a lightproof cover if using a glass carboy.)

13. After 7 to 10 days or when the kräusen has fallen, gently rack the beer into the secondary fermenter to avoid aerating it, leaving as much of the sediment behind as possible. Seal and keep at room temperature, covered or in a dark place, to allow fermentation to continue.

14. Once the bubbling in the airlock has slowed, confirm completion of fermentation by using the hydrometer to take final gravity readings. (Hydrometer readings should be the same for several days in a row.)

15. Prime and bottle the beer (see page 91) and condition it for 3 to 4 weeks.

Brewer's Tips

No special equipment is required to crack the grains. Place them in a gallon-sized, sealable plastic bag (so there's room for them to move but they can't escape) and use the malt can or a heavy rolling pin to lightly crush them. The goal is to crack the outer shells and break them apart lightly, not to make flour. Cracked grains should have a coarse texture. Alternatively, your homebrew supplier can crack them for you. Just don't use a food processor to pulse them.

If you want to get all the possible goodness out of your grain after the steeping process, sparge the grain. To sparge, place the grain bag in a colander or strainer and gently rinse the bag over the kettle with about 1 US qt (1 L) of 170°F (77°C) brewing water before discarding the bag. Don't wring the bag out; wringing it out will release harsh tannins.

Multi-Grain Stout

Michigan's Founders' Brewery pioneered this new style with their renowned Breakfast Stout. In the UK, brewers often produced oatmeal stouts. The oats add a nice flavor and texture to the brew, and it was a logical extension to include other cereal grains. Get your spoon, it's breakfast time!

Estimated Original Gravity: 1.056

Equipment

- **brew kettle**
- **fermentation gear (page 14)**

As you build your brewing skills, switching to liquid yeast products (from Wyeast or White Labs) will give you a brew that is more complex than the ones made with the dry yeast (from Fermentis or Danstar) in the Absolute Beginner recipes. See page 86 for more information about liquid yeasts.

Yeast

1 pack	Wyeast 1187 or White Labs WLP006 or Fermentis S-33	1 pack

Grains

8 oz	brown malt or other dark-toasted (50 to 70 Lovibond)	224 g
8 oz	crystal or caramel malt (60 Lovibond)	224 g
8 oz	Cararye® malt	224 g
8 oz	roast barley	224 g
8 oz	oat flakes (do not crack)	224 g
5.5 US gal	brewing water (page 89)	21 L

Malt Extracts

3.3 lbs	any brand wheat	1.5 kg
3.3 lbs	any brand light	1.5 kg

Bittering Hops

6 to 8 AAUs	medium-alpha acid	6 to 8 AAUs

Later Additions

1 tsp	Irish moss	5 mL
1 tsp	yeast nutrient	5 mL

Aroma Hops

1 oz	Bramling Cross, Fuggle or Kent Golding	28 g

1. Prepare the liquid yeast in advance, according to the package directions (if using).
2. Coarsely crack the grains and place them in a cheesecloth or nylon grain bag. Add oat flakes.
3. In a brew kettle, bring at least 3 US gal (11 L) brewing water to steeping temperature (150 to 160°F/65 to 71°C). Turn off the heat, add the grain bag, cover and steep for 30 minutes. (If the temperature drops below steeping temperature, turn the element back on briefly to bring it back up.) Remove grain bag and discard.
4. Increase the heat and bring grain tea to a boil. Remove from heat, add the malt extract and stir until dissolved completely.
5. Return kettle to the burner and increase the heat until the wort begins to boil. Using a spoon, clear any foam to one side. Reduce heat until a rolling boil can be maintained without foam buildup.
6. Add the bittering hops, stirring to combine. Boil for 45 minutes, uncovered. Monitor to prevent boiling over.

7. Meanwhile, prepare fermentation gear and cooling bath or wort chiller.

8. After 45 minutes, remove the kettle from the heat and add Irish moss and yeast nutrient. Stir to ensure that the nutrient has dissolved. Return the kettle to the burner and bring back to a rolling boil. Boil for 15 minutes, then stir in the aroma hops, turn off the heat and cover.

9. To cool the brew, place the covered kettle in the prepared cooling tub or use a wort chiller according to the manufacturer's directions. Cool to the desired temperature, 75°F (24°C), within 30 to 45 minutes.

10. While the wort is cooling, clean and sanitize the brewing spoon. When the wort has cooled, move the kettle to a counter and stir the wort briskly in one direction for about 5 minutes. After stirring, cover and let rest for 10 to 15 minutes as the hops and trub form a cone.

11. Using a racking cane and siphon, rack as much wort as possible into the sanitized primary fermenter. Using the sanitized funnel and straining screen, strain the rest of the wort into the fermenter. Top off with brewing water to bring the volume to around 5.5 US gal (21 L). Using the hydrometer, take a reading of the specific gravity and record it in your brewing journal.

12. Add the yeast; vigorously stir it with a sanitized spoon to distribute it throughout the wort. Seal the fermenter with lid, stopper and airlock. Keep the fermenter at room temperature (68 to 72°F/20 to 22°C) during primary fermentation (which typically lasts 1 to 4 days after fermentation begins). (Keep in a dark place or under a lightproof cover if using a glass carboy.)

13. After 1 to 4 days or when the kräusen has fallen, gently rack the beer into the secondary fermenter to avoid aerating it, leaving as much of the sediment behind as possible. Seal and keep at room temperature, covered or in a dark place, to allow fermentation to continue.

14. Once the bubbling in the airlock has slowed, confirm completion of fermentation by using the hydrometer to take final gravity readings. (Hydrometer readings should be the same for several days in a row.)

15. Prime and bottle the beer (see page 91) and condition it for 3 to 4 weeks.

Brewer's Tips

No special equipment is required to crack the grains. Place them in a gallon-sized, sealable plastic bag (so there's room for them to move but they can't escape) and use the malt can or a heavy rolling pin to lightly crush them. The goal is to crack the outer shells and break them apart lightly, not to make flour. Cracked grains should have a coarse texture. Alternatively, your homebrew supplier can crack them for you. Just don't use a food processor to pulse them.

If you want to get all the possible goodness out of your grain after the steeping process, sparge the grain. To sparge, place the grain bag in a colander or strainer and gently rinse the bag over the kettle with about 1 US qt (1 L) of 170°F (77°C) brewing water before discarding the bag. Don't wring the bag out; wringing it out will release harsh tannins.

Rye IPA

This modern beer combines the spicy notes of rye with the hoppy bite of an IPA. These beers allow a little more malt flavor than normal IPAs so the rye notes can be detected. This is a great beer to enjoy with barbecued food.

Estimated Original Gravity: 1.076

Equipment

- **brew kettle**
- **fermentation gear (page 14)**

Beers with an estimated original gravity higher than 1.065 require a longer time in both primary and secondary fermentation. Primary fermentation will take 7 to 10 days, and secondary fermentation will take about 2 weeks longer than weaker brews.

Yeast

| 1 pack | Wyeast 1056 or White Labs WLP001 or or Fermentis S-05 | 1 pack |

Grains

1 lb	rye malt	450 g
1 lb	Pilsner malt	450 g
1 lb	Cararye®	450 g
1 lb	dark Munich malt	450 g
1 lb	Melanoidin® malt or any toasted (25 to 50 Lovibond)	450 g
1 lb	crystal or caramel malt (40 to 50 Lovibond)	450 g
5.5 US gal	brewing water (page 89)	21 L

Malt Extract

| 6.6 lbs | any brand extra-light, divided in half | 3 kg |

Bittering Hops

| 10 to 12 AAUs | medium- to high-alpha acid | 10 to 12 AAUs |

Later Additions

| 1 tsp | Irish moss | 5 mL |
| 1 tsp | yeast nutrient | 5 mL |

Aroma and Dry Hops

| 4 oz | Amarillo, Citra or Sorachi, divided in half | 112 g |

1. Prepare the liquid yeast in advance, according to the package directions (if using).
2. Coarsely crack the malt grains and place them in a cheesecloth or nylon grain bag.
3. In a brew kettle, bring at least 3 US gal (11 L) brewing water to steeping temperature (150 to 160°F/65 to 71°C). Turn off the heat, add the grain bag, cover and steep for 90 minutes. (If the temperature drops below steeping temperature, reheat briefly.) Remove and rinse grain bag (see Tips) and discard.
4. Increase the heat and bring grain tea to a boil. Remove from heat, add half of the malt extract and stir until dissolved completely.
5. Return kettle to the burner and increase the heat until the wort begins to boil. Using a spoon, clear any foam to one side. Reduce heat until a rolling boil can be maintained without foam buildup.

6. Add the bittering hops, stirring to combine. Boil for 45 minutes, uncovered. Monitor to prevent boiling over.

7. Meanwhile, prepare fermentation gear and cooling bath or wort chiller.

8. After 45 minutes, remove the kettle from the heat and add the remaining half of the extract, Irish moss and yeast nutrient. Stir to ensure that the extract and nutrient are dissolved. Return the kettle to the burner and bring back to a rolling boil. Boil for 15 minutes, then stir in half of the aroma hops, turn off the heat and cover.

9. To cool the brew, place the covered kettle in the prepared cooling tub or use a wort chiller according to the manufacturer's directions. Cool to the desired temperature, 75°F (24°C), within 30 to 45 minutes.

10. While the wort is cooling, clean and sanitize the brewing spoon. When the wort has cooled, move the kettle to a counter and stir the wort briskly in one direction for about 5 minutes. After stirring, cover and let rest for 10 to 15 minutes as the hops and trub form a cone.

11. Using a racking cane and siphon, rack as much wort as possible into the sanitized primary fermenter. Using the sanitized funnel and straining screen, strain the rest of the wort into the fermenter. Top off with brewing water to bring the volume to around 5.5 US gal (21 L). Using the hydrometer, take a reading of the specific gravity and record it in your brewing journal.

12. Add the yeast; vigorously stir it with a sanitized spoon to distribute it throughout the wort. Seal the fermenter with lid, stopper and airlock. Keep the fermenter at room temperature (68 to 72°F/20 to 22°C) during primary fermentation (which typically lasts 7 to 10 days after fermentation begins). (Keep in a dark place or under a lightproof cover if using a glass carboy.)

13. After 7 to 10 days or when the kräusen has fallen, gently rack the beer into the secondary fermenter to avoid aerating it, leaving as much of the sediment behind as possible. Seal and keep at room temperature, covered or in a dark place, to allow fermentation to continue.

14. Once the bubbling in the airlock has slowed, gently add the remainder of the hops, reseal and leave it for about 2 more weeks. Confirm completion of fermentation by using the hydrometer to take final gravity readings. (Hydrometer readings should be the same for several days in a row.)

15. Prime and bottle the beer (see page 91) and condition it for 3 to 4 weeks.

Brewer's Tips

No special equipment is required to crack the grains. Place them in a gallon-sized, sealable plastic bag (so there's room for them to move but they can't escape) and use the malt can or a heavy rolling pin to lightly crush them. The goal is to crack the outer shells and break them apart lightly, not to make flour. Cracked grains should have a coarse texture. Alternatively, your homebrew supplier can crack them for you. Just don't use a food processor to pulse them.

If you want to get all the possible goodness out of your grain after the steeping process, sparge the grain. To sparge, place the grain bag in a colander or strainer and gently rinse the bag over the kettle with about 1 US qt (1 L) of 170°F (77°C) brewing water before discarding the bag. Don't wring the bag out; wringing it out will release harsh tannins.

India Brown Ale

This is an American brown ale with the hops turned up to IPA status. Add half the aroma hops at the end of the boil and the other half to the secondary fermenter as a dry hop.

Estimated Original Gravity: 1.061

Equipment

- **brew kettle**
- **fermentation gear (page 14)**

As you build your brewing skills, switching to liquid yeast products (from Wyeast or White Labs) will give you a brew that is more complex than the ones made with the dry yeast (from Fermentis or Danstar) in the Absolute Beginner recipes. See page 86 for more information about liquid yeasts.

Yeast

1 pack	Wyeast 1056 or White Labs WLP001 or Fermentis S-05	1 pack

Grains

1 lb	crystal malt (40 Lovibond)	450 g
1 lb	Special Roast Malt	450 g
4 oz	chocolate malt	112 g
5.5 US gal	brewing water (page 89)	21 L

Malt Extract

6.6 lbs	any brand extra-light	3 kg

Bittering Hops

10 to 12 AAUs	medium- to high-alpha acid	10 to 12 AAUs

Later Additions

1 tsp	Irish moss	5 mL
1 tsp	yeast nutrient	5 mL

Aroma and Dry Hops

4 oz	Amarillo, Citra or Sorachi, divided in half	112 g

1. Prepare the liquid yeast in advance, according to the package directions (if using).
2. Coarsely crack the malt grains and place them in a cheesecloth or nylon grain bag.
3. In a brew kettle, bring at least 3 US gal (11 L) brewing water to steeping temperature (150 to 160°F/65 to 71°C). Turn off the heat, add the grain bag, cover and steep for 30 minutes. (If the temperature drops below steeping temperature, turn the element back on briefly to bring it back up.) Remove grain bag and discard.
4. Increase the heat and bring grain tea to a boil. Remove from heat, add the malt extract and stir until dissolved completely.
5. Return kettle to the burner and increase the heat until the wort begins to boil. Using a spoon, clear any foam to one side. Reduce heat until a rolling boil can be maintained without foam buildup.
6. Add the bittering hops, stirring to combine. Boil for 45 minutes, uncovered. Monitor to prevent boiling over.
7. Meanwhile, prepare fermentation gear and cooling bath or wort chiller.

8. After 45 minutes, remove the kettle from the heat and add Irish moss and yeast nutrient. Stir to ensure that the nutrient has dissolved. Return the kettle to the burner and bring back to a rolling boil. Boil for 15 minutes, then stir in half of the aroma hops, turn off the heat and cover.

9. To cool the brew, place the covered kettle in the prepared cooling tub or use a wort chiller according to the manufacturer's directions. Cool to the desired temperature, 75°F (24°C), within 30 to 45 minutes.

10. While the wort is cooling, clean and sanitize the brewing spoon. When the wort has cooled, move the kettle to a counter and stir the wort briskly in one direction for about 5 minutes. After stirring, cover and let rest for 10 to 15 minutes as the hops and trub form a cone.

11. Using a racking cane and siphon, rack as much wort as possible into the sanitized primary fermenter. Using the sanitized funnel and straining screen, strain the rest of the wort into the fermenter. Top off with brewing water to bring the volume to around 5.5 US gal (21 L). Using the hydrometer, take a reading of the specific gravity and record it in your brewing journal.

12. Add the yeast; vigorously stir it with a sanitized spoon to distribute it throughout the wort. Seal the fermenter with lid, stopper and airlock. Keep the fermenter at room temperature (68 to 72°F/20 to 22°C) during primary fermentation (which typically lasts 5 to 7 days after fermentation begins). (Keep in a dark place or under a lightproof cover if using a glass carboy.)

13. When the kräusen has fallen, gently rack the beer into the secondary fermenter to avoid aerating it, leaving as much of the sediment behind as possible. Seal and keep at room temperature, covered or in a dark place, to allow fermentation to continue.

14. Once the bubbling in the airlock has slowed, gently add the remainder of the hops, reseal and leave it for about 2 more weeks. Confirm completion of fermentation by using the hydrometer to take final gravity readings. (Hydrometer readings should be the same for several days in a row.)

15. Prime and bottle the beer (see page 91) and condition it for 3 to 4 weeks.

Brewer's Tips

No special equipment is required to crack the grains. Place them in a gallon-sized, sealable plastic bag (so there's room for them to move but they can't escape) and use the malt can or a heavy rolling pin to lightly crush them. The goal is to crack the outer shells and break them apart lightly, not to make flour. Cracked grains should have a coarse texture. Alternatively, your homebrew supplier can crack them for you. Just don't use a food processor to pulse them.

If you want to get all the possible goodness out of your grain after the steeping process, sparge the grain. To sparge, place the grain bag in a colander or strainer and gently rinse the bag over the kettle with about 1 US qt (1 L) of 170°F (77°C) brewing water before discarding the bag. Don't wring the bag out; wringing it out will release harsh tannins.

Black IPA

Invented in the Pacific Northwest, this latest take on the popular hop bomb brings the rich flavor of dark malts to the table. (Dehusked Carafa II™ is the preferred grain; substitute any dark roast if it is not available.) This is a great beer to enjoy with spicy shellfish dishes.

Estimated Original Gravity: 1.068

Equipment

- **brew kettle**
- **fermentation gear (page 14)**

Beers with an estimated original gravity higher than 1.065 require a longer time in both primary and secondary fermentation. Primary fermentation will take 7 to 10 days, and secondary fermentation will take about 2 weeks longer than weaker brews.

Yeast

1 pack	Wyeast 1056 or White Labs WLP001 or Fermentis S-05	1 pack

Grains

1 lb	crystal malt (60 Lovibond)	450 g
1 lb	brown or other dark-toasted malt (50 to 70 Lovibond)	450 g
12 oz	dehusked Carafa II® malt	336 g
5.5 US gal	brewing water (page 89)	21 L

Malt Extract

6.6 lbs	any brand light	3 kg

Bittering Hops

12 to 14 AAUs	any high-alpha acid	12 to 14 AAUs

Later Additions

1 lb	Demerara or other dark raw sugar	450 g
1 tsp	Irish moss	5 mL
1 tsp	yeast nutrient	5 mL

Aroma and Dry Hops

3 oz	Amarillo, Cascade, Citra (or other citrusy), divided in half	85 g

1. Prepare the liquid yeast in advance, according to the package directions (if using).
2. Coarsely crack the malt grains and place them in a cheesecloth or nylon grain bag.
3. In a brew kettle, bring at least 3 US gal (11 L) brewing water to steeping temperature (150 to 160°F/65 to 71°C). Turn off the heat, add the grain bag, cover and steep for 30 minutes. (If the temperature drops below steeping temperature, turn the element back on briefly to bring it back up.) Remove grain bag and discard.
4. Increase the heat and bring grain tea to a boil. Remove from heat, add the malt extract and stir until dissolved completely.
5. Return kettle to the burner and increase the heat until the wort begins to boil. Using a spoon, clear any foam to one side. Reduce heat until a rolling boil can be maintained without foam buildup.
6. Add the bittering hops, stirring to combine. Boil for 45 minutes, uncovered. Monitor to prevent boiling over.

7. Meanwhile, prepare fermentation gear and cooling bath or wort chiller.

8. After 45 minutes, remove the kettle from the heat and add sugar, Irish moss and yeast nutrient. Stir to ensure that the sugar and nutrient are dissolved. Return the kettle to the burner and bring back to a rolling boil. Boil for 15 minutes, then stir in half of the aroma hops, turn off the heat and cover.

9. To cool the brew, place the covered kettle in the prepared cooling tub or use a wort chiller according to the manufacturer's directions. Cool to the desired temperature, 75°F (24°C), within 30 to 45 minutes.

10. While the wort is cooling, clean and sanitize the brewing spoon. When the wort has cooled, move the kettle to a counter and stir the wort briskly in one direction for about 5 minutes. After stirring, cover and let rest for 10 to 15 minutes as the hops and trub form a cone.

11. Using a racking cane and siphon, rack as much wort as possible into the sanitized primary fermenter. Using the sanitized funnel and straining screen, strain the rest of the wort into the fermenter. Top off with brewing water to bring the volume to around 5.5 US gal (21 L). Using the hydrometer, take a reading of the specific gravity and record it in your brewing journal.

12. Add the yeast; vigorously stir it with a sanitized spoon to distribute it throughout the wort. Seal the fermenter with lid, stopper and airlock. Keep the fermenter at room temperature (68 to 72°F/20 to 22°C) during primary fermentation (which typically lasts 7 to 10 days after fermentation begins). (Keep in a dark place or under a lightproof cover if using a glass carboy.)

13. After 7 to 10 days or when the kräusen has fallen, gently rack the beer into the secondary fermenter to avoid aerating it, leaving as much of the sediment behind as possible. Seal and keep at room temperature, covered or in a dark place, to allow fermentation to continue.

14. Once the bubbling in the airlock has slowed, gently add the remaining half of the hops, reseal and leave it for about 2 more weeks. Confirm completion of fermentation by using the hydrometer to take final gravity readings. (Hydrometer readings should be the same for several days in a row.)

15. Prime and bottle the beer (see page 91) and condition it for 3 to 4 weeks.

Brewer's Tips

No special equipment is required to crack the grains. Place them in a gallon-sized, sealable plastic bag (so there's room for them to move but they can't escape) and use the malt can or a heavy rolling pin to lightly crush them. The goal is to crack the outer shells and break them apart lightly, not to make flour. Cracked grains should have a coarse texture. Alternatively, your homebrew supplier can crack them for you. Just don't use a food processor to pulse them.

If you want to get all the possible goodness out of your grain after the steeping process, sparge the grain. To sparge, place the grain bag in a colander or strainer and gently rinse the bag over the kettle with about 1 US qt (1 L) of 170°F (77°C) brewing water before discarding the bag. Don't wring the bag out; wringing it out will release harsh tannins.

Imperial IPA

This is the beer for those who say, "too much of everything is just enough." It was developed as homebrewers and craft brewers competed to produce progressively stronger and hoppier IPAs. As brewers continued to "turn it up to eleven," a new style was born. If you don't like hoppy beers, this is not for you!

This recipe produces a fairly pale version; use darker toasted and crystal malts if you prefer a darker color. The aroma hops are divided into thirds: add 2 oz (56 g) hops with 15 minutes remaining on the boil, 2 oz (56 g) at the end of the boil and 2 oz (56 g) to the secondary fermenter.

Estimated Original Gravity: 1.097

Equipment

- **brew kettle**
- **fermentation gear (page 14)**

Beers with an estimated original gravity higher than 1.065 require a longer time in both primary and secondary fermentation. Primary fermentation will take 7 to 10 days, and secondary fermentation will take about 2 weeks longer than weaker brews.

Yeast

2 packs	Wyeast 1056 or White Labs WLP001 (or 1 pack in starter) or Fermentis S-05	2 packs

Grains

1 lb	Carafoam®, Carapils® or dextrin malt	450 g
1 lb	Vienna malt	450 g
1 lb	Carahelles® or other crystal malt (9 to 15 Lovibond)	450 g
5.5 US gal	brewing water (page 89)	21 L

Malt Extract

9.9 lbs	any brand extra-light, divided $1/3$:$2/3$	4.5 kg

Bittering Hops

20 to 25 AAUs	any high-alpha acid (such as Columbus, Summit or Warrior)	20 to 25 AAUs

Later Additions

1 lb	turbinado or other light raw sugar	450 g
1 tsp	Irish moss	5 mL
1 tsp	yeast nutrient	5 mL

Flavor, Aroma and Dry Hops

6 oz	Amarillo, Cascade, Citra or Simcoe, divided in thirds	168 g

1. Prepare the liquid yeast in advance, according to the package directions (if using).
2. Coarsely crack the malt grains and place them in a cheesecloth or nylon grain bag.
3. In a brew kettle, bring at least 3 US gal (11 L) brewing water to steeping temperature (150 to 160°F/65 to 71°C). Turn off the heat, add the grain bag, cover and steep for 30 minutes. (If the temperature drops below steeping temperature, turn the element back on briefly to bring it back up.) Remove grain bag and discard.
4. Increase the heat and bring grain tea to a boil. Remove from heat, add $1/3$ (3.3 lbs/1.5 kg) of the malt extract and stir until dissolved completely.
5. Return kettle to the burner and increase the heat until the wort begins to boil. Using a spoon, clear any foam to one side. Reduce heat until a rolling boil can be maintained without foam buildup.
6. Add the bittering hops, stirring to combine. Boil for 45 minutes, uncovered. Monitor to prevent boiling over.

7. Prepare fermentation gear and cooling bath or wort chiller.

8. After 45 minutes, remove the kettle from the heat and add remaining $2/3$ (6.6 lbs/3 kg) of malt extract, $1/3$ (2 oz/56 g) of the aroma hops, sugar, Irish moss and yeast nutrient. Stir to ensure that the extract, sugar and nutrient are dissolved. Return the kettle to the burner and bring back to a rolling boil. Boil for 15 minutes, then stir in $1/3$ (2 oz/56 g) of the aroma hops, turn off the heat and cover.

9. To cool the brew, place the covered kettle in the prepared cooling tub or use a wort chiller according to the manufacturer's directions. Cool to the desired temperature, 75°F (24°C), within 30 to 45 minutes.

10. While the wort is cooling, clean and sanitize the brewing spoon. When the wort has cooled, move the kettle to a counter and stir the wort briskly in one direction for about 5 minutes. After stirring, cover and let rest for 10 to 15 minutes as the hops and trub form a cone.

11. Using a racking cane and siphon, rack as much wort as possible into the sanitized primary fermenter. Using the sanitized funnel and straining screen, strain the rest of the wort into the fermenter. Top off with brewing water to bring the volume to around 5.5 US gal (21 L). Using the hydrometer, take a reading of the specific gravity and record it in your brewing journal.

12. Add the yeast; vigorously stir it with a sanitized spoon to distribute it throughout the wort. Seal the fermenter with lid, stopper and airlock. Keep the fermenter at room temperature (68 to 72°F/20 to 22°C) during primary fermentation (which typically lasts 7 to 10 days after fermentation begins). (Keep in a dark place or under a lightproof cover if using a glass carboy.)

13. After 7 to 10 days or when the kräusen has fallen, gently rack the beer into the secondary fermenter to avoid aerating it, leaving as much of the sediment behind as possible. Seal and keep at room temperature, covered or in a dark place, to allow fermentation to continue.

14. Once the bubbling in the airlock has slowed, gently add the remaining $1/3$ (2 oz/56 g) of the hops, reseal and leave it for about 2 more weeks. Confirm completion of fermentation by using the hydrometer to take final gravity readings. (Hydrometer readings should be the same for several days in a row.)

15. Prime and bottle the beer (see page 91) and condition it for 3 to 4 weeks.

Variation

Imperial Rye IPA: Follow the Imperial IPA recipe but add 1 lb/450 g Cararye® malt to the grains. (Estimated) Original Gravity 1.102

Brewer's Tips

For more information on preparing a yeast starter, see page 89.

If active fermentation backs up into the airlock, replace airlock with blow-off hose (see page 16). Change water as needed; re-install airlock when fermentation settles down.

Imperial Pilsner

To my knowledge, this beer style was first brewed by super-rock-star brewer Sam Calagione of Delaware's Dogfish Head Craft Brewery. He produced the beer for several years at the brewpub. Now in commercial production, the beer is called Golden Era. The aroma hops are divided into thirds: add 2 oz (56 g) hops with 15 minutes remaining on the boil, 2 oz (56 g) at the end of the boil and 2 oz (56 g) to the secondary fermenter.

Estimated Original Gravity: 1.084

Equipment

- **brew kettle**
- **fermentation gear (page 14)**

Lagers feature cold fermentation and longer fermentation times. See page 88 for more information.

Yeast

2 packs	Wyeast 2206 or White Labs WLP940 (or 1 pack in starter) or Fermentis S-23	2 packs

Grains

1 lb	Carafoam®, Carapils® or dextrin malt	450 g
1 lb	Carahelles® or other crystal malt (9 to 15 Lovibond)	450 g
5.5 US gal	brewing water (page 89)	21 L

Malt Extract

9.9 lbs	any brand extra-light, divided $\frac{1}{3}$:$\frac{2}{3}$	4.5 kg

Bittering Hops

20 to 25 AAUs	Horizon, Northern Brewer, Perle or Premiant	20 to 25 AAUs

Later Additions

1 tsp	Irish moss	5 mL
1 tsp	yeast nutrient	5 mL

Flavor, Aroma and Dry Hops

6 oz	Saaz (or any Noble Hops that you prefer), divided in thirds	168 g

1. Prepare the liquid yeast in advance, according to the package directions (if using).
2. Coarsely crack the malt grains and place them in a cheesecloth or nylon grain bag.
3. In a brew kettle, bring at least 3 US gal (11 L) brewing water to steeping temperature (150 to 160°F/65 to 71°C). Turn off the heat, add the grain bag, cover and steep for 30 minutes. (If the temperature drops below steeping temperature, turn the element back on briefly to bring it back up.) Remove grain bag and discard.
4. Increase heat and bring grain tea to a boil. Remove from heat, add $\frac{1}{3}$ (3.3 lbs/1.5 kg) of malt extract and stir until dissolved.
5. Return kettle to burner and increase heat until wort begins to boil. Using a spoon, clear foam to one side. Reduce heat until a rolling boil is maintained without foam buildup.
6. Add the bittering hops, stirring to combine. Boil for 45 minutes, uncovered. Monitor to prevent boiling over.
7. Meanwhile, prepare fermentation gear and cooling bath or wort chiller.

8. After 45 minutes, remove the kettle from the heat and add the remaining $\frac{2}{3}$ (6.6 lbs/3 kg) of malt extract, $\frac{1}{3}$ (2 oz/56 g) of the aroma hops, Irish moss and yeast nutrient. Stir to ensure that the extract and nutrient are dissolved. Return the kettle to the burner and bring back to a rolling boil. Boil for 15 minutes, then stir in $\frac{1}{3}$ (2 oz/56 g) of the aroma hops, turn off the heat and cover.

9. To cool the brew, place the covered kettle in the prepared cooling tub or use a wort chiller according to the manufacturer's directions. Cool to the desired temperature, 75°F (24°C), within 30 to 45 minutes.

10. While the wort is cooling, clean and sanitize the brewing spoon. When the wort has cooled, move the kettle to a counter and stir it briskly in one direction for about 5 minutes. After stirring, cover and let rest for 10 to 15 minutes as the hops and trub form a cone.

11. Using a racking cane and siphon, rack as much wort as possible into the sanitized primary fermenter. Using the sanitized funnel and straining screen, strain the rest of the wort into the fermenter. Top off with brewing water to bring the volume to around 5.5 US gal (21 L). Using the hydrometer, take a reading of the specific gravity and record it in your brewing journal.

12. Add the yeast; vigorously stir it with a sanitized spoon to distribute it throughout the wort. Seal the fermenter with lid, stopper and airlock. Keep the fermenter at room temperature (68 to 72°F/20 to 22°C) until fermentation begins (bubbles will be moving through the airlock). (Keep it in a dark place or under a lightproof cover if using a glass carboy.) Once fermentation begins, drop the temperature to 46 to 55°F (8 to 13°C) for one week of primary fermentation.

13. Gently rack the beer into the secondary fermenter to avoid aerating it, leaving as much of the sediment behind as possible. Seal and drop the temperature to 35 to 45°F (2 to 7°C); keep it at that temperature, covered or in a dark place, to allow fermentation to continue for 4 weeks.

14. Once the bubbling in the airlock has slowed, gently add the remaining $\frac{1}{3}$ (2 oz/56 g) of the hops, reseal and leave it for about 2 more weeks. Confirm completion of fermentation by using the hydrometer to take final gravity readings. (Hydrometer readings should be the same for several days in a row.)

15. Prime and bottle the beer (see page 91). Store it in the refrigerator for 3 to 4 weeks to condition it.

Noble Hops

Noble Hops is a term used to describe the aroma hops popular in Europe. Typically they have an alpha acid below 5% and exhibit pleasant aromas. The pungent Czech grown Saaz is the classic hop for Pilsner. German hops grown in the Hallertau (soft and floral) and Tettnang (woody and spicy) regions are also part of this group, which includes a number of others.

Brewer's Tips

For more information on preparing a yeast starter, see page 89.

If active fermentation backs up into the airlock, replace airlock with blow-off hose (see page 16). Change water as needed; re-install airlock when fermentation settles down.

Imperial Amber

As the word implies, "Imperial" refers to an amped-up version of the style. This is a great beer to enjoy in late autumn.

Estimated Original Gravity: 1.084

Equipment

- **brew kettle**
- **fermentation gear (page 14)**

Beers with an estimated original gravity higher than 1.065 require a longer time in both primary and secondary fermentation. Primary fermentation will take 7 to 10 days, and secondary fermentation will take about 2 weeks longer than weaker brews.

Yeast

2 packs	Wyeast 1056 or White Labs WLP001 (or 1 pack in starter) or Fermentis S-05	2 packs

Grains

1 lb	Melanoidin® malt or other toasted malt (25 to 40 Lovibond)	450 g
1 lb	crystal or caramel malt (40 to 60 Lovibond)	450 g
1 oz	any dark-roasted malt (such as chocolate, black patent, Carafa® or roast barley)	28 g
5.5 US gal	brewing water (page 89)	21 L

Malt Extract

9.9 lbs	light or gold (such as Briess, Coopers or Northwestern); divided $1/3$:$2/3$	4.5 kg

Bittering Hops

14 to 16 AAUs	any medium-alpha acid	14 to 16 AAUs

Later Additions

1 lb	Demerara or other dark raw sugar	450 g
1 tsp	Irish moss	5 mL
1 tsp	yeast nutrient	5 mL

Aroma Hops

1.5 oz	Cascade, Liberty, Mt Hood or Willamette	42 g

1. Prepare liquid yeast in advance, according to directions.
2. Coarsely crack the malt grains and place them in a cheesecloth or nylon grain bag.
3. In a brew kettle, bring at least 3 US gal (11 L) brewing water to steeping temperature (150 to 160°F/65 to 71°C). Turn off the heat, add the grain bag, cover and steep for 30 minutes. (If the temperature drops below steeping temperature, turn the element back on briefly to bring it back up.) Remove grain bag and discard.
4. Increase the heat and bring grain tea to a boil. Remove from heat, add $1/3$ (3.3 lbs/1.5 kg) of the malt extract and stir until dissolved completely.
5. Return kettle to burner and increase heat until wort begins to boil. Using a spoon, clear foam. Reduce heat until a rolling boil is maintained without foam buildup.
6. Add the bittering hops, stirring to combine. Boil for 45 minutes, uncovered. Monitor to prevent boiling over.
7. Prepare fermentation gear and cooling bath or wort chiller.

8. After 45 minutes, remove the kettle from the heat and add the remaining ⅔ (6.6 lbs/3 kg) of malt extract, sugar, Irish moss and yeast nutrient. Stir to ensure that the extract, sugar and nutrient are dissolved. Return the kettle to the burner and bring back to a rolling boil. Boil for 15 minutes, then stir in the aroma hops, turn off the heat and cover.

9. To cool the brew, place the covered kettle in the prepared cooling tub or use a wort chiller according to the manufacturer's directions. Cool to the desired temperature, 75°F (24°C), within 30 to 45 minutes.

10. While the wort is cooling, clean and sanitize the brewing spoon. When the wort has cooled, move the kettle to a counter and stir the wort briskly in one direction for about 5 minutes. After stirring, cover and let rest for 10 to 15 minutes as the hops and trub form a cone.

11. Using a racking cane and siphon, rack as much wort as possible into the sanitized primary fermenter. Using the sanitized funnel and straining screen, strain the rest of the wort into the fermenter. Top off with brewing water to bring the volume to around 5.5 US gal (21 L). Using the hydrometer, take a reading of the specific gravity and record it in your brewing journal.

12. Add the yeast; vigorously stir it with a sanitized spoon to distribute it throughout the wort. Seal the fermenter with lid, stopper and airlock. Keep the fermenter at room temperature (68 to 72°F/20 to 22°C) during primary fermentation (which typically lasts 7 to 10 days after fermentation begins). (Keep in a dark place or under a lightproof cover if using a glass carboy.)

13. After 7 to 10 days or when the kräusen has fallen, gently rack the beer into the secondary fermenter to avoid aerating it, leaving as much of the sediment behind as possible. Seal and keep at room temperature, covered or in a dark place, to allow fermentation to continue.

14. Once the bubbling in the airlock has slowed, confirm completion of fermentation by using the hydrometer to take final gravity readings. (Hydrometer readings should be the same for several days in a row.)

15. Prime and bottle the beer (see page 91) and condition it for 3 to 4 weeks.

Variation

Imperial Brown Ale: To brew an Imperial Brown ale, follow the recipe for Imperial Amber, increasing the dark-roasted malt to 4 oz (112 g).

Brewer's Tips

For information on preparing a yeast starter, see page 89.

If active fermentation backs up into the airlock, replace airlock with blow-off hose (see page 16). Change water as needed; re-install airlock when fermentation settles down.

American Barley Wine

This is a style that vexes the alcohol registration authorities. "No, it's not wine. It's beer! It's just a strong beer with a wine-like strength." The original renditions of this brew hail from the UK (see in the next section). On this side of the pond, the style becomes more extreme.

Estimated Original Gravity: 1.099

Equipment

- **brew kettle**
- **fermentation gear (page 14)**

Beers with an estimated original gravity higher than 1.065 require a longer time in both primary and secondary fermentation. Primary fermentation will take 7 to 10 days, and secondary fermentation will take about 2 weeks longer than weaker brews.

To Hydrate Lalvin Yeast

In a sanitized bowl or measuring cup, dissolve Lalvin yeast in 1.5 US fl oz (50 mL) of boiled water cooled to 104 to 109°F (40 to 43°C). Let stand for 15 minutes without stirring; then stir with a sanitized spoon to distribute yeast in water.

Yeast

2 packs	Wyeast 1056 or White Labs 001 (or 1 pack in starter) or Fermentis US-05	2 packs
2 packs	Lalvin EC-1118 Champagne yeast (14 g) (add to secondary fermenter)	2 packs

Grains

1 lb	crystal malt (30 Lovibond)	450 g
1 lb	Victory malt	450 g
5.5 US gal	brewing water (page 89)	21 L

Malt Extract

12.2 lbs	any brand extra-light, divided $^1/_3$:$^2/_3$	5.5 kg

Bittering Hops

25 to 35 AAUs	high-alpha acid (such as Columbus, Summit or Warrior)	25 to 35 AAUs

Later Additions

1 tsp	Irish moss	5 mL
1 tsp	yeast nutrient	5 mL
5 tsp	yeast energizer (add to secondary fermenter)	25 mL

Aroma and Dry Hops

1.5 oz	Cascade or Willamette (reserve .5 oz/14 g as dry hop)	42 g

1. Prepare the first liquid yeast addition in advance, according to the package directions (if using liquid yeast).
2. Coarsely crack the malt grains and place them in a cheesecloth or nylon grain bag.
3. In a brew kettle, bring at least 3 US gal (11 L) brewing water to steeping temperature (150 to 160°F/65 to 71°C). Turn off the heat, add the grain bag, cover and steep for 30 minutes. (If the temperature drops below steeping temperature, turn the element back on briefly to bring it back up.) Remove grain bag and discard.
4. Increase heat and bring grain tea to a boil. Remove from heat, add $^1/_3$ (4 lbs/1.8 kg) of malt extract and dissolve.
5. Return kettle to the burner and increase the heat until the wort begins to boil. Using a spoon, clear any foam to one side. Reduce heat until a rolling boil can be maintained without foam buildup.
6. Add the bittering hops, stirring to combine. Boil for 45 minutes, uncovered. Monitor to prevent boiling over.

7. Meanwhile, prepare fermentation gear and cooling bath or wort chiller.

8. After 45 minutes, remove the kettle from the heat and add the remaining ⅔ (8.2 lbs/3.7 kg) of the malt extract, Irish moss and yeast nutrient. Stir to ensure that the extract and nutrient are dissolved. Return the kettle to the burner and bring back to a rolling boil. Boil for 15 minutes, then stir in 1 oz (28 g) of the aroma hops, turn off the heat and cover.

9. To cool the brew, place the covered kettle in the prepared cooling tub or use a wort chiller according to the manufacturer's directions. Cool to the desired temperature, 75°F (24°C), within 30 to 45 minutes.

10. While the wort is cooling, clean and sanitize the brewing spoon. When the wort has cooled, move the kettle to a counter and stir the wort briskly in one direction for about 5 minutes. After stirring, cover and let rest for 10 to 15 minutes as the hops and trub form a cone.

11. Using a racking cane and siphon, rack as much wort as possible into the sanitized primary fermenter. Using the sanitized funnel and straining screen, strain the rest of the wort into the fermenter. Top off with brewing water to bring the volume to around 5.5 US gal (21 L). Using the hydrometer, take a reading of the specific gravity and record it in your brewing journal.

12. Add the yeast; vigorously stir it with a sanitized spoon to distribute it throughout the wort. Seal the fermenter with lid, stopper and airlock or blow-off hose. Keep the fermenter at room temperature (68 to 72°F/20 to 22°C) during primary fermentation (which typically lasts 7 to 10 days after fermentation begins). (Keep in a dark place or under a lightproof cover if using a glass carboy.)

13. After 7 to 10 days or when the kräusen has fallen, gently rack the beer into the secondary fermenter to avoid aerating it, leaving as much of the sediment behind as possible. Seal and keep at room temperature, covered or in a dark place, to allow fermentation to continue.

14. Once the bubbling in the airlock has slowed, gently add the remaining .5 oz (14 g) of the hops, yeast energizer and the Lalvin yeast, reseal and leave it for about 2 more weeks. Confirm completion of fermentation by using the hydrometer to take final gravity readings. (Hydrometer readings should be the same for several days in a row.)

15. Prime and bottle the beer (see page 91) and condition it for 3 to 4 weeks.

Variation

Wheat Wine:
Wheat wine is a beer that's so retro, it's modern. Popular in merry old England, the style has seen a revival among home and craft brewers.

To produce one of your own, make the following modifications to the Barley Wine recipe:

- Change the malt extract from extra-light to wheat
- Change the bittering hops to 10 to 15 AAUs
- Use mellower aroma hop like Liberty, Mt Hood or Willamette

Brewer's Tips

For information on preparing a yeast starter, see page 89.

If active fermentation backs up into the airlock, replace airlock with blow-off hose (see page 16). Change water as needed; re-install airlock when fermentation settles down.

Hop Harvest Ale

Inevitably, you (or someone you know) will get some hop rhizomes, and you'll try your hand at brewing a "wet-hopped" beer with homegrown, fresh-picked hops. (The hop vine is propagated by planting rhizomes.)

Since you probably won't have the fresh hops analyzed for their alpha acid by a lab, use hops with a known alpha acid to bitter the brew, as called for in the recipe. We'll use the fresh hops for flavor and aroma. We'll even employ a version of an esoteric German procedure called "mash hopping."

Estimated Original Gravity: 1.064

Equipment

- **brew kettle**
- **fermentation gear (page 14)**

Yeast

1 pack	Wyeast 1056 or White Labs 001 or Fermentis S-05	1 pack

Grains

1 lb	pale malted barley	450 g
1 lb	dark Munich malt	450 g
1 lb	Caraamber® or other toasted malt (25 to 30 Lovibond)	450 g
1 lb	crystal or caramel malt (20 to 30 Lovibond)	450 g

Flavor and Aroma Hops

6[+] oz	fresh "wet" hops (i.e., not dried), divided	168[+] g
5.5 US gal	brewing water (page 89)	21 L

Malt Extract

6.6 lbs	any brand light, divided in half	3 kg

Bittering Hops

6 to 8 AAUs	medium-alpha acid	6 to 8 AAUs

Later Additions

1 tsp	Irish moss	5 mL
1 tsp	yeast nutrient	5 mL

1. Prepare the liquid yeast in advance, according to the package directions (if using).
2. Coarsely crack the malt grains and place them in a cheesecloth or nylon grain bag. Add 2 oz (56 g) of fresh hops to the bag.
3. In a brew kettle, bring at least 3 US gal (11 L) brewing water to steeping temperature (150 to 160°F/65 to 71°C). Turn off the heat, add the bag with the grain and hops, cover and steep for 60 minutes. (If the temperature drops below steeping temperature, turn the element back on briefly to bring it back up.) Remove bag and discard.
4. Increase the heat and bring grain and hop tea to a boil. Remove from heat, add half of the malt extract and stir until dissolved completely.
5. Return kettle to the burner and increase the heat until the wort begins to boil. Using a spoon, clear any foam to one side. Reduce heat until a rolling boil can be maintained without foam buildup.
6. Add the bittering hops, stirring to combine. Boil for 30 minutes, uncovered. Monitor to prevent boiling over. Place 1 oz (28 g) fresh hops in a muslin bag and add to the wort. Continue the boil for another 15 minutes.

7. Meanwhile, prepare fermentation gear and cooling bath or wort chiller.

8. After a total of 45 minutes, remove the kettle from the heat and add the other half of the malt extract, Irish moss and yeast nutrient. Stir to ensure that the extract and nutrient are dissolved. Add another bag with 1 oz (28 g) of fresh hops to the kettle. Return the kettle to the burner and bring back to a rolling boil. Boil for 10 minutes, then add another bag with 1 oz (28 g) of fresh hops for the final 5 minutes of the boil. Turn off the heat and cover.

9. To cool the brew, place the covered kettle in the prepared cooling tub or use a wort chiller according to the manufacturer's directions. Cool to the desired temperature, 75°F (24°C), within 30 to 45 minutes.

10. While the wort is cooling, clean and sanitize the brewing spoon. When the wort has cooled, move the kettle to a counter and stir the wort briskly in one direction for about 5 minutes. After stirring, cover and let rest for 10 to 15 minutes as the hops and trub form a cone.

11. Using a racking cane and siphon, rack as much wort as possible into the sanitized primary fermenter. Using the sanitized funnel and straining screen, strain the rest of the wort into the fermenter. Top off with brewing water to bring the volume to around 5.5 US gal (21 L). Using the hydrometer, take a reading of the specific gravity and record it in your brewing journal.

12. Add the yeast; vigorously stir it with a sanitized spoon to distribute it throughout the wort. Seal the fermenter with lid, stopper and airlock. Keep the fermenter at room temperature (68 to 72°F/20 to 22°C) during primary fermentation (which typically lasts 5 to 7 days after fermentation begins). (Keep in a dark place or under a lightproof cover if using a glass carboy.)

13. When the kräusen has fallen, gently rack the beer into the secondary fermenter to avoid aerating it, leaving as much of the sediment behind as possible. Seal and keep at room temperature, covered or in a dark place, to allow fermentation to continue.

14. Once the bubbling in the airlock has slowed, place the last 1 oz (28 g) of fresh hops in a sanitized muslin bag and add to the fermenter; reseal and leave it for about 2 more weeks. Confirm completion of fermentation by using the hydrometer to take final gravity readings. (Hydrometer readings should be the same for several days in a row.)

15. Prime and bottle the beer (see page 91) and condition it for 3 to 4 weeks.

Brewer's Tip

It is best to use muslin hop bags to contain the hop cones. Add 2 oz (56 g) of fresh hops to the grain bag and steep the hops and grains for 60 minutes instead of 30. 1 oz (28 g) hops will be added at each of the 30, 15 and 5 minutes remaining in the boil. Another 1 oz (28 g) will be added to the secondary fermentation as a dry hop. Is that hoppy enough for you? If you're a hophead with a big bag of hops, ignore those numbers and go crazy!

Pre-Prohibition Lager

Before Prohibition, the Great Depression and two world wars left North Americans drinking watered-down light lager beers, our grandfathers and great-grandfathers drank a different, more robust beer. My grandfather was the brewmaster for a brewery in Philadelphia. Brew this one up and enjoy "beer the way it used to be."

Estimated Original Gravity: 1.078

Equipment

- **brew kettle**
- **fermentation gear (page 14)**

Lagers feature cold fermentation and longer fermentation times. See page 88 for more information.

Yeast

| 2 packs | Wyeast 2035 or White Labs WLP840 (or 1 pack in starter) or Fermentis S-23 | 2 packs |

Grains

1 lb	Carafoam®, Carapils® or dextrin malt	450 g
1 lb	Vienna malt	450 g
5.5 US gal	brewing water (page 89)	21 L

Malt Extract

| 8 lbs | Alexander's Sun Country Pale Malt Extract, divided in half | 3.6 kg |

Bittering Hops

| 8 to 10 AAUs | Cluster or Northern Brewer | 8 to 10 AAUs |

Later Additions

1 lb	rice syrup	450 g
1 tsp	Irish moss	5 mL
1 tsp	yeast nutrient	5 mL

Aroma Hops

| 1.5 oz | Hallertau, Liberty or Mt Hood | 42 g |

1. Prepare the liquid yeast in advance, according to the package directions (if using).
2. Coarsely crack the malt grains and place them in a cheesecloth or nylon grain bag.
3. In a brew kettle, bring at least 3 US gal (11 L) brewing water to steeping temperature (150 to 160°F/65 to 71°C). Turn off the heat, add the grain bag, cover and steep for 30 minutes. (If the temperature drops below steeping temperature, turn the element back on briefly to bring it back up.) Remove grain bag and discard.
4. Increase the heat and bring grain tea to a boil. Remove from heat, add half of the malt extract and stir until dissolved completely.
5. Return kettle to the burner and increase the heat until the wort begins to boil. Using a spoon, clear any foam to one side. Reduce the heat until a rolling boil can be maintained without foam buildup.
6. Add the bittering hops, stirring to combine. Boil for 45 minutes, uncovered. Monitor to prevent boiling over.
7. Meanwhile, prepare fermentation gear and cooling bath or wort chiller.

8. After 45 minutes, remove the kettle from the heat and add the remaining half of the malt extract, rice syrup, Irish moss and yeast nutrient. Stir to ensure that the extract, syrup and nutrient are dissolved. Return the kettle to the burner and bring back to a rolling boil. Boil for 15 minutes, then stir in the aroma hops, turn off the heat and cover.

9. To cool the brew, place the covered kettle in the prepared cooling tub or use a wort chiller according to the manufacturer's directions. Cool to the desired temperature, 75°F (24°C), within 30 to 45 minutes.

10. While the wort is cooling, clean and sanitize the brewing spoon. When the wort has cooled, move the kettle to a counter and stir it briskly in one direction for about 5 minutes. After stirring, cover and let rest for 10 to 15 minutes as the hops and trub form a cone.

11. Using a racking cane and siphon, rack as much wort as possible into the sanitized primary fermenter. Using the sanitized funnel and straining screen, strain the rest of the wort into the fermenter. Top off with brewing water to bring the volume to around 5.5 US gal (21 L). Using the hydrometer, take a reading of the specific gravity and record it in your brewing journal.

12. Add the yeast; vigorously stir it with a sanitized spoon to distribute it throughout the wort. Seal the fermenter with lid, stopper and airlock. Keep the fermenter at room temperature (68 to 72°F/20 to 22°C) until fermentation begins (bubbles will be moving through the airlock). (Keep it in a dark place or under a lightproof cover if using a glass carboy.) Once fermentation begins, drop the temperature to 46 to 55°F (8 to 13°C) for one week of primary fermentation.

13. Gently rack the beer into the secondary fermenter to avoid aerating it, leaving as much of the sediment behind as possible. Seal and drop the temperature to 35 to 45°F (2 to 7°C); keep it at that temperature, covered or in a dark place, to allow fermentation to continue for 4 weeks.

14. Once the bubbling in the airlock has slowed, confirm completion of fermentation by using the hydrometer to take final gravity readings. (Hydrometer readings should be the same for several days in a row.)

15. Prime and bottle the beer (see page 91). Condition it in the refrigerator for 3 to 4 weeks.

Brewer's Tips

For information on preparing a yeast starter, see page 89.

No special equipment is required to crack the grains. Place them in a gallon-sized, sealable plastic bag (so there's room for them to move but they can't escape) and use the malt can or a heavy rolling pin to lightly crush them. The goal is to crack the outer shells and break them apart lightly, not to make flour. Cracked grains should have a coarse texture. Alternatively, your homebrew supplier can crack them for you. Just don't use a food processor to pulse them.

If you want to get all the possible goodness out of your grain after the steeping process, sparge the grain. To sparge, place the grain bag in a colander or strainer and gently rinse the bag over the kettle with about 1 US qt (1 L) of 170°F (77°C) brewing water before discarding the bag. Don't wring the bag out; wringing it out will release harsh tannins.

The brewers in the UK brew ales for the most part. Just like on our side of the pond, most UK lager beers are lame interpretations of north European lagers. In contrast, UK ales are very much about balance, showcasing the flavors of each ingredient.

Needless to say, we've specified UK malts to produce UK beers. Use whatever UK brand is available, and feel free to use whatever grains are available. If possible, however, try to stick with the hops and yeast that have been specified.

Brews from the British Isles

We spent some time discussing and brewing American-style IPAs because that is often the style that fledgling homebrewers want to emulate. Now, let's take a step back in time and try to duplicate the original. It was produced at Burton-on-Trent, using water that is particularly hard, which enhanced the beer's hoppy character. Drink a pint of this ale and step out into the noonday sun with the mad dogs and Englishmen! Add half the aroma hops at the end of the boil and the other half to the secondary fermenter as a dry hop.

Estimated Original Gravity: 1.066

Equipment

- **brew kettle**
- **fermentation gear (page 14)**

Beers with an estimated original gravity higher than 1.065 require a longer time in both primary and secondary fermentation. Primary fermentation will take 7 to 10 days, and secondary fermentation will take about 2 weeks longer than weaker brews.

UK IPA

Yeast

1 pack	Wyeast 1098 or White Labs 005 or Fermentis S-04	1 pack

Grains

1 lb	UK caramalt or crystal malt (15 to 25 Lovibond)	450 g
1 lb	UK amber or any toasted malt (25 to 30 Lovibond)	450 g
5.5 US gal	brewing water (page 89)	21 L

Malt Extract

6.6 lbs	UK light, divided in half	3 kg

Bittering Hops

12 to 16 AAUs	Northern Brewer or other medium- to high-alpha UK hops	12 to 16 AAUs

Later Additions

1 lb	Demerara or other raw sugar	450 g
1 tsp	Irish moss	5 mL
1 tsp	yeast nutrient	5 mL
2 tsp	Burton Salts or gypsum	10 mL

Aroma and Dry Hops

3 oz	Fuggle, Kent Golding, or a blend of both, divided in half	85 g

1. Prepare the liquid yeast in advance, according to the package directions (if using).
2. Coarsely crack the malt grains and place them in a cheesecloth or nylon grain bag.
3. In a brew kettle, bring at least 3 US gal (11 L) brewing water to steeping temperature (150 to 160°F/65 to 71°C). Turn off the heat, add the grain bag, cover and steep for 30 minutes. (If the temperature drops below steeping temperature, turn the element back on briefly to bring it back up.) Remove grain bag and discard.
4. Increase the heat and bring grain tea to a boil. Remove from heat, add half of the malt extract and stir until dissolved completely.
5. Return kettle to the burner and increase the heat until the wort begins to boil. Using a spoon, clear any foam to one side. Reduce heat until a rolling boil can be maintained without foam buildup.
6. Add the bittering hops, stirring to combine. Boil for 45 minutes, uncovered. Monitor to prevent boiling over.

7. Meanwhile, prepare the fermentation gear and cooling bath or wort chiller.

8. After 45 minutes, remove the kettle from the heat and add the remaining half of the malt extract, sugar, Irish moss, yeast nutrient and Burton Salts. Stir to ensure that the extract, sugar, nutrient and salts are dissolved. Return the kettle to the burner and bring back to a rolling boil. Boil for 15 minutes, then stir in half of the aroma hops, turn off the heat and cover.

9. To cool the brew, place the covered kettle in the prepared cooling tub or use a wort chiller according to the manufacturer's directions. Cool to the desired temperature, 75°F (24°C), within 30 to 45 minutes.

10. While the wort is cooling, clean and sanitize the brewing spoon. When the wort has cooled, move the kettle to a counter and stir the wort briskly in one direction for about 5 minutes. After stirring, cover and let rest for 10 to 15 minutes as the hops and trub form a cone.

11. Using a racking cane and siphon, rack as much wort as possible into the sanitized primary fermenter. Using the sanitized funnel and straining screen, strain the rest of the wort into the fermenter. Top off with brewing water to bring the volume to around 5.5 US gal (21 L). Using the hydrometer, take a reading of the specific gravity and record it in your brewing journal.

12. Add the yeast; vigorously stir it with a sanitized spoon to distribute it throughout the wort. Seal the fermenter with lid, stopper and airlock. Keep the fermenter at room temperature (68 to 72°F/20 to 22°C) during primary fermentation (which typically lasts 7 to 10 days after fermentation begins). (Keep in a dark place or under a lightproof cover if using a glass carboy.)

13. After 7 to 10 days or when the kräusen has fallen, gently rack the beer into the secondary fermenter to avoid aerating it, leaving as much of the sediment behind as possible. Seal and keep at room temperature, covered or in a dark place, to allow fermentation to continue.

14. Once the bubbling in the airlock has slowed, gently add the remainder of the hops, reseal and leave it for about 2 more weeks. Confirm completion of fermentation by using the hydrometer to take final gravity readings. (Hydrometer readings should be the same for several days in a row.)

15. Prime and bottle the beer (see page 91) and condition it for 3 to 4 weeks.

To Oak or Not To Oak? (...and how to)

There is much debate over the oak character in IPA. Yes, it spent many weeks aging in an oak barrel. Some say that the brewers would have lined those barrels with pitch, negating the absorption of oak flavor, and thus oak was not a part of the flavor profile. Others say the oak was noticeable.

The truth is that anyone who actually drank the original IPAs is long dead and can tell no tales. If you like oak flavors in your wine and spirits, most likely you'll enjoy them in your beer. Take 2 to 4 oz (56 to 112 g) light-toasted oak chips, such as those used in winemaking. Put them in a cheesecloth hop bag, put the bag in a jar and cover the chips with vodka (generic is fine). Allow the chips to stand for a few days and then add the bag and the oaky vodka to the secondary fermenter. Taste the beer every few days. If it starts to become too oaky, rack the beer to another fermenter and discard the bag.

Remember, too little oak is better than too much. Too much oak will result in an overly harsh tannic flavor.

In recent years UK brewers have produced lighter, hoppier ales for summer consumption. They've taken their inspiration from North American craft brewers.

Estimated Original Gravity: 1.053

Equipment

- **brew kettle**
- **fermentation gear (page 14)**

As you build your brewing skills, switching to liquid yeast products (from Wyeast or White Labs) will give you a brew that is more complex than the ones made with the dry yeast (from Fermentis or Danstar) in the Absolute Beginner recipes. See page 86 for more information about liquid yeasts.

Summer Ale

Yeast

1 pack	Wyeast 1098 or White Labs 005 or Fermentis S-04	1 pack

Grains

1 lb	UK Caramalt	450 g
5.5 US gal	brewing water (page 89)	21 L

Malt Extract

6.6 lbs	UK extra-light, divided in half	3 kg

Bittering Hops

12 to 14 AAUs	Target, Pilgrim or Northern Brewer	12 to 14 AAUs

Later Additions

1 tsp	Irish moss	5 mL
1 tsp	yeast nutrient	5 mL

Aroma and Dry Hops

2 oz	Kent Golding or Fuggle (reserve .5 oz/14 g as a dry hop)	56 g

1. Prepare the liquid yeast in advance, according to the package directions (if using).
2. Coarsely crack the malt grains and place them in a cheesecloth or nylon grain bag.
3. In a brew kettle, bring at least 3 US gal (11 L) brewing water to steeping temperature (150 to 160°F/65 to 71°C). Turn off the heat, add the grain bag, cover and steep for 30 minutes. (If the temperature drops below steeping temperature, turn the element back on briefly to bring it back up.) Remove grain bag and discard.
4. Increase the heat and bring grain tea to a boil. Remove from heat, add half of the malt extract and stir until dissolved completely.
5. Return kettle to the burner and increase the heat until the wort begins to boil. Using a spoon, clear any foam to one side. Reduce heat until a rolling boil can be maintained without foam buildup.
6. Add the bittering hops, stirring to combine. Boil for 45 minutes, uncovered. Monitor to prevent boiling over.
7. Meanwhile, prepare the fermentation gear and cooling bath or wort chiller.

8. After 45 minutes, remove the kettle from the heat and add the remaining half of the malt extract, Irish moss and yeast nutrient. Stir to ensure that the extract, sugar and nutrient are dissolved. Return the kettle to the burner and bring back to a rolling boil. Boil for 15 minutes, then stir in 1.5 oz (42 g) of the aroma hops, turn off the heat and cover.

9. To cool the brew, place the covered kettle in the prepared cooling tub or use a wort chiller according to the manufacturer's directions. Cool to the desired temperature, 75°F (24°C), within 30 to 45 minutes.

10. While the wort is cooling, clean and sanitize the brewing spoon. When the wort has cooled, move the kettle to a counter and stir the wort briskly in one direction for about 5 minutes. After stirring, cover and let rest for 10 to 15 minutes as the hops and trub form a cone.

11. Using a racking cane and siphon, rack as much wort as possible into the sanitized primary fermenter. Using the sanitized funnel and straining screen, strain the rest of the wort into the fermenter. Top off with brewing water to bring the volume to around 5.5 US gal (21 L). Using the hydrometer, take a reading of the specific gravity and record it in your brewing journal.

12. Add the yeast; vigorously stir it with a sanitized spoon to distribute it throughout the wort. Seal the fermenter with lid, stopper and airlock. Keep the fermenter at room temperature (68 to 72°F/20 to 22°C) during primary fermentation (which typically lasts 1 to 4 days after fermentation begins). (Keep in a dark place or under a lightproof cover if using a glass carboy.)

13. After 1 to 4 days or when the kräusen has fallen, gently rack the beer into the secondary fermenter to avoid aerating it, leaving as much of the sediment behind as possible. Seal and keep at room temperature, covered or in a dark place, to allow fermentation to continue.

14. Once the bubbling in the airlock has slowed, gently add the remaining .5 oz (14 g) hops, reseal and leave it for about 2 more weeks. Confirm completion of fermentation by using the hydrometer to take final gravity readings. (Hydrometer readings should be the same for several days in a row.)

15. Prime and bottle the beer (see page 91) and condition it for 3 to 4 weeks.

Golden Mild

This is the first of a trio of recipes for mild ales. This style is often given the brush-off by drinkers of robust craft beers. They don't view themselves as wanting a "mild" experience.

Many brewers of the style use tough-sounding names for marketing purposes. Pioneering brewer Bert Grant called his dark mild Celtic Ale and the Yards Brewery in Philadelphia calls their ruby mild Brawler. What these social beverages are is simple: lower alcohol, easy-drinking beers for session drinking.

Estimated Original Gravity: 1.054

Equipment

- **brew kettle**
- **fermentation gear (page 14)**

As you build your brewing skills, switching to liquid yeast products (from Wyeast or White Labs) will give you a brew that is more complex than the ones made with the dry yeast (from Fermentis or Danstar) in the Absolute Beginner recipes. See page 86 for more information about liquid yeasts.

Yeast

1 pack	Wyeast 1098 or White Labs 005 or Fermentis S-04	1 pack

Grains

1 lb	UK caramalt or crystal malt (15 to 25 Lovibond)	450 g
1 lb	Carafoam®, Carapils® or dextrin malt	450 g
5.5 US gal	brewing water (page 89)	21 L

Malt Extracts

1 lb	UK extra-light DME	450 g
4 lbs	UK light (reserve for late extract addition)	1.8 kg

Bittering Hops

4 to 5 AAUs	Fuggle or Kent Golding	4 to 5 AAUs

Later Additions

8 oz	turbinado or other light raw sugar	224 g
1 tsp	Irish moss	5 mL
1 tsp	yeast nutrient	5 mL

Aroma Hops

.5 oz	Fuggle or Kent Golding	14 g

1. Prepare the liquid yeast in advance, according to the package directions (if using).
2. Coarsely crack the malt grains and place them in a cheesecloth or nylon grain bag.
3. In a brew kettle, bring at least 3 US gal (11 L) brewing water to steeping temperature (150 to 160°F/65 to 71°C). Turn off the heat, add the grain bag, cover and steep for 30 minutes. (If the temperature drops below steeping temperature, turn the element back on briefly to bring it back up.) Remove grain bag and discard.
4. Increase the heat and bring grain tea to a boil. Remove from heat, add the extra-light DME and stir until dissolved completely.
5. Return kettle to the burner and increase the heat until the wort begins to boil. Using a spoon, clear any foam to one side. Reduce heat until a rolling boil can be maintained without foam buildup.
6. Add the bittering hops, stirring to combine. Boil for 45 minutes, uncovered. Monitor to prevent boiling over.
7. Meanwhile, prepare the fermentation gear and cooling bath or wort chiller.

8. After 45 minutes, remove the kettle from the heat and add the light malt extract, sugar, Irish moss and yeast nutrient. Stir to ensure that the extract, sugar and nutrient are dissolved. Return the kettle to the burner and bring back to a rolling boil. Boil for 15 minutes, then stir in the aroma hops, turn off the heat and cover.

9. To cool the brew, place the covered kettle in the prepared cooling tub or use a wort chiller according to the manufacturer's directions. Cool to the desired temperature, 75°F (24°C), within 30 to 45 minutes.

10. While the wort is cooling, clean and sanitize the brewing spoon. When the wort has cooled, move the kettle to a counter and stir the wort briskly in one direction for about 5 minutes. After stirring, cover and let rest for 10 to 15 minutes as the hops and trub form a cone.

11. Using a racking cane and siphon, rack as much wort as possible into the sanitized primary fermenter. Using the sanitized funnel and straining screen, strain the rest of the wort into the fermenter. Top off with brewing water to bring the volume to around 5.5 US gal (21 L). Using the hydrometer, take a reading of the specific gravity and record it in your brewing journal.

12. Add the yeast; vigorously stir it with a sanitized spoon to distribute it throughout the wort. Seal the fermenter with lid, stopper and airlock. Keep the fermenter at room temperature (68 to 72°F/20 to 22°C) during primary fermentation (which typically lasts 1 to 4 days after fermentation begins). (Keep in a dark place or under a lightproof cover if using a glass carboy.)

13. After 1 to 4 days or when the kräusen has fallen, gently rack the beer into the secondary fermenter to avoid aerating it, leaving as much of the sediment behind as possible. Seal and keep at room temperature, covered or in a dark place, to allow fermentation to continue.

14. Once the bubbling in the airlock has slowed, confirm completion of fermentation by using the hydrometer to take final gravity readings. (Hydrometer readings should be the same for several days in a row.)

15. Prime and bottle the beer (see page 91) and condition it for 3 to 4 weeks.

Ruby Mild

Estimated Original Gravity: 1.053

Equipment

- **brew kettle**
- **fermentation gear (page 14)**

As you build your brewing skills, switching to liquid yeast products (from Wyeast or White Labs) will give you a brew that is more complex than the ones made with the dry yeast (from Fermentis or Danstar) in the Absolute Beginner recipes. See page 86 for more information about liquid yeasts

Yeast

1 pack	Wyeast 1098 or White Labs 005 or Fermentis S-04	1 pack

Grains

1 lb	UK amber malt	450 g
1 lb	UK crystal malt (60 Lovibond)	450 g
1 oz	UK roast barley	28 g
5.5 US gal	brewing water (page 89)	21 L

Malt Extracts

4 lbs	UK light	1.8 kg
1 lb	UK extra-light DME	450 g

Bittering Hops

4 to 5 AAUs	Fuggle or Kent Golding	4 to 5 AAUs

Later Additions

8 oz	Demerara or other dark raw sugar	224 g
1 tsp	Irish moss	5 mL
1 tsp	yeast nutrient	5 mL

Aroma Hops

.5 oz	Fuggle or Kent Golding	14 g

1. Prepare the liquid yeast in advance, according to the package directions (if using).
2. Coarsely crack the malt grains and place them in a cheesecloth or nylon grain bag.
3. In a brew kettle, bring at least 3 US gal (11 L) brewing water to steeping temperature (150 to 160°F/65 to 71°C). Turn off the heat, add the grain bag, cover and steep for 30 minutes. (If the temperature drops below steeping temperature, turn the element back on briefly to bring it back up.) Remove grain bag and discard.
4. Increase the heat and bring grain tea to a boil. Remove from heat, add the malt extracts and stir until dissolved completely.
5. Return kettle to the burner and increase the heat until the wort begins to boil. Using a spoon, clear any foam to one side. Reduce heat until a rolling boil can be maintained without foam buildup.
6. Add the bittering hops, stirring to combine. Boil for 45 minutes, uncovered. Monitor to prevent boiling over.
7. Meanwhile, prepare the fermentation gear and cooling bath or wort chiller.

8. After 45 minutes, remove the kettle from the heat and add sugar, Irish moss and yeast nutrient. Stir to ensure that the sugar and nutrient are dissolved. Return the kettle to the burner and bring back to a rolling boil. Boil for 15 minutes, then stir in the aroma hops, turn off the heat and cover.

9. To cool the brew, place the covered kettle in the prepared cooling tub or use a wort chiller according to the manufacturer's directions. Cool to the desired temperature, 75°F (24°C), within 30 to 45 minutes.

10. While the wort is cooling, clean and sanitize the brewing spoon. When the wort has cooled, move the kettle to a counter and stir the wort briskly in one direction for about 5 minutes. After stirring, cover and let rest for 10 to 15 minutes as the hops and trub form a cone.

11. Using a racking cane and siphon, rack as much wort as possible into the sanitized primary fermenter. Using the sanitized funnel and straining screen, strain the rest of the wort into the fermenter. Top off with brewing water to bring the volume to around 5.5 US gal (21 L). Using the hydrometer, take a reading of the specific gravity and record it in your brewing journal.

12. Add the yeast; vigorously stir it with a sanitized spoon to distribute it throughout the wort. Seal the fermenter with lid, stopper and airlock. Keep the fermenter at room temperature (68 to 72°F/20 to 22°C) during primary fermentation (which typically lasts 1 to 4 days after fermentation begins). (Keep in a dark place or under a lightproof cover if using a glass carboy.)

13. After 1 to 4 days or when the kräusen has fallen, gently rack the beer into the secondary fermenter to avoid aerating it, leaving as much of the sediment behind as possible. Seal and keep at room temperature, covered or in a dark place, to allow fermentation to continue.

14. Once the bubbling in the airlock has slowed, confirm completion of fermentation by using the hydrometer to take final gravity readings. (Hydrometer readings should be the same for several days in a row.)

15. Prime and bottle the beer (see page 91) and condition it for 3 to 4 weeks.

Dark Mild

Equipment

- **brew kettle**
- **fermentation gear (page 14)**

As you build your brewing skills, switching to liquid yeast products (from Wyeast or White Labs) will give you a brew that is more complex than the ones made with the dry yeast (from Fermentis or Danstar) in the Absolute Beginner recipes. See page 86 for more information about liquid yeasts.

Yeast

1 pack	Wyeast 1098 or White Labs 005 or Fermentis S-04	1 pack

Grains

1 lb	UK brown malt	450 g
1 lb	UK crystal malt (60 Lovibond)	450 g
4 oz	UK chocolate malt	112 g
5.5 US gal	brewing water (page 89)	21 L

Malt Extracts

4 lbs	UK light	1.8 kg
1 lb	extra-light DME	450 g

Bittering Hops

4 to 5 AAUs	Fuggle or Kent Golding	4 to 5 AAUs

Later Additions

8 oz	Demerara or other dark raw sugar	224 g
1 tsp	Irish moss	5 mL
1 tsp	yeast nutrient	5 mL

Aroma Hops

.5 oz	Fuggle or Kent Golding	14 g

1. Prepare the liquid yeast in advance, according to the package directions (if using).
2. Coarsely crack the malt grains and place them in a cheesecloth or nylon grain bag.
3. In a brew kettle, bring at least 3 US gal (11 L) brewing water to steeping temperature (150 to 160°F/65 to 71°C). Turn off the heat, add the grain bag, cover and steep for 30 minutes. (If the temperature drops below steeping temperature, turn the element back on briefly to bring it back up.) Remove grain bag and discard.
4. Increase the heat and bring grain tea to a boil. Remove from heat, add the malt extracts and stir until dissolved completely.
5. Return kettle to the burner and increase the heat until the wort begins to boil. Using a spoon, clear any foam to one side. Reduce heat until a rolling boil can be maintained without foam buildup.
6. Add the bittering hops, stirring to combine. Boil for 45 minutes, uncovered. Monitor to prevent boiling over.
7. Meanwhile, prepare the fermentation gear and cooling bath or wort chiller.

8. After 45 minutes, remove the kettle from the heat and add sugar, Irish moss and yeast nutrient. Stir to ensure that the sugar and nutrient are dissolved. Return the kettle to the burner and bring back to a rolling boil. Boil for 15 minutes, then stir in the aroma hops, turn off the heat and cover.

9. To cool the brew, place the covered kettle in the prepared cooling tub or use a wort chiller according to the manufacturer's directions. Cool to the desired temperature, 75°F (24°C), within 30 to 45 minutes.

10. While the wort is cooling, clean and sanitize the brewing spoon. When the wort has cooled, move the kettle to a counter and stir the wort briskly in one direction for about 5 minutes. After stirring, cover and let rest for 10 to 15 minutes as the hops and trub form a cone.

11. Using a racking cane and siphon, rack as much wort as possible into the sanitized primary fermenter. Using the sanitized funnel and straining screen, strain the rest of the wort into the fermenter. Top off with brewing water to bring the volume to around 5.5 US gal (21 L). Using the hydrometer, take a reading of the specific gravity and record it in your brewing journal.

12. Add the yeast; vigorously stir it with a sanitized spoon to distribute it throughout the wort. Seal the fermenter with lid, stopper and airlock. Keep the fermenter at room temperature (68 to 72°F/20 to 22°C) during primary fermentation (which typically lasts 1 to 4 days after fermentation begins). (Keep in a dark place or under a lightproof cover if using a glass carboy.)

13. After 1 to 4 days or when the kräusen has fallen, gently rack the beer into the secondary fermenter to avoid aerating it, leaving as much of the sediment behind as possible. Seal and keep at room temperature, covered or in a dark place, to allow fermentation to continue.

14. Once the bubbling in the airlock has slowed, confirm completion of fermentation by using the hydrometer to take final gravity readings. (Hydrometer readings should be the same for several days in a row.)

15. Prime and bottle the beer (see page 91) and condition it for 3 to 4 weeks.

60 Shilling

The beers of Scotland developed a flavor profile of their own, in part because, being the northernmost part of the British Isles, it's a bit chillier. Consequently, Scottish ales ferment at lower temperatures.

Hops were imported from the southern part of England and treated with traditional Scottish frugality. Beers were taxed by their strength, so the tradition was to name the beers for the taxes paid on a barrel. Considering the world economy, one imagines these were taxes from a different century!

Estimated Original Gravity: 1.056

Equipment

- **brew kettle**
- **fermentation gear (page 14)**

As you build your brewing skills, switching to liquid yeast products (from Wyeast or White Labs) will give you a brew that is more complex than the ones made with the dry yeast (from Fermentis or Danstar) in the Absolute Beginner recipes. See page 86 for more information about liquid yeasts.

Liquid Yeast

1 pack	Wyeast 1728 or White Labs WLP028	1 pack

Grains

1 lb	UK Caramalt	450 g
8 oz	UK amber malt	224 g
4 oz	UK dark crystal malt	112 g
5.5 US gal	brewing water (page 89)	21 L

Malt Extract

5 lbs	UK amber DME	2.25 kg

Bittering Hops

4 to 6 AAUs	Challenger, Northern Brewer or Target	4 to 6 AAUs

Later Additions

1 tsp	Irish moss	5 mL
1 tsp	yeast nutrient	5 mL

Aroma Hops

.5 oz	Fuggle or Willamette	14 g

1. Prepare the liquid yeast in advance, according to the package directions.
2. Coarsely crack the malt grains and place them in a cheesecloth or nylon grain bag.
3. In a brew kettle, bring at least 3 US gal (11 L) brewing water to steeping temperature (150 to 160°F/65 to 71°C). Turn off the heat, add the grain bag, cover and steep for 30 minutes. (If the temperature drops below steeping temperature, turn the element back on briefly to bring it back up.) Remove grain bag and discard.
4. Increase the heat and bring grain tea to a boil. Remove from heat, add the malt extract and stir until dissolved completely.
5. Return kettle to the burner and increase the heat until the wort begins to boil. Using a spoon, clear any foam to one side. Reduce heat until a rolling boil can be maintained without foam buildup.
6. Add the bittering hops, stirring to combine. Boil for 45 minutes, uncovered. Monitor to prevent boiling over.
7. Meanwhile, prepare the fermentation gear and cooling bath or wort chiller.

8. After 45 minutes, remove the kettle from the heat and add Irish moss and yeast nutrient. Stir to ensure that the nutrient has dissolved. Return the kettle to the burner and bring back to a rolling boil. Boil for 15 minutes, then stir in the aroma hops, turn off the heat and cover.

9. To cool the brew, place the covered kettle in the prepared cooling tub or use a wort chiller according to the manufacturer's directions. Cool to the desired temperature, 75°F (24°C), within 30 to 45 minutes.

10. While the wort is cooling, clean and sanitize the brewing spoon. When the wort has cooled, move the kettle to a counter and stir the wort briskly in one direction for about 5 minutes. After stirring, cover and let rest for 10 to 15 minutes as the hops and trub form a cone.

11. Using a racking cane and siphon, rack as much wort as possible into the sanitized primary fermenter. Using the sanitized funnel and straining screen, strain the rest of the wort into the fermenter. Top off with brewing water to bring the volume to around 5.5 US gal (21 L). Using the hydrometer, take a reading of the specific gravity and record it in your brewing journal.

12. Add the yeast; vigorously stir it with a sanitized spoon to distribute it throughout the wort. Seal the fermenter with lid, stopper and airlock. Keep the fermenter at room temperature (65 to 68°F/18 to 20°C) during primary fermentation (which typically lasts 7 to 10 days after fermentation begins). (Keep in a dark place or under a lightproof cover if using a glass carboy.)

13. After 7 to 10 days or when the kräusen has fallen, gently rack the beer into the secondary fermenter to avoid aerating it, leaving as much of the sediment behind as possible. Seal and keep at room temperature, covered or in a dark place, to allow fermentation to continue.

14. Once the bubbling in the airlock has slowed, confirm completion of fermentation by using the hydrometer to take final gravity readings. (Hydrometer readings should be the same for several days in a row.)

15. Prime and bottle the beer (see page 91) and condition it for 3 to 4 weeks.

Brewer's Tip

Many modern brewers incorporate a portion of the peat-smoked malt that is used to make Scotch whisky. This is not traditional Scottish ale; for that, you'll find a peated recipe, in the Smoked Beers section, on page 338 of the book.

80 Shilling

Estimated Original Gravity: 1.073

Equipment

- **brew kettle**
- **fermentation gear (page 14)**
- **blow-off hose (page 16)**

Beers with an estimated original gravity higher than 1.065 require a longer time in both primary and secondary fermentation. Primary fermentation will take 7 to 10 days, and secondary fermentation will take about 2 weeks longer than weaker brews.

Liquid Yeast

1 pack	Wyeast 1728 or White Labs WLP028	1 pack

Grains

1 lb	UK crystal malt (60 Lovibond)	450 g
8 oz	UK amber malt	224 g
4 oz	UK dark crystal malt	112 g
5.5 US gal	brewing water (page 89)	21 L

Malt Extract

6 lbs	UK amber DME	2.7 kg

Bittering Hops

6 to 8 AAUs	Challenger, Northern Brewer or Target	6 to 8 AAUs

Later Additions

1 lb	Demerara or other dark raw sugar	450 g
1 tsp	Irish moss	5 mL
1 tsp	yeast nutrient	5 mL

Aroma Hops

.5 oz	Fuggle or Willamette	14 g

1. Prepare the liquid yeast in advance, according to the package directions.
2. Coarsely crack the malt grains and place them in a cheesecloth or nylon grain bag.
3. In a brew kettle, bring at least 3 US gal (11 L) brewing water to steeping temperature (150 to 160°F/65 to 71°C). Turn off the heat, add the grain bag, cover and steep for 30 minutes. (If the temperature drops below steeping temperature, turn the element back on briefly to bring it back up.) Remove grain bag and discard.
4. Increase the heat and bring grain tea to a boil. Remove from heat, add the malt extract and stir until dissolved completely.
5. Return kettle to the burner and increase the heat until the wort begins to boil. Using a spoon, clear any foam to one side. Reduce heat until a rolling boil can be maintained without foam buildup.
6. Add the bittering hops, stirring to combine. Boil for 45 minutes, uncovered. Monitor to prevent boiling over.
7. Mcanwhile, prepare the fermentation gear and cooling bath or wort chiller.

8. After 45 minutes, remove the kettle from the heat and add sugar, Irish moss and yeast nutrient. Stir to ensure that the sugar and nutrient are dissolved. Return the kettle to the burner and bring back to a rolling boil. Boil for 15 minutes, then stir in the aroma hops, turn off the heat and cover.

9. To cool the brew, place the covered kettle in the prepared cooling tub or use a wort chiller according to the manufacturer's directions. Cool to the desired temperature, 75°F (24°C), within 30 to 45 minutes.

10. While the wort is cooling, clean and sanitize the brewing spoon. When the wort has cooled, move the kettle to a counter and stir the wort briskly in one direction for about 5 minutes. After stirring, cover and let rest for 10 to 15 minutes as the hops and trub form a cone.

11. Using a racking cane and siphon, rack as much wort as possible into the sanitized primary fermenter. Using the sanitized funnel and straining screen, strain the rest of the wort into the fermenter. Top off with brewing water to bring the volume to around 5.5 US gal (21 L). Using the hydrometer, take a reading of the specific gravity and record it in your brewing journal.

12. Add the yeast; vigorously stir it with a sanitized spoon to distribute it throughout the wort. Seal the fermenter with lid, stopper and airlock or blow-off hose. Keep the fermenter at room temperature (65 to 68°F/18 to 20°C) during primary fermentation (which typically lasts 7 to 10 days after fermentation begins). (Keep in a dark place or under a lightproof cover if using a glass carboy.)

13. After 7 to 10 days or when the kräusen has fallen, gently rack the beer into the secondary fermenter to avoid aerating it, leaving as much of the sediment behind as possible. Seal and keep at room temperature, covered or in a dark place, to allow fermentation to continue.

14. Once the bubbling in the airlock has slowed, confirm completion of fermentation by using the hydrometer to take final gravity readings. (Hydrometer readings should be the same for several days in a row.)

15. Prime and bottle the beer (see page 91) and condition it for 3 to 4 weeks.

Brewer's Tip

If active fermentation backs up into the airlock, replace airlock with blow-off hose (see page 16). Change water as needed; re-install airlock when fermentation settles down.

Strong Ale

Equipment

- **brew kettle**
- **fermentation gear (page 14)**
- **blow-off hose (page 16)**

Beers with an estimated original gravity higher than 1.065 require a longer time in both primary and secondary fermentation. Primary fermentation will take 7 to 10 days, and secondary fermentation will take about 2 weeks longer than weaker brews.

Liquid Yeast

2 packs	Wyeast 1728 or White Labs WLP028 (or 1 pack in starter)	2 packs

Grains

1 lb	UK crystal malt (60 Lovibond)	450 g
8 oz	UK brown malt	224 g
8 oz	UK dark crystal malt	224 g
5.5 US gal	brewing water (page 89)	21 L

Malt Extract

8 lbs	UK amber DME	3.6 kg

Bittering Hops

8 to 10 AAUs	Challenger, Northern Brewer or Target	8 to 10 AAUs

Later Additions

1 lb	Demerara or other dark raw sugar	450 g
1 tsp	Irish moss	5 mL
1 tsp	yeast nutrient	5 mL

Aroma Hops

.5 oz	Fuggle or Willamette	14 g

1. Prepare the liquid yeast in advance, according to the package directions.
2. Coarsely crack the malt grains and place them in a cheesecloth or nylon grain bag.
3. In a brew kettle, bring at least 3 US gal (11 L) brewing water to steeping temperature (150 to 160°F/65 to 71°C). Turn off the heat, add the grain bag, cover and steep for 30 minutes. (If the temperature drops below steeping temperature, turn the element back on briefly to bring it back up.) Remove grain bag and discard.
4. Increase the heat and bring grain tea to a boil. Remove from heat, add the malt extract and stir until dissolved completely.
5. Return kettle to the burner and increase the heat until the wort begins to boil. Using a spoon, clear any foam to one side. Reduce heat until a rolling boil can be maintained without foam buildup.
6. Add the bittering hops, stirring to combine. Boil for 45 minutes, uncovered. Monitor to prevent boiling over.
7. Meanwhile, prepare the fermentation gear and cooling bath or wort chiller.

8. After 45 minutes, remove the kettle from the heat and add sugar, Irish moss and yeast nutrient. Stir to ensure that the sugar and nutrient are dissolved. Return the kettle to the burner and bring back to a rolling boil. Boil for 15 minutes, then stir in the aroma hops, turn off the heat and cover.

9. To cool the brew, place the covered kettle in the prepared cooling tub or use a wort chiller according to the manufacturer's directions. Cool to the desired temperature, 75°F (24°C), within 30 to 45 minutes.

10. While the wort is cooling, clean and sanitize the brewing spoon. When the wort has cooled, move the kettle to a counter and stir the wort briskly in one direction for about 5 minutes. After stirring, cover and let rest for 10 to 15 minutes as the hops and trub form a cone.

11. Using a racking cane and siphon, rack as much wort as possible into the sanitized primary fermenter. Using the sanitized funnel and straining screen, strain the rest of the wort into the fermenter. Top off with brewing water to bring the volume to around 5.5 US gal (21 L). Using the hydrometer, take a reading of the specific gravity and record it in your brewing journal.

12. Add the yeast; vigorously stir it with a sanitized spoon to distribute it throughout the wort. Seal the fermenter with lid, stopper and airlock or blow-off hose. Keep the fermenter at room temperature (65 to 68°F/18 to 20°C) during primary fermentation (which typically lasts 7 to 10 days after fermentation begins). (Keep in a dark place or under a lightproof cover if using a glass carboy.)

13. After 7 to 10 days or when the kräusen has fallen, gently rack the beer into the secondary fermenter to avoid aerating it, leaving as much of the sediment behind as possible. Seal and keep at room temperature, covered or in a dark place, to allow fermentation to continue.

14. Once the bubbling in the airlock has slowed, confirm completion of fermentation by using the hydrometer to take final gravity readings. (Hydrometer readings should be the same for several days in a row.)

15. Prime and bottle the beer (see page 91) and condition it for 3 to 4 weeks.

Variation

120 Shilling: Add another 1 lb (450 g) UK amber DME for the "Big Daddy" of the Scottish ales. Estimated Original Gravity: 1.101

Brewer's Tips

For information on preparing a yeast starter, see page 89.

If active fermentation backs up into the airlock, replace airlock with blow-off hose (see page 16). Change water as needed; re-install airlock when fermentation settles down.

Brown Porter

In London in the 1700s, a dark ale was popular among those who worked as porters. The brew, known as "Three Threads," was a blend of three different ales. Bar owners got tired of visiting three faucets to draw a single draft and asked brewers for a beer that would taste the same as the blend. The new beer was called "Entire Butt" (a butt is an archaic term for a cask or keg), but soon the brew became known by the name of the men who ordered it.

Estimated Original Gravity: 1.058

Equipment

- **brew kettle**
- **fermentation gear (page 14)**

As you build your brewing skills, switching to liquid yeast products (from Wyeast or White Labs) will give you a brew that is more complex than the ones made with the dry yeast (from Fermentis or Danstar) in the Absolute Beginner recipes. See page 86 for more information about liquid yeasts.

Yeast

1 pack	Wyeast 1028 or White Labs WLP013 or Fermentis S-04	1 pack

Grains

1 lb	UK crystal malt (60 Lovibond)	450 g
1 lb	UK brown malt	450 g
4 oz	UK dark crystal malt (150 Lovibond)	112 g
4 oz	UK chocolate malt	112 g
2 oz	UK black patent malt	56 g
5.5 US gal	brewing water (page 89)	21 L

Malt Extract

6.6 lbs	UK light	1.5 kg

Bittering Hops

8 to 10 AAUs	medium-alpha acid (such as Northern Brewer)	8 to 10 AAUs

Later Additions

1 tsp	Irish moss	5 mL
1 tsp	yeast nutrient	5 mL

Aroma Hops

.5 oz	Fuggle or Kent Golding	14 g

1. Prepare the liquid yeast in advance, according to the package directions (if using).
2. Coarsely crack the malt grains and place them in a cheesecloth or nylon grain bag.
3. In a brew kettle, bring at least 3 US gal (11 L) brewing water to steeping temperature (150 to 160°F/65 to 71°C). Turn off the heat, add the grain bag, cover and steep for 30 minutes. (If the temperature drops below steeping temperature, turn the element back on briefly to bring it back up.) Remove grain bag and discard.
4. Increase the heat and bring grain tea to a boil. Remove from heat, add the malt extract and stir until dissolved completely.
5. Return kettle to the burner and increase the heat until the wort begins to boil. Using a spoon, clear any foam to one side. Reduce heat until a rolling boil can be maintained without foam buildup.
6. Add the bittering hops, stirring to combine. Boil for 45 minutes, uncovered. Monitor to prevent boiling over.

7. Meanwhile, prepare the fermentation gear and cooling bath or wort chiller.

8. After 45 minutes, remove the kettle from the heat and add Irish moss and yeast nutrient. Stir to ensure that the nutrient has dissolved. Return the kettle to the burner and bring back to a rolling boil. Boil for 15 minutes, then stir in the aroma hops, turn off the heat and cover.

9. To cool the brew, place the covered kettle in the prepared cooling tub or use a wort chiller according to the manufacturer's directions. Cool to the desired temperature, 75°F (24°C), within 30 to 45 minutes.

10. While the wort is cooling, clean and sanitize the brewing spoon. When the wort has cooled, move the kettle to a counter and stir the wort briskly in one direction for about 5 minutes. After stirring, cover and let rest for 10 to 15 minutes as the hops and trub form a cone.

11. Using a racking cane and siphon, rack as much wort as possible into the sanitized primary fermenter. Using the sanitized funnel and straining screen, strain the rest of the wort into the fermenter. Top off with brewing water to bring the volume to around 5.5 US gal (21 L). Using the hydrometer, take a reading of the specific gravity and record it in your brewing journal.

12. Add the yeast; vigorously stir it with a sanitized spoon to distribute it throughout the wort. Seal the fermenter with lid, stopper and airlock. Keep the fermenter at room temperature (68 to 72°F/20 to 22°C) during primary fermentation (which typically lasts 1 to 4 days after fermentation begins). (Keep in a dark place or under a lightproof cover if using a glass carboy.)

13. After 1 to 4 days or when the kräusen has fallen, gently rack the beer into the secondary fermenter to avoid aerating it, leaving as much of the sediment behind as possible. Seal and keep at room temperature, covered or in a dark place, to allow fermentation to continue.

14. Once the bubbling in the airlock has slowed, confirm completion of fermentation by using the hydrometer to take final gravity readings. (Hydrometer readings should be the same for several days in a row.)

15. Prime and bottle the beer (see page 91) and condition it for 3 to 4 weeks.

Robust Porter

Equipment

- **brew kettle**
- **fermentation gear
  (page 14)**

As you build your brewing skills, switching to liquid yeast products (from Wyeast or White Labs) will give you a brew that is more complex than the ones made with the dry yeast (from Fermentis or Danstar) in the Absolute Beginner recipes. See page 86 for more information about liquid yeasts.

Yeast

1 pack	Wyeast 1028 or White Labs WLP013 or Fermentis S-04	1 pack

Grains

1 lb	UK crystal malt (60 Lovibond)	450 g
1 lb	UK brown malt	450 g
8 oz	UK dark crystal malt (150 Lovibond)	224 g
8 oz	UK chocolate malt	224 g
4 oz	UK black patent malt	112 g
5.5 US gal	brewing water (page 89)	21 L

Malt Extract

6.6 lbs	UK light	3 kg

Bittering Hops

10 to 12 AAUs	medium-alpha acid (such as Northern Brewer)	10 to 12 AAUs

Later Additions

1 tsp	Irish moss	5 mL
1 tsp	yeast nutrient	5 mL

Aroma Hops

.5 oz	Fuggle or Kent Golding	14 g

1. Prepare the liquid yeast in advance, according to the package directions (if using).
2. Coarsely crack the malt grains and place them in a cheesecloth or nylon grain bag.
3. In a brew kettle, bring at least 3 US gal (11 L) brewing water to steeping temperature (150 to 160°F/65 to 71°C). Turn off the heat, add the grain bag, cover and steep for 30 minutes. (If the temperature drops below steeping temperature, turn the element back on briefly to bring it back up.) Remove grain bag and discard.
4. Increase the heat and bring grain tea to a boil. Remove from heat, add the malt extract and stir until dissolved completely.
5. Return kettle to the burner and increase the heat until the wort begins to boil. Using a spoon, clear any foam to one side. Reduce heat until a rolling boil can be maintained without foam buildup.
6. Add the bittering hops, stirring to combine. Boil for 45 minutes, uncovered. Monitor to prevent boiling over.

7. Meanwhile, prepare the fermentation gear and cooling bath or wort chiller.

8. After 45 minutes, remove the kettle from the heat and add Irish moss and yeast nutrient. Stir to ensure that the nutrient has dissolved. Return the kettle to the burner and bring back to a rolling boil. Boil for 15 minutes, then stir in the aroma hops, turn off the heat and cover.

9. To cool the brew, place the covered kettle in the prepared cooling tub or use a wort chiller according to the manufacturer's directions. Cool to the desired temperature, 75°F (24°C), within 30 to 45 minutes.

10. While the wort is cooling, clean and sanitize the brewing spoon. When the wort has cooled, move the kettle to a counter and stir the wort briskly in one direction for about 5 minutes. After stirring, cover and let rest for 10 to 15 minutes as the hops and trub form a cone.

11. Using a racking cane and siphon, rack as much wort as possible into the sanitized primary fermenter. Using the sanitized funnel and straining screen, strain the rest of the wort into the fermenter. Top off with brewing water to bring the volume to around 5.5 US gal (21 L). Using the hydrometer, take a reading of the specific gravity and record it in your brewing journal.

12. Add the yeast; vigorously stir it with a sanitized spoon to distribute it throughout the wort. Seal the fermenter with lid, stopper and airlock. Keep the fermenter at room temperature (68 to 72°F/20 to 22°C) during primary fermentation (which typically lasts 1 to 4 days after fermentation begins). (Keep in a dark place or under a lightproof cover if using a glass carboy.)

13. After 1 to 4 days or when the kräusen has fallen, gently rack the beer into the secondary fermenter to avoid aerating it, leaving as much of the sediment behind as possible. Seal and keep at room temperature, covered or in a dark place, to allow fermentation to continue.

14. Once the bubbling in the airlock has slowed, confirm completion of fermentation by using the hydrometer to take final gravity readings. (Hydrometer readings should be the same for several days in a row.)

15. Prime and bottle the beer (see page 91) and condition it for 3 to 4 weeks.

Dry (Irish) Stout

When Mr. Guinness came along with a particularly beefy porter, it became known as "Stout Porter," eventually shortened to just "Stout." When the stout recipes call for flaked unmalted grains, they needn't be milled. Simply add them to the grain bag with other grains.

Estimated Original Gravity: 1.050

Equipment

- **brew kettle**
- **fermentation gear (page 14)**

As you build your brewing skills, switching to liquid yeast products (from Wyeast or White Labs) will give you a brew that is more complex than the ones made with the dry yeast (from Fermentis or Danstar) in the Absolute Beginner recipes. See page 86 for more information about liquid yeasts.

Yeast

| 1 pack | Wyeast 1084 or White Labs WLP004 or Fermentis S-04 | 1 pack |

Grains

12 oz	UK roast barley	336 g
8 oz	barley flakes (do not crack)	224 g
5.5 US gal	brewing water (page 89)	21 L

Malt Extracts

| 4 lbs | Mountmellick Irish Light Malt Extract or any brand | 1.8 kg |
| 1.5 lbs | UK light DME | 680 g |

Bittering Hops

| 8 to 10 AAUs | Challenger, Progress or any UK | 8 to 10 AAUs |

Later Additions

| 1 tsp | Irish moss | 5 mL |
| 1 tsp | yeast nutrient | 5 mL |

Aroma Hops

None

1. Prepare the liquid yeast in advance, according to the package directions (if using).
2. Coarsely crack the grains and place them and the barley flakes in a cheesecloth or nylon grain bag.
3. In a brew kettle, bring at least 3 US gal (11 L) brewing water to steeping temperature (150 to 160°F/65 to 71°C). Turn off the heat, add the grain bag, cover and steep for 30 minutes. (If the temperature drops below steeping temperature, turn the element back on briefly to bring it back up.) Remove grain bag and discard.
4. Increase the heat and bring grain tea to a boil. Remove from heat, add the malt extracts and stir until dissolved completely.
5. Return kettle to the burner and increase the heat until the wort begins to boil. Using a spoon, clear any foam to one side. Reduce heat until a rolling boil can be maintained without foam buildup.
6. Add the bittering hops, stirring to combine. Boil for 45 minutes, uncovered. Monitor to prevent boiling over.
7. Meanwhile, prepare the fermentation gear and cooling bath or wort chiller.

8. After 45 minutes, remove the kettle from the heat and add Irish moss and yeast nutrient. Stir to ensure that the nutrient has dissolved. Return the kettle to the burner and bring back to a rolling boil. Boil for 15 minutes, then turn off the heat and cover.

9. To cool the brew, place the covered kettle in the prepared cooling tub or use a wort chiller according to the manufacturer's directions. Cool to the desired temperature, 75°F (24°C), within 30 to 45 minutes.

10. While the wort is cooling, clean and sanitize the brewing spoon. When the wort has cooled, move the kettle to a counter and stir the wort briskly in one direction for about 5 minutes. After stirring, cover and let rest for 10 to 15 minutes as the hops and trub form a cone.

11. Using a racking cane and siphon, rack as much wort as possible into the sanitized primary fermenter. Using the sanitized funnel and straining screen, strain the rest of the wort into the fermenter. Top off with brewing water to bring the volume to around 5.5 US gal (21 L). Using the hydrometer, take a reading of the specific gravity and record it in your brewing journal.

12. Add the yeast; vigorously stir it with a sanitized spoon to distribute it throughout the wort. Seal the fermenter with lid, stopper and airlock. Keep the fermenter at room temperature (68 to 72°F/20 to 22°C) during primary fermentation (which typically lasts 1 to 4 days after fermentation begins). (Keep in a dark place or under a lightproof cover if using a glass carboy.)

13. After 1 to 4 days or when the kräusen has fallen, gently rack the beer into the secondary fermenter to avoid aerating it, leaving as much of the sediment behind as possible. Seal and keep at room temperature, covered or in a dark place, to allow fermentation to continue.

14. Once the bubbling in the airlock has slowed, confirm completion of fermentation by using the hydrometer to take final gravity readings. (Hydrometer readings should be the same for several days in a row.)

15. Prime and bottle the beer (see page 91) and condition it for 3 to 4 weeks.

Foreign Export Stout

Estimated Original Gravity: 1.066

Equipment

- **brew kettle**
- **fermentation gear (page 14)**

Beers with an estimated original gravity higher than 1.065 require a longer time in both primary and secondary fermentation. Primary fermentation will take 7 to 10 days, and secondary fermentation will take about 2 weeks longer than weaker brews.

Yeast

1 pack	Wyeast 1084 or White Labs WLP004 or Fermentis S-04	1 pack

Grains

12 oz	UK roast barley	336 g
8 oz	UK crystal malt (60 Lovibond)	224 g
4 oz	UK chocolate malt	112 g
8 oz	barley flakes (do not crack)	224 g
5.5 US gal	brewing water (page 89)	21 L

Malt Extract

8 lbs	Mountmellick Irish Light Malt Extract or any brand	3.6 kg

Bittering Hops

12 to 14 AAUs	Challenger, Progress or any UK	12 to 14 AAUs

Later Additions

1 tsp	Irish moss	5 mL
1 tsp	yeast nutrient	5 mL

Aroma Hops

None

1. Prepare the liquid yeast in advance, according to the package directions (if using).
2. Coarsely crack the grains and place them and the barley flakes in a cheesecloth or nylon grain bag.
3. In a brew kettle, bring at least 3 US gal (11 L) brewing water to steeping temperature (150 to 160°F/65 to 71°C). Turn off the heat, add the grain bag, cover and steep for 30 minutes. (If the temperature drops below steeping temperature, turn the element back on briefly to bring it back up.) Remove grain bag and discard.
4. Increase the heat and bring grain tea to a boil. Remove from heat, add the malt extract and stir until dissolved completely.
5. Return kettle to the burner and increase the heat until the wort begins to boil. Using a spoon, clear any foam to one side. Reduce heat until a rolling boil can be maintained without foam buildup.
6. Add the bittering hops, stirring to combine. Boil for 45 minutes, uncovered. Monitor to prevent boiling over.

7. Meanwhile, prepare the fermentation gear and cooling bath or wort chiller.

8. After 45 minutes, remove the kettle from the heat and add Irish moss and yeast nutrient. Stir to ensure that the nutrient has dissolved. Return the kettle to the burner and bring back to a rolling boil. Boil for 15 minutes, then turn off the heat and cover.

9. To cool the brew, place the covered kettle in the prepared cooling tub or use a wort chiller according to the manufacturer's directions. Cool to the desired temperature, 75°F (24°C), within 30 to 45 minutes.

10. While the wort is cooling, clean and sanitize the brewing spoon. When the wort has cooled, move the kettle to a counter and stir the wort briskly in one direction for about 5 minutes. After stirring, cover and let rest for 10 to 15 minutes as the hops and trub form a cone.

11. Using a racking cane and siphon, rack as much wort as possible into the sanitized primary fermenter. Using the sanitized funnel and straining screen, strain the rest of the wort into the fermenter. Top off with brewing water to bring the volume to around 5.5 US gal (21 L). Using the hydrometer, take a reading of the specific gravity and record it in your brewing journal.

12. Add the yeast; vigorously stir it with a sanitized spoon to distribute it throughout the wort. Seal the fermenter with lid, stopper and airlock. Keep the fermenter at room temperature (68 to 72°F/20 to 22°C) during primary fermentation (which typically lasts 7 to 10 days after fermentation begins). (Keep in a dark place or under a lightproof cover if using a glass carboy.)

13. After 7 to 10 days or when the kräusen has fallen, gently rack the beer into the secondary fermenter to avoid aerating it, leaving as much of the sediment behind as possible. Seal and keep at room temperature, covered or in a dark place, to allow fermentation to continue.

14. Once the bubbling in the airlock has slowed, confirm completion of fermentation by using the hydrometer to take final gravity readings. (Hydrometer readings should be the same for several days in a row.)

15. Prime and bottle the beer (see page 91) and condition it for 3 to 4 weeks.

Sweet Stout

Equipment

- **brew kettle**
- **fermentation gear (page 14)**

As you build your brewing skills, switching to liquid yeast products (from Wyeast or White Labs) will give you a brew that is more complex than the ones made with the dry yeast (from Fermentis or Danstar) in the Absolute Beginner recipes. See page 86 for more information about liquid yeasts.

Yeast

1 pack	Wyeast 1028 or White Labs WLP013 or Fermentis S-04	1 pack

Grains

1 lb	UK crystal malt (60 Lovibond)	450 g
8 oz	UK brown malt	224 g
4 oz	UK chocolate malt	112 g
4 oz	UK black patent malt	112 g
4 oz	UK roast barley	112 g
5.5 US gal	brewing water (page 89)	21 L

Malt Extract

6.6 lbs	UK light	3 kg

Bittering Hops

6 to 8 AAUs	medium-alpha acid (such as Northern Brewer)	6 to 8 AAUs

Later Additions

1 tsp	Irish moss	5 mL
1 tsp	yeast nutrient	5 mL

Aroma Hops

.5 oz	Fuggle or Kent Golding	14 g

1. Prepare the liquid yeast in advance, according to the package directions (if using).
2. Coarsely crack the grains and place them in a cheesecloth or nylon grain bag.
3. In a brew kettle, bring at least 3 US gal (11 L) brewing water to steeping temperature (150 to 160°F/65 to 71°C). Turn off the heat, add the grain bag, cover and steep for 30 minutes. (If the temperature drops below steeping temperature, turn the element back on briefly to bring it back up.) Remove grain bag and discard.
4. Increase the heat and bring grain tea to a boil. Remove from heat, add the malt extract and stir until dissolved completely.
5. Return kettle to the burner and increase the heat until the wort begins to boil. Using a spoon, clear any foam to one side. Reduce heat until a rolling boil can be maintained without foam buildup.
6. Add the bittering hops, stirring to combine. Boil for 45 minutes, uncovered. Monitor to prevent boiling over.

7. Meanwhile, prepare the fermentation gear and cooling bath or wort chiller.

8. After 45 minutes, remove the kettle from the heat and add Irish moss and yeast nutrient. Stir to ensure that the nutrient has dissolved. Return the kettle to the burner and bring back to a rolling boil. Boil for 15 minutes, then stir in the aroma hops, turn off the heat and cover.

9. To cool the brew, place the covered kettle in the prepared cooling tub or use a wort chiller according to the manufacturer's directions. Cool to the desired temperature, 75°F (24°C), within 30 to 45 minutes.

10. While the wort is cooling, clean and sanitize the brewing spoon. When the wort has cooled, move the kettle to a counter and stir the wort briskly in one direction for about 5 minutes. After stirring, cover and let rest for 10 to 15 minutes as the hops and trub form a cone.

11. Using a racking cane and siphon, rack as much wort as possible into the sanitized primary fermenter. Using the sanitized funnel and straining screen, strain the rest of the wort into the fermenter. Top off with brewing water to bring the volume to around 5.5 US gal (21 L). Using the hydrometer, take a reading of the specific gravity and record it in your brewing journal.

12. Add the yeast; vigorously stir it with a sanitized spoon to distribute it throughout the wort. Seal the fermenter with lid, stopper and airlock. Keep the fermenter at room temperature (68 to 72°F/20 to 22°C) during primary fermentation (which typically lasts 1 to 4 days after fermentation begins). (Keep in a dark place or under a lightproof cover if using a glass carboy.)

13. After 1 to 4 days or when the kräusen has fallen, gently rack the beer into the secondary fermenter to avoid aerating it, leaving as much of the sediment behind as possible. Seal and keep at room temperature, covered or in a dark place, to allow fermentation to continue.

14. Once the bubbling in the airlock has slowed, confirm completion of fermentation by using the hydrometer to take final gravity readings. (Hydrometer readings should be the same for several days in a row.)

15. Prime and bottle the beer (see page 91) and condition it for 3 to 4 weeks.

Variations

Milk Stout: Milk Stouts were brewed in England as a health tonic for nursing mothers. The addition of lactose (milk sugar) adds sweetness and texture to the beer. Therefore, it is probably wise not to serve this beer to any of your lactose-intolerant friends. Add 1 lb (450 g) lactose during the final 15 minutes of the boil in the Sweet Stout recipe.

Oyster Stout: This is another old-school beer that's seen a recent revival. Follow the Sweet Stout recipe but add one dozen fresh oysters, in a grain bag for ease of removal, to the brew kettle for the entire boil. There's a special brewers treat at the end — you get to enjoy the wort-stewed oysters at the end of your brew session. (*Do not serve this beer to anyone with shellfish allergies.*)

Oatmeal Stout

**Estimated Original
Gravity: 1.061**

Equipment

- **brew kettle**
- **fermentation gear
  (page 14)**

As you build your brewing skills, switching to liquid yeast products (from Wyeast or White Labs) will give you a brew that is more complex than the ones made with the dry yeast (from Fermentis or Danstar) in the Absolute Beginner recipes. See page 86 for more information about liquid yeasts.

Yeast

1 pack	Wyeast 1028 or White Labs WLP013 or Fermentis S-04	1 pack

Grains

1 lb	UK crystal malt (60 Lovibond)	450 g
8 oz	UK brown malt	224 g
4 oz	UK chocolate malt	112 g
4 oz	UK black patent malt	112 g
4 oz	UK roast barley	112 g
1 lb	Brewer's Oat Flakes (or thick rolled oats from grocery store) (do not crack)	450 g
5.5 US gal	brewing water (page 89)	21 L

Malt Extract

6.6 lbs	UK light	3 kg

Bittering Hops

6 to 8 AAUs	medium-alpha acid (such as Northern Brewer)	6 to 8 AAUs

Later Additions

1 tsp	Irish moss	5 mL
1 tsp	yeast nutrient	5 mL

Aroma Hops

.5 oz	Fuggle or Kent Golding	14 g

1. Prepare the liquid yeast in advance, according to the package directions (if using).
2. Coarsely crack the grains and place them in a cheesecloth or nylon grain bag. Add the oat flakes.
3. In a brew kettle, bring at least 3 US gal (11 L) brewing water to steeping temperature (150 to 160°F/65 to 71°C). Turn off the heat, add the grain bag, cover and steep for 30 minutes. (If the temperature drops below steeping temperature, turn the element back on briefly to bring it back up.) Remove grain bag and discard.
4. Increase the heat and bring grain tea to a boil. Remove from heat, add the malt extract and stir until dissolved completely.
5. Return kettle to the burner and increase the heat until the wort begins to boil. Using a spoon, clear any foam to one side. Reduce heat until a rolling boil can be maintained without foam buildup.

6. Add the bittering hops, stirring to combine. Boil for 45 minutes, uncovered. Monitor to prevent boiling over.

7. Meanwhile, prepare the fermentation gear and cooling bath or wort chiller.

8. After 45 minutes, remove the kettle from the heat and add Irish moss and yeast nutrient. Stir to ensure that the nutrient has dissolved. Return the kettle to the burner and bring back to a rolling boil. Boil for 15 minutes, then stir in the aroma hops, turn off the heat and cover.

9. To cool the brew, place the covered kettle in the prepared cooling tub or use a wort chiller according to the manufacturer's directions. Cool to the desired temperature, 75°F (24°C), within 30 to 45 minutes.

10. While the wort is cooling, clean and sanitize the brewing spoon. When the wort has cooled, move the kettle to a counter and stir the wort briskly in one direction for about 5 minutes. After stirring, cover and let rest for 10 to 15 minutes as the hops and trub form a cone.

11. Using a racking cane and siphon, rack as much wort as possible into the sanitized primary fermenter. Using the sanitized funnel and straining screen, strain the rest of the wort into the fermenter. Top off with brewing water to bring the volume to around 5.5 US gal (21 L). Using the hydrometer, take a reading of the specific gravity and record it in your brewing journal.

12. Add the yeast; vigorously stir it with a sanitized spoon to distribute it throughout the wort. Seal the fermenter with lid, stopper and airlock. Keep the fermenter at room temperature (68 to 72°F/20 to 22°C) during primary fermentation (which typically lasts 1 to 4 days after fermentation begins). (Keep in a dark place or under a lightproof cover if using a glass carboy.)

13. After 1 to 4 days or when the kräusen has fallen, gently rack the beer into the secondary fermenter to avoid aerating it, leaving as much of the sediment behind as possible. Seal and keep at room temperature, covered or in a dark place, to allow fermentation to continue.

14. Once the bubbling in the airlock has slowed, confirm completion of fermentation by using the hydrometer to take final gravity readings. (Hydrometer readings should be the same for several days in a row.)

15. Prime and bottle the beer (see page 91) and condition it for 3 to 4 weeks.

Imperial Stout

During the days of Tsarist Russia, a strong stout brewed in London by the John Courage Brewery became very popular in the imperial court. In honor of their most prestigious customer, they dubbed this strong, dark brew Russian Imperial Stout. In modern times, the word Imperial has been adopted to indicate a beer that's been amped up.

Estimated Original Gravity: 1.101

Equipment

- **brew kettle**
- **fermentation gear (page 14)**
- **blow-off hose (page 16)**

Beers with an estimated original gravity higher than 1.065 require a longer time in both primary and secondary fermentation. Primary fermentation will take 7 to 10 days, and secondary fermentation will take about 2 weeks longer than weaker brews.

Yeast

2 packs	Wyeast 1028 or White Labs WLP013 (or 1 pack in starter) or Fermentis S-04	2 packs
2 packs	Lalvin Champagne yeast (14 g) (add to secondary fermenter)	2 packs

Grains

1 lb	UK crystal malt (60 Lovibond)	450 g
8 oz	UK brown malt	224 g
4 oz	UK chocolate malt	112 g
4 oz	UK black patent malt	112 g
4 oz	UK roast barley	112 g
1 lb	flaked barley (do not crack)	450 g
5.5 US gal	brewing water (page 89)	21 L

Malt Extract

9.9 lbs	UK light	4.5 kg

Bittering Hops

14 to 16 AAUs	medium-alpha acid (such as Northern Brewer)	14 to 16 AAUs

Later Additions

1.5 lb	Demerara or other dark raw sugar	680 g
1 tsp	Irish moss	5 mL
1 tsp	yeast nutrient	5 mL

Aroma Hops

.5 oz	Fuggle or Kent Golding	14 g
5 tsp	yeast energizer (add to secondary fermenter)	25 mL

1. Prepare first liquid yeast in advance, according to directions.
2. Coarsely crack the grains and place them and the flaked barley in a cheesecloth or nylon grain bag.
3. In a brew kettle, bring at least 3 US gal (11 L) brewing water to steeping temperature (150 to 160°F/65 to 71°C). Turn off the heat, add the grain bag, cover and steep for 30 minutes. (Turn element back on briefly to bring temperature up, if necessary.) Remove grain bag and discard.
4. Increase heat and bring grain tea to a boil. Remove from heat, add malt extract and stir until dissolved.
5. Return kettle to burner and increase heat until wort begins to boil. Using a spoon, clear any foam to one side. Reduce heat until rolling boil is maintained without foam buildup.

6. Add the bittering hops, stirring to combine. Boil for 45 minutes, uncovered. Monitor to prevent boiling over.

7. Meanwhile, prepare the fermentation gear and cooling bath or wort chiller.

8. After 45 minutes, remove the kettle from the heat and add sugar, Irish moss and yeast nutrient. Stir to ensure that the sugar and nutrient are dissolved. Return the kettle to the burner and bring back to a rolling boil. Boil for 15 minutes, then stir in the aroma hops, turn off the heat and cover.

9. To cool the brew, place the covered kettle in the prepared cooling tub or use a wort chiller according to the manufacturer's directions. Cool to the desired temperature, 75°F (24°C), within 30 to 45 minutes.

10. While the wort is cooling, clean and sanitize the brewing spoon. When the wort has cooled, move the kettle to a counter and stir the wort briskly in one direction for about 5 minutes. After stirring, cover and let rest for 10 to 15 minutes as the hops and trub form a cone.

11. Using a racking cane and siphon, rack as much wort as possible into the sanitized primary fermenter. Using the sanitized funnel and straining screen, strain the rest of the wort into the fermenter. Top off with brewing water to bring the volume to around 5.5 US gal (21 L). Using the hydrometer, take a reading of the specific gravity and record it in your brewing journal.

12. Add the first yeast; vigorously stir it with a sanitized spoon to distribute it throughout the wort. Seal the fermenter with lid, stopper and airlock or blow-off hose. Keep the fermenter at room temperature (68 to 72°F/20 to 22°C) during primary fermentation (which typically lasts 7 to 10 days after fermentation begins). (Keep in a dark place or under a lightproof cover if using a glass carboy.)

13. After 7 to 10 days or when the kräusen has fallen, gently rack the beer into the secondary fermenter to avoid aerating it, leaving as much of the sediment behind as possible. Seal and keep at room temperature, covered or in a dark place, to allow fermentation to continue.

14. Once the bubbling in the airlock has slowed, prepare the Lalvin yeast, gently add the yeast energizer and the Lalvin yeast, reseal and leave it for about 2 more weeks. Confirm completion of fermentation by using the hydrometer to take final gravity readings. (Hydrometer readings should be the same for several days in a row.)

15. Prime and bottle the beer (see page 91) and condition it for 3 to 4 weeks.

Brewer's Tips

For information on preparing a yeast starter, see page 89.

If active fermentation backs up into the airlock, replace airlock with blow-off hose (see page 16). Change water as needed; re-install airlock when fermentation settles down.

To Hydrate Lalvin Yeast

In a sanitized bowl or measuring cup, dissolve Lalvin yeast in 1.5 US fl oz (50 mL) of boiled water cooled to 104 to 109°F (40 to 43°C). Let stand for 15 minutes without stirring; then stir with a sanitized spoon to distribute yeast in water.

Barley Wine

Equipment

- **brew kettle**
- **fermentation gear (page 14)**
- **blow-off hose (page 16)**

Beers with an estimated original gravity higher than 1.065 require a longer time in both primary and secondary fermentation. Primary fermentation will take 7 to 10 days, and secondary fermentation will take about 2 weeks longer than weaker brews.

Yeast

| 2 packs | Wyeast 1098 or White Labs WLP005 (or 1 pack in starter) or Fermentis S-04 | 2 packs |
| 2 packs | Lalvin Champagne yeast (14 g) (add to secondary fermenter) | 2 packs |

Grains

1 lb	UK crystal malt (60 Lovibond)	450 g
8 oz	UK amber malt	224 g
5.5 US gal	brewing water (page 89)	21 L

Malt Extract

| 9.9 lbs | UK extra-light | 4.5 kg |

Bittering Hops

| 16 to 18 AAUs | medium-alpha acid (such as Northern Brewer) | 16 to 18 AAUs |

Later Additions

1.5 lb	Demerara or other dark raw sugar	680 g
1 tsp	Irish moss	5 mL
1 tsp	yeast nutrient	5 mL

Aroma Hops

| .5 oz | Fuggle or Kent Golding | 14 g |
| 5 tsp | yeast energizer (add to secondary fermenter) | 25 mL |

1. Prepare the first liquid yeast in advance, according to the package directions (if using liquid).

2. Coarsely crack the malt grains and place them in a cheesecloth or nylon grain bag.

3. In a brew kettle, bring at least 3 US gal (11 L) brewing water to steeping temperature (150 to 160°F/65 to 71°C). Turn off the heat, add the grain bag, cover and steep for 30 minutes. (If the temperature drops below steeping temperature, turn the element back on briefly to bring it back up.) Remove grain bag and discard.

4. Increase the heat and bring grain tea to a boil. Remove from heat, add the malt extract and stir until dissolved completely.

5. Return kettle to the burner and increase the heat until the wort begins to boil. Using a spoon, clear any foam to one side. Reduce heat until a rolling boil can be maintained without foam buildup.

6. Add the bittering hops, stirring to combine. Boil for 45 minutes, uncovered. Monitor to prevent boiling over.

7. Meanwhile, prepare the fermentation gear and cooling bath or wort chiller.

8. After 45 minutes, remove the kettle from the heat and add sugar, Irish moss and yeast nutrient. Stir to ensure that the sugar and nutrient are dissolved. Return the kettle to the burner and bring back to a rolling boil. Boil for 15 minutes, then stir in the aroma hops, turn off the heat and cover.

9. To cool the brew, place the covered kettle in the prepared cooling tub or use a wort chiller according to the manufacturer's directions. Cool to the desired temperature, 75°F (24°C), within 30 to 45 minutes.

10. While the wort is cooling, clean and sanitize the brewing spoon. When the wort has cooled, move the kettle to a counter and stir the wort briskly in one direction for about 5 minutes. After stirring, cover and let rest for 10 to 15 minutes as the hops and trub form a cone.

11. Using a racking cane and siphon, rack as much wort as possible into the sanitized primary fermenter. Using the sanitized funnel and straining screen, strain the rest of the wort into the fermenter. Top off with brewing water to bring the volume to around 5.5 US gal (21 L). Using the hydrometer, take a reading of the specific gravity and record it in your brewing journal.

12. Add the yeast; vigorously stir it with a sanitized spoon to distribute it throughout the wort. Seal the fermenter with lid, stopper and airlock or blow-off hose. Keep the fermenter at room temperature (68 to 72°F/20 to 22°C) during primary fermentation (which typically lasts 7 to 10 days after fermentation begins). (Keep in a dark place or under a lightproof cover if using a glass carboy.)

13. After 7 to 10 days or when the kräusen has fallen, gently rack the beer into the secondary fermenter to avoid aerating it, leaving as much of the sediment behind as possible. Seal and keep at room temperature, covered or in a dark place, to allow fermentation to continue.

14. Once the bubbling in the airlock has slowed, prepare the Lalvin yeast and gently add yeast energizer and the Lalvin yeast. Reseal and leave it for about 2 more weeks. Confirm completion of fermentation by using the hydrometer to take final gravity readings. (Hydrometer readings should be the same for several days in a row.)

15. Prime and bottle the beer (see page 91) and condition it for 3 to 4 weeks.

Brewer's Tip

For information on preparing a yeast starter, see page 89.

If active fermentation backs up into the airlock, replace airlock with blow-off hose (see page 16). Change water as needed; re-install airlock when fermentation settles down.

To Hydrate Lalvin Yeast

In a sanitized bowl or measuring cup, dissolve Lalvin yeast in 1.5 US fl oz (50 mL) of boiled water cooled to 104 to 109°F (40 to 43°C). Let stand for 15 minutes without stirring; then stir with a sanitized spoon to distribute yeast in water.

Some of the most exciting beers produced in the world come from Belgium or from brewers elsewhere brewing Belgian-style beers. Unlike their German brethren, who are confined to brewing with basic beer ingredients by the German Purity Law, Belgian brewers play with different spices, sugars, fruits and unusual yeast strains.

These brewers may be steeped in traditions dating back to the Middle Ages, but they playfully embrace new ingredients and ideas from brewers everywhere. Their small batch beers can be a little pricey, so you can save some serious cash by making your own versions.

The Weyermann grains, such as Caramunich®, Carapils® or Carabelge®, specified in this section are especially suited to the beers that call for them. They are widely distributed in North America and Europe. If not available, refer to the grain chart on page 77 or ask your brewing supplies retailer for his or her best substitute.

Brews from Belgium and Northern France

Abbey Style

Wit/White/Blanche

This is a great beer for summer drinking. For those wishing to produce a beer quickly, it's one of the few Belgian styles not in need of extended aging. Beer in this style had vanished by the 1960s, when Belgian milkman Pierre Celis opened the Hoergaarden brewery.

The spices used date to the pre-hopped beers of the Middle Ages. Add them during the final 15 minutes of the boil.

Estimated Original Gravity: 1.063

Equipment

- **brew kettle**
- **fermentation gear (page 14)**

As you build your brewing skills, switching to liquid yeast products (from Wyeast or White Labs) will give you a brew that is more complex than the ones made with the dry yeast (from Fermentis or Danstar) in the Absolute Beginner recipes. See page 86 for more information about liquid yeasts.

Yeast

1 pack	Wyeast 3944 or White Labs WLP400 or Fermentis T-58	1 pack

Grains

2 lbs	Pilsner malt	900 g
1 lb	flaked wheat (do not crack)	450 g
1 lb	flaked oats (do not crack)	450 g
5.5 US gal	brewing water (page 89)	21 L

Malt Extracts

1.4 lbs	Alexander's Sun Country Pale	635 g
4 lbs	Alexander's Sun Country Wheat	1.8 kg

Bittering Hops

2 to 3 AAUs	Hallertau, Tettnang, Saaz or Styrian Golding	2 to 3 AAUs

Later Additions

1 lb	orange blossom honey	450 g
1 oz	coriander seed, crushed	28 g
.5 oz	Bitter Orange Peel	14 g
.5 oz	Sweet Orange Peel	14 g
.5 oz	chamomile flowers, crushed	14 g
	Grains of Paradise (or black peppercorns)	2 g
1 tsp	yeast nutrient	5 mL

Aroma Hops

None

1. Prepare the liquid yeast in advance, according to the package directions (if using).
2. Coarsely crack the malt grains and place them in a cheesecloth or nylon grain bag. Add wheat and oat flakes.
3. In a brew kettle, bring at least 3 US gal (11 L) brewing water to steeping temperature (150 to 160°F/65 to 71°C). Turn off the heat, add the grain bag, cover and steep for 30 minutes. (If the temperature drops below steeping temperature, turn the element back on briefly to bring it back up.) Remove grain bag and discard.
4. Increase heat and bring grain tea to a boil. Remove from heat, add pale malt extract only and stir until dissolved.
5. Return kettle to the burner and increase the heat until the wort begins to boil. Using a spoon, clear any foam to one side. Reduce heat until a rolling boil can be maintained without foam buildup.

6. Add the bittering hops, stirring to combine. Boil for 45 minutes, uncovered. Monitor to prevent boiling over.

7. Meanwhile, prepare the fermentation gear and cooling bath or wort chiller.

8. After 45 minutes, remove the kettle from the heat and add the wheat malt and extract and honey. Place coriander seed, orange peels, chamomile and Grains of Paradise in a hop bag. Add bag and yeast nutrient. Stir to ensure extract, honey and nutrient are dissolved. Return the kettle to the burner and bring back to a rolling boil. Boil for 15 minutes, then turn off the heat and cover.

9. To cool the brew, place the covered kettle in the prepared cooling tub or use a wort chiller according to the manufacturer's directions. Cool to the desired temperature, 75°F (24°C), within 30 to 45 minutes.

10. While the wort is cooling, clean and sanitize the brewing spoon. When the wort has cooled, move the kettle to a counter and stir the wort briskly in one direction for about 5 minutes. After stirring, cover and let rest for 10 to 15 minutes as the hops and trub form a cone.

11. Using a racking cane and siphon, rack as much wort as possible into the sanitized primary fermenter. Using the sanitized funnel and straining screen, strain the rest of the wort into the fermenter. Top off with brewing water to bring the volume to around 5.5 US gal (21 L). Using the hydrometer, take a reading of the specific gravity and record it in your brewing journal.

12. Add the yeast; vigorously stir it with a sanitized spoon to distribute it throughout the wort. Seal the fermenter with lid, stopper and airlock. Keep the fermenter at room temperature (68 to 72°F/20 to 22°C) during primary fermentation, which typically lasts 1 to 4 days after fermentation begins. (Keep in a dark place or under a lightproof cover if using a glass carboy.)

13. After 1 to 4 days or when the kräusen has fallen, gently rack the beer into the secondary fermenter to avoid aerating it, leaving as much of the sediment behind as possible. Seal and keep at room temperature, covered or in a dark place, to allow fermentation to continue.

14. Once the bubbling in the airlock has slowed, confirm completion of fermentation by using the hydrometer to take final gravity readings. (Hydrometer readings should be the same for several days in a row.)

15. Prime and bottle the beer (see page 91) and condition it for 6 to 8 weeks.

Funky Beers

Historically, Wit was likely one of the sour beers of Belgium. Modern versions use more neutral yeasts, as we have here. If you are interested in brewing the sour styles and fruited lambic beers, consult the sections on funky and fruited beers in Part 3.

Belgian Pale Ale

This beer is very similar to other pale ales but has the distinctive character of Belgian yeast. De Koenick and Straffe Hendrick are brewed in this style.

Estimated Original Gravity: 1.067

Equipment

- **brew kettle**
- **fermentation gear (page 14)**

Beers with an estimated original gravity higher than 1.065 require a longer time in both primary and secondary fermentation. Primary fermentation should take 7 to 10 days, and secondary fermentation should take about 2 weeks longer than weaker brews.

Yeast

1 pack	Wyeast 3522 or White Labs WLP550 or Fermentis T-58	1 pack

Grains

1 lb	Caraamber® malt	450 g
1 lb	Caramunich I® malt	450 g
5.5 US gal	brewing water (page 89)	21 L

Malt Extract

6.6 lbs	any brand extra-light, divided in half	3 kg

Bittering Hops

8 to 10 AAUs	Northern Brewer or Perle	8 to 10 AAUs

Later Additions

1 lb	clear Belgian candi sugar	450 g
1 tsp	Irish moss	5 mL
1 tsp	yeast nutrient	5 mL

Aroma Hops

1.5 oz	Fuggle, Kent Golding or Styrian Golding	42 g

1. Prepare the liquid yeast in advance, according to the package directions (if using).
2. Coarsely crack the malt grains and place them in a cheesecloth or nylon grain bag.
3. In a brew kettle, bring at least 3 US gal (11 L) brewing water to steeping temperature (150 to 160°F/65 to 71°C). Turn off the heat, add the grain bag, cover and steep for 30 minutes. (If the temperature drops below steeping temperature, turn the element back on briefly to bring it back up.) Remove grain bag and discard.
4. Increase the heat and bring grain tea to a boil. Remove from heat, add half of the malt extract and stir until dissolved completely.
5. Return kettle to the burner and increase the heat until the wort begins to boil. Using a spoon, clear any foam to one side. Reduce heat until a rolling boil can be maintained without foam buildup.
6. Add the bittering hops, stirring to combine. Boil for 45 minutes, uncovered. Monitor to prevent boiling over.
7. Meanwhile, prepare the fermentation gear and cooling bath or wort chiller.

8. After 45 minutes, remove the kettle from the heat and add remaining half of the malt extract, candi sugar, Irish moss and yeast nutrient. Stir to ensure that the extract, sugar and nutrient are dissolved. Return the kettle to the burner and bring back to a rolling boil. Boil for 15 minutes, then stir in the aroma hops, turn off the heat and cover.

9. To cool the brew, place the covered kettle in the prepared cooling tub or use a wort chiller according to the manufacturer's directions. Cool to the desired temperature, 75°F (24°C), within 30 to 45 minutes.

10. While the wort is cooling, clean and sanitize the brewing spoon. When the wort has cooled, move the kettle to a counter and stir the wort briskly in one direction for about 5 minutes. After stirring, cover and let rest for 10 to 15 minutes as the hops and trub form a cone.

11. Using a racking cane and siphon, rack as much wort as possible into the sanitized primary fermenter. Using the sanitized funnel and straining screen, strain the rest of the wort into the fermenter. Top off with brewing water to bring the volume to around 5.5 US gal (21 L). Using the hydrometer, take a reading of the specific gravity and record it in your brewing journal.

12. Add the yeast; vigorously stir it with a sanitized spoon to distribute it throughout the wort. Seal the fermenter with lid, stopper and airlock. Keep the fermenter at room temperature (68 to 72°F/20 to 22°C) during primary fermentation, which typically lasts 7 to 10 days after fermentation begins. (Keep in a dark place or under a lightproof cover if using a glass carboy.)

13. After 7 to 10 days or when the kräusen has fallen, gently rack the beer into the secondary fermenter to avoid aerating it, leaving as much of the sediment behind as possible. Seal and keep at room temperature, covered or in a dark place, to allow fermentation to continue.

14. Once the bubbling in the airlock has slowed, confirm completion of fermentation by using the hydrometer to take final gravity readings. (Hydrometer readings should be the same for several days in a row.)

15. Prime and bottle the beer (see page 91) and condition it for 6 to 8 weeks.

Brewer's Tip

If the specified brands of grains are not available, use the grains chart on page 77 to find substitutes.

Estimated Original Gravity: 1.053

Equipment

- **brew kettle**
- **fermentation gear (page 14)**

As you build your brewing skills, switching to liquid yeast products (from Wyeast or White Labs) will give you a brew that is more complex than the ones made with the dry yeast (from Fermentis or Danstar) in the Absolute Beginner recipes. See page 86 for more information about liquid yeasts.

Belgian Bitter

Yeast

1 pack	Wyeast 3522 or White Labs WLP510 or Fermentis T-58	1 pack

Grains

1 lb	Carafoam®, Carapils® or dextrin malt	450 g
5.5 US gal	brewing water (page 89)	21 L

Malt Extract

6.6 lbs	any brand extra-light, divided in half	3 kg

Bittering Hops

12 to 14 AAUs	Target, Pilgrim or Northern Brewer	12 to 14 AAUs

Later Additions

1 tsp	Irish moss	5 mL
1 tsp	yeast nutrient	5 mL

Aroma and Dry Hops

2 oz	Kent Golding or Fuggle (reserve .5 oz/14 g as a dry hop)	56 g

1. Prepare the liquid yeast in advance, according to the package directions (if using).
2. Coarsely crack the malt grains and place them in a cheesecloth or nylon grain bag.
3. In a brew kettle, bring at least 3 US gal (11 L) brewing water to steeping temperature (150 to 160°F/65 to 71°C). Turn off the heat, add the grain bag, cover and steep for 30 minutes. (If the temperature drops below steeping temperature, turn the element back on briefly to bring it back up.) Remove grain bag and discard.
4. Increase the heat and bring grain tea to a boil. Remove from heat, add half of the malt extract and stir until dissolved completely.
5. Return kettle to the burner and increase the heat until the wort begins to boil. Using a spoon, clear any foam to one side. Reduce heat until a rolling boil can be maintained without foam buildup.
6. Add the bittering hops, stirring to combine. Boil for 45 minutes, uncovered. Monitor to prevent boiling over.
7. Meanwhile, prepare the fermentation gear and cooling bath or wort chiller.

8. After 45 minutes, remove the kettle from the heat and add the remaining half of the malt extract, Irish moss and yeast nutrient. Stir to ensure that the extract and nutrient are dissolved. Return the kettle to the burner and bring back to a rolling boil. Boil for 15 minutes, then stir in 1.5 oz (42 g) of the aroma hops, turn off the heat and cover.

9. To cool the brew, place the covered kettle in the prepared cooling tub or use a wort chiller according to the manufacturer's directions. Cool to the desired temperature, 75°F (24°C), within 30 to 45 minutes.

10. While the wort is cooling, clean and sanitize the brewing spoon. When the wort has cooled, move the kettle to a counter and stir the wort briskly in one direction for about 5 minutes. After stirring, cover and let rest for 10 to 15 minutes as the hops and trub form a cone.

11. Using a racking cane and siphon, rack as much wort as possible into the sanitized primary fermenter. Using the sanitized funnel and straining screen, strain the rest of the wort into the fermenter. Top off with brewing water to bring the volume to around 5.5 US gal (21 L). Using the hydrometer, take a reading of the specific gravity and record it in your brewing journal.

12. Add the yeast; vigorously stir it with a sanitized spoon to distribute it throughout the wort. Seal the fermenter with lid, stopper and airlock. Keep the fermenter at room temperature (68 to 72°F/20 to 22°C) during primary fermentation, which typically lasts 1 to 4 days after fermentation begins. (Keep in a dark place or under a lightproof cover if using a glass carboy.)

13. After 1 to 4 days or when the kräusen has fallen, gently rack the beer into the secondary fermenter to avoid aerating it, leaving as much of the sediment behind as possible. Seal and keep at room temperature, covered or in a dark place, to allow fermentation to continue.

14. Once the bubbling in the airlock has slowed, gently add remaining .5 oz (14 g) of the hops, reseal and leave it for about 2 more weeks. Confirm completion of fermentation by using the hydrometer to take final gravity readings. (Hydrometer readings should be the same for several days in a row.)

15. Prime and bottle the beer (see page 91) and condition it for 6 to 8 weeks.

Belgian IPA

Inspired by brews in North America, brewers combined strong Belgian ale with American-style IPA. The beer has been embraced on both sides of the Atlantic. Belgian examples are Urthel's Hop It and Achouffe's Houbolon; American examples are brewed by Allagash, Captain Lawrence and Flying Fish.

There are two takes on the style: one school says to load in the flavor, and aroma American hop varieties such as Amarillo, Cascade or Centennial are used; others prefer to load in European hops like Hallertau, Tettnang or Saaz.

Estimated Original Gravity: 1.083

Equipment

- **brew kettle**
- **fermentation gear (page 14)**

Beers with an estimated original gravity higher than 1.065 require a longer time in both primary and secondary fermentation. Primary fermentation should take 7 to 10 days, and secondary fermentation should take about 2 weeks longer than weaker brews.

Yeast

1 pack	Wyeast 3522 or White Labs WLP550 or Fermentis T-58	1 pack

Grains

1 lb	Carabelge® malt	450 g
1 lb	Abbey® malt	450 g
1 lb	Carahell® malt	450 g
5.5 US gal	brewing water (page 89)	21 L

Malt Extract

8 lbs	Alexander's Sun Country Pale, divided in half	3.6 kg

Bittering Hops

12 to 16 AAUs	Northern Brewer, Palisades or Perle	12 to 16 AAUs

Flavor, Aroma and Dry Hops

1.5 oz	any European variety low-alpha hops for flavor (add as late addition)	42 g
1.5 oz	any European variety low-alpha hops for aroma (add at end of boil)	42 g
1.5 oz	any European variety for dry hopping	42 g

Later Additions

1 lb	clear Belgian candi sugar	450 g
1 tsp	Irish moss	5 mL
1 tsp	yeast nutrient	5 mL

1. Prepare the liquid yeast in advance, according to the package directions (if using).
2. Coarsely crack the malt grains and place them in a cheesecloth or nylon grain bag.
3. In a brew kettle, bring at least 3 US gal (11 L) brewing water to steeping temperature (150 to 160°F/65 to 71°C). Turn off the heat, add the grain bag, cover and steep for 30 minutes. (If the temperature drops below steeping temperature, turn the element back on briefly to bring it back up.) Remove grain bag and discard.
4. Increase the heat and bring grain tea to a boil. Remove from heat, add half of the malt extract and stir until dissolved completely.
5. Return kettle to the burner and increase the heat until the wort begins to boil. Using a spoon, clear any foam to one side. Reduce heat until a rolling boil can be maintained without foam buildup.

6. Add the bittering hops, stirring to combine. Boil for 45 minutes, uncovered. Monitor to prevent boiling over.

7. Meanwhile, prepare the fermentation gear and cooling bath or wort chiller.

8. After 45 minutes, remove the kettle from the heat and add the remaining half of the malt extract, 1.5 oz (42 g) hops for flavor, candi sugar, Irish moss and yeast nutrient. Stir to ensure that the extract, sugar and nutrient are dissolved. Return the kettle to the burner and bring back to a rolling boil. Boil for 15 minutes, then stir in 1.5 (42 g) aroma hops, turn off the heat and cover.

9. To cool the brew, place the covered kettle in the prepared cooling tub or use a wort chiller according to the manufacturer's directions. Cool to the desired temperature, 75°F (24°C), within 30 to 45 minutes.

10. While the wort is cooling, clean and sanitize the brewing spoon. When the wort has cooled, move the kettle to a counter and stir the wort briskly in one direction for about 5 minutes. After stirring, cover and let rest for 10 to 15 minutes as the hops and trub form a cone.

11. Using a racking cane and siphon, rack as much wort as possible into the sanitized primary fermenter. Using the sanitized funnel and straining screen, strain the rest of the wort into the fermenter. Top off with brewing water to bring the volume to around 5.5 US gal (21 L). Using the hydrometer, take a reading of the specific gravity and record it in your brewing journal.

12. Add the yeast; vigorously stir it with a sanitized spoon to distribute it throughout the wort. Seal the fermenter with lid, stopper and airlock. Keep the fermenter at room temperature (68 to 72°F/20 to 22°C) during primary fermentation, which typically lasts 7 to 10 days after fermentation begins. (Keep in a dark place or under a lightproof cover if using a glass carboy.)

13. After 7 to 10 days or when the kräusen has fallen, gently rack the beer into the secondary fermenter to avoid aerating it, leaving as much of the sediment behind as possible. Seal and keep at room temperature, covered or in a dark place, to allow fermentation to continue.

14. Once the bubbling in the airlock has slowed, gently add the remaining 1.5 oz (42 g) of the hops, reseal and leave it for about 2 more weeks. Confirm completion of fermentation by using the hydrometer to take final gravity readings. (Hydrometer readings should be the same for several days in a row.)

15. Prime and bottle the beer (see page 91) and condition it for 6 to 8 weeks.

Brewer's Tips

If the specified brands of grains are not available, use the grains chart on page 77 to find substitutes.

When choosing the flavor and aroma hops for this beer, minimize the number of hop varieties you use until you learn which flavors you like. In general, choose low-alpha acid hops to combine. Use the hop varieties charts starting on page 79 to give you some ideas.

Estimated Original Gravity: 1.069

Equipment

- **brew kettle**
- **fermentation gear (page 14)**

Beers with an estimated original gravity higher than 1.065 require a longer time in both primary and secondary fermentation. Primary fermentation should take 7 to 10 days, and secondary fermentation should take about 2 weeks longer than weaker brews.

Belgian Stout

Yeast

1 pack	Wyeast 1214 or White Labs WLP500 or Fermentis T-58	1 pack

Grains

12 oz	roast barley	336 g
8 oz	crystal malt (60 Lovibond)	224 g
8 oz	barley flakes (do not crack)	224 g
4 oz	chocolate malt	112 g
5.5 US gal	brewing water (page 89)	21 L

Malt Extract

8 lbs	any brand light	3.6 kg

Bittering Hops

12 to 14 AAUs	Challenger, Progress or any UK	12 to 14 AAUs

Later Additions

1 tsp	Irish moss	5 mL
1 tsp	yeast nutrient	5 mL

Aroma Hops

None

1. Prepare the liquid yeast in advance, according to the package directions (if using).
2. Coarsely crack the grains and place them in a cheesecloth or nylon grain bag. Add barley flakes.
3. In a brew kettle, bring at least 3 US gal (11 L) brewing water to steeping temperature (150 to 160°F/65 to 71°C). Turn off the heat, add the grain bag, cover and steep for 30 minutes. (If the temperature drops below steeping temperature, turn the element back on briefly to bring it back up.) Remove grain bag and discard.
4. Increase the heat and bring grain tea to a boil. Remove from heat, add the malt extract and stir until dissolved completely.
5. Return kettle to the burner and increase the heat until the wort begins to boil. Using a spoon, clear any foam to one side. Reduce heat until a rolling boil can be maintained without foam buildup.
6. Add the bittering hops, stirring to combine. Boil for 45 minutes, uncovered. Monitor to prevent boiling over.
7. Meanwhile, prepare the fermentation gear and cooling bath or wort chiller.

8. After 45 minutes, remove the kettle from the heat and add Irish moss and yeast nutrient. Stir to ensure that the nutrient has dissolved. Return the kettle to the burner and bring back to a rolling boil. Boil for 15 minutes, turn off the heat and cover.

9. To cool the brew, place the covered kettle in the prepared cooling tub or use a wort chiller according to the manufacturer's directions. Cool to the desired temperature, 75°F (24°C), within 30 to 45 minutes.

10. While the wort is cooling, clean and sanitize the brewing spoon. When the wort has cooled, move the kettle to a counter and stir the wort briskly in one direction for about 5 minutes. After stirring, cover and let rest for 10 to 15 minutes as the hops and trub form a cone.

11. Using a racking cane and siphon, rack as much wort as possible into the sanitized primary fermenter. Using the sanitized funnel and straining screen, strain the rest of the wort into the fermenter. Top off with brewing water to bring the volume to around 5.5 US gal (21 L). Using the hydrometer, take a reading of the specific gravity and record it in your brewing journal.

12. Add the yeast; vigorously stir it with a sanitized spoon to distribute it throughout the wort. Seal the fermenter with lid, stopper and airlock. Keep the fermenter at room temperature (68 to 72°F/20 to 22°C) during primary fermentation, which typically lasts 7 to 10 days after fermentation begins. (Keep in a dark place or under a lightproof cover if using a glass carboy.)

13. After 7 to 10 days or when the kräusen has fallen, gently rack the beer into the secondary fermenter to avoid aerating it, leaving as much of the sediment behind as possible. Seal and keep at room temperature, covered or in a dark place, to allow fermentation to continue.

14. Once the bubbling in the airlock has slowed, confirm completion of fermentation by using the hydrometer to take final gravity readings. (Hydrometer readings should be the same for several days in a row.)

15. Prime and bottle the beer (see page 91) and condition it for 6 to 8 weeks.

Saison (Farmhouse)

The classic country ales of Belgium were made by farmers in the spring, to be enjoyed during the summer and fall harvest. Saison DuPont is the beer that all others are judged by. These beers are very food-friendly. Try them with grilled seafood and chicken or with double-crème cheeses.

Estimated Original Gravity: 1.077

Equipment

- **brew kettle**
- **fermentation gear (page 14)**
- **blow-off hose (page 16)**

Beers with an estimated original gravity higher than 1.065 require a longer time in both primary and secondary fermentation. Primary fermentation should take 7 to 10 days, and secondary fermentation should take about 2 weeks longer than weaker brews.

Yeast

1 pack	Wyeast 3711 or White Labs WLP565 or Fermentis T-58	1 pack

Grains

1 lb	Vienna malt	450 g
1 lb	Carabelge® malt	450 g
5.5 US gal	brewing water (page 89)	21 L

Malt Extracts

4 lbs	Alexander's Sun Country Wheat	1.8 kg
4 lbs	Alexander's Sun Country Pale (late extract addition)	1.8 kg

Bittering Hops

8 to 10 AAUs	Northern Brewer or Perle	8 to 10 AAUs

Later Additions

1 lb	orange blossom honey	450 g
1 tsp	Irish moss	5 mL
1 tsp	yeast nutrient	5 mL

Aroma Hops

1.5 oz	Hallertau, Saaz, Strisselspalt or Styrian Golding	42 g

1. Prepare the liquid yeast in advance, according to the package directions (if using).
2. Coarsely crack the malt grains and place them in a cheesecloth or nylon grain bag.
3. In a brew kettle, bring at least 3 US gal (11 L) brewing water to steeping temperature (150 to 160°F/65 to 71°C). Turn off the heat, add the grain bag, cover and steep for 30 minutes. (If the temperature drops below steeping temperature, turn the element back on briefly to bring it back up.) Remove grain bag and discard.
4. Increase the heat and bring grain tea to a boil. Remove from heat, add the wheat malt extract only and stir until dissolved completely.
5. Return kettle to the burner and increase the heat until the wort begins to boil. Using a spoon, clear any foam to one side. Reduce heat until a rolling boil can be maintained without foam buildup.
6. Add the bittering hops, stirring to combine. Boil for 45 minutes, uncovered. Monitor to prevent boiling over.
7. Meanwhile, prepare the fermentation gear and cooling bath or wort chiller.

8. After 45 minutes, remove the kettle from the heat and add the pale malt extract, honey, Irish moss and yeast nutrient. Stir to ensure that the extract, honey and nutrient are dissolved. Return the kettle to the burner and bring back to a rolling boil. Boil for 15 minutes, then stir in the aroma hops, turn off the heat and cover.

9. To cool the brew, place the covered kettle in the prepared cooling tub or use a wort chiller according to the manufacturer's directions. Cool to the desired temperature, 75°F (24°C), within 30 to 45 minutes.

10. While the wort is cooling, clean and sanitize the brewing spoon. When the wort has cooled, move the kettle to a counter and stir the wort briskly in one direction for about 5 minutes. After stirring, cover and let rest for 10 to 15 minutes as the hops and trub form a cone.

11. Using a racking cane and siphon, rack as much wort as possible into the sanitized primary fermenter. Using the sanitized funnel and straining screen, strain the rest of the wort into the fermenter. Top off with brewing water to bring the volume to around 5.5 US gal (21 L). Using the hydrometer, take a reading of the specific gravity and record it in your brewing journal.

12. Add the yeast; vigorously stir it with a sanitized spoon to distribute it throughout the wort. Seal the fermenter with lid, stopper and airlock or blow-off hose. Keep the fermenter at room temperature (68 to 72°F/20 to 22°C) during primary fermentation, which typically lasts 7 to 10 days after fermentation begins. (Keep in a dark place or under a lightproof cover if using a glass carboy.)

13. After 7 to 10 days or when the kräusen has fallen, gently rack the beer into the secondary fermenter to avoid aerating it, leaving as much of the sediment behind as possible. Seal and keep at room temperature, covered or in a dark place, to allow fermentation to continue.

14. Once the bubbling in the airlock has slowed, confirm completion of fermentation by using the hydrometer to take final gravity readings. (Hydrometer readings should be the same for several days in a row.)

15. Prime and bottle the beer (see page 91) and condition it for up to 8 weeks or longer.

Variation

Black Saison: To brew a dark version of this beer, include 8 oz (224 g) Dehusked Carafa® to the grain bill.

Brewer's Tips

If the specified brands of grains are not available, use the grains chart on page 77 to find substitutes.

If active fermentation backs up into the airlock, replace airlock with blow-off hose (see page 16). Change water as needed; re-install airlock when fermentation settles down.

Bière de Garde

Very similar to Saison, this Northern French beer is a kissing cousin when it comes to why they were brewed and their flavor profile. Mainly the richer, more copper-tinted color is what separates these beers from the Saisons to the north.

Estimated Original Gravity: 1.085

Equipment

- **brew kettle**
- **fermentation gear (page 14)**
- **blow-off hose (page 16)**

Beers with an estimated original gravity higher than 1.065 require a longer time in both primary and secondary fermentation. Primary fermentation should take 7 to 10 days, and secondary fermentation should take about 2 weeks longer than weaker brews.

Yeast

1 pack	Wyeast 3522 or White Labs WLP550 or Fermentis T-58	1 pack

Grains

1 lb	Carabelge® malt	450 g
1 lb	Abbey® malt	450 g
1 lb	Caramunich II® malt	450 g
5.5 US gal	brewing water (page 89)	21 L

Malt Extracts

4 lbs	Alexander's Sun Country Wheat	1.8 kg
4 lbs	Alexander's Sun Country Pale (late extract addition)	1.8 kg

Bittering Hops

8 to 10 AAUs	Northern Brewer or Perle	8 to 10 AAUs

Later Additions

1 lb	Belgian amber candi sugar	450 g
1 tsp	Irish moss	5 mL
1 tsp	yeast nutrient	5 mL

Aroma Hops

1.5 oz	Hallertau, Saaz, Strisselspalt or Styrian Golding	42 g

1. Prepare the liquid yeast in advance, according to the package directions (if using).
2. Coarsely crack the malt grains and place them in a cheesecloth or nylon grain bag.
3. In a brew kettle, bring at least 3 US gal (11 L) brewing water to steeping temperature (150 to 160°F/65 to 71°C). Turn off the heat, add the grain bag, cover and steep for 30 minutes. (If the temperature drops below steeping temperature, turn the element back on briefly to bring it back up.) Remove grain bag and discard.
4. Increase the heat and bring grain tea to a boil. Remove from heat, add the wheat malt extract only and stir until dissolved completely.
5. Return kettle to the burner and increase the heat until the wort begins to boil. Using a spoon, clear any foam to one side. Reduce heat until a rolling boil can be maintained without foam buildup.
6. Add the bittering hops, stirring to combine. Boil for 45 minutes, uncovered. Monitor to prevent boiling over.

7. Meanwhile, prepare the fermentation gear and cooling bath or wort chiller.

8. After 45 minutes, remove the kettle from the heat and add the pale malt extract, candi sugar, Irish moss and yeast nutrient. Stir to ensure that the extract, sugar and nutrient are dissolved. Return the kettle to the burner and bring back to a rolling boil. Boil for 15 minutes, then stir in the aroma hops, turn off heat and cover.

9. To cool the brew, place the covered kettle in the prepared cooling tub or use a wort chiller according to the manufacturer's directions. Cool to the desired temperature, 75°F (24°C), within 30 to 45 minutes.

10. While the wort is cooling, clean and sanitize the brewing spoon. When the wort has cooled, move the kettle to a counter and stir the wort briskly in one direction for about 5 minutes. After stirring, cover and let rest for 10 to 15 minutes as the hops and trub form a cone.

11. Using a racking cane and siphon, rack as much wort as possible into the sanitized primary fermenter. Using the sanitized funnel and straining screen, strain the rest of the wort into the fermenter. Top off with brewing water to bring the volume to around 5.5 US gal (21 L). Using the hydrometer, take a reading of the specific gravity and record it in your brewing journal.

12. Add the yeast; vigorously stir it with a sanitized spoon to distribute it throughout the wort. Seal the fermenter with lid, stopper and airlock or blow-off hose. Keep the fermenter at room temperature (68 to 72°F/20 to 22°C) during primary fermentation, which typically lasts 7 to 10 days after fermentation begins. (Keep in a dark place or under a lightproof cover if using a glass carboy.)

13. After 7 to 10 days or when the kräusen has fallen, gently rack the beer into the secondary fermenter to avoid aerating it, leaving as much of the sediment behind as possible. Seal and keep at room temperature, covered or in a dark place, to allow fermentation to continue.

14. Once the bubbling in the airlock has slowed, confirm completion of fermentation by using the hydrometer to take final gravity readings. (Hydrometer readings should be the same for several days in a row.)

15. Prime and bottle the beer (see page 91) and condition it for up to 8 weeks or longer.

Brewer's Tips

If the specified brands of grains are not available, use the grains chart on page 77 to find substitutes.

If active fermentation backs up into the airlock, replace airlock with blow-off hose (see page 16). Change water as needed; re-install airlock when fermentation settles down.

Strong Golden Ale

The original version of this beer was Moorgaat's Duvel. It is said that when the brewer tasted the prototype he exclaimed, "That's a devil of beer!" Others agreed, and the beer was given the Flemish name for the devil. Imitators often give their versions devilish names, like Lucifer or Damnation. Although light in color, this beer is a heavy hitter when it comes to alcohol.

Estimated Original Gravity: 1.097

Equipment

- **brew kettle**
- **fermentation gear (page 14)**
- **blow-off hose (page 16)**

Beers with an estimated original gravity higher than 1.065 require a longer time in both primary and secondary fermentation. Primary fermentation should take 7 to 10 days, and secondary fermentation should take about 2 weeks longer than weaker brews.

Yeast

2 packs	Wyeast 1388 or White Labs WLP570 (or 1 pack in starter) or Fermentis T-58	2 packs

Grains

1 lb	Carafoam®, Carapils® or dextrin malt	450 g
5.5 US gal	brewing water (page 89)	21 L

Malt Extract

9.9 lbs	any brand extra-light, divided $^1/_3$:$^2/_3$	4.5 kg

Bittering Hops

12 to 14 AAUs	Northern Brewer or Perle	12 to 14 AAUs

Later Additions

2 lbs	dextrose, divided in half	900 g
1 tsp	Irish moss	5 mL
1 tsp	yeast nutrient	5 mL

Aroma Hops

1.5 oz	Saaz	42 g

1. Prepare the liquid yeast in advance, according to the package directions (if using).
2. Coarsely crack the malt grains and place them in a cheesecloth or nylon grain bag.
3. In a brew kettle, bring at least 3 US gal (11 L) brewing water to steeping temperature (150 to 160°F/65 to 71°C). Turn off the heat, add the grain bag, cover and steep for 30 minutes. (If the temperature drops below steeping temperature, turn the element back on briefly to bring it back up.) Remove grain bag and discard.
4. Increase the heat and bring grain tea to a boil. Remove from heat, add 3.3 lbs (1.5 kg) of the malt extract and stir until dissolved completely.
5. Return kettle to the burner and increase the heat until the wort begins to boil. Using a spoon, clear any foam to one side. Reduce heat until a rolling boil can be maintained without foam buildup.
6. Add the bittering hops, stirring to combine. Boil for 45 minutes, uncovered. Monitor to prevent boiling over.
7. Meanwhile, prepare the fermentation gear and cooling bath or wort chiller.

8. After 45 minutes, remove the kettle from the heat and add the remaining 6.6 lbs (3 kg) of the malt extract, 1 lb (500 g) of the dextrose, Irish moss and yeast nutrient. Stir to ensure that the extract, sugars and nutrient are dissolved. Return the kettle to the burner and bring back to a rolling boil. Boil for 15 minutes, then stir in the aroma hops, turn off the heat and cover.

9. To cool the brew, place the covered kettle in the prepared cooling tub or use a wort chiller according to the manufacturer's directions. Cool to the desired temperature, 75°F (24°C), within 30 to 45 minutes.

10. While the wort is cooling, clean and sanitize the brewing spoon. When the wort has cooled, move the kettle to a counter and stir the wort briskly in one direction for about 5 minutes. After stirring, cover and let rest for 10 to 15 minutes as the hops and trub form a cone.

11. Using a racking cane and siphon, rack as much wort as possible into the sanitized primary fermenter. Using the sanitized funnel and straining screen, strain the rest of the wort into the fermenter. Top off with brewing water to bring the volume to around 5.5 US gal (21 L). Using the hydrometer, take a reading of the specific gravity and record it in your brewing journal.

12. Add the yeast; vigorously stir it with a sanitized spoon to distribute it throughout the wort. Seal the fermenter with lid, stopper and airlock or blow-off hose. Keep the fermenter at room temperature (68 to 72°F/20 to 22°C) during primary fermentation, which typically lasts 7 to 10 days after fermentation begins. (Keep in a dark place or under a lightproof cover if using a glass carboy.)

13. After 7 to 10 days or when the kräusen has fallen, gently rack the beer into the secondary fermenter to avoid aerating it, leaving as much of the sediment behind as possible. Boil enough water or wort to dissolve the remaining 1 lb (450 g) of dextrose. Add dextrose and stir until it is completely dissolved. Add dextrose solution and seal fermenter with blow-off hose. When fermentation calms down, replace blow-off hose with airlock and keep at room temperature, covered or in a dark place; allow fermentation to continue.

14. Once the bubbling in the airlock has slowed, confirm completion of fermentation by using the hydrometer to take final gravity readings. (Hydrometer readings should be the same for several days in a row.)

15. Prime and bottle the beer (see page 91) and condition it for a minimum of 3 months.

Brewer's Tips

For information on preparing a yeast starter, see page 89.

If active fermentation backs up into the airlock, replace airlock with blow-off hose (see page 16). Change water as needed; re-install airlock when fermentation settles down.

Grand Cru

Grand Cru is not a specific beer style. Belgian brewers use this distinction for beer they consider to be their best. Usually it's a higher-alcohol beer with ramped-up flavors. When my friends at the Nodding Head brewpub in Philadelphia approached me to co-brew a beer with them, I suggested a Grand Cru. They called this beer George's Fault, and it has won both gold and bronze medals at the Great American Beer Festival, a competition of commercial beers held each year in Denver.

This recipe is one that I've developed over many years. It is hugely popular with beer lovers as well as those who don't even like beer.

Estimated Original Gravity: 1.089

Equipment

- **brew kettle**
- **fermentation gear (page 14)**
- **blow-off hose (page 16)**

Beers with an estimated original gravity higher than 1.065 require a longer time in both primary and secondary fermentation. Primary fermentation should take 7 to 10 days, and secondary fermentation should take about 2 weeks longer than weaker brews.

Yeast

2 packs	Wyeast 3522 or White Labs WLP550 (or 1 pack in starter) or Fermentis T-58	2 packs

Grains

1 lb	Carafoam®, Carapils® or dextrin malt	450 g
5.5 US gal	brewing water (page 89)	21 L

Malt Extracts

1.4 lbs	Alexander's Sun Country Pale	635 g
8 lbs	Alexander's Sun Country Wheat	3.6 kg

Bittering Hops

6 to 8 AAUs	Styrian Golding	6 to 8 AAUs

Later Additions

1 oz	Bitter Orange Peel	28 g
1 oz	Sweet Orange Peel	28 g
.5 oz	chamomile flowers, crushed	14 g
1 oz	coriander seed, crushed	28 g
	Grains of Paradise seeds (OR black peppercorns), crushed	2 g
2 lbs	orange blossom honey	900 g
1 tsp	Irish moss	5 mL
1 tsp	yeast nutrient	5 mL

Aroma Hops

.5 oz	Styrian Golding	14 g

1. Prepare the liquid yeast in advance, according to the package directions (if using).
2. Coarsely crack the malt grains and place them in a cheesecloth or nylon grain bag.
3. In a brew kettle, bring at least 3 US gal (11 L) brewing water to steeping temperature (150 to 160°F/65 to 71°C). Turn off the heat, add the grain bag, cover and steep for 30 minutes. (If the temperature drops below steeping temperature, turn the element back on briefly to bring it back up.) Remove grain bag and discard.
4. Increase the heat and bring grain tea to a boil. Remove from heat, add the pale malt extract only and stir until dissolved completely.
5. Return kettle to the burner and increase the heat until the wort begins to boil. Using a spoon, clear any foam to one side. Reduce heat until a rolling boil can be maintained without foam buildup.

6. Add the bittering hops, stirring to combine. Boil for 45 minutes, uncovered. Monitor to prevent boiling over.

7. Meanwhile, prepare the fermentation gear and cooling bath or wort chiller.

8. After 45 minutes, remove the kettle from the heat. Place the peel, flowers and seeds in a hop bag. Add the wheat malt extract, honey, spice bag, Irish moss and yeast nutrient to the kettle. Stir to ensure that the extract, honey and nutrient are dissolved. Return the kettle to the burner and bring back to a rolling boil. Boil for 15 minutes, then stir in the aroma hops, turn off the heat and cover.

9. To cool the brew, place the covered kettle in the prepared cooling tub or use a wort chiller according to the manufacturer's directions. Cool to the desired temperature, 75°F (24°C), within 30 to 45 minutes.

10. While the wort is cooling, clean and sanitize the brewing spoon. When the wort has cooled, move the kettle to a counter and stir the wort briskly in one direction for about 5 minutes. After stirring, cover and let rest for 10 to 15 minutes as the hops and trub form a cone.

11. Using a racking cane and siphon, rack as much wort as possible into the sanitized primary fermenter. Using the sanitized funnel and straining screen, strain the rest of the wort into the fermenter. Top off with brewing water to bring the volume to around 5.5 US gal (21 L). Using the hydrometer, take a reading of the specific gravity and record it in your brewing journal.

12. Add the yeast; vigorously stir it with a sanitized spoon to distribute it throughout the wort. Seal the fermenter with lid, stopper and airlock or blow-off hose. Keep the fermenter at room temperature (68 to 72°F/20 to 22°C) during primary fermentation, which typically lasts 7 to 10 days after fermentation begins. (Keep in a dark place or under a lightproof cover if using a glass carboy.)

13. After 7 to 10 days or when the kräusen has fallen, gently rack the beer into the secondary fermenter to avoid aerating it, leaving as much of the sediment behind as possible. Seal and keep at room temperature, covered or in a dark place, to allow fermentation to continue.

14. Once the bubbling in the airlock has slowed, confirm completion of fermentation by using the hydrometer to take final gravity readings. (Hydrometer readings should be the same for several days in a row.)

15. Prime and bottle the beer (see page 91) and condition it for a minimum of 3 months.

Variation

This version of Grand Cru is on the light side; it's more like an Imperial Wit beer. If you want a darker version, include up to 1 lb (450 g) each of a toasted and crystal/caramel malt for a copper color and add 4 oz (112 g) of a dark-roasted malt such as Carafara® to the grains for a dark beer.

Brewer's Tips

For information on preparing a yeast starter, see page 89.

If active fermentation backs up into the airlock, replace airlock with blow-off hose (see page 16). Change water as needed; re-install airlock when fermentation settles down.

Strong Dark Ale

Equipment

- **brew kettle**
- **fermentation gear
  (page 14)**
- **blow-off hose
  (page 16)**

Beers with an estimated original gravity higher than 1.065 require a longer time in both primary and secondary fermentation. Primary fermentation should take 7 to 10 days, and secondary fermentation should take about 2 weeks longer than weaker brews.

Yeast

2 packs	Wyeast1388 or White Labs WLP545 (or 1 pack in starter) or Fermentis T-58	2 packs

Grains

1 lb	Carabohemian® malt	450 g
1 lb	Caraaroma® malt	450 g
4 oz	dehusked Carafa III® malt	112 g
5.5 US gal	brewing water (page 89)	21 L

Malt Extract

12.2 lbs	any brand extra-light, divided in half	5.5 kg

Bittering Hops

12 to 14 AAUs	Northern Brewer or Perle	12 to 14 AAUs

Later Additions

1 tsp	Irish moss	5 mL
1 tsp	yeast nutrient	5 mL

Aroma Hops

1.5 oz	Styrian Golding	42 g

1. Prepare the liquid yeast in advance, according to the package directions (if using).

2. Coarsely crack the malt grains and place them in a cheesecloth or nylon grain bag.

3. In a brew kettle, bring at least 3 US gal (11 L) brewing water to steeping temperature (150 to 160°F/65 to 71°C). Turn off the heat, add the grain bag, cover and steep for 30 minutes. (If the temperature drops below steeping temperature, turn the element back on briefly to bring it back up.) Remove grain bag and discard.

4. Increase the heat and bring grain tea to a boil. Remove from heat, add half (6.1 lbs/2.75 kg) of the malt extract and stir until dissolved completely.

5. Return kettle to the burner and increase the heat until the wort begins to boil. Using a spoon, clear any foam to one side. Reduce heat until a rolling boil can be maintained without foam buildup.

6. Add the bittering hops, stirring to combine. Boil for 45 minutes, uncovered. Monitor to prevent boiling over.

7. Meanwhile, prepare the fermentation gear and cooling bath or wort chiller.

8. After 45 minutes, remove the kettle from the heat and add the remaining 6.1 lbs/2.75 kg) of the malt extract, Irish moss and yeast nutrient. Stir to ensure that the extract and nutrient are dissolved. Return the kettle to the burner and bring back to a rolling boil. Boil for 15 minutes, then stir in the aroma hops, turn off the heat and cover.

9. To cool the brew, place the covered kettle in the prepared cooling tub or use a wort chiller according to the manufacturer's directions. Cool to the desired temperature, 75°F (24°C), within 30 to 45 minutes.

10. While the wort is cooling, clean and sanitize the brewing spoon. When the wort has cooled, move the kettle to a counter and stir the wort briskly in one direction for about 5 minutes. After stirring, cover and let rest for 10 to 15 minutes as the hops and trub form a cone.

11. Using a racking cane and siphon, rack as much wort as possible into the sanitized primary fermenter. Using the sanitized funnel and straining screen, strain the rest of the wort into the fermenter. Top off with brewing water to bring the volume to around 5.5 US gal (21 L). Using the hydrometer, take a reading of the specific gravity and record it in your brewing journal.

12. Add the yeast; vigorously stir it with a sanitized spoon to distribute it throughout the wort. Seal the fermenter with lid, stopper and airlock or blow-off hose. Keep the fermenter at room temperature (68 to 72°F/20 to 22°C) during primary fermentation, which typically lasts 7 to 10 days after fermentation begins. (Keep in a dark place or under a lightproof cover if using a glass carboy.)

13. After 7 to 10 days or when the kräusen has fallen, gently rack the beer into the secondary fermenter to avoid aerating it, leaving as much of the sediment behind as possible. Seal and keep at room temperature, covered or in a dark place, to allow fermentation to continue.

14. Once the bubbling in the airlock has slowed, confirm completion of fermentation by using the hydrometer to take final gravity readings. (Hydrometer readings should be the same for several days in a row.)

15. Prime and bottle the beer (see page 91) and condition it for a minimum of 3 months.

Brewer's Tips

For information on preparing a yeast starter, see page 89.

If the specified brands of grains are not available, use the grains chart on page 77 to find substitutes.

If active fermentation backs up into the airlock, replace airlock with blow-off hose (see page 16). Change water as needed; re-install airlock when fermentation settles down.

Belgian Bock (Bok Ale)

Unlike the bock and dopplebock beers of Germany, the Belgian bocks are rich, malty ales. The spicing is optional.

Estimated Original Gravity: 1.073

Equipment

- **brew kettle**
- **fermentation gear (page 14)**
- **blow-off hose (page 16)**

Beers with an estimated original gravity higher than 1.065 require a longer time in both primary and secondary fermentation. Primary fermentation should take 7 to 10 days, and secondary fermentation should take about 2 weeks longer than weaker brews.

Yeast

2 packs	Wyeast 3522 or White Labs WLP550 (or 1 pack in starter) or Fermentis T-58	2 packs

Grains

1 lb	Abbey® malt	450 g
1 lb	Carabohemian® malt	450 g
1 lb	Caraaroma® malt	450 g
5.5 US gal	brewing water (page 89)	21 L

Malt Extract

8 lbs	any brand UK light	3.6 kg

Bittering Hops

6 to 8 AAUs	Perle or Northern Brewer	6 to 8 AAUs

Later Additions

.5 oz	coriander seed, crushed	14 g
2 ea	star anise, whole	2 ea
1 lb	dark Belgian candi sugar	450 g
1 tsp	Irish moss	5 mL
1 tsp	yeast nutrient	5 mL

Aroma Hops

.5 oz	Hallertau	14 g

1. Prepare the liquid yeast in advance, according to the package directions (if using).
2. Coarsely crack the malt grains and place them in a cheesecloth or nylon grain bag.
3. In a brew kettle, bring at least 3 US gal (11 L) brewing water to steeping temperature (150 to 160°F/65 to 71°C). Turn off the heat, add the grain bag, cover and steep for 30 minutes. (If the temperature drops below steeping temperature, turn the element back on briefly to bring it back up.) Remove grain bag and discard.
4. Increase the heat and bring grain tea to a boil. Remove from heat, add the malt extract and stir until dissolved completely.
5. Return kettle to the burner and increase the heat until the wort begins to boil. Using a spoon, clear any foam to one side. Reduce heat until a rolling boil can be maintained without foam buildup.
6. Add the bittering hops, stirring to combine. Boil for 45 minutes, uncovered. Monitor to prevent boiling over.

7. Meanwhile, prepare the fermentation gear and cooling bath or wort chiller.

8. After 45 minutes, remove the kettle from the heat. Place the crushed seeds and star anise in a hop bag. Add candi sugar, bag, Irish moss and yeast nutrient to the kettle. Stir to ensure that the sugar and nutrient are dissolved. Return the kettle to the burner and bring back to a rolling boil. Boil for 15 minutes, then stir in the aroma hops, turn off the heat and cover.

9. To cool the brew, place the covered kettle in the prepared cooling tub or use a wort chiller according to the manufacturer's directions. Cool to the desired temperature, 75°F (24°C), within 30 to 45 minutes.

10. While the wort is cooling, clean and sanitize the brewing spoon. When the wort has cooled, move the kettle to a counter and stir the wort briskly in one direction for about 5 minutes. After stirring, cover and let rest for 10 to 15 minutes as the hops and trub form a cone.

11. Using a racking cane and siphon, rack as much wort as possible into the sanitized primary fermenter. Using the sanitized funnel and straining screen, strain the rest of the wort into the fermenter. Top off with brewing water to bring the volume to around 5.5 US gal (21 L). Using the hydrometer, take a reading of the specific gravity and record it in your brewing journal.

12. Add the yeast; vigorously stir it with a sanitized spoon to distribute it throughout the wort. Seal the fermenter with lid, stopper and airlock or blow-off hose. Keep the fermenter at room temperature (68 to 72°F/20 to 22°C) during primary fermentation, which typically lasts 7 to 10 days after fermentation begins. (Keep in a dark place or under a lightproof cover if using a glass carboy.)

13. After 7 to 10 days or when the kräusen has fallen, gently rack the beer into the secondary fermenter to avoid aerating it, leaving as much of the sediment behind as possible. Seal and keep at room temperature, covered or in a dark place, to allow fermentation to continue.

14. Once the bubbling in the airlock has slowed, confirm completion of fermentation by using the hydrometer to take final gravity readings. (Hydrometer readings should be the same for several days in a row.)

15. Prime and bottle the beer (see page 91) and condition it for a minimum of 3 months.

Brewer's Tips

For information on preparing a yeast starter, see page 89.

If the specified brands of grains are not available, use the grains chart on page 77 to find substitutes.

If active fermentation backs up into the airlock, replace airlock with blow-off hose (see page 16). Change water as needed; re-install airlock when fermentation settles down.

This is a strongly spiced holiday beer to be brewed over the summer for winter enjoyment.

Estimated Original Gravity: 1.113

Equipment

- **brew kettle**
- **fermentation gear (page 14)**
- **blow-off hose (page 16)**

Beers with an estimated original gravity higher than 1.065 require a longer time in both primary and secondary fermentation. Primary fermentation should take 7 to 10 days, and secondary fermentation should take about 2 weeks longer than weaker brews.

Belgian Christmas Ale

Yeast

1 pack	Wyeast 3522 or White Labs WLP545 or Fermentis T-58	1 pack

Grains

1 lb	Abbey® malt	450 g
1 lb	Caraamber® malt	450 g
1 lb	Caramunich III® malt	450 g
5.5 US gal	brewing water (page 89)	21 L

Malt Extract

12.2 lbs	any brand extra-light, divided ⅓:⅔	5.5 kg

Bittering Hops

10 to 12 AAUs	Northern Brewer or Perle	10 to 12 AAUs

Later Additions

.5 oz	coriander seed, crushed	14 g
	caraway seed, crushed	2 g
	cumin seed, crushed	1 g
.1 lb	Belgian dark candi sugar	450 g
1 tsp	Irish moss	5 mL
1 tsp	yeast nutrient	5 mL

Aroma Hops

None

1. Prepare the liquid yeast in advance, according to the package directions (if using).
2. Coarsely crack the malt grains and place them in a cheesecloth or nylon grain bag.
3. In a brew kettle, bring at least 3 US gal (11 L) brewing water to steeping temperature (150 to 160°F/65 to 71°C). Turn off the heat, add the grain bag, cover and steep for 30 minutes. (If the temperature drops below steeping temperature, turn the element back on briefly to bring it back up.) Remove grain bag and discard.
4. Increase the heat and bring grain tea to a boil. Remove from heat, add ⅓ (4 lbs/1.8 kg) of the malt extract and stir until dissolved completely.
5. Return kettle to the burner and increase the heat until the wort begins to boil. Using a spoon, clear any foam to one side. Reduce heat until a rolling boil can be maintained without foam buildup.

6. Add the bittering hops, stirring to combine. Boil for 45 minutes, uncovered. Monitor to prevent boiling over.

7. Meanwhile, prepare the fermentation gear and cooling bath or wort chiller.

8. After 45 minutes, remove the kettle from the heat. Place the spice seeds in a hop bag. Add the remaining $\frac{2}{3}$ (8.1 lbs/3.7 kg) of the malt extract, spice bag, sugar, Irish moss and yeast nutrient. Stir to ensure that the extract, sugar and nutrient are dissolved. Return the kettle to the burner and bring back to a rolling boil. Boil for 15 minutes, then turn off the heat and cover.

9. To cool the brew, place the covered kettle in the prepared cooling tub or use a wort chiller according to the manufacturer's directions. Cool to the desired temperature, 75°F (24°C), within 30 to 45 minutes.

10. While the wort is cooling, clean and sanitize the brewing spoon. When the wort has cooled, move the kettle to a counter and stir the wort briskly in one direction for about 5 minutes. After stirring, cover and let rest for 10 to 15 minutes as the hops and trub form a cone.

11. Using a racking cane and siphon, rack as much wort as possible into the sanitized primary fermenter. Using the sanitized funnel and straining screen, strain the rest of the wort into the fermenter. Top off with brewing water to bring the volume to around 5.5 US gal (21 L). Using the hydrometer, take a reading of the specific gravity and record it in your brewing journal.

12. Add the yeast; vigorously stir it with a sanitized spoon to distribute it throughout the wort. Seal the fermenter with lid, stopper and airlock or blow-off hose. Keep the fermenter at room temperature (68 to 72°F/20 to 22°C) during primary fermentation, which typically lasts 7 to 10 days after fermentation begins. (Keep in a dark place or under a lightproof cover if using a glass carboy.)

13. When the kräusen has fallen, gently rack the beer into the secondary fermenter to avoid aerating it, leaving as much of the sediment behind as possible. Seal and keep at room temperature, covered or in a dark place, to allow fermentation to continue.

14. Once the bubbling in the airlock has slowed, confirm completion of fermentation by using the hydrometer to take final gravity readings. (Hydrometer readings should be the same for several days in a row.)

15. Prime and bottle the beer (see page 91) and condition it for a minimum of 3 months.

> ### Brewer's Tips
>
> If the specified brands of grains are not available, use the grains chart on page 77 to find substitutes.
>
> If active fermentation backs up into the airlock, replace airlock with blow-off hose (see page 16). Change water as needed; re-install airlock when fermentation settles down.

Dubbel

From ancient to medieval times, brewing was done by religious orders. As beer production shifted to secular operations, some monastic orders maintained their brewing tradition. Today a handful of Trappist monasteries in Belgium and the Netherlands still produce beers. They fiercely protect the Trappist designation (as well they should). When secular brewers produce beers in this style, the results are called Abbey beers.

Estimated Original Gravity: 1.083

Equipment

- **brew kettle**
- **fermentation gear (page 14)**
- **blow-off hose (page 16)**

Bring your patience to this beer. Both fermentation and conditioning take longer than your average homebrews. (The early days of primary fermentation can also be violent. Have the blow-off hose handy.) The reward for those who can wait is a beer that will continue to improve for years to come.

Yeast

2 packs	Wyeast 1214 or White Labs WLP500 (or 1 pack in starter) or Fermentis T-58	2 packs

Grains

1 lb	Caramunich III® malt	450 g
1 lb	Carabohemian® malt	450 g
1 lb	Caraaroma or Special B® malt	450 g
5.5 US gal	brewing water (page 89)	21 L

Malt Extract

8 lbs	any brand light	3.6 kg

Bittering Hops

6 to 8 AAUs	Northern Brewer or Perle	6 to 8 AAUs

Later Additions

1 lb	Belgian amber or dark candi sugar	450 g
1 tsp	Irish moss	5 mL
1 tsp	yeast nutrient	5 mL

Aroma Hops

.5 oz	Styrian Golding, Saaz or other Noble Hops	14 g

1. Prepare the liquid yeast in advance, according to the package directions (if using).
2. Coarsely crack the malt grains and place them in a cheesecloth or nylon grain bag.
3. In a brew kettle, bring at least 3 US gal (11 L) brewing water to steeping temperature (150 to 160°F/65 to 71°C). Turn off the heat, add the grain bag, cover and steep for 30 minutes. (If the temperature drops below steeping temperature, turn the element back on briefly to bring it back up.) Remove grain bag and discard.
4. Increase the heat and bring grain tea to a boil. Remove from heat, add the malt extract and stir until dissolved completely.
5. Return kettle to the burner and increase the heat until the wort begins to boil. Using a spoon, clear any foam to one side. Reduce the heat until a rolling boil can be maintained without foam buildup.
6. Add the bittering hops, stirring to combine. Boil for 45 minutes, uncovered. Monitor to prevent boiling over.
7. Meanwhile, prepare the fermentation gear and cooling bath or wort chiller.

8. After 45 minutes, remove the kettle from the heat and add candi sugar, Irish moss and yeast nutrient. Stir to ensure that the sugar and nutrient are dissolved. Return the kettle to the burner and bring back to a rolling boil. Boil for 15 minutes, then stir in the aroma hops, turn off the heat and cover.

9. To cool the brew, place the covered kettle in the prepared cooling tub or use a wort chiller according to the manufacturer's directions. Cool to the desired temperature, 75°F (24°C), within 30 to 45 minutes.

10. While the wort is cooling, clean and sanitize the brewing spoon. When the wort has cooled, move the kettle to a counter and stir it briskly in a clockwise direction for about 5 minutes. After stirring, cover and let rest for 10 to 15 minutes; the hops and trub should form a cone in the bottom of the kettle.

11. Using a racking cane and siphon, rack as much wort as possible into the sanitized primary fermenter. Using the sanitized funnel and straining screen, strain the rest of the wort into the fermenter. Top off with brewing water to bring the volume to around 5.5 US gal (21 L). Using the hydrometer, take a reading of the specific gravity and record it in your brewing journal.

12. Add the yeast; vigorously stir it with a sanitized spoon to distribute it throughout the wort. Seal the fermenter with lid, stopper and airlock or blow-off hose. Keep the fermenter at room temperature (68 to 72°F/20 to 22°C) during primary fermentation, which typically lasts 7 to 10 days after fermentation begins. (Keep in a dark place or under a lightproof cover if using a glass carboy.) If fermentation becomes very active, substitute the blow-off hose and a small bucket of sanitizer for the airlock until it slows.

13. After 7 to 10 days or when the kräusen has fallen and left a ring on the inside of the bucket, gently rack the beer into the secondary fermenter to avoid aerating it, leaving most of the sediment behind. Seal and keep at room temperature, covered or in a dark place, to allow fermentation to continue for several weeks.

14. Once the bubbling in the airlock has slowed, confirm completion of fermentation by using the hydrometer to take final gravity readings. (Hydrometer readings should be the same for several days in a row.)

15. Prime and bottle the beer (see page 91). Store the bottles in an upright position, away from the light and condition the beer for 6 to 9 months. (Sample it after 3 months.)

Brewer's Tips

If the specified brands of grains are not available, use the grains chart on page 77 to find substitutes.

If active fermentation backs up into the airlock, replace airlock with blow-off hose (see page 16). Change water as needed; re-install airlock when fermentation settles down.

Trippel

These beers don't mind elevated fermentation temperatures. Many homebrewers produce Abbey-style beers in the summer, when it's too warm for other brews, and enjoy them in the winter and early spring.

Estimated Original Gravity: 1.090

Equipment

- **brew kettle**
- **fermentation gear (page 14)**
- **blow-off hose (page 16)**

Bring your patience to this beer. Both fermentation and conditioning take longer than your average homebrews. (The early days of primary fermentation can also be violent. Have the blow-off hose handy.) The reward for those who can wait is a beer that will continue to improve for years to come.

Yeast

2 packs	Wyeast 1214 or White Labs WLP500 (or 1 pack in starter) or Fermentis T-58	2 packs

Grains

1 lb	Carafoam®, Carapils® or dextrin malt	450 g
1 lb	Carabelge® malt	450 g
5.5 US gal	brewing water (page 89)	21 L

Malt Extracts

3.3 lbs	any brand wheat	1.5 kg
6.6 lbs	any brand extra-light (late extract addition)	3 kg

Bittering Hops

10 to 12 AAUs	Northern Brewer or Perle	10 to 12 AAUs

Later Additions

1 lb	Belgian clear candi sugar	450 g
1 tsp	Irish moss	5 mL
1 tsp	yeast nutrient	5 mL

Aroma Hops

1 oz	Hallertau, Saaz or other Noble Hops	28 g

1. Prepare the liquid yeast in advance, according to the package directions (if using).
2. Coarsely crack the malt grains and place them in a cheesecloth or nylon grain bag.
3. In a brew kettle, bring at least 3 US gal (11 L) brewing water to steeping temperature (150 to 160°F/65 to 71°C). Turn off the heat, add the grain bag, cover and steep for 30 minutes. (If the temperature drops below steeping temperature, turn the element back on briefly to bring it back up.) Remove grain bag and discard.
4. Increase the heat and bring grain tea to a boil. Remove from heat, add the wheat malt extract only and stir until dissolved completely.
5. Return kettle to the burner and increase the heat until the wort begins to boil. Using a spoon, clear any foam to one side. Reduce the heat until a rolling boil can be maintained without foam buildup.
6. Add the bittering hops, stirring to combine. Boil for 45 minutes, uncovered. Monitor to prevent boiling over.
7. Meanwhile, prepare the fermentation gear and cooling bath or wort chiller.

8. After 45 minutes, remove the kettle from the heat and add extra-light malt extract, candi sugar, Irish moss and yeast nutrient. Stir to ensure that the extract, sugar and nutrient are dissolved. Return the kettle to the burner and bring back to a rolling boil. Boil for 15 minutes, then stir in the aroma hops, turn off the heat and cover.

9. To cool the brew, place the covered kettle in the prepared cooling tub or use a wort chiller according to the manufacturer's directions. Cool to the desired temperature, 75°F (24°C), within 30 to 45 minutes.

10. While the wort is cooling, clean and sanitize the brewing spoon. When the wort has cooled, move the kettle to a counter and stir it briskly in a clockwise direction for about 5 minutes. After stirring, cover and let rest for 10 to 15 minutes; the hops and trub should form a cone in the bottom of the kettle.

11. Using a racking cane and siphon, rack as much wort as possible into the sanitized primary fermenter. Using the sanitized funnel and straining screen, strain the rest of the wort into the fermenter. Top off with brewing water to bring the volume to around 5.5 US gal (21 L). Using the hydrometer, take a reading of the specific gravity and record it in your brewing journal.

12. Add the yeast; vigorously stir it with a sanitized spoon to distribute it throughout the wort. Seal the fermenter with lid, stopper and airlock or blow-off hose. Keep the fermenter at room temperature (68 to 72°F/20 to 22°C) during primary fermentation, which typically lasts 7 to 10 days after fermentation begins. (Keep in a dark place or under a lightproof cover if using a glass carboy.) If fermentation becomes very active, substitute the blow-off hose and a small bucket of sanitizer for the airlock until it slows.

13. After 7 to 10 days or when the kräusen (brownish foam on top of the wort) has fallen and left a ring on the inside of the bucket, gently rack the beer into the secondary fermenter to avoid aerating it, leaving most of the sediment behind. Seal and keep at room temperature, covered or in a dark place, to allow fermentation to continue for several weeks.

14. Once the bubbling in the airlock has slowed, confirm completion of fermentation by using the hydrometer to take final gravity readings. (Hydrometer readings should be the same for several days in a row.)

15. Prime and bottle the beer (see page 91). Store the bottles in an upright position, away from the light and condition the beer for 6 to 9 months. (Sample it after 3 months.)

Brewer's Tips

For information on preparing a yeast starter, see page 89.

If active fermentation backs up into the airlock, replace airlock with blow-off hose. Change water as needed; re-install airlock when fermentation settles down.

Quad

Makes 5 US gal (19 L)

Typically the Brothers produce a table or small beer called a Single or a Pater. This would be a lighter version of a Belgian Pale Ale. They produce a Dubbel, which is a dark ale around 8% alcohol by volume (abv); and a Trippel, which is a blonde ale around 10% abv. Only one brewer produces a Quadruple, which by sheer viscosity alone is dark and huge! The Quad style is emulated by many secular brewers.

Estimated Original Gravity: 1.130

Equipment

- **brew kettle**
- **fermentation gear (page 14)**
- **blow-off hose (page 16)**

Bring your patience to this beer. Both fermentation and conditioning take longer than your average homebrews. (The early days of primary fermentation can also be violent. Have the blow-off hose handy.) The reward for those who can wait is a beer that will continue to improve for years to come.

Yeast

2 packs	Wyeast 1214 or White Labs WLP500 (or 1 pack in starter) or Fermentis T-58	2 packs
2 packs	Lalvin Champagne yeast (14 g) (add to secondary fermenter)	2 packs

Grains

1 lb	Carabelge® malt	450 g
1 lb	Abbey® malt	450 g
1 lb	Caramunich I® malt	450 g
5.5 US gal	brewing water (page 89)	21 L

Malt Extracts

3.3 lbs	any brand wheat	1.5 kg
9.9 lbs	any brand extra-light (late extract addition)	4.5 kg

Bittering Hops

14 to 16 AAUs	Northern Brewer or Perle	14 to 16 AAUs

Later Additions

1 lb	Belgian clear candi sugar	450 g
1 lb	Belgian amber or dark candi sugar	450 g
1 tsp	Irish moss	5 mL
1 tsp	yeast nutrient	5 mL

Aroma Hops

1 oz	Styrian Golding, Saaz or other Noble Hops	28 g
5 tsp	yeast energizer (add to secondary fermenter)	25 mL

1. Prepare first liquid yeast in advance, according to directions.
2. Coarsely crack the malt grains and place them in a cheesecloth or nylon grain bag.
3. In a brew kettle, bring at least 3 US gal (11 L) brewing water to steeping temperature (150 to 160°F/65 to 71°C). Turn off the heat, add the grain bag, cover and steep for 30 minutes. Remove grain bag and discard.
4. Increase heat and bring grain tea to a boil. Remove from heat, add wheat malt extract only and stir until dissolved.
5. Return kettle to burner and increase heat until wort begins to boil. Using a spoon, clear foam to one side. Reduce heat until a rolling boil is maintained without foam buildup.
6. Add the bittering hops, stirring to combine. Boil for 45 minutes, uncovered. Monitor to prevent boiling over.
7. Meanwhile, prepare the fermentation gear and cooling bath or wort chiller.

8. After 45 minutes, remove the kettle from the heat and add extra-light malt extract, candi or amber sugars, Irish moss and yeast nutrient. Stir to ensure that the extract, sugars and nutrient are dissolved. Return the kettle to the burner and bring back to a rolling boil. Boil for 15 minutes, then stir in the aroma hops, turn off the heat and cover.

9. To cool the brew, place the covered kettle in the prepared cooling tub or use a wort chiller according to the manufacturer's directions. Cool to the desired temperature, 75°F (24°C), within 30 to 45 minutes.

10. While the wort is cooling, clean and sanitize the brewing spoon. When the wort has cooled, move the kettle to a counter and stir it briskly in a clockwise direction for about 5 minutes. After stirring, cover and let rest for 10 to 15 minutes; the hops and trub should form a cone.

11. Using a racking cane and siphon, rack as much wort as possible into sanitized primary fermenter. Using the sanitized funnel and straining screen, strain remainder of wort into fermenter. Top off with brewing water to around 5.5 US gal (21 L). Using the hydrometer, take a reading of the specific gravity and record it.

12. Add first yeast; vigorously stir it with a sanitized spoon to distribute throughout. Seal fermenter with lid, stopper and airlock or blow-off hose. Keep fermenter at room temperature (68 to 72°F/20 to 22°C) during primary fermentation, which typically lasts 7 to 10 days after fermentation begins. (Keep in a dark place or under a lightproof cover if using a glass carboy.) If fermentation becomes very active, substitute blow-off hose and small bucket of sanitizer for the airlock until it slows.

13. After 7 to 10 days or when the kräusen has fallen, gently rack beer into secondary fermenter to avoid aerating it, leaving most of the sediment behind. Seal and keep at room temperature, covered or in a dark place, to allow fermentation to continue for several weeks.

14. Once the bubbling in the airlock has slowed, add yeast energizer and Lalvin yeast. Reseal and leave for about 2 more weeks. Confirm completion of fermentation by using the hydrometer to take final gravity readings. (Hydrometer readings should be the same for several days in a row.)

15. Prime and bottle the beer (see page 91). Store the bottles in an upright position, away from the light and condition the beer for 6 to 9 months. (Sample it after 3 months.)

Brewer's Tips

For information on preparing a yeast starter, see page 89.

If the specified brands of grains are not available, use the grains chart on page 77 to find substitutes.

If active fermentation backs up into the airlock, replace airlock with blow-off hose. Change water as needed; re-install airlock when fermentation settles down.

To Hydrate Lalvin Yeast

In a sanitized bowl or measuring cup, dissolve Lalvin yeast in 1.5 US fl oz (50 mL) of boiled water cooled to 104 to 109°F (40 to 43°C). Let stand for 15 minutes without stirring; then stir with a sanitized spoon to distribute yeast in water.

The great lager beers of the world can trace their roots to the German/Czech part of Europe. Unlike American and Belgian styles, German brewing is about subtlety and balance, and that distinction makes them a bit trickier to brew. If you aren't able to cold-ferment lager beers, use a clean, neutral ale yeast (such as Wyeast 1056 or 1007) and increase the aroma hop addition by about one-third.

Altbier, Kölsch and the various incarnations of wheat beer are the only top-fermenting ales produced in this part of the world. In the ales section I have also included a lager yeast version of a Baltic Porter.

The Weyermann grains, such as Caramunich®, Carapils® or Carabelge®, specified in this section are especially suited to the beers that call for them. They are widely distributed in North America and Europe. If not available, refer to the grain chart on page 77 or ask your brewing supplies retailer for his or her best substitute.

Brews from the German and Czech Regions

Lagers

Ales

Bohemian Pilsner

The next two recipes will take the Pilsner brew back to its richly flavored roots. The Industrial Revolution made Pilsner possible: malting processes became industrialized and better controlled, producing lighter-colored malt. Refrigeration was invented, and lager beers could be brewed year round. Glass, formerly handmade and only affordable for the wealthy, was mass-produced.

All the factors came together in the city of Pilsen (Plzn) in the state of Bohemia (part of the modern Czech Republic), and the result was a light-colored, crisp lager beer poured into a clear vessel that showed off its deep golden color.

Estimated Original Gravity: 1.064

Equipment

- **brew kettle**
- **fermentation gear (page 14)**

Yeast

2 packs	Wyeast 2124 or White Labs WLP800 (or 1 pack in starter) or Fermentis S-23	2 packs

Grains

1 lb	Carafoam®, Carapils® or dextrin malt	450 g
5.5 US gal	brewing water (page 89)	21 L

Malt Extract

8 lbs	Alexander's Sun Country Pale, divided in half	3.6 kg

Bittering Hops

12 to 14 AAUs	Northern Brewer or Perle	12 to 14 AAUs

Later Additions

1 tsp	Irish moss	5 mL
1 tsp	yeast nutrient	5 mL

Aroma Hops

1.5 oz	Saaz	42 g

1. Prepare the liquid yeast in advance, according to the package directions (if using).

2. Coarsely crack the malt grains and place them in a cheesecloth or nylon grain bag.

3. In a brew kettle, bring at least 3 US gal (11 L) brewing water to steeping temperature (150 to 160°F/65 to 71°C). Turn off the heat, add the grain bag, cover and steep for 30 minutes. (If the temperature drops below steeping temperature, turn the element back on briefly to bring it back up.) Remove grain bag and discard.

4. Increase the heat and bring grain tea to a boil. Remove from heat, add half (4 lbs/1.8 kg) of the malt extract and stir until dissolved completely.

5. Return kettle to the burner and increase the heat until the wort begins to boil. Using a spoon, clear any foam to one side. Reduce the heat until a rolling boil can be maintained without foam buildup.

6. Add the bittering hops, stirring to combine. Boil for 45 minutes, uncovered. Monitor to prevent boiling over.

7. Meanwhile, prepare the fermentation gear and cooling bath or wort chiller.

8. After 45 minutes, remove the kettle from the heat and add the remaining half (4 lbs/1.8 kg) of the malt extract, Irish moss and yeast nutrient. Stir to ensure that the extract and nutrient are dissolved. Return the kettle to the burner and bring back to a rolling boil. Boil for 15 minutes, then stir in the aroma hops, turn off the heat and cover.

9. To cool the brew, place the covered kettle in the prepared cooling tub or use a wort chiller according to the manufacturer's directions. Cool to the desired temperature, 75°F (24°C), within 30 to 45 minutes.

10. While the wort is cooling, clean and sanitize the brewing spoon. When the wort has cooled, move the kettle to a counter and stir it briskly in one direction for about 5 minutes. After stirring, cover and let rest for 10 to 15 minutes as the hops and trub form a cone.

11. Using a racking cane and siphon, rack as much wort as possible into the sanitized primary fermenter. Using the sanitized funnel and straining screen, strain the rest of the wort into the fermenter. Top off with brewing water to bring the volume to around 5.5 US gal (21 L). Using the hydrometer, take a reading of the specific gravity and record it in your brewing journal.

12. Add the yeast; vigorously stir it with a sanitized spoon to distribute it throughout the wort. Seal the fermenter with lid, stopper and airlock. Keep the fermenter at room temperature (68 to 72°F/20 to 22°C) until fermentation begins (bubbles will be moving through the airlock). (Keep it in a dark place or under a lightproof cover if using a glass carboy.) Once fermentation begins, drop the temperature to 46 to 55°F (8 to 13°C) for one week of primary fermentation.

13. Gently rack the beer into the secondary fermenter to avoid aerating it, leaving as much of the sediment behind as possible. Seal and drop the temperature to 35 to 45°F (2 to 7°C); keep it at that temperature, covered or in a dark place, to allow fermentation to continue for 4 weeks.

14. Once the bubbling in the airlock has slowed, confirm completion of fermentation by using the hydrometer to take final gravity readings. (Hydrometer readings should be the same for several days in a row.)

15. Prime and bottle the beer (see page 91). Store it in the refrigerator to condition for 3 to 4 weeks or longer.

Brewer's Tips

For information on preparing a yeast starter, see page 89.

Some brewers like to dry hop their Pilsner beer for additional aroma. Although not traditional, you could dry hop with .5 to 1.5 oz (14 to 42 g) of Saaz or any other Noble Hop.

Northern European Pils

Estimated Original Gravity: 1.053

Equipment

- **brew kettle**
- **fermentation gear (page 14)**

As you build your brewing skills, switching to liquid yeast products (from Wyeast or White Labs) will give you a brew that is more complex than the ones made with the dry yeast (from Fermentis or Danstar) in the Absolute Beginner recipes.

See page 86 for more information about liquid yeasts. See page 89 for information on preparing a yeast starter.

Yeast

2 packs	Wyeast 2206 or White Labs WLP838 (or 1 pack in starter) or Fermentis S-23	2 packs

Grains

1 lb	Carafoam®, Carapils® or dextrin malt	450 g
5.5 US gal	brewing water (page 89)	21 L

Malt Extract

6.6 lbs	any brand extra-light, divided in half	3 kg

Bittering Hops

8 to 10 AAUs	Northern Brewer or Perle	8 to 10 AAUs

Later Additions

1 tsp	Irish moss	5 mL
1 tsp	yeast nutrient	5 mL

Aroma Hops

1 oz	any German Noble Hops	28 g

1. Prepare the liquid yeast in advance, according to the package directions (if using).
2. Coarsely crack the malt grains and place them in a cheesecloth or nylon grain bag.
3. In a brew kettle, bring at least 3 US gal (11 L) brewing water to steeping temperature (150 to 160°F/65 to 71°C). Turn off the heat, add the grain bag, cover and steep for 30 minutes. (If the temperature drops below steeping temperature, turn the element back on briefly to bring it back up.) Remove grain bag and discard.
4. Increase the heat and bring grain tea to a boil. Remove from heat, add half (3.3 lbs/1.5 kg) of the malt extract and stir until dissolved completely.
5. Return kettle to the burner and increase the heat until the wort begins to boil. Using a spoon, clear any foam to one side. Reduce the heat until a rolling boil can be maintained without foam buildup.
6. Add the bittering hops, stirring to combine. Boil for 45 minutes, uncovered. Monitor to prevent boiling over.
7. Meanwhile, prepare the fermentation gear and cooling bath or wort chiller.

8. After 45 minutes, remove the kettle from the heat and add the remaining half (3.3 lbs/1.5 kg) of the malt extract, Irish moss and yeast nutrient. Stir to ensure that the extract and nutrient are dissolved. Return the kettle to the burner and bring back to a rolling boil. Boil for 15 minutes, then stir in the aroma hops, turn off the heat and cover.

9. To cool the brew, place the covered kettle in the prepared cooling tub or use a wort chiller according to the manufacturer's directions. Cool to the desired temperature, 75°F (24°C), within 30 to 45 minutes.

10. While the wort is cooling, clean and sanitize the brewing spoon. When the wort has cooled, move the kettle to a counter and stir it briskly in one direction for about 5 minutes. After stirring, cover and let rest for 10 to 15 minutes as the hops and trub form a cone.

11. Using a racking cane and siphon, rack as much wort as possible into the sanitized primary fermenter. Using the sanitized funnel and straining screen, strain the rest of the wort into the fermenter. Top off with brewing water to bring the volume to around 5.5 US gal (21 L). Using the hydrometer, take a reading of the specific gravity and record it in your brewing journal.

12. Add the yeast; vigorously stir it with a sanitized spoon to distribute it throughout the wort. Seal the fermenter with lid, stopper and airlock. Keep the fermenter at room temperature (68 to 72°F/20 to 22°C) until fermentation begins (bubbles will be moving through the airlock). (Keep it in a dark place or under a lightproof cover if using a glass carboy.) Once fermentation begins, drop the temperature to 46 to 55°F (8 to 13°C) for one week of primary fermentation.

13. Gently rack the beer into the secondary fermenter to avoid aerating it, leaving as much of the sediment behind as possible. Seal and drop the temperature to 35 to 45°F (2 to 7°C); keep it at that temperature, covered or in a dark place, to allow fermentation to continue for 4 weeks.

14. Once the bubbling in the airlock has slowed, confirm completion of fermentation by using the hydrometer to take final gravity readings. (Hydrometer readings should be the same for several days in a row.)

15. Prime and bottle the beer (see page 91). Store it in the refrigerator to condition for 3 to 4 weeks or longer.

Noble Hops

Noble Hops is a term used to describe the aroma hops popular in Europe. Typically they have an alpha acid below 5% and exhibit pleasant aromas. The pungent Czech grown Saaz is the classic hop for Pilsner. German hops grown in the Hallertau (soft and floral) and Tettnang (woody and spicy) regions are also part of this group, which includes a number of others.

Munich Helles

The German or Northern European approach to lagers is a little more restrained. The presentation of German beers begins by featuring the world-famous cold-fermented lager beers. The Munich Helles is the classic light lager of the Bavarian capital. It's more about malt and balance than hops.

Estimated Original Gravity: 1.048

Equipment

- **brew kettle**
- **fermentation gear (page 14)**

As you build your brewing skills, switching to liquid yeast products (from Wyeast or White Labs) will give you a brew that is more complex than the ones made with the dry yeast (from Fermentis or Danstar) in the Absolute Beginner recipes.

See page 86 for more information about liquid yeasts. See page 89 for information on preparing a yeast starter.

Yeast
2 packs	Wyeast 2206 or White Labs WLP838 (or 1 pack in starter) or Fermentis S-23	2 packs

Grains
1 lb	Carafoam®, Carapils® or dextrin malt	450 g
8 oz	Vienna malt	224 g
5.5 US gal	brewing water (page 89)	21 L

Malt Extract
5.4 lbs	Alexander's Sun Country Pale, divided ¼:¾	2.5 kg

Bittering Hops
4 to 6 AAUs	Tettnang, Spalt or other German Noble Hops	4 to 6 AAUs

Flavor and Aroma Hops
1 oz	Tettnang, Spalt or other German Noble Hops, divided in half	28 g

Later Additions
1 tsp	Irish moss	5 mL
1 tsp	yeast nutrient	5 mL

1. Prepare the liquid yeast in advance, according to the package directions (if using).
2. Coarsely crack the malt grains and place them in a cheesecloth or nylon grain bag.
3. In a brew kettle, bring at least 3 US gal (11 L) brewing water to steeping temperature (150 to 160°F/65 to 71°C). Turn off the heat, add the grain bag, cover and steep for 30 minutes. (If the temperature drops below steeping temperature, turn the element back on briefly to bring it back up.) Remove grain bag and discard.
4. Increase the heat and bring grain tea to a boil. Remove from heat, add 1.4 lbs (635 g) of the malt extract and stir until dissolved completely.
5. Return kettle to the burner and increase the heat until the wort begins to boil. Using a spoon, clear any foam to one side. Reduce the heat until a rolling boil can be maintained without foam buildup.
6. Add the bittering hops, stirring to combine. Boil for 45 minutes, uncovered. Monitor to prevent boiling over.
7. Meanwhile, prepare the fermentation gear and cooling bath or wort chiller.

8. After 45 minutes, remove the kettle from the heat and add the remaining 4 lbs (1.8 kg) of the malt extract, .5 oz (14 g) flavor hops, Irish moss and yeast nutrient. Stir to ensure that the extract and nutrient are dissolved. Return the kettle to the burner and bring back to a rolling boil. Boil for 15 minutes, then stir in the remaining .5 oz (14 g) as aroma hops, turn off the heat and cover.

9. To cool the brew, place the covered kettle in the prepared cooling tub or use a wort chiller according to the manufacturer's directions. Cool to the desired temperature, 75°F (24°C), within 30 to 45 minutes.

10. While the wort is cooling, clean and sanitize the brewing spoon. When the wort has cooled, move the kettle to a counter and stir it briskly in one direction for about 5 minutes. After stirring, cover and let rest for 10 to 15 minutes as the hops and trub form a cone.

11. Using a racking cane and siphon, rack as much wort as possible into the sanitized primary fermenter. Using the sanitized funnel and straining screen, strain the rest of the wort into the fermenter. Top off with brewing water to bring the volume to around 5.5 US gal (21 L). Using the hydrometer, take a reading of the specific gravity and record it in your brewing journal.

12. Add the yeast; vigorously stir it with a sanitized spoon to distribute it throughout the wort. Seal the fermenter with lid, stopper and airlock. Keep the fermenter at room temperature (68 to 72°F/20 to 22°C) until fermentation begins (bubbles will be moving through the airlock). (Keep it in a dark place or under a lightproof cover if using a glass carboy.) Once fermentation begins, drop the temperature to 46 to 55°F (8 to 13°C) for one week of primary fermentation.

13. Gently rack the beer into the secondary fermenter to avoid aerating it, leaving as much of the sediment behind as possible. Seal and drop the temperature to 35 to 45°F (2 to 7°C); keep it at that temperature, covered or in a dark place, to allow fermentation to continue for 4 weeks.

14. Once the bubbling in the airlock has slowed, confirm completion of fermentation by using the hydrometer to take final gravity readings. (Hydrometer readings should be the same for several days in a row.)

15. Prime and bottle the beer (see page 91). Store it in the refrigerator to condition for 3 to 4 weeks or longer.

Dortmund Export

The more robust lagers of Dortmund were the first to be shipped to other towns. Hence, it became known as Export.

Estimated Original Gravity: 1.056

Equipment

- **brew kettle**
- **fermentation gear (page 14)**

As you build your brewing skills, switching to liquid yeast products (from Wyeast or White Labs) will give you a brew that is more complex than the ones made with the dry yeast (from Fermentis or Danstar) in the Absolute Beginner recipes.

See page 86 for more information about liquid yeasts. See page 89 for information on preparing a yeast starter.

Yeast

2 packs	Wyeast 2206 or White Labs WLP838 (or 1 pack in starter) or Fermentis S-23	2 packs

Grains

1 lb	Vienna malt	450 g
8 oz	Caravienne® malt	224 g
5.5 US gal	brewing water (page 89)	21 L

Malt Extract

6.6 lbs	any brand extra-light, divided in half	3 kg

Bittering Hops

6 to 8 AAUs	Northern Brewer or Perle	6 to 8 AAUs

Flavor and Aroma Hops

1 oz	Tettnang, Spalt or other German Noble hops, divided in half	28 g

Later Additions

1 tsp	Irish moss	5 mL
1 tsp	yeast nutrient	5 mL

1. Prepare the liquid yeast in advance, according to the package directions (if using).
2. Coarsely crack the malt grains and place them in a cheesecloth or nylon grain bag.
3. In a brew kettle, bring at least 3 US gal (11 L) brewing water to steeping temperature (150 to 160°F/65 to 71°C). Turn off the heat, add the grain bag, cover and steep for 30 minutes. (If the temperature drops below steeping temperature, turn the element back on briefly to bring it back up.) Remove grain bag and discard.
4. Increase the heat and bring grain tea to a boil. Remove from heat, add half (3.3 lbs/1.5 kg) of the malt extract and stir until dissolved completely.
5. Return kettle to the burner and increase the heat until the wort begins to boil. Using a spoon, clear any foam to one side. Reduce the heat until a rolling boil can be maintained without foam buildup.
6. Add the bittering hops, stirring to combine. Boil for 45 minutes, uncovered. Monitor to prevent boiling over.
7. Meanwhile, prepare the fermentation gear and cooling bath or wort chiller.

8. After 45 minutes, remove the kettle from the heat and add the remaining 3.3 lbs (1.5 kg) of the malt extract, .5 oz (14 g) of the hops for flavor, Irish moss and yeast nutrient. Stir to ensure that the extract and nutrient are dissolved. Return the kettle to the burner and bring back to a rolling boil. Boil for 15 minutes, then stir in the remaining .5 oz (14 g) of the hops for aroma, turn off the heat and cover.

9. To cool the brew, place the covered kettle in the prepared cooling tub or use a wort chiller according to the manufacturer's directions. Cool to the desired temperature, 75°F (24°C), within 30 to 45 minutes.

10. While the wort is cooling, clean and sanitize the brewing spoon. When the wort has cooled, move the kettle to a counter and stir it briskly in one direction for about 5 minutes. After stirring, cover and let rest for 10 to 15 minutes as the hops and trub form a cone.

11. Using a racking cane and siphon, rack as much wort as possible into the sanitized primary fermenter. Using the sanitized funnel and straining screen, strain the rest of the wort into the fermenter. Top off with brewing water to bring the volume to around 5.5 US gal (21 L). Using the hydrometer, take a reading of the specific gravity and record it in your brewing journal.

12. Add the yeast; vigorously stir it with a sanitized spoon to distribute it throughout the wort. Seal the fermenter with lid, stopper and airlock. Keep the fermenter at room temperature (68 to 72°F/20 to 22°C) until fermentation begins (bubbles will be moving through the airlock). (Keep it in a dark place or under a lightproof cover if using a glass carboy.) Once fermentation begins, drop the temperature to 46 to 55°F (8 to 13°C) for one week of primary fermentation.

13. Gently rack the beer into the secondary fermenter to avoid aerating it, leaving as much of the sediment behind as possible. Seal and drop the temperature to 35 to 45°F (2 to 7°C); keep it at that temperature, covered or in a dark place, to allow fermentation to continue for 4 weeks.

14. Once the bubbling in the airlock has slowed, confirm completion of fermentation by using the hydrometer to take final gravity readings. (Hydrometer readings should be the same for several days in a row.)

15. Prime and bottle the beer (see page 91). Store it in the refrigerator to condition for 3 to 4 weeks or longer.

Munich Dunkel

This is the classic, easy-drinking dark lager of Bavaria. If you want a bigger, dark beer, look ahead to the bock and dopplebock recipes.

Estimated Original Gravity: 1.050

Equipment

- **brew kettle**
- **fermentation gear (page 14)**

As you build your brewing skills, switching to liquid yeast products (from Wyeast or White Labs) will give you a brew that is more complex than the ones made with the dry yeast (from Fermentis or Danstar) in the Absolute Beginner recipes.

See page 86 for more information about liquid yeasts. See page 89 for information on preparing a yeast starter.

Yeast

2 packs	Wyeast 2206 or White Labs WLP838 (or 1 pack in starter) or Fermentis S-23	2 packs

Grains

1 lb	Melanoidin® malt	450 g
1 lb	Caramunich III® malt	450 g
4 oz	dehusked Carafa I® malt	112 g
5.5 US gal	brewing water (page 89)	21 L

Malt Extract

5.4 lbs	Alexander's Sun Country Pale	2.5 kg

Bittering Hops

4 to 6 AAUs	Tettnang, Spalt or other German Noble Hops	4 to 6 AAUs

Flavor and Aroma Hops

1 oz	Tettnang, Spalt or other German Noble Hops, divided in half	28 g

Later Additions

1 tsp	Irish moss	5 mL
1 tsp	yeast nutrient	5 mL

1. Prepare the liquid yeast in advance, according to the package directions (if using).
2. Coarsely crack the malt grains and place them in a cheesecloth or nylon grain bag.
3. In a brew kettle, bring at least 3 US gal (11 L) brewing water to steeping temperature (150 to 160°F/65 to 71°C). Turn off the heat, add the grain bag, cover and steep for 30 minutes. (If the temperature drops below steeping temperature, turn the element back on briefly to bring it back up.) Remove grain bag and discard.
4. Increase the heat and bring grain tea to a boil. Remove from heat, add the malt extract and stir until dissolved completely.
5. Return kettle to the burner and increase the heat until the wort begins to boil. Using a spoon, clear any foam to one side. Reduce the heat until a rolling boil can be maintained without foam buildup.
6. Add the bittering hops, stirring to combine. Boil for 45 minutes, uncovered. Monitor to prevent boiling over.
7. Meanwhile, prepare the fermentation gear and cooling bath or wort chiller.

8. After 45 minutes, remove the kettle from the heat and add .5 oz (14 g) hops for flavor, Irish moss and yeast nutrient. Stir to ensure that the nutrient has dissolved. Return the kettle to the burner and bring back to a rolling boil. Boil for 15 minutes, then stir in the remaining .5 oz (14 g) of hops for aroma, turn off the heat and cover.

9. To cool the brew, place the covered kettle in the prepared cooling tub or use a wort chiller according to the manufacturer's directions. Cool to the desired temperature, 75°F (24°C), within 30 to 45 minutes.

10. While the wort is cooling, clean and sanitize the brewing spoon. When the wort has cooled, move the kettle to a counter and stir it briskly in one direction for about 5 minutes. After stirring, cover and let rest for 10 to 15 minutes as the hops and trub form a cone.

11. Using a racking cane and siphon, rack as much wort as possible into the sanitized primary fermenter. Using the sanitized funnel and straining screen, strain the rest of the wort into the fermenter. Top off with brewing water to bring the volume to around 5.5 US gal (21 L). Using the hydrometer, take a reading of the specific gravity and record it in your brewing journal.

12. Add the yeast; vigorously stir it with a sanitized spoon to distribute it throughout the wort. Seal the fermenter with lid, stopper and airlock. Keep the fermenter at room temperature (68 to 72°F/20 to 22°C) until fermentation begins (bubbles will be moving through the airlock). (Keep it in a dark place or under a lightproof cover if using a glass carboy.) Once fermentation begins, drop the temperature to 46 to 55°F (8 to 13°C) for one week of primary fermentation.

13. Gently rack the beer into the secondary fermenter to avoid aerating it, leaving as much of the sediment behind as possible. Seal and drop the temperature to 35 to 45°F (2 to 7°C); keep it at that temperature, covered or in a dark place, to allow fermentation to continue for 4 weeks.

14. Once the bubbling in the airlock has slowed, confirm completion of fermentation by using the hydrometer to take final gravity readings. (Hydrometer readings should be the same for several days in a row.)

15. Prime and bottle the beer (see page 91). Store it in the refrigerator to condition for 3 to 4 weeks or longer.

Brewer's Tips

If the specified brands of grains are not available, use the grains chart on page 77 to find substitutes.

Schwartzbier

This black lager is considered by many to be the porter of Germany. The flavor is fuller than a Munich Dunkel but not as heavy as the bock beers that follow.

Estimated Original Gravity: 1.070

Equipment

- **brew kettle**
- **fermentation gear (page 14)**
- **blow-off hose (page 16)**

Beers with an estimated original gravity higher than 1.065 require a longer time in both primary and secondary fermentation. Primary fermentation should take up to 10 days, and secondary fermentation should take about 2 weeks longer than weaker brews.

Yeast

2 packs	Wyeast 2206 or White Labs WLP838 (or 1 pack in starter) or Fermentis S-23	2 packs

Grains

1 lb	Caramunich III® malt	450 g
8 oz	Melanoidin® malt	224 g
8 oz	dehusked Carafa I® malt	224 g
5.5 US gal	brewing water (page 89)	21 L

Malt Extract

6.6 lbs	any brand light	3 kg

Bittering Hops

6 to 8 AAUs	Northern Brewer or Perle	6 to 8 AAUs

Flavor and Aroma Hops

2 oz	Tettnang, Spalt or other German Noble Hops, divided in half	56 g

Later Additions

1 tsp	Irish moss	5 mL
1 tsp	yeast nutrient	5 mL

1. Prepare the liquid yeast in advance, according to the package directions (if using).
2. Coarsely crack the malt grains and place them in a cheesecloth or nylon grain bag.
3. In a brew kettle, bring at least 3 US gal (11 L) brewing water to steeping temperature (150 to 160°F/65 to 71°C). Turn off the heat, add the grain bag, cover and steep for 30 minutes. (If the temperature drops below steeping temperature, turn the element back on briefly to bring it back up.) Remove grain bag and discard.
4. Increase the heat and bring grain tea to a boil. Remove from heat, add the malt extract and stir until dissolved completely.
5. Return kettle to the burner and increase the heat until the wort begins to boil. Using a spoon, clear any foam to one side. Reduce the heat until a rolling boil can be maintained without foam buildup.
6. Add the bittering hops, stirring to combine. Boil for 45 minutes, uncovered. Monitor to prevent boiling over.
7. Meanwhile, prepare the fermentation gear and cooling bath or wort chiller.

8. After 45 minutes, remove the kettle from the heat and add 1 oz (28 g) hops for flavor, Irish moss, and yeast nutrient. Stir to ensure that the nutrient has dissolved. Return the kettle to the burner and bring back to a rolling boil. Boil for 15 minutes, then stir in the remaining 1 oz (28 g) hops for aroma, turn off the heat and cover.

9. To cool the brew, place the covered kettle in the prepared cooling tub or use a wort chiller according to the manufacturer's directions. Cool to the desired temperature, 75°F (24°C), within 30 to 45 minutes.

10. While the wort is cooling, clean and sanitize the brewing spoon. When the wort has cooled, move the kettle to a counter and stir it briskly in one direction for about 5 minutes. After stirring, cover and let rest for 10 to 15 minutes as the hops and trub form a cone.

11. Using a racking cane and siphon, rack as much wort as possible into the sanitized primary fermenter. Using the sanitized funnel and straining screen, strain the rest of the wort into the fermenter. Top off with brewing water to bring the volume to around 5.5 US gal (21 L). Using the hydrometer, take a reading of the specific gravity and record it in your brewing journal.

12. Add the yeast; vigorously stir it with a sanitized spoon to distribute it throughout the wort. Seal the fermenter with lid, stopper and airlock or blow-off hose. Keep the fermenter at room temperature (68 to 72°F/20 to 22°C) until fermentation begins (bubbles will be moving through the airlock). (Keep it in a dark place or under a lightproof cover if using a glass carboy.) Once fermentation begins, drop the temperature to 46 to 55°F (8 to 13°C) for up to 2 weeks of primary fermentation.

13. Gently rack the beer into the secondary fermenter to avoid aerating it, leaving as much of the sediment behind as possible. Seal and drop the temperature to 35 to 45°F (2 to 7°C); keep it at that temperature, covered or in a dark place, to allow fermentation to continue for 6 to 8 weeks.

14. Once the bubbling in the airlock has slowed, confirm completion of fermentation by using the hydrometer to take final gravity readings. (Hydrometer readings should be the same for several days in a row.)

15. Prime and bottle the beer (see page 91). Store it in the refrigerator to condition for 3 to 4 weeks or longer.

> **Brewer's Tips**
>
> For information on preparing a yeast starter, see page 89.
>
> If the specified brands of grains are not available, use the grains chart on page 77 to find substitutes.

Bock

German bock beers are so notorious they are sometimes the subject of urban legend. If you sit at a bar and drink dark beer, some bar-stool expert will tell you that bock beer is made once a year from the lees at the bottom of the brewer's tanks. This is simply not true. Any brewer who only cleaned his tanks once a year would have been closed before that year was out! Brewers (and homebrewers) clean and sanitize their tanks before and after each use!

Estimated Original Gravity: 1.064

Equipment

- **brew kettle**
- **fermentation gear (page 14)**
- **blow-off hose (page 16)**

Yeast

| 2 packs | Wyeast 2206 or White Labs WLP833 (or 1 pack in starter) or Fermentis S-23 | 2 packs |

Grains

1 lb	Carabohemian® malt	450 g
1 lb	Caraaroma® malt	450 g
5.5 US gal	brewing water (page 89)	21 L

Malt Extracts

| 6.6 lbs | any brand amber | 3 kg |
| 1 lb | light DME | 450 g |

Bittering Hops

| 6 to 8 AAUs | Northern Brewer or Perle | 6 to 8 AAUs |

Flavor and Aroma Hops

| 1 oz | Tettnang, Spalt or other German Noble Hops, divided in half | 28 g |

Later Additions

| 1 tsp | Irish moss | 5 mL |
| 1 tsp | yeast nutrient | 5 mL |

1. Prepare the liquid yeast in advance, according to the package directions (if using).
2. Coarsely crack the malt grains and place them in a cheesecloth or nylon grain bag.
3. In a brew kettle, bring at least 3 US gal (11 L) brewing water to steeping temperature (150 to 160°F/65 to 71°C). Turn off the heat, add the grain bag, cover and steep for 30 minutes. (If the temperature drops below steeping temperature, turn the element back on briefly to bring it back up.) Remove grain bag and discard.
4. Increase the heat and bring grain tea to a boil. Remove from heat, add the malt extract and stir until dissolved completely.
5. Return kettle to the burner and increase the heat until the wort begins to boil. Using a spoon, clear any foam to one side. Reduce the heat until a rolling boil can be maintained without foam buildup.
6. Add the bittering hops, stirring to combine. Boil for 45 minutes, uncovered. Monitor to prevent boiling over.
7. Meanwhile, prepare the fermentation gear and cooling bath or wort chiller.

8. After 45 minutes, remove the kettle from the heat and add .5 oz (14 g) hops for flavor, Irish moss, and yeast nutrient. Stir to ensure that the nutrient has dissolved. Return the kettle to the burner and bring back to a rolling boil. Boil for 15 minutes, then stir in the remaining .5 oz (14 g) of the hops for aroma, turn off the heat and cover.

9. To cool the brew, place the covered kettle in the prepared cooling tub or use a wort chiller according to the manufacturer's directions. Cool to the desired temperature, 75°F (24°C), within 30 to 45 minutes.

10. While the wort is cooling, clean and sanitize the brewing spoon. When the wort has cooled, move the kettle to a counter and stir it briskly in one direction for about 5 minutes. After stirring, cover and let rest for 10 to 15 minutes as the hops and trub form a cone.

11. Using a racking cane and siphon, rack as much wort as possible into the sanitized primary fermenter. Using the sanitized funnel and straining screen, strain the rest of the wort into the fermenter. Top off with brewing water to bring the volume to around 5.5 US gal (21 L). Using the hydrometer, take a reading of the specific gravity and record it in your brewing journal.

12. Add the yeast; vigorously stir it with a sanitized spoon to distribute it throughout the wort. Seal the fermenter with lid, stopper and airlock or blow-off hose. Keep the fermenter at room temperature (68 to 72°F/20 to 22°C) until fermentation begins (bubbles will be moving through the airlock). (Keep it in a dark place or under a lightproof cover if using a glass carboy.) Once fermentation begins, drop the temperature to 46 to 55°F (8 to 13°C) for up to 2 weeks of primary fermentation.

13. Gently rack the beer into the secondary fermenter to avoid aerating it, leaving as much of the sediment behind as possible. Seal and drop the temperature to 35 to 45°F (2 to 7°C); keep it at that temperature, covered or in a dark place, to allow fermentation to continue for about 6 to 8 weeks.

14. Once the bubbling in the airlock has slowed, confirm completion of fermentation by using the hydrometer to take final gravity readings. (Hydrometer readings should be the same for several days in a row.)

15. Prime and bottle the beer (see page 91). Store it in the refrigerator to condition for 3 to 4 weeks or longer.

Brewer's Tips

For information on preparing a yeast starter, see page 89.

If the specified brands of grains are not available, use the grains chart on page 77 to find substitutes.

If active fermentation backs up into the airlock, replace airlock with blow-off hose (see page 16). Change water as needed; re-install airlock when fermentation settles down.

Maibock

This is the blonde member of the bock family

Estimated Original Gravity: 1.070

Equipment

- **brew kettle**
- **fermentation gear (page 14)**
- **blow-off hose (page 16)**

Beers with an estimated original gravity higher than 1.065 require a longer time in both primary and secondary fermentation. Primary fermentation should take 7 to 10 days, and secondary fermentation should take about 2 weeks longer than weaker brews.

Yeast

2 packs	Wyeast 2206 or White Labs WLP833 (or 1 pack in starter) or Fermentis S-23	2 packs

Grains

1 lb	Carafoam® malt	450 g
1 lb	Vienna malt	450 g
1 lb	Carahell® malt	450 g
5.5 US gal	brewing water (page 89)	21 L

Malt Extract

9.4 lbs	Alexander Sun Country Pale, divided 1.4 lbs (635 g):8 lbs (3.62 kg)	4.25 kg

Bittering Hops

8 to 10 AAUs	Northern Brewer or Perle	8 to 10 AAUs

Flavor and Aroma Hops

1 oz	Tettnang, Spalt or other German Noble Hops, divided in half	28 g

Later Additions

1 tsp	Irish moss	5 mL
1 tsp	yeast nutrient	5 mL

1. Prepare the liquid yeast in advance, according to the package directions (if using).
2. Coarsely crack the malt grains and place them in a cheesecloth or nylon grain bag.
3. In a brew kettle, bring at least 3 US gal (11 L) brewing water to steeping temperature (150 to 160°F/65 to 71°C). Turn off the heat, add the grain bag, cover and steep for 30 minutes. (If the temperature drops below steeping temperature, turn the element back on briefly to bring it back up.) Remove grain bag and discard.
4. Increase the heat and bring grain tea to a boil. Remove from heat, add 1.4 lbs (635 g) of the malt extract and stir until dissolved completely.
5. Return kettle to the burner and increase the heat until the wort begins to boil. Using a spoon, clear any foam to one side. Reduce the heat until a rolling boil can be maintained without foam buildup.
6. Add the bittering hops, stirring to combine. Boil for 45 minutes, uncovered. Monitor to prevent boiling over.
7. Meanwhile, prepare the fermentation gear and cooling bath or wort chiller.

8. After 45 minutes, remove the kettle from the heat and add the remaining 8 lbs (3.62 kg) of malt extract, .5 oz (14 g) hops for flavor, Irish moss, and yeast nutrient. Stir to ensure that the extract and nutrient are dissolved. Return the kettle to the burner and bring back to a rolling boil. Boil for 15 minutes, then stir in the remaining .5 oz (14 g) hops for aroma, turn off the heat and cover.

9. To cool the brew, place the covered kettle in the prepared cooling tub or use a wort chiller according to the manufacturer's directions. Cool to the desired temperature, 75°F (24°C), within 30 to 45 minutes.

10. While the wort is cooling, clean and sanitize the brewing spoon. When the wort has cooled, move the kettle to a counter and stir it briskly in one direction for about 5 minutes. After stirring, cover and let rest for 10 to 15 minutes as the hops and trub form a cone.

11. Using a racking cane and siphon, rack as much wort as possible into the sanitized primary fermenter. Using the sanitized funnel and straining screen, strain the rest of the wort into the fermenter. Top off with brewing water to bring the volume to around 5.5 US gal (21 L). Using the hydrometer, take a reading of the specific gravity and record it in your brewing journal.

12. Add the yeast; vigorously stir it with a sanitized spoon to distribute it throughout the wort. Seal the fermenter with lid, stopper and airlock or blow-off hose. Keep the fermenter at room temperature (68 to 72°F/20 to 22°C) until fermentation begins (bubbles will be moving through the airlock). (Keep it in a dark place or under a lightproof cover if using a glass carboy.) Once fermentation begins, drop the temperature to 46 to 55°F (8 to 13°C) for up to 2 weeks of primary fermentation.

13. Gently rack the beer into the secondary fermenter to avoid aerating it, leaving as much of the sediment behind as possible. Seal and drop the temperature to 35 to 45°F (2 to 7°C); keep it at that temperature, covered or in a dark place, to allow fermentation to continue for 6 to 8 weeks.

14. Once the bubbling in the airlock has slowed, confirm completion of fermentation by using the hydrometer to take final gravity readings. (Hydrometer readings should be the same for several days in a row.)

15. Prime and bottle the beer (see page 91). Store it in the refrigerator to condition for 3 to 4 weeks or longer.

Brewer's Tips

For information on preparing a yeast starter, see page 89.

If the specified brands of grains are not available, use the grains chart on page 77 to find substitutes.

If active fermentation backs up into the airlock, replace airlock with blow-off hose (see page 16). Change water as needed; re-install airlock when fermentation settles down.

Dopplebock

This brew is the "Big Daddy" of the bock family!

Estimated Original Gravity: 1.079

Equipment

- **brew kettle**
- **fermentation gear (page 14)**
- **blow-off hose (page 16)**

Beers with an estimated original gravity higher than 1.065 require a longer time in both primary and secondary fermentation. Primary fermentation should take 7 to 10 days, and secondary fermentation should take about 2 weeks longer than weaker brews.

Yeast

| 2 packs | Wyeast 2206 or White Labs WLP833 (or 1 pack in starter) or Fermentis S-23 | 2 packs |

Grains

1 lb	Carabohemian® malt	450 g
1 lb	Caraaroma® malt	450 g
5.5 US gal	brewing water (page 89)	21 L

Malt Extract

| 9.9 lbs | any brand light | 4.5 kg |

Bittering Hops

| 6 to 8 AAUs | Northern Brewer or Perle | 6 to 8 AAUs |

Flavor and Aroma Hops

| 1 oz | Tettnang, Spalt or other German Noble Hops, divided in half | 28 g |

Later Additions

| 1 tsp | Irish moss | 5 mL |
| 1 tsp | yeast nutrient | 5 mL |

1. Prepare the liquid yeast in advance, according to the package directions (if using).
2. Coarsely crack the malt grains and place them in a cheesecloth or nylon grain bag.
3. In a brew kettle, bring at least 3 US gal (11 L) brewing water to steeping temperature (150 to 160°F/65 to 71°C). Turn off the heat, add the grain bag, cover and steep for 30 minutes. (If the temperature drops below steeping temperature, turn the element back on briefly to bring it back up.) Remove grain bag and discard.
4. Increase the heat and bring grain tea to a boil. Remove from heat, add the malt extract and stir until dissolved completely.
5. Return kettle to the burner and increase the heat until the wort begins to boil. Using a spoon, clear any foam to one side. Reduce the heat until a rolling boil can be maintained without foam buildup.
6. Add the bittering hops, stirring to combine. Boil for 45 minutes, uncovered. Monitor to prevent boiling over.
7. Meanwhile, prepare the fermentation gear and cooling bath or wort chiller.

8. After 45 minutes, remove the kettle from the heat and add .5 oz (14 g) of the hops for flavor, Irish moss, and yeast nutrient. Stir to ensure that the nutrient has dissolved. Return the kettle to the burner and bring back to a rolling boil. Boil for 15 minutes, then stir in the remaining .5 oz (14 g) of hops for aroma, turn off the heat and cover.

9. To cool the brew, place the covered kettle in the prepared cooling tub or use a wort chiller according to the manufacturer's directions. Cool to the desired temperature, 75°F (24°C), within 30 to 45 minutes.

10. While the wort is cooling, clean and sanitize the brewing spoon. When the wort has cooled, move the kettle to a counter and stir it briskly in one direction for about 5 minutes. After stirring, cover and let rest for 10 to 15 minutes as the hops and trub form a cone.

11. Using a racking cane and siphon, rack as much wort as possible into the sanitized primary fermenter. Using the sanitized funnel and straining screen, strain the rest of the wort into the fermenter. Top off with brewing water to bring the volume to around 5.5 US gal (21 L). Using the hydrometer, take a reading of the specific gravity and record it in your brewing journal.

12. Add the yeast; vigorously stir it with a sanitized spoon to distribute it throughout the wort. Seal the fermenter with lid, stopper and airlock or blow-off hose. Keep the fermenter at room temperature (68 to 72°F/20 to 22°C) until fermentation begins (bubbles will be moving through the airlock). (Keep it in a dark place or under a lightproof cover if using a glass carboy.) Once fermentation begins, drop the temperature to 46 to 55°F (8 to 13°C) for up to 2 weeks of primary fermentation.

13. Gently rack the beer into the secondary fermenter to avoid aerating it, leaving as much of the sediment behind as possible. Seal and drop the temperature to 35 to 45°F (2 to 7°C); keep it at that temperature, covered or in a dark place, to allow fermentation to continue for 6 to 8 weeks.

14. Once the bubbling in the airlock has slowed, confirm completion of fermentation by using the hydrometer to take final gravity readings. (Hydrometer readings should be the same for several days in a row.)

15. Prime and bottle the beer (see page 91). Store it in the refrigerator to condition for 3 to 4 weeks or longer.

Variation

Schwartz Bock: A new take on the style brings in the toasted notes of the Schwartz style with the added heft of the dopplebock. Add 8 oz (224 g) dehusked Carafa I® to the grain bill. May the Schwartz be with you!

Brewer's Tips

For information on preparing a yeast starter, see page 89.

If the specified brands of grains are not available, use the grains chart on page 77 to find substitutes.

If active fermentation backs up into the airlock, replace airlock with blow-off hose (see page 16). Change water as needed; re-install airlock when fermentation settles down.

Dunkel Weizen

Moving from German lagers to German ales, this is an amber-colored take on the classic wheat ales of Bavaria.

Estimated Original Gravity: 1.056

Equipment

- **brew kettle**
- **fermentation gear (page 14)**
- **blow-off hose (page 16)**

As you build your brewing skills, switching to liquid yeast products (from Wyeast or White Labs) will give you a brew that is more complex than the ones made with the dry yeast (from Fermentis or Danstar) in the Absolute Beginner recipes. See page 86 for more information about liquid yeasts.

Yeast

1 pack	Wyeast 3056 or White Labs WLP351 or Fermentis WB-06	1 pack

Grains

1 lb	Caraamber® malt	450 g
1 lb	Caramunich II® malt	450 g
5.5 US gal	brewing water (page 89)	21 L

Malt Extract

6.6 lbs	wheat/weizen	3 kg

Bittering Hops

4 to 6 AAUs	Tettnang, Spalt or other German Noble Hops	4 to 6 AAUs

Flavor and Aroma Hops

1 oz	Tettnang, Spalt or other German Noble Hops, divided in half	28 g

Later Additions

1 tsp	Irish moss	5 mL
1 tsp	yeast nutrient	5 mL

1. Prepare the liquid yeast in advance, according to the package directions (if using).
2. Coarsely crack the malt grains and place them in a cheesecloth or nylon grain bag.
3. In a brew kettle, bring at least 3 US gal (11 L) brewing water to steeping temperature (150 to 160°F/65 to 71°C). Turn off the heat, add the grain bag, cover and steep for 30 minutes. (If the temperature drops below steeping temperature, turn the element back on briefly to bring it back up.) Remove grain bag and discard.
4. Increase the heat and bring grain tea to a boil. Remove from heat, add the malt extract and stir until dissolved completely.
5. Return kettle to the burner and increase the heat until the wort begins to boil. Using a spoon, clear any foam to one side. Reduce heat until a rolling boil can be maintained without foam buildup.
6. Add the bittering hops, stirring to combine. Boil for 45 minutes, uncovered. Monitor to prevent boiling over.
7. Meanwhile, prepare the fermentation gear and cooling bath or wort chiller.

8. After 45 minutes, remove the kettle from the heat and add .5 oz (14 g) of the hops for flavor, Irish moss and yeast nutrient. Stir to ensure that the nutrient has dissolved. Return the kettle to the burner and bring back to a rolling boil. Boil for 15 minutes, then stir in the remaining .5 oz (14 g) of the hops for aroma, turn off the heat and cover.

9. To cool the brew, place the covered kettle in the prepared cooling tub or use a wort chiller according to the manufacturer's directions. Cool to the desired temperature, 75°F (24°C), within 30 to 45 minutes.

10. While the wort is cooling, clean and sanitize the brewing spoon. When the wort has cooled, move the kettle to a counter and stir the wort briskly in one direction for about 5 minutes. After stirring, cover and let rest for 10 to 15 minutes as the hops and trub form a cone.

11. Using a racking cane and siphon, rack as much wort as possible into the sanitized primary fermenter. Using the sanitized funnel and straining screen, strain the rest of the wort into the fermenter. Top off with brewing water to bring the volume to around 5.5 US gal (21 L). Using the hydrometer, take a reading of the specific gravity and record it in your brewing journal.

12. Add the yeast; vigorously stir it with a sanitized spoon to distribute it throughout the wort. Seal the fermenter with lid, stopper and airlock or blow-off hose. Keep the fermenter at room temperature (68 to 72°F/20 to 22°C) during primary fermentation, which typically lasts 1 to 4 days after fermentation begins. (Keep in a dark place or under a lightproof cover if using a glass carboy.)

13. After 1 to 4 days or when the kräusen has fallen, gently rack the beer into the secondary fermenter to avoid aerating it, leaving as much of the sediment behind as possible. Seal and keep at room temperature, covered or in a dark place, to allow fermentation to continue.

14. Once the bubbling in the airlock has slowed, confirm completion of fermentation by using the hydrometer to take final gravity readings. (Hydrometer readings should be the same for several days in a row.)

15. Prime and bottle the beer (see page 91) and condition it for 3 to 4 weeks.

Brewer's Tips
If the specified brands of grains are not available, use the grains chart on page 77 to find substitutes.

Dusseldorf Altbier

This amber ale is brewed in the town of Dusseldorf. Alt literally means "old." These are the old-style ales of Germany that predate modern lagers. Like a US steam beer, the traits of ale and lager are combined. Cold condition for 30 days after carbonation.

Estimated Original Gravity: 1.058

Equipment

- **brew kettle**
- **fermentation gear (page 14)**

As you build your brewing skills, switching to liquid yeast products (from Wyeast or White Labs) will give you a brew that is more complex than the ones made with the dry yeast (from Fermentis or Danstar) in the Absolute Beginner recipes. See page 86 for more information about liquid yeasts.

Yeast
1 pack	Wyeast1007 or White Labs WLP036 or Fermentis US-56	1 pack

Grains
1 lb	Caraamber® malt	450 g
1 lb	Caramunich I® malt	450 g
5.5 US gal	brewing water (page 89)	21 L

Malt Extracts
3.3 lbs	wheat/weizen	1.5 kg
3.3 lbs	extra-light (late extract addition)	1.5 kg

Bittering Hops
6 to 8 AAUs	Northern Brewer or Perle	6 to 8 AAUs

Flavor and Aroma Hops
2 oz	Tettnang, Spalt or other German Noble Hops, divided in half	56 g

Later Additions
1 tsp	Irish moss	5 mL
1 tsp	yeast nutrient	5 mL

1. Prepare the liquid yeast in advance, according to the package directions (if using).
2. Coarsely crack the malt grains and place them in a cheesecloth or nylon grain bag.
3. In a brew kettle, bring at least 3 US gal (11 L) brewing water to steeping temperature (150 to 160°F/65 to 71°C). Turn off the heat, add the grain bag, cover and steep for 30 minutes. (If the temperature drops below steeping temperature, turn the element back on briefly to bring it back up.) Remove grain bag and discard.
4. Increase the heat and bring grain tea to a boil. Remove from heat, add the wheat malt extract only and stir until dissolved completely.
5. Return kettle to the burner and increase the heat until the wort begins to boil. Using a spoon, clear any foam to one side. Reduce heat until a rolling boil can be maintained without foam buildup.
6. Add the bittering hops, stirring to combine. Boil for 45 minutes, uncovered. Monitor to prevent boiling over.
7. Meanwhile, prepare the fermentation gear and cooling bath or wort chiller.

8. After 45 minutes, remove the kettle from the heat and add the extra-light malt extract, 1 oz (28 g) of the hops for flavor, Irish moss and yeast nutrient. Stir to ensure that the extract, sugar and nutrient are dissolved. Return the kettle to the burner and bring back to a rolling boil. Boil for 15 minutes, then stir in the remaining 1 oz (28 g) of the hops for aroma, turn off the heat and cover.

9. To cool the brew, place the covered kettle in the prepared cooling tub or use a wort chiller according to the manufacturer's directions. Cool to the desired temperature, 75°F (24°C), within 30 to 45 minutes.

10. While the wort is cooling, clean and sanitize the brewing spoon. When the wort has cooled, move the kettle to a counter and stir the wort briskly in one direction for about 5 minutes. After stirring, cover and let rest for 10 to 15 minutes as the hops and trub form a cone.

11. Using a racking cane and siphon, rack as much wort as possible into the sanitized primary fermenter. Using the sanitized funnel and straining screen, strain the rest of the wort into the fermenter. Top off with brewing water to bring the volume to around 5.5 US gal (21 L). Using the hydrometer, take a reading of the specific gravity and record it in your brewing journal.

12. Add the yeast; vigorously stir it with a sanitized spoon to distribute it throughout the wort. Seal the fermenter with lid, stopper and airlock. Keep the fermenter at room temperature (68 to 72°F/20 to 22°C) during primary fermentation, which typically lasts 1 to 4 days after fermentation begins. (Keep in a dark place or under a lightproof cover if using a glass carboy.)

13. After 1 to 4 days or when the kräusen has fallen, gently rack the beer into the secondary fermenter to avoid aerating it, leaving as much of the sediment behind as possible. Seal and keep at room temperature, covered or in a dark place, to allow fermentation to continue.

14. Once the bubbling in the airlock has slowed, confirm completion of fermentation by using the hydrometer to take final gravity readings. (Hydrometer readings should be the same for several days in a row.)

15. Prime and bottle the beer (see page 91) and condition it for 3 to 4 weeks. Once beer is carbonated, cold condition for another 30 days.

> **Brewer's Tips**
>
> If the specified brands of grains are not available, use the grains chart on page 77 to find substitutes.

Sticke Altbier

Altbier brewers occasionally produce a special, stronger version and discreetly offer it to their best customers. The chance to sample these "secret" beers is highly coveted.

Estimated Original Gravity: 1.074

Equipment

- **brew kettle**
- **fermentation gear (page 14)**
- **blow-off hose (page 16)**

Beers with an estimated original gravity higher than 1.065 require a longer time in both primary and secondary fermentation. Primary fermentation should take 7 to 10 days, and secondary fermentation should take about 2 weeks longer than weaker brews.

Yeast

1 pack	Wyeast1007 or White Labs WLP036 or Fermentis US-56	1 pack

Grains

1 lb	dark Munich malt	450 g
1 lb	Caraamber® malt	450 g
1 lb	Caramunich I® malt	450 g
5.5 US gal	brewing water (page 89)	21 L

Malt Extracts

4 lbs	Alexander's Sun Country Wheat	1.8 kg
4 lbs	Alexander's Sun Country Pale (late extract addition)	1.8 kg

Bittering Hops

8 to 10 AAUs	Northern Brewer or Perle	8 to 10 AAUs

Flavor and Aroma Hops

2 oz	Tettnang, Spalt or other German Noble Hops, divided in half	56 g

Later Additions

1 tsp	Irish moss	5 mL
1 tsp	yeast nutrient	5 mL

1. Prepare the liquid yeast in advance, according to the package directions (if using).
2. Coarsely crack the malt grains and place them in a cheesecloth or nylon grain bag.
3. In a brew kettle, bring at least 3 US gal (11 L) brewing water to steeping temperature (150 to 160°F/65 to 71°C). Turn off the heat, add the grain bag, cover and steep for 30 minutes. (If the temperature drops below steeping temperature, turn the element back on briefly to bring it back up.) Remove grain bag and discard.
4. Increase the heat and bring grain tea to a boil. Remove from heat, add the wheat malt extract only and stir until dissolved completely.
5. Return kettle to the burner and increase the heat until the wort begins to boil. Using a spoon, clear any foam to one side. Reduce heat until a rolling boil can be maintained without foam buildup.
6. Add the bittering hops, stirring to combine. Boil for 45 minutes, uncovered. Monitor to prevent boiling over.

7. Meanwhile, prepare the fermentation gear and cooling bath or wort chiller.

8. After 45 minutes, remove the kettle from the heat and add the pale malt extract, 1 oz (28 g) of the hops for flavor, Irish moss and yeast nutrient. Stir to ensure that the extract and nutrient are dissolved. Return the kettle to the burner and bring back to a rolling boil. Boil for 15 minutes, then stir in the remaining 1 oz (28 g) of hops for aroma, turn off the heat and cover.

9. To cool the brew, place the covered kettle in the prepared cooling tub or use a wort chiller according to the manufacturer's directions. Cool to the desired temperature, 75°F (24°C), within 30 to 45 minutes.

10. While the wort is cooling, clean and sanitize the brewing spoon. When the wort has cooled, move the kettle to a counter and stir the wort briskly in one direction for about 5 minutes. After stirring, cover and let rest for 10 to 15 minutes as the hops and trub form a cone.

11. Using a racking cane and siphon, rack as much wort as possible into the sanitized primary fermenter. Using the sanitized funnel and straining screen, strain the rest of the wort into the fermenter. Top off with brewing water to bring the volume to around 5.5 US gal (21 L). Using the hydrometer, take a reading of the specific gravity and record it in your brewing journal.

12. Add the yeast; vigorously stir it with a sanitized spoon to distribute it throughout the wort. Seal the fermenter with lid, stopper and airlock or blow-off hose. Keep the fermenter at room temperature (68 to 72°F/20 to 22°C) during primary fermentation, which typically lasts 7 to 10 days after fermentation begins. (Keep in a dark place or under a lightproof cover if using a glass carboy.)

13. After 7 to 10 days or when the kräusen has fallen, gently rack the beer into the secondary fermenter to avoid aerating it, leaving as much of the sediment behind as possible. Seal and keep at room temperature, covered or in a dark place, to allow fermentation to continue.

14. Once the bubbling in the airlock has slowed, confirm completion of fermentation by using the hydrometer to take final gravity readings. (Hydrometer readings should be the same for several days in a row.)

15. Prime and bottle the beer (see page 91) and condition it for 3 to 4 weeks.

Brewer's Tip

For information on preparing a yeast starter, see page 89.

If the specified brands of grains are not available, use the grains chart on page 77 to find substitutes.

If active fermentation backs up into the airlock, replace airlock with blow-off hose (see page 16). Change water as needed; re-install airlock when fermentation settles down.

Kölsch

The classic blonde ale of the city of Cologne (Köln) is very lager-like. In fact, it's a style that's been adopted by many an "ale-only" brewpub owner who wishes to pour something for lager drinkers.

Estimated Original Gravity: 1.053

Equipment

- **brew kettle**
- **fermentation gear (page 14)**

As you build your brewing skills, switching to liquid yeast products (from Wyeast or White Labs) will give you a brew that is more complex than the ones made with the dry yeast (from Fermentis or Danstar) in the Absolute Beginner recipes. See page 86 for more information about liquid yeasts.

Yeast

1 pack	Wyeast 2565 or White Labs WLP029 or Fermentis US-56	1 pack

Grains

1 lb	Carafoam®, Carapils® or dextrin malt	450 g
5.5 US gal	brewing water (page 89)	21 L

Malt Extracts

3.3 lbs	wheat/weizen	1.5 kg
3.3 lbs	any brand extra-light (late extract addition)	1.5 kg

Bittering Hops

6 to 8 AAUs	Northern Brewer or Perle	6 to 8 AAUs

Flavor and Aroma Hops

2 oz	Tettnang, Spalt or other German Noble Hops, divided in half	56 g

Later Additions

1 tsp	Irish moss	5 mL
1 tsp	yeast nutrient	5 mL

1. Prepare the liquid yeast in advance, according to the package directions (if using).
2. Coarsely crack the malt grains and place them in a cheesecloth or nylon grain bag.
3. In a brew kettle, bring at least 3 US gal (11 L) brewing water to steeping temperature (150 to 160°F/65 to 71°C). Turn off the heat, add the grain bag, cover and steep for 30 minutes. (If the temperature drops below steeping temperature, turn the element back on briefly to bring it back up.) Remove grain bag and discard.
4. Increase the heat and bring grain tea to a boil. Remove from heat, add the wheat malt extract only and stir until dissolved completely.
5. Return kettle to the burner and increase the heat until the wort begins to boil. Using a spoon, clear any foam to one side. Reduce heat until a rolling boil can be maintained without foam buildup.
6. Add the bittering hops, stirring to combine. Boil for 45 minutes, uncovered. Monitor to prevent boiling over.
7. Meanwhile, prepare the fermentation gear and cooling bath or wort chiller.

8. After 45 minutes, remove the kettle from the heat and add the extra-light malt extract, 1 oz (28 g) of the hops for flavor, Irish moss and yeast nutrient. Stir to ensure that the extract, sugar and nutrient are dissolved. Return the kettle to the burner and bring back to a rolling boil. Boil for 15 minutes, then stir in the remaining 1 oz (28 g) hops for aroma, turn off the heat and cover.

9. To cool the brew, place the covered kettle in the prepared cooling tub or use a wort chiller according to the manufacturer's directions. Cool to the desired temperature, 75°F (24°C), within 30 to 45 minutes.

10. While the wort is cooling, clean and sanitize the brewing spoon. When the wort has cooled, move the kettle to a counter and stir the wort briskly in one direction for about 5 minutes. After stirring, cover and let rest for 10 to 15 minutes as the hops and trub form a cone.

11. Using a racking cane and siphon, rack as much wort as possible into the sanitized primary fermenter. Using the sanitized funnel and straining screen, strain the rest of the wort into the fermenter. Top off with brewing water to bring the volume to around 5.5 US gal (21 L). Using the hydrometer, take a reading of the specific gravity and record it in your brewing journal.

12. Add the yeast; vigorously stir it with a sanitized spoon to distribute it throughout the wort. Seal the fermenter with lid, stopper and airlock. Keep the fermenter at room temperature (68 to 72°F/20 to 22°C) during primary fermentation, which typically lasts 1 to 4 days after fermentation begins. (Keep in a dark place or under a lightproof cover if using a glass carboy.)

13. After 1 to 4 days or when the kräusen has fallen, gently rack the beer into the secondary fermenter to avoid aerating it, leaving as much of the sediment behind as possible. Seal and keep at room temperature, covered or in a dark place, to allow fermentation to continue.

14. Once the bubbling in the airlock has slowed, confirm completion of fermentation by using the hydrometer to take final gravity readings. (Hydrometer readings should be the same for several days in a row.)

15. Prime and bottle the beer (see page 91) and condition it for 3 to 4 weeks.

Weizenbock

This is the big bruiser of the wheat beer family. The classic commercial example is Schneider Aventinus. This is the traditional New Year beer of Germany.

Estimated Original Gravity: 1.080

Equipment

- **brew kettle**
- **fermentation gear (page 14)**
- **blow-off hose (page 16)**

Beers with an estimated original gravity higher than 1.065 require a longer time in both primary and secondary fermentation. Primary fermentation should take 7 to 10 days, and secondary fermentation should take about 2 weeks longer than weaker brews.

Yeast

2 packs	Wyeast 3068 or White Labs WLP351 (or 1 pack in starter) or Fermentis WB-06	2 packs

Grains

1 lb	Melanoidin® malt	450 g
1 lb	Caramunich III® malt	450 g
4 oz	dehusked Carafa I® malt	112 g
5.5 US gal	brewing water (page 89)	21 L

Malt Extract

9.9 lbs	wheat/weizen	4.5 kg

Bittering Hops

8 to 10 AAUs	Northern Brewer or Perle	8 to 10 AAUs

Flavor and Aroma Hops

.5 oz	Tettnang, Spalt or other German Noble Hops, divided in half	14 g

Later Additions

1 tsp	Irish moss	5 mL
1 tsp	yeast nutrient	5 mL

1. Prepare the liquid yeast in advance, according to the package directions (if using).
2. Coarsely crack the malt grains and place them in a cheesecloth or nylon grain bag.
3. In a brew kettle, bring at least 3 US gal (11 L) brewing water to steeping temperature (150 to 160°F/65 to 71°C). Turn off the heat, add the grain bag, cover and steep for 30 minutes. (If the temperature drops below steeping temperature, turn the element back on briefly to bring it back up.) Remove grain bag and discard.
4. Increase the heat and bring grain tea to a boil. Remove from heat, add the malt extract and stir until dissolved completely.
5. Return kettle to the burner and increase the heat until the wort begins to boil. Using a spoon, clear any foam to one side. Reduce heat until a rolling boil can be maintained without foam buildup.
6. Add the bittering hops, stirring to combine. Boil for 45 minutes, uncovered. Monitor to prevent boiling over.
7. Meanwhile, prepare the fermentation gear and cooling bath or wort chiller.

8. After 45 minutes, remove the kettle from the heat and add .25 oz (7 g) of the hops for flavor, Irish moss and yeast nutrient. Stir to ensure that the nutrient has dissolved. Return the kettle to the burner and bring back to a rolling boil. Boil for 15 minutes, then stir in the remaining .25 oz (7 g) of hops for aroma, turn off the heat and cover.

9. To cool the brew, place the covered kettle in the prepared cooling tub or use a wort chiller according to the manufacturer's directions. Cool to the desired temperature, 75°F (24°C), within 30 to 45 minutes.

10. While the wort is cooling, clean and sanitize the brewing spoon. When the wort has cooled, move the kettle to a counter and stir the wort briskly in one direction for about 5 minutes. After stirring, cover and let rest for 10 to 15 minutes as the hops and trub form a cone.

11. Using a racking cane and siphon, rack as much wort as possible into the sanitized primary fermenter. Using the sanitized funnel and straining screen, strain the rest of the wort into the fermenter. Top off with brewing water to bring the volume to around 5.5 US gal (21 L). Using the hydrometer, take a reading of the specific gravity and record it in your brewing journal.

12. Add the yeast; vigorously stir it with a sanitized spoon to distribute it throughout the wort. Seal the fermenter with lid, stopper and airlock or blow-off hose. Keep the fermenter at room temperature (68 to 72°F/20 to 22°C) during primary fermentation, which typically lasts 7 to 10 days after fermentation begins. (Keep in a dark place or under a lightproof cover if using a glass carboy.)

13. After 7 to 10 days or when the kräusen has fallen, gently rack the beer into the secondary fermenter to avoid aerating it, leaving as much of the sediment behind as possible. Seal and keep at room temperature, covered or in a dark place, to allow fermentation to continue.

14. Once the bubbling in the airlock has slowed, confirm completion of fermentation by using the hydrometer to take final gravity readings. (Hydrometer readings should be the same for several days in a row.)

15. Prime and bottle the beer (see page 91) and condition it for 3 to 4 weeks.

Brewer's Tips

For information on preparing a yeast starter, see page 89.

If the specified brands of grains are not available, use the grains chart on page 77 to find substitutes.

If active fermentation backs up into the airlock, replace airlock with blow-off hose (see page 16). Change water as needed; re-install airlock when fermentation settles down.

Roggen Bier

**Estimated Original
Gravity: 1.059**

Equipment

- **brew kettle**
- **fermentation gear
  (page 14)**

Yeast

2 packs	Wyeast 3056 or White Labs WLP351 (or 1 pack in starter) or Fermentis WB-06	2 packs

Grains

2 lbs	6-Row malted barley	900 g
2 lbs	rye malt	900 g
1 lb	light Munich malt	450 g
1 lb	Cararye® malt	450 g
1 qt	rice hulls	1 L
5.5 US gal	brewing water (page 89)	21 L

Malt Extract

4 lbs	Alexander's Sun Country Pale	1.8 kg

Bittering Hops

3 to 4 AAUs	Tettnang or Spalt	3 to 4 AAUs

Later Additions

1 tsp	Irish moss	5 mL
1 tsp	yeast nutrient	5 mL

Aroma Hops

None

1. Prepare the liquid yeast in advance, according to the package directions (if using).
2. Coarsely crack the malt grains and place them in a cheesecloth or nylon grain bag with rice hulls. Mix thoroughly.
3. In a brew kettle, bring at least 3 US gal (11 L) brewing water to steeping temperature (150 to 160°F/65 to 71°C). Turn off the heat, add the grain bag, cover and steep for 90 minutes. (If the temperature drops below steeping temperature, turn the element back on briefly to bring it back up.) Remove grain bag, gently rinse it over the kettle with about 1 US qt (1 L) of 170°F (77°C) temperature brewing water and discard.
4. Increase the heat and bring grain tea to a boil. Remove from heat, add the malt extract and stir until dissolved completely.
5. Return kettle to the burner and increase the heat until the wort begins to boil. Using a spoon, clear any foam to one side. Reduce heat until a rolling boil can be maintained without foam buildup.

6. Add the bittering hops, stirring to combine. Boil for 45 minutes, uncovered. Monitor to prevent boiling over.

7. Meanwhile, prepare the fermentation gear and cooling bath or wort chiller.

8. After 45 minutes, remove the kettle from the heat and add Irish moss and yeast nutrient. Stir to ensure that the nutrient has dissolved. Return the kettle to the burner and bring back to a rolling boil. Boil for 15 minutes, turn off the heat and cover.

9. To cool the brew, place the covered kettle in the prepared cooling tub or use a wort chiller according to the manufacturer's directions. Cool to the desired temperature, 75°F (24°C), within 30 to 45 minutes.

10. While the wort is cooling, clean and sanitize the brewing spoon. When the wort has cooled, move the kettle to a counter and stir the wort briskly in one direction for about 5 minutes. After stirring, cover and let rest for 10 to 15 minutes as the hops and trub form a cone.

11. Using a racking cane and siphon, rack as much wort as possible into the sanitized primary fermenter. Using the sanitized funnel and straining screen, strain the rest of the wort into the fermenter. Top off with brewing water to bring the volume to around 5.5 US gal (21 L). Using the hydrometer, take a reading of the specific gravity and record it in your brewing journal.

12. Add the yeast; vigorously stir it with a sanitized spoon to distribute it throughout the wort. Seal the fermenter with lid, stopper and airlock. Keep the fermenter at room temperature (68 to 72°F/20 to 22°C) during primary fermentation, which typically lasts 1 to 4 days after fermentation begins. (Keep in a dark place or under a lightproof cover if using a glass carboy.)

13. After 1 to 4 days or when the kräusen has fallen, gently rack the beer into the secondary fermenter to avoid aerating it, leaving as much of the sediment behind as possible. Seal and keep at room temperature, covered or in a dark place, to allow fermentation to continue.

14. Once the bubbling in the airlock has slowed, confirm completion of fermentation by using the hydrometer to take final gravity readings. (Hydrometer readings should be the same for several days in a row.)

15. Prime and bottle the beer (see page 91) and condition it for 3 to 4 weeks.

Brewer's Tips

For information on preparing a yeast starter, see page 89.

This rye ale will be a little trickier to brew because you're going to actually convert the starch in the rye malt. To help the process, be sure the different grains are well combined before wetting and steep the grains for 90 minutes instead of the usual 30. Rinse the grains carefully. The rice hulls are included to keep the grains from gumming up.

Baltic Porter

Baltic porter is one of the great, forgotten styles. It is difficult to find, even in its region of origin. Victory Brewing Co. of Downingtown, Pennsylvania produces an excellent version called Baltic Thunder.

These are malty beers, often produced with lager yeast. They are dark brews that combine the worlds of bock beer and porter. Ferment at cool room temperatures.

Estimated Original Gravity: 1.077

Equipment

- **brew kettle**
- **fermentation gear (page 14)**
- **blow-off hose (page 16)**

Yeast

1 pack	Wyeast 2112 or White Labs WLP810 or Fermentis S-23	1 pack

Grains

1 lb	Carabohemian® malt	450 g
8 oz	Caraaroma® or other dark crystal malt	224 g
8 oz	dehusked Carafa I® malt	224 g
5.5 US gal	brewing water (page 89)	21 L

Malt Extract

8 lbs	any brand UK light	3.6 kg

Bittering Hops

6 to 8 AAUs	Northern Brewer, Perle or other medium-alpha acid	6 to 8 AAUs

Later Additions

1 lb	Demerara sugar	450 g
1 tsp	Irish moss	5 mL
1 tsp	yeast nutrient	5 mL

Aroma Hops

.5 oz	Styrian Golding, Fuggle or Kent Golding	14 g

1. Prepare the liquid yeast in advance, according to the package directions (if using).
2. Coarsely crack the malt grains and place them in a cheesecloth or nylon grain bag.
3. In a brew kettle, bring at least 3 US gal (11 L) brewing water to steeping temperature (150 to 160°F/65 to 71°C). Turn off the heat, add the grain bag, cover and steep for 30 minutes. (If the temperature drops below steeping temperature, turn the element back on briefly to bring it back up.) Remove grain bag, rinse gently into the kettle and discard.
4. Increase the heat and bring grain tea to a boil. Remove from heat, add the malt extract and stir until dissolved completely.
5. Return kettle to the burner and increase the heat until the wort begins to boil. Using a spoon, clear any foam to one side. Reduce heat until a rolling boil can be maintained without foam buildup.
6. Add the bittering hops, stirring to combine. Boil for 45 minutes, uncovered. Monitor to prevent boiling over.

7. Meanwhile, prepare the fermentation gear and cooling bath or wort chiller.

8. After 45 minutes, remove the kettle from the heat and add sugar, Irish moss and yeast nutrient. Stir to ensure that the sugar and nutrient are dissolved. Return the kettle to the burner and bring back to a rolling boil. Boil for 15 minutes, then stir in the aroma hops, turn off the heat and cover.

9. To cool the brew, place the covered kettle in the prepared cooling tub or use a wort chiller according to the manufacturer's directions. Cool to the desired temperature, 75°F (24°C), within 30 to 45 minutes.

10. While the wort is cooling, clean and sanitize the brewing spoon. When the wort has cooled, move the kettle to a counter and stir the wort briskly in one direction for about 5 minutes. After stirring, cover and let rest for 10 to 15 minutes as the hops and trub form a cone.

11. Using a racking cane and siphon, rack as much wort as possible into the sanitized primary fermenter. Using the sanitized funnel and straining screen, strain the rest of the wort into the fermenter. Top off with brewing water to bring the volume to around 5.5 US gal (21 L). Using the hydrometer, take a reading of the specific gravity and record it in your brewing journal.

12. Add the yeast; vigorously stir it with a sanitized spoon to distribute it throughout the wort. Seal the fermenter with lid, stopper and airlock or blow-off hose. Keep the fermenter at a cool room temperature (60 to 65°F/15 to 18°C) during primary fermentation, which typically lasts 7 to 10 days after fermentation begins. (Keep in a dark place or under a lightproof cover if using a glass carboy.)

13. After 7 to 10 days or when the kräusen has fallen, gently rack the beer into the secondary fermenter to avoid aerating it, leaving as much of the sediment behind as possible. Seal and keep at cool room temperature, covered or in a dark place, to allow fermentation to continue.

14. Once the bubbling in the airlock has slowed, confirm completion of fermentation by using the hydrometer to take final gravity readings. (Hydrometer readings should be the same for several days in a row.)

15. Prime and bottle the beer (see page 91) and condition it for 3 to 4 weeks.

Brewer's Tips

If the specified brands of grains are not available, use the grains chart on page 77 to find substitutes.

If active fermentation backs up into the airlock, replace airlock with blow-off hose (see page 16). Change water as needed; re-install airlock when fermentation settles down.

Now that you've enjoyed the glories of grains in the brewing process, you might want to revisit a favorite recipe from Part 1. The ingredient upgrades in this section will allow you to bring greater flavor to your beers as you switch from dry yeast to liquid and include malted grains instead of only using extracts. If the original recipe did not call for extra-light, gold, light or pale malt extract, we'll be switching to it in these enhanced versions.

Beginner Ales Made with Grains

Irish (Red) Amber

Estimated Original Gravity: 1.047

Equipment

- **brew kettle**
- **fermentation gear (page 14)**

As you build your brewing skills, switching to liquid yeast products (from Wyeast or White Labs) will give you a brew that is more complex than the ones made with the dry yeast (from Fermentis or Danstar) in the Absolute Beginner recipes. See page 86 for more information about liquid yeasts.

Liquid Yeast

1 pack	Wyeast 1084 or White Labs WLP004	1 pack

Grains

8 oz	toasted malt (25 to 50 Lovibond)	224 g
8 oz	crystal or caramel malt (40 to 60 Lovibond)	224 g
2 oz	dark-roasted malt	56 g
5.5 US gal	brewing water (page 89)	21 L

Malt Extract

4 lbs	any brand UK light	1.8 kg

Bittering Hops

6 to 7 AAUs	UK hops (such as Bramling Cross, East Kent Golding, Fuggle or other)	6 to 7 AAUs

Flavor and Aroma Hops

1 oz	UK hops (such as Bramling Cross, East Kent Golding, Fuggle or other), divided in half	28 g

Later Additions

1 lb	Demerara sugar (or turbinado or unrefined brown cane sugar)	450 g
1 tsp	Irish moss	5 mL
1 tsp	yeast nutrient	5 mL

1. Prepare liquid yeast in advance, according to package directions.
2. Coarsely crack the grains and place them in a cheesecloth or nylon grain bag.
3. In a brew kettle, bring at least 3 US gal (11 L) brewing water to steeping temperature (150 to 160°F/65 to 71°C). Turn off the heat, add the grain bag, cover and steep for 30 minutes. (If the temperature drops below steeping temperature, reheat briefly.) Remove grain bag. Place it in a strainer, rinse it over the kettle with steeping water and then discard it.
4. Increase the heat and bring grain tea to a boil. Remove from heat, add the malt extract and stir until dissolved completely.
5. Return kettle to the burner and increase the heat until the wort begins to boil. Using a spoon, clear any foam to one side. Reduce heat until a rolling boil can be maintained without foam buildup.
6. Add the bittering hops, stirring to combine. Boil for 45 minutes, uncovered. Monitor to prevent boiling over.

7. Meanwhile, prepare the fermentation gear and cooling bath or wort chiller.

8. After 45 minutes, remove the kettle from the heat and add half the aroma hops for flavor (.5 oz/14 g), sugar, Irish moss and yeast nutrient. Stir to ensure that the sugar and nutrient have dissolved. Return the kettle to the burner and bring back to a rolling boil. Boil for 15 minutes; stir in the remaining aroma hops (.5 oz/14 g), turn off the heat and cover.

9. To cool the brew, place the covered kettle in the prepared cooling tub or use a wort chiller according to the manufacturer's directions. Cool to the desired temperature, 75°F (24°C), within 30 to 45 minutes.

10. While the wort is cooling, clean and sanitize the brewing spoon. When the wort has cooled, move the kettle to a counter and stir the wort briskly in one direction for about 5 minutes. After stirring, cover and let rest for 10 to 15 minutes as the hops and trub form a cone.

11. Using sanitized racking cane and siphon, rack as much wort as possible into the sanitized primary fermenter. Using the sanitized funnel and straining screen, strain the rest of the wort into the fermenter. Top off with brewing water to bring the volume to around 5.5 US gal (21 L). Using the hydrometer, take a reading of the specific gravity and record it in your brewing journal.

12. Add the yeast; vigorously stir it with a sanitized spoon to distribute it throughout the wort. Seal the fermenter with lid, stopper and airlock. Keep the fermenter at room temperature (68 to 72°F/20 to 22°C) during primary fermentation, which typically lasts 1 to 4 days after fermentation begins. (Keep in a dark place or under a lightproof cover if using a glass carboy.)

13. After 1 to 4 days or when the kräusen has fallen, use a sanitized racking cane and siphon to gently rack the beer into the sanitized secondary fermenter. Avoid aerating it, and leave as much of the sediment behind as possible. Seal and keep at room temperature, covered or in a dark place, to allow fermentation to continue.

14. Once the bubbling in the airlock has slowed, confirm completion of fermentation by using the hydrometer to take final gravity readings. (Hydrometer readings should be the same for several days in a row.)

15. Prime and bottle the beer (see page 91) and condition it for 3 to 4 weeks.

American Amber

For a sweeter, maltier brew, use the lower end of the recommended AAUs; for a more bitter approach, use the higher number. The Briess and Northwestern extracts are the same product packaged by different companies.

Estimated Original Gravity: 1.053

Equipment

- **brew kettle**
- **fermentation gear (page 14)**

As you build your brewing skills, switching to liquid yeast products (from Wyeast or White Labs) will give you a brew that is more complex than the ones made with the dry yeast (from Fermentis or Danstar) in the Absolute Beginner recipes. See page 86 for more information about liquid yeasts.

Liquid Yeast

1 pack	Wyeast 1056 or White Labs WLP001	1 pack

Grains

8 oz	toasted malt (25 to 50 Lovibond)	224 g
8 oz	crystal or caramel malt (40 to 60 Lovibond)	224 g
2 oz	dark-roasted malt	56 g
5.5 US gal	brewing water (page 89)	21 L

Malt Extract

6.6 lbs	light (such as Briess, Coopers or Northwestern or any brand), divided in half	3 kg

Bittering Hops

8 to 10 AAUs	high-alpha acid American hops (such as Amarillo, Centennial, Chinook or Columbus)	8 to 10 AAUs

Later Additions

1 tsp	Irish moss	5 mL
1 tsp	yeast nutrient	5 mL

Aroma Hops

2 oz	American hops (such as Ahtanum, Amarillo, Cascade or Willamette)	56 g

1. Prepare the liquid yeast in advance, according to the package directions.
2. Coarsely crack the grains and place them in a cheesecloth or nylon grain bag.
3. In a brew kettle, bring at least 3 US gal (11 L) brewing water to steeping temperature (150 to 160°F/65 to 71°C). Turn off the heat, add the grain bag, cover and steep for 30 minutes. (If the temperature drops below steeping temperature, reheat briefly.) Remove grain bag. Place it in a strainer, rinse it over the kettle with steeping water and then discard it.
4. Increase the heat and bring grain tea to a boil. Remove from heat, add half the malt extract (3.3 lbs/1.5 kg) and stir until dissolved completely.
5. Return kettle to the burner and increase the heat until the wort begins to boil. Using a spoon, clear any foam to one side. Reduce heat until a rolling boil can be maintained without foam buildup.
6. Add the bittering hops, stirring to combine. Boil for 45 minutes, uncovered. Monitor to prevent boiling over.

7. Meanwhile, prepare the fermentation gear and cooling bath or wort chiller.

8. After 45 minutes, remove the kettle from the heat and add remaining half of the malt extract (3.3 lbs/1.5 kg), Irish moss and yeast nutrient. Stir to ensure that the extract and nutrient have dissolved. Return the kettle to the burner and bring back to a rolling boil. Boil for 15 minutes; stir in the aroma hops, turn off the heat and cover.

9. To cool the brew, place the covered kettle in the prepared cooling tub or use a wort chiller according to the manufacturer's directions. Cool to the desired temperature, 75°F (24°C), within 30 to 45 minutes.

10. While the wort is cooling, clean and sanitize the brewing spoon. When the wort has cooled, move the kettle to a counter and stir the wort briskly in one direction for about 5 minutes. After stirring, cover and let rest for 10 to 15 minutes as the hops and trub form a cone.

11. Using sanitized racking cane and siphon, rack as much wort as possible into the sanitized primary fermenter. Using the sanitized funnel and straining screen, strain the rest of the wort into the fermenter. Top off with brewing water to bring the volume to around 5.5 US gal (21 L). Using the hydrometer, take a reading of the specific gravity and record it in your brewing journal.

12. Add the yeast; vigorously stir it with a sanitized spoon to distribute it throughout the wort. Seal the fermenter with lid, stopper and airlock. Keep the fermenter at room temperature (68 to 72°F/20 to 22°C) during primary fermentation, which typically lasts 1 to 4 days after fermentation begins. (Keep in a dark place or under alightproof cover if using a glass carboy.)

13. After 1 to 4 days or when the kräusen has fallen, use a sanitized racking cane and siphon to gently rack the beer into the sanitized secondary fermenter. Avoid aerating it, and leave as much of the sediment behind as possible. Seal and keep at room temperature, covered or in a dark place, to allow fermentation to continue.

14. Once the bubbling in the airlock has slowed, confirm completion of fermentation by using the hydrometer to take final gravity readings. (Hydrometer readings should be the same for several days in a row.)

15. Prime and bottle the beer (see page 91) and condition it for 3 to 4 weeks.

British Brown Ale

Equipment

- **brew kettle**
- **fermentation gear
  (page 14)**

As you build your brewing skills, switching to liquid yeast products (from Wyeast or White Labs) will give you a brew that is more complex than the ones made with the dry yeast (from Fermentis or Danstar) in the Absolute Beginner recipes. See page 86 for more information about liquid yeasts.

Liquid Yeast

1 pack	Wyeast 1028 or White Labs WLP013	1 pack

Grains

1 lb	toasted malt (25 to 50 Lovibond)	450 g
1 lb	crystal or caramel malt (40 to 60 Lovibond)	450 g
4 oz	dark-roasted malt	112 g
5.5 US gal	brewing water (page 89)	21 L

Malt Extract

6.6 lbs	any brand UK light	3 kg

Bittering Hops

6 to 8 AAUs	UK hops (such as Challenger, First Gold, Northern Brewer, Pilgrim or Target)	6 to 8 AAUs

Later Additions

8 oz.	Demerara sugar (or turbinado or other raw cane sugar)	224 g
1 tsp	Irish moss	5 mL
1 tsp	yeast nutrient	5 mL

Aroma Hops

0.5 oz	UK hops (such as Bramling Cross, Fuggle or East Kent Golding)	14 g

1. Prepare the liquid yeast in advance, according to the package directions.
2. Coarsely crack the grains and place them in a cheesecloth or nylon grain bag.
3. In a brew kettle, bring at least 3 US gal (11 L) brewing water to steeping temperature (150 to 160°F/65 to 71°C). Turn off the heat, add the grain bag, cover and steep for 30 minutes. (If the temperature drops below steeping temperature, reheat briefly.) Remove grain bag. Place it in a strainer, rinse it over the kettle with steeping water and then discard it.
4. Increase the heat and bring grain tea to a boil. Remove from heat, add the malt extract and stir until dissolved completely.
5. Return kettle to the burner and increase the heat until the wort begins to boil. Using a spoon, clear any foam to one side. Reduce heat until a rolling boil can be maintained without foam buildup.

6. Add the bittering hops, stirring to combine. Boil for 45 minutes, uncovered. Monitor to prevent boiling over.

7. Meanwhile, prepare the fermentation gear and cooling bath or wort chiller.

8. After 45 minutes, remove the kettle from the heat and add sugar, Irish moss and yeast nutrient. Stir to ensure that the sugar and nutrient have dissolved. Return the kettle to the burner and bring back to a rolling boil. Boil for 15 minutes; stir in the aroma hops, turn off the heat and cover.

9. To cool the brew, place the covered kettle in the prepared cooling tub or use a wort chiller according to the manufacturer's directions. Cool to the desired temperature, 75°F (24°C), within 30 to 45 minutes.

10. While the wort is cooling, clean and sanitize the brewing spoon. When the wort has cooled, move the kettle to a counter and stir the wort briskly in one direction for about 5 minutes. After stirring, cover and let rest for 10 to 15 minutes as the hops and trub form a cone.

11. Using sanitized racking cane and siphon, rack as much wort as possible into the sanitized primary fermenter. Using the sanitized funnel and straining screen, strain the rest of the wort into the fermenter. Top off with brewing water to bring the volume to around 5.5 US gal (21 L). Using the hydrometer, take a reading of the specific gravity and record it in your brewing journal.

12. Add the yeast; vigorously stir it with a sanitized spoon to distribute it throughout the wort. Seal the fermenter with lid, stopper and airlock. Keep the fermenter at room temperature (68 to 72°F/20 to 22°C) during primary fermentation, which typically lasts 1 to 4 days after fermentation begins. (Keep in a dark place or under a lightproof cover if using a glass carboy.)

13. After 1 to 4 days or when the kräusen has fallen, use a sanitized racking cane and siphon to gently rack the beer into the sanitized secondary fermenter. Avoid aerating it, and leave as much of the sediment behind as possible. Seal and keep at room temperature, covered or in a dark place, to allow fermentation to continue.

14. Once the bubbling in the airlock has slowed, confirm completion of fermentation by using the hydrometer to take final gravity readings. (Hydrometer readings should be the same for several days in a row.)

15. Prime and bottle the beer (see page 91) and condition it for 3 to 4 weeks.

American (Texas) Brown

Estimated Original Gravity: 1.045

Equipment

- **brew kettle**
- **fermentation gear (page 14)**

As you build your brewing skills, switching to liquid yeast products (from Wyeast or White Labs) will give you a brew that is more complex than the ones made with the dry yeast (from Fermentis or Danstar) in the Absolute Beginner recipes. See page 86 for more information about liquid yeasts.

Liquid Yeast

1 pack	Wyeast 1056 or White Labs WLP001	1 pack

Grains

1 lb	toasted malt (25 to 50 Lovibond)	450 g
1 lb	crystal or caramel malt (40 to 60 Lovibond)	450 g
4 oz	dark-roasted malt	112 g
5.5 US gal	brewing water (page 89)	21 L

Malt Extract

6.6 lbs	light (such as Briess, Coopers or Northwestern or any brand), divided in half	3 kg

Bittering Hops

8 to 10 AAUs	high-alpha acid American hops (such as Amarillo, Centennial, Chinook or Columbus)	8 to 10 AAUs

Later Additions

1 tsp	Irish moss	5 mL
1 tsp	yeast nutrient	5 mL

Aroma Hops

1.5 oz	citrusy American hops (such as Ahtanum, Amarillo or Cascade)	42 g

1. Prepare the liquid yeast in advance, according to the package directions.
2. Coarsely crack the grains and place them in a cheesecloth or nylon grain bag.
3. In a brew kettle, bring at least 3 US gal (11 L) brewing water to steeping temperature (150 to 160°F/65 to 71°C). Turn off the heat, add the grain bag, cover and steep for 30 minutes. (If the temperature drops below steeping temperature, reheat briefly.) Remove grain bag. Place it in a strainer, rinse it over the kettle with steeping water and then discard it.
4. Increase the heat and bring grain tea to a boil. Remove from heat, add half the malt extract (3.3 lbs/1.5 kg) and stir until dissolved completely.
5. Return kettle to the burner and increase the heat until the wort begins to boil. Using a spoon, clear any foam to one side. Reduce heat until a rolling boil can be maintained without foam buildup.
6. Add the bittering hops, stirring to combine. Boil for 45 minutes, uncovered. Monitor to prevent boiling over.

7. Meanwhile, prepare the fermentation gear and cooling bath or wort chiller.

8. After 45 minutes, remove the kettle from the heat and add remaining half of the malt extract (3.3 lbs/1.5 kg), Irish moss and yeast nutrient. Stir to ensure that the extract and nutrient have dissolved. Return the kettle to the burner and bring back to a rolling boil. Boil for 15 minutes; stir in the aroma hops, turn off the heat and cover.

9. To cool the brew, place the covered kettle in the prepared cooling tub or use a wort chiller according to the manufacturer's directions. Cool to the desired temperature, 75°F (24°C), within 30 to 45 minutes.

10. While the wort is cooling, clean and sanitize the brewing spoon. When the wort has cooled, move the kettle to a counter and stir the wort briskly in one direction for about 5 minutes. After stirring, cover and let rest for 10 to 15 minutes as the hops and trub form a cone.

11. Using sanitized racking cane and siphon, rack as much wort as possible into the sanitized primary fermenter. Using the sanitized funnel and straining screen, strain the rest of the wort into the fermenter. Top off with brewing water to bring the volume to around 5.5 US gal (21 L). Using the hydrometer, take a reading of the specific gravity and record it in your brewing journal.

12. Add the yeast; vigorously stir it with a sanitized spoon to distribute it throughout the wort. Seal the fermenter with lid, stopper and airlock. Keep the fermenter at room temperature (68 to 72°F/20 to 22°C) during primary fermentation, which typically lasts 1 to 4 days after fermentation begins. (Keep in a dark place or under a lightproof cover if using a glass carboy.)

13. After 1 to 4 days or when the kräusen has fallen, use a sanitized racking cane and siphon to gently rack the beer into the sanitized secondary fermenter. Avoid aerating it, and leave as much of the sediment behind as possible. Seal and keep at room temperature, covered or in a dark place, to allow fermentation to continue.

14. Once the bubbling in the airlock has slowed, confirm completion of fermentation by using the hydrometer to take final gravity readings. (Hydrometer readings should be the same for several days in a row.)

15. Prime and bottle the beer (see page 91) and condition it for 3 to 4 weeks.

**Estimated Original
Gravity: 1.048**

Equipment

- **brew kettle**
- **fermentation gear
  (page 14)**

As you build your brewing skills, switching to liquid yeast products (from Wyeast or White Labs) will give you a brew that is more complex than the ones made with the dry yeast (from Fermentis or Danstar) in the Absolute Beginner recipes. See page 86 for more information about liquid yeasts.

British Pale Ale (Special Bitter)

Liquid Yeast

1 pack	Wyeast 1098 or White Labs WLP005	1 pack

Grains

8 oz	toasted malt (20 to 30 Lovibond)	224 g
8 oz	crystal or caramel malt (20 to 60 Lovibond)	224 g
5.5 US gal	brewing water (page 89)	21 L

Malt Extract

6.6 lbs	any brand UK light, divided in half	3 kg

Bittering Hops

10 to 12 AAUs	UK hops (such as Challenger, First Gold, Northern Brewer, Pilgrim or Target)	10 to 12 AAUs

Later Additions

1 tsp	Irish moss	5 mL
1 tsp	yeast nutrient	5 mL

Aroma Hops

1.5 oz	UK hops (such as Bramling Cross, Fuggle or East Kent Golding)	42 g

1. Prepare the liquid yeast in advance, according to the package directions.
2. Coarsely crack the grains and place them in a cheesecloth or nylon grain bag.
3. In a brew kettle, bring at least 3 US gal (11 L) brewing water to steeping temperature (150 to 160°F/65 to 71°C). Turn off the heat, add the grain bag, cover and steep for 30 minutes. (If the temperature drops below steeping temperature, reheat briefly.) Remove grain bag. Place it in a strainer, rinse it over the kettle with steeping water and then discard it.
4. Increase the heat and bring grain tea to a boil. Remove from heat, add half the malt extract (3.3 lbs/1.5 kg) and stir until dissolved completely.
5. Return kettle to the burner and increase the heat until the wort begins to boil. Using a spoon, clear any foam to one side. Reduce heat until a rolling boil can be maintained without foam buildup.
6. Add the bittering hops, stirring to combine. Boil for 45 minutes, uncovered. Monitor to prevent boiling over.

7. Meanwhile, prepare the fermentation gear and cooling bath or wort chiller.

8. After 45 minutes, remove the kettle from the heat and add remaining half of the malt extract (3.3 lbs/1.5 kg), Irish moss and yeast nutrient. Stir to ensure that the extract and nutrient have dissolved. Return the kettle to the burner and bring back to a rolling boil. Boil for 15 minutes; stir in the aroma hops, turn off the heat and cover.

9. To cool the brew, place the covered kettle in the prepared cooling tub or use a wort chiller according to the manufacturer's directions. Cool to the desired temperature, 75°F (24°C), within 30 to 45 minutes.

10. While the wort is cooling, clean and sanitize the brewing spoon. When the wort has cooled, move the kettle to a counter and stir the wort briskly in one direction for about 5 minutes. After stirring, cover and let rest for 10 to 15 minutes as the hops and trub form a cone.

11. Using sanitized racking cane and siphon, rack as much wort as possible into the sanitized primary fermenter. Using the sanitized funnel and straining screen, strain the rest of the wort into the fermenter. Top off with brewing water to bring the volume to around 5.5 US gal (21 L). Using the hydrometer, take a reading of the specific gravity and record it in your brewing journal.

12. Add the yeast; vigorously stir it with a sanitized spoon to distribute it throughout the wort. Seal the fermenter with lid, stopper and airlock. Keep the fermenter at room temperature (68 to 72°F/20 to 22°C) during primary fermentation, which typically lasts 1 to 4 days after fermentation begins. (Keep in a dark place or under a lightproof cover if using a glass carboy.)

13. After 1 to 4 days or when the kräusen has fallen, use a sanitized racking cane and siphon to gently rack the beer into the sanitized secondary fermenter. Avoid aerating it, and leave as much of the sediment behind as possible. Seal and keep at room temperature, covered or in a dark place, to allow fermentation to continue.

14. Once the bubbling in the airlock has slowed, confirm completion of fermentation by using the hydrometer to take final gravity readings. (Hydrometer readings should be the same for several days in a row.)

15. Prime and bottle the beer (see page 91) and condition it for 3 to 4 weeks.

Variation

ESB or Strong Bitter: Follow the recipe for Bitter, but add 1.5 lbs (680 g) Demerara sugar.

Ordinary Bitter

Equipment

- **brew kettle**
- **fermentation gear (page 14)**

Estimated Original Gravity: 1.043

As you build your brewing skills, switching to liquid yeast products (from Wyeast or White Labs) will give you a brew that is more complex than the ones made with the dry yeast (from Fermentis or Danstar) in the Absolute Beginner recipes. See page 86 for more information about liquid yeasts.

Liquid Yeast

1 pack	Wyeast 1098 or White Labs WLP005	1 pack

Grains

8 oz	toasted malt (20 to 30 Lovibond)	224 g
8 oz	crystal or caramel malt (20 to 60 Lovibond)	224 g
5.5 US gal	brewing water (page 89)	21 L

Malt Extracts

1 lb	any brand UK light dry malt extract (DME)	450 g
4 lbs	any brand UK light malt extract syrup (late addition)	1.8 kg

Bittering Hops

6 to 7 AAUs	UK hops (such as Bramling Cross, East Kent Golding, Fuggle or other)	6 to 7 AAUs

Flavor and Aroma Hops

1 oz	UK hops (such as Bramling Cross, East Kent Golding, Fuggle or other), divided in half	28 g

Later Additions

8 oz	Demerara sugar (or turbinado or raw brown cane sugar)	224 g
1 tsp	Irish moss	5 mL
1 tsp	yeast nutrient	5 mL

1. Prepare the liquid yeast in advance, according to the package directions.
2. Coarsely crack the grains and place them in a cheesecloth or nylon grain bag.
3. In a brew kettle, bring at least 3 US gal (11 L) brewing water to steeping temperature (150 to 160°F/65 to 71°C). Turn off the heat, add the grain bag, cover and steep for 30 minutes. (If the temperature drops below steeping temperature, reheat briefly.) Remove grain bag. Place it in a strainer, rinse it over the kettle with steeping water and then discard it.
4. Increase the heat and bring grain tea to a boil. Remove from heat, add the dry malt extract only and stir until dissolved completely.
5. Return kettle to the burner and increase the heat until the wort begins to boil. Using a spoon, clear any foam to one side. Reduce heat until a rolling boil can be maintained without foam buildup.

6. Add the bittering hops, stirring to combine. Boil for 45 minutes, uncovered. Monitor to prevent boiling over.

7. Meanwhile, prepare the fermentation gear and cooling bath or wort chiller.

8. After 45 minutes, remove the kettle from the heat and add light malt extract syrup, half of the hops (.5 oz/14 g) for flavor, sugar, Irish moss and yeast nutrient. Stir to ensure that the extract, sugar and nutrient have dissolved. Return the kettle to the burner and bring back to a rolling boil. Boil for 15 minutes; stir in the remaining half of the hops (.5 oz/14 g), turn off the heat and cover.

9. To cool the brew, place the covered kettle in the prepared cooling tub or use a wort chiller according to the manufacturer's directions. Cool to the desired temperature, 75°F (24°C), within 30 to 45 minutes.

10. While the wort is cooling, clean and sanitize the brewing spoon. When the wort has cooled, move the kettle to a counter and stir the wort briskly in one direction for about 5 minutes. After stirring, cover and let rest for 10 to 15 minutes as the hops and trub form a cone.

11. Using sanitized racking cane and siphon, rack as much wort as possible into the sanitized primary fermenter. Using the sanitized funnel and straining screen, strain the rest of the wort into the fermenter. Top off with brewing water to bring the volume to around 5.5 US gal (21 L). Using the hydrometer, take a reading of the specific gravity and record it in your brewing journal.

12. Add the yeast; vigorously stir it with a sanitized spoon to distribute it throughout the wort. Seal the fermenter with lid, stopper and airlock. Keep the fermenter at room temperature (68 to 72°F/20 to 22°C) during primary fermentation, which typically lasts 1 to 4 days after fermentation begins. (Keep in a dark place or under a lightproof cover if using a glass carboy.)

13. After 1 to 4 days or when the kräusen has fallen, use a sanitized racking cane and siphon to gently rack the beer into the sanitized secondary fermenter. Avoid aerating it, and leave as much of the sediment behind as possible. Seal and keep at room temperature, covered or in a dark place, to allow fermentation to continue.

14. Once the bubbling in the airlock has slowed, confirm completion of fermentation by using the hydrometer to take final gravity readings. (Hydrometer readings should be the same for several days in a row.)

15. Prime and bottle the beer (see page 91) and condition it for 3 to 4 weeks.

American Pale Ale (APA)

**Estimated Original
Gravity: 1.046**

Equipment

- **brew kettle**
- **fermentation gear
  (page 14)**

As you build your brewing
skills, switching to liquid
yeast products (from
Wyeast or White Labs)
will give you a brew
that is more complex
than the ones made
with the dry yeast (from
Fermentis or Danstar) in
the Absolute Beginner
recipes. See page 86 for
more information about
liquid yeasts.

Liquid Yeast

1 pack	Wyeast 1056 or White Labs WLP001	1 pack

Grains

8 oz	toasted malt (25 to 50 Lovibond)	224 g
8 oz	crystal or caramel malt (40 to 60 Lovibond)	224 g
5.5 US gal	brewing water (page 89)	21 L

Malt Extract

6.6 lbs	light (such as Briess, Coopers or Northwestern or any brand), divided in half	3 kg

Bittering Hops

12 to 14 AAUs	high-alpha acid American hops (such as Amarillo, Centennial, Chinook or Columbus)	12 to 14 AAUs

Later Additions

1 tsp	Irish moss	5 mL
1 tsp	yeast nutrient	5 mL

Aroma Hops

2 oz	citrusy American hops (such as Ahtanum, Amarillo or Cascade)	56 g

1. Prepare the liquid yeast in advance, according to the package directions.
2. Coarsely crack the grains and place them in a cheesecloth or nylon grain bag.
3. In a brew kettle, bring at least 3 US gal (11 L) brewing water to steeping temperature (150 to 160°F/65 to 71°C). Turn off the heat, add the grain bag, cover and steep for 30 minutes. (If the temperature drops below steeping temperature, reheat briefly.) Remove grain bag. Place it in a strainer, rinse it over the kettle with steeping water and then discard it.
4. Increase the heat and bring grain tea to a boil. Remove from heat, add half the malt extract (3.3 lbs/1.5 kg) and stir until dissolved completely.
5. Return kettle to the burner and increase the heat until the wort begins to boil. Using a spoon, clear any foam to one side. Reduce heat until a rolling boil can be maintained without foam buildup.
6. Add the bittering hops, stirring to combine. Boil for 45 minutes, uncovered. Monitor to prevent boiling over.

7. Meanwhile, prepare the fermentation gear and cooling bath or equipment.

8. After 45 minutes, remove the kettle from the heat and add remaining half of the malt extract (3.3 lbs/1.5 kg), Irish moss and yeast nutrient. Stir to ensure that the extract, and nutrient have dissolved. Return the kettle to the burner and bring back to a rolling boil. Boil for 15 minutes; stir in the aroma hops, turn off the heat and cover.

9. To cool the brew, place the covered kettle in the prepared cooling tub or use a wort chiller according to the manufacturer's directions. Cool to the desired temperature, 75°F (24°C), within 30 to 45 minutes.

10. While the wort is cooling, clean and sanitize the brewing spoon. When the wort has cooled, move the kettle to a counter and stir the wort briskly in one direction for about 5 minutes. After stirring, cover and let rest for 10 to 15 minutes as the hops and trub form a cone.

11. Using sanitized racking cane and siphon, rack as much wort as possible into the sanitized primary fermenter. Using the sanitized funnel and straining screen, strain the rest of the wort into the fermenter. Top off with brewing water to bring the volume to around 5.5 US gal (21 L). Using the hydrometer, take a reading of the specific gravity and record it in your brewing journal.

12. Add the yeast; vigorously stir it with a sanitized spoon to distribute it throughout the wort. Seal the fermenter with lid, stopper and airlock. Keep the fermenter at room temperature (68 to 72°F/20 to 22°C) during primary fermentation, which typically lasts 1 to 4 days after fermentation begins. (Keep in a dark place or under a lightproof cover if using a glass carboy.)

13. After 1 to 4 days or when the kräusen has fallen, use a sanitized racking cane and siphon to gently rack the beer into the sanitized secondary fermenter. Avoid aerating it, and leave as much of the sediment behind as possible. Seal and keep at room temperature, covered or in a dark place, to allow fermentation to continue.

14. Once the bubbling in the airlock has slowed, confirm completion of fermentation by using the hydrometer to take final gravity readings. (Hydrometer readings should be the same for several days in a row.)

15. Prime and bottle the beer (see page 91) and condition it for 3 to 4 weeks.

India Pale Ale (IPA)

For a more traditional English approach, check out the UK IPA recipe on page 128. Feel free to tone the hops up or down as your taste dictates. For a darker color, use some or all amber extract; to go paler switch to extra-light.

Estimated Original Gravity: 1.068

Equipment

- **brew kettle**
- **fermentation gear (page 14)**

Liquid Yeast

1 pack	Wyeast 1056 or White Labs WLP001	1 pack

Grains

8 oz	toasted malt (25 to 50 Lovibond)	224 g
8 oz	crystal or caramel malt (40 to 60 Lovibond)	224 g
5.5 US gal	brewing water (page 89)	21 L

Malt Extract

6.6 lbs	light (such as Briess, Coopers or Northwestern or any brand)	3 kg

Bittering Hops

15 to 25 AAUs	super high-alpha acid hops (such as Chinook, Columbus, Summit, Tomahawk or Warrior)	15 to 25 AAUs

Later Additions

1 lb	turbinado (or other raw sugar)	450 g
1 tsp	Irish moss	5 mL
1 tsp	yeast nutrient	5 mL

Aroma and Dry Hops

4 oz	citrusy American hops (such as Ahtanum, Amarillo, or Cascade), divided in half	112 g

1. Prepare the liquid yeast in advance, according to the package directions.
2. Coarsely crack the grains and place them in a cheesecloth or nylon grain bag.
3. In a brew kettle, bring at least 3 US gal (11 L) brewing water to steeping temperature (150 to 160°F/65 to 71°C). Turn off the heat, add the grain bag, cover and steep for 30 minutes. (If the temperature drops below steeping temperature, reheat briefly.) Remove grain bag. Place it in a strainer, rinse it over the kettle with steeping water and then discard it.
4. Increase the heat and bring grain tea to a boil. Remove from heat, add the malt extract and stir until dissolved completely.
5. Return kettle to the burner and increase the heat until the wort begins to boil. Using a spoon, clear any foam to one side. Reduce heat until a rolling boil can be maintained without foam buildup.

6. Add the bittering hops, stirring to combine. Boil for 45 minutes, uncovered. Monitor to prevent boiling over.

7. Meanwhile, prepare the fermentation gear and cooling bath or wort chiller.

8. After 45 minutes, remove the kettle from the heat and add sugar, Irish moss and yeast nutrient. Stir to ensure that the sugar and nutrient have dissolved. Return the kettle to the burner and bring back to a rolling boil. Boil for 15 minutes; stir in half of the aroma hops, turn off the heat and cover.

9. To cool the brew, place the covered kettle in the prepared cooling tub or use a wort chiller according to the manufacturer's directions. Cool to the desired temperature, 75°F (24°C), within 30 to 45 minutes.

10. While the wort is cooling, clean and sanitize the brewing spoon. When the wort has cooled, move the kettle to a counter and stir the wort briskly in one direction for about 5 minutes. After stirring, cover and let rest for 10 to 15 minutes as the hops and trub form a cone.

11. Using sanitized racking cane and siphon, rack as much wort as possible into the sanitized primary fermenter. Using the sanitized funnel and straining screen, strain the rest of the wort into the fermenter. Top off with brewing water to bring the volume to around 5.5 US gal (21 L). Using the hydrometer, take a reading of the specific gravity and record it in your brewing journal.

12. Add the yeast; vigorously stir it with a sanitized spoon to distribute it throughout the wort. Seal the fermenter with lid, stopper and airlock. Keep the fermenter at room temperature (68 to 72°F/20 to 22°C) during primary fermentation, which typically lasts 7 to 10 days after fermentation begins. (Keep in a dark place or under a lightproof cover if using a glass carboy.)

13. After 7 to 10 days or when the kräusen has fallen, use a sanitized racking cane and siphon to gently rack the beer into the sanitized secondary fermenter. Avoid aerating it, and leave as much of the sediment behind as possible. Gently add remaining hops (2 oz/56 g). Seal and keep at room temperature, covered or in a dark place, for another 2 weeks.

14. Once the bubbling in the airlock has slowed, confirm completion of fermentation by using the hydrometer to take final gravity readings. (Hydrometer readings should be the same for several days in a row.)

15. Prime and bottle the beer (see page 91) and condition it for 3 to 4 weeks.

Dry Hopping

IPA brewers shipping beer to India dosed the casks with hops prior to shipping. This dry hopping was done to take advantage of the preservative character of the hops, but it was soon discovered that, because the hops weren't boiled, they contributed an intense hop aroma to the beer.

If the beer you love has a hoppy floral aroma, you'll want to experiment with dry hopping. It is best to add dry hops to the secondary fermenter when activity has slowed. Allow another week or two for the beer to clear. Sometimes when pellet hops are added, your beer will foam for a little while. No, it didn't start to re-ferment; it's just acting as a nucleation point for dissolved CO_2 in the beer. Use a blow-off hose briefly, if needed.

Fest Bier

**Estimated Original
Gravity: 1.061**

Equipment

- **brew kettle**
- **fermentation gear
  (page 14)**

As you build your brewing
skills, switching to liquid
yeast products (from
Wyeast or White Labs)
will give you a brew
that is more complex
than the ones made
with the dry yeast (from
Fermentis or Danstar) in
the Absolute Beginner
recipes. See page 86 for
more information about
liquid yeasts.

Liquid Yeast

1 pack	Wyeast 1007 or White Labs WLP036	1 pack

Grains

1 lb	dark Munich malt	450 g
1 lb	toasted malt (25 to 50 Lovibond)	450 g
1 lb	crystal or caramel malt (40 to 60 Lovibond)	450 g
5.5 US gal	brewing water (page 89)	21 L

Malt Extracts

8.8 lbs	Weyermann Pilsner (or Briess Pilsner Light)	4 kg

Bittering Hops

8 to 10 AAUs	Perle, Northern Brewer or Saphir	8 to 10 AAUs

Flavor and Aroma Hops

1 oz	Noble European hops (such as Hallertau, Saaz, Spalt or Tettnang), divided in half	28 g

Later Additions

1 tsp	Irish moss	5 mL
1 tsp	yeast nutrient	5 mL

1. Prepare the liquid yeast in advance, according to the package directions.
2. Coarsely crack the grains and place them in a cheesecloth or nylon grain bag.
3. In a brew kettle, bring at least 3 US gal (11 L) brewing water to steeping temperature (150 to 160°F/65 to 71°C). Turn off the heat, add the grain bag, cover and steep for 30 minutes. (If the temperature drops below steeping temperature, reheat briefly.) Remove grain bag. Place it in a strainer, rinse it over the kettle with steeping water and then discard it.
4. Increase the heat and bring grain tea to a boil. Remove from heat, add the malt extracts and stir until dissolved completely.
5. Return kettle to the burner and increase the heat until the wort begins to boil. Using a spoon, clear any foam to one side. Reduce heat until a rolling boil can be maintained without foam buildup.
6. Add the bittering hops, stirring to combine. Boil for 45 minutes, uncovered. Monitor to prevent boiling over.
7. Meanwhile, prepare the fermentation gear and cooling bath or wort chiller.

8. After 45 minutes, remove the kettle from the heat and add half the hops (.5 oz/14 g) for flavor, Irish moss and yeast nutrient. Stir to ensure that the nutrient has dissolved. Return the kettle to the burner and bring back to a rolling boil. Boil for 15 minutes; stir in the remaining hops (.5 oz/14 g), turn off the heat and cover.

9. To cool the brew, place the covered kettle in the prepared cooling tub or use a wort chiller according to the manufacturer's directions. Cool to the desired temperature, 75°F (24°C), within 30 to 45 minutes.

10. While the wort is cooling, clean and sanitize the brewing spoon. When the wort has cooled, move the kettle to a counter and stir the wort briskly in one direction for about 5 minutes. After stirring, cover and let rest for 10 to 15 minutes as the hops and trub form a cone.

11. Using sanitized racking cane and siphon, rack as much wort as possible into the sanitized primary fermenter. Using the sanitized funnel and straining screen, strain the rest of the wort into the fermenter. Top off with brewing water to bring the volume to around 5.5 US gal (21 L). Using the hydrometer, take a reading of the specific gravity and record it in your brewing journal.

12. Add the yeast; vigorously stir it with a sanitized spoon to distribute it throughout the wort. Seal the fermenter with lid, stopper and airlock. Keep the fermenter at room temperature (68 to 72°F/20 to 22°C) during primary fermentation, which typically lasts 7 to 10 days after fermentation begins. (Keep in a dark place or under a lightproof cover if using a glass carboy.)

13. After 7 to 10 days or when the kräusen has fallen, use a sanitized racking cane and siphon to gently rack the beer into the sanitized secondary fermenter. Avoid aerating it, and leave as much of the sediment behind as possible. Seal and keep at room temperature, covered or in a dark place, to allow fermentation to continue.

14. Once the bubbling in the airlock has slowed, confirm completion of fermentation by using the hydrometer to take final gravity readings. (Hydrometer readings should be the same for several days in a row.)

15. Prime and bottle the beer (see page 91) and condition it for 3 to 4 weeks.

Ale or Lager?

The difference between ale and lager is determined by yeast, temperature and time. Lager yeasts ferment at colder temperatures than ale yeasts. This means you must ferment lagers in a refrigerator if you're not brewing during cold weather.

To brew a lager, select a lager yeast such as Wyeast 2206 or White Labs WLP830. Store your primary fermenter at room temperature until fermentation begins, then refrigerate (or otherwise chill) it to a temperature between 46 and 55°F (8 and 13°C.) After 7 days, rack to a secondary fermenter and drop the temperature to 35 to 45°F (2 to 7° C). Expect the ferment to continue for another 4 to 6 weeks. If you're not sure it's ready for bottling, wait!

Store bottled beer in the refrigerator for 3 to 4 weeks.

Colonial Porter

Estimated Original Gravity: 1.077

Equipment

- **brew kettle**
- **fermentation gear (page 14)**

Beers with an estimated original gravity higher than 1.065 require a longer time in both primary and secondary fermentation. Primary fermentation should take 7 to 10 days, and secondary fermentation should take about 2 weeks longer than weaker brews.

Liquid Yeast

1 pack	Wyeast 1187 or White Labs WLP013	1 pack

Grains

1 lb	toasted malt (25 to 50 Lovibond)	450 g
1 lb	crystal and caramel malt (40 to 60 Lovibond)	450 g
8 oz	chocolate malt	224 g
5.5 US gal	brewing water (page 89)	21 L

Malt Extract

8 lbs	any brand UK light	3.6 kg

Bittering Hops

8 to 10 AAUs	UK hops (such as Challenger, First Gold, Pilgrim or Target)	8 to 10 AAUs

Later Additions

8 oz	blackstrap molasses	224 g
1 tsp	Irish moss	5 mL
1 tsp	yeast nutrient	5 mL

Aroma Hops

1.5 oz	UK hops (such as Bramling Cross, Fuggle or East Kent Golding)	42 g

1. Prepare the liquid yeast in advance, according to the package directions.
2. Coarsely crack the grains and place them in a cheesecloth or nylon grain bag.
3. In a brew kettle, bring at least 3 US gal (11 L) brewing water to steeping temperature (150 to 160°F/65 to 71°C). Turn off the heat, add the grain bag, cover and steep for 30 minutes. (If the temperature drops below steeping temperature, reheat briefly.) Remove grain bag. Place it in a strainer, rinse it over the kettle with steeping water and then discard it.
4. Increase the heat and bring grain tea to a boil. Remove from heat, add the malt extract and stir until dissolved completely.
5. Return kettle to the burner and increase the heat until the wort begins to boil. Using a spoon, clear any foam to one side. Reduce heat until a rolling boil can be maintained without foam buildup.
6. Add the bittering hops, stirring to combine. Boil for 45 minutes, uncovered. Monitor to prevent boiling over.

7. Meanwhile, prepare the fermentation gear and cooling bath or wort chiller.

8. After 45 minutes, remove the kettle from the heat and add molasses, Irish moss and yeast nutrient. Stir to ensure that the molasses and nutrient have dissolved. Return the kettle to the burner and bring back to a rolling boil. Boil for 15 minutes; stir in the aroma hops, turn off the heat and cover.

9. To cool the brew, place the covered kettle in the prepared cooling tub or use a wort chiller according to the manufacturer's directions. Cool to the desired temperature, 75°F (24°C), within 30 to 45 minutes.

10. While the wort is cooling, clean and sanitize the brewing spoon. When the wort has cooled, move the kettle to a counter and stir the wort briskly in one direction for about 5 minutes. After stirring, cover and let rest for 10 to 15 minutes as the hops and trub form a cone.

11. Using sanitized racking cane and siphon, rack as much wort as possible into the sanitized primary fermenter. Using the sanitized funnel and straining screen, strain the rest of the wort into the fermenter. Top off with brewing water to bring the volume to around 5.5 US gal (21 L). Using the hydrometer, take a reading of the specific gravity and record it in your brewing journal.

12. Add the yeast; vigorously stir it with a sanitized spoon to distribute it throughout the wort. Seal the fermenter with lid, stopper and airlock. Keep the fermenter at room temperature (68 to 72°F/20 to 22°C) during primary fermentation, which typically lasts 7 to 10 days after fermentation begins. (Keep in a dark place or under a lightproof cover if using a glass carboy.)

13. After 7 to 10 days or when the kräusen has fallen, use a sanitized racking cane and siphon to gently rack the beer into the sanitized secondary fermenter. Avoid aerating it, and leave as much of the sediment behind as possible. Seal and keep at room temperature, covered or in a dark place, to allow fermentation to continue.

14. Once the bubbling in the airlock has slowed, confirm completion of fermentation by using the hydrometer to take final gravity readings. (Hydrometer readings should be the same for several days in a row.)

15. Prime and bottle the beer (see page 91) and condition it for 3 to 4 weeks.

Old or Stock Ale

Estimated Original Gravity: 1.064

Equipment

- **brew kettle**
- **fermentation gear (page 14)**

As you build your brewing skills, switching to liquid yeast products (from Wyeast or White Labs) will give you a brew that is more complex than the ones made with the dry yeast (from Fermentis or Danstar) in the Absolute Beginner recipes. See page 86 for more information about liquid yeasts.

Liquid Yeast

1 pack	Wyeast 1028 or White Labs WLP013	1 pack

Grains

8 oz	toasted malt (25 to 50 Lovibond)	224 g
8 oz	crystal or caramel malt (40 to 60 Lovibond)	224 g
2 oz	dark-roasted malt	56 g
5.5 US gal	brewing water (page 89)	21 L

Malt Extract

8 lbs	any brand UK light	3.6 kg

Bittering Hops

6 to 7 AAUs	UK hops (such as Bramling Cross, East Kent Golding, Fuggle or other)	6 to 7 AAUs

Later Additions

2 lbs	amber, Barbados or baking molasses	900 g
1 tsp	Irish moss	5 mL
1 tsp	yeast nutrient	5 mL

Aroma Hops

.5 oz	UK hops (such as Bramling Cross, East Kent Golding or Fuggle)	14 g

1. Prepare the liquid yeast in advance, according to the package directions.
2. Coarsely crack the grains and place them in a cheesecloth or nylon grain bag.
3. In a brew kettle, bring at least 3 US gal (11 L) brewing water to steeping temperature (150 to 160°F/65 to 71°C). Turn off the heat, add the grain bag, cover and steep for 30 minutes. (If the temperature drops below steeping temperature, reheat briefly.) Remove grain bag. Place it in a strainer, rinse it over the kettle with steeping water and then discard it.
4. Increase the heat and bring grain tea to a boil. Remove from heat, add the malt extract and stir until dissolved completely.
5. Return kettle to the burner and increase the heat until the wort begins to boil. Using a spoon, clear any foam to one side. Reduce heat until a rolling boil can be maintained without foam buildup.
6. Add the bittering hops, stirring to combine. Boil for 45 minutes, uncovered. Monitor to prevent boiling over.

7. Meanwhile, prepare the fermentation gear and cooling bath or wort chiller.

8. After 45 minutes, remove the kettle from the heat and add molasses, Irish moss and yeast nutrient. Stir to ensure that the sugar and nutrient have dissolved. Return the kettle to the burner and bring back to a rolling boil. Boil for 15 minutes; stir in the aroma hops, turn off the heat and cover.

9. To cool the brew, place the covered kettle in the prepared cooling tub or use a wort chiller according to the manufacturer's directions. Cool to the desired temperature, 75°F (24°C), within 30 to 45 minutes.

10. While the wort is cooling, clean and sanitize the brewing spoon. When the wort has cooled, move the kettle to a counter and stir the wort briskly in one direction for about 5 minutes. After stirring, cover and let rest for 10 to 15 minutes as the hops and trub form a cone.

11. Using sanitized racking cane and siphon, rack as much wort as possible into the sanitized primary fermenter. Using the sanitized funnel and straining screen, strain the rest of the wort into the fermenter. Top off with brewing water to bring the volume to around 5.5 US gal (21 L). Using the hydrometer, take a reading of the specific gravity and record it in your brewing journal.

12. Add the yeast; vigorously stir it with a sanitized spoon to distribute it throughout the wort. Seal the fermenter with lid, stopper and airlock. Keep the fermenter at room temperature (68 to 72°F/20 to 22°C) during primary fermentation, which typically lasts 1 to 4 days after fermentation begins. (Keep in a dark place or under a lightproof cover if using a glass carboy.)

13. After 1 to 4 days or when the kräusen has fallen, use a sanitized racking cane and siphon to gently rack the beer into the sanitized secondary fermenter. Avoid aerating it, and leave as much of the sediment behind as possible. Seal and keep at room temperature, covered or in a dark place, to allow fermentation to continue.

14. Once the bubbling in the airlock has slowed, confirm completion of fermentation by using the hydrometer to take final gravity readings. (Hydrometer readings should be the same for several days in a row.)

15. Prime and bottle the beer (see page 91) and condition it for 3 to 4 weeks.

Variation

Christmas Spice Ale: This is often the beer style that is served with mulling spices for a Winter Solstice beer. While there is a more complex recipe later in the book, if you want an easy version now, add two or three of your favorite spiced herbal tea bags during the last 15 minutes of the boil. (Use herbal tea, not black or green tea!) These beers make great holiday gifts.

California Blonde

The Alexander's extracts are widely distributed and work best for the recipes that call for it. If not available, substitute the lightest extra-light extract you can find.

Estimated Original Gravity: 1.059

Equipment

- **brew kettle**
- **fermentation gear (page 14)**

As you build your brewing skills, switching to liquid yeast products (from Wyeast or White Labs) will give you a brew that is more complex than the ones made with the dry yeast (from Fermentis or Danstar) in the Absolute Beginner recipes. See page 86 for more information about liquid yeasts.

Liquid Yeast

| 1 pack | Wyeast 1056 or White Labs WLP001 | 1 pack |

Grains

1 lb	Carafoam®, Carapils® or dextrin malt	450 g
8 oz	Vienna malt	224 g
5.5 US gal	brewing water (page 89)	21 L

Malt Extract

| 8 lbs | Alexander's Sun Country Pale (or any brand extra-light), divided in half | 3.6 kg |

Bittering Hops

| 12 to 14 AAUs | high-alpha acid American hops (such as Amarillo, Centennial, Chinook or Columbus) | 12 to 14 AAUs |

Later Additions

| 1 tsp | Irish moss | 5 mL |
| 1 tsp | yeast nutrient | 5 mL |

Aroma Hops

| 2 oz | citrusy American hops (such as Ahtanum, Amarillo, Cascade or Williamette) | 56 g |

1. Prepare the liquid yeast in advance, according to the package directions.
2. Coarsely crack the grains and place them in a cheesecloth or nylon grain bag.
3. In a brew kettle, bring at least 3 US gal (11 L) brewing water to steeping temperature (150 to 160°F/65 to 71°C). Turn off the heat, add the grain bag, cover and steep for 30 minutes. (If the temperature drops below steeping temperature, reheat briefly.) Remove grain bag. Place it in a strainer, rinse it over the kettle with steeping water and then discard it.
4. Increase the heat and bring grain tea to a boil. Remove from heat, add half the malt extract (4 lbs/1.8 kg) and stir until dissolved completely.
5. Return kettle to the burner and increase the heat until the wort begins to boil. Using a spoon, clear any foam to one side. Reduce heat until a rolling boil can be maintained without foam buildup.
6. Add the bittering hops, stirring to combine. Boil for 45 minutes, uncovered. Monitor to prevent boiling over.

7. Meanwhile, prepare the fermentation gear and cooling bath or wort chiller.

8. After 45 minutes, remove the kettle from the heat and add the remaining half of the malt extract (4 lbs/1.8 kg), Irish moss and yeast nutrient. Stir to ensure that the extract and nutrient have dissolved. Return the kettle to the burner and bring back to a rolling boil. Boil for 15 minutes; stir in the aroma hops, turn off the heat and cover.

9. To cool the brew, place the covered kettle in the prepared cooling tub or use a wort chiller according to the manufacturer's directions. Cool to the desired temperature, 75°F (24°C), within 30 to 45 minutes.

10. While the wort is cooling, clean and sanitize the brewing spoon. When the wort has cooled, move the kettle to a counter and stir the wort briskly in one direction for about 5 minutes. After stirring, cover and let rest for 10 to 15 minutes as the hops and trub form a cone.

11. Using sanitized racking cane and siphon, rack as much wort as possible into the sanitized primary fermenter. Using the sanitized funnel and straining screen, strain the rest of the wort into the fermenter. Top off with brewing water to bring the volume to around 5.5 US gal (21 L). Using the hydrometer, take a reading of the specific gravity and record it in your brewing journal.

12. Add the yeast; vigorously stir it with a sanitized spoon to distribute it throughout the wort. Seal the fermenter with lid, stopper and airlock. Keep the fermenter at room temperature (68 to 72°F/20 to 22°C) during primary fermentation, which typically lasts 1 to 4 days after fermentation begins. (Keep in a dark place or under a lightproof cover if using a glass carboy.)

13. After 1 to 4 days or when the kräusen has fallen, use a sanitized racking cane and siphon to gently rack the beer into the sanitized secondary fermenter. Avoid aerating it, and leave as much of the sediment behind as possible. Seal and keep at room temperature, covered or in a dark place, to allow fermentation to continue.

14. Once the bubbling in the airlock has slowed, confirm completion of fermentation by using the hydrometer to take final gravity readings. (Hydrometer readings should be the same for several days in a row.)

15. Prime and bottle the beer (see page 91) and condition it for 3 to 4 weeks.

Bavarian Hefeweizen

Estimated Original Gravity: 1.048

Equipment

- **brew kettle**
- **fermentation gear (page 14)**

As you build your brewing skills, switching to liquid yeast products (from Wyeast or White Labs) will give you a brew that is more complex than the ones made with the dry yeast (from Fermentis or Danstar) in the Absolute Beginner recipes. See page 86 for more information about liquid yeasts.

Liquid Yeast

1 pack	Wyeast 3056 or White Labs WLP300	1 pack

Grains

1 lb	Pilsner malt	450 g
1 lb	light wheat malt	450 g
5.5 US gal	brewing water (page 89)	21 L

Malt Extract

6.6 lbs	Coopers or Munton's wheat, divided in half	3 kg

Bittering Hops

3 to 4 AAUs	European hops (such as Hallertau, Tettnang, Saaz or Spalt)	3 to 4 AAUs

Later Additions

1 tsp	yeast nutrient	5 mL

Aroma Hops

.5 oz	European hops (such as Hallertau, Tettnang, Saaz or Spalt)	14 g

1. Prepare the liquid yeast in advance, according to the package directions.
2. Coarsely crack the grains and place them in a cheesecloth or nylon grain bag.
3. In a brew kettle, bring at least 3 US gal (11 L) brewing water to steeping temperature (150 to 160°F/65 to 71°C). Turn off the heat, add the grain bag, cover and steep for 30 minutes. (If the temperature drops below steeping temperature, reheat briefly.) Remove grain bag. Place it in a strainer, rinse it over the kettle with steeping water and then discard it.
4. Increase the heat and bring grain tea to a boil. Remove from heat, add half the malt extract (3.3 lbs/1.5 kg) and stir until dissolved completely.
5. Return kettle to the burner and increase the heat until the wort begins to boil. Using a spoon, clear any foam to one side. Reduce heat until a rolling boil can be maintained without foam buildup.
6. Add the bittering hops, stirring to combine. Boil for 45 minutes, uncovered. Monitor to prevent boiling over.
7. Meanwhile, prepare the fermentation gear and cooling bath or wort chiller.

8. After 45 minutes, remove the kettle from the heat and add the remaining half of the malt extract (3.3 lbs/1.5 kg), Irish moss and yeast nutrient. Stir to ensure that the extract and nutrient have dissolved. Return the kettle to the burner and bring back to a rolling boil. Boil for 15 minutes; stir in the aroma hops, turn off the heat and cover.

9. To cool the brew, place the covered kettle in the prepared cooling tub or use a wort chiller according to the manufacturer's directions. Cool to the desired temperature, 75°F (24°C), within 30 to 45 minutes.

10. While the wort is cooling, clean and sanitize the brewing spoon. When the wort has cooled, move the kettle to a counter and stir the wort briskly in one direction for about 5 minutes. After stirring, cover and let rest for 10 to 15 minutes as the hops and trub form a cone.

11. Using sanitized racking cane and siphon, rack as much wort as possible into the sanitized primary fermenter. Using the sanitized funnel and straining screen, strain the rest of the wort into the fermenter. Top off with brewing water to bring the volume to around 5.5 US gal (21 L). Using the hydrometer, take a reading of the specific gravity and record it in your brewing journal.

12. Add the yeast; vigorously stir it with a sanitized spoon to distribute it throughout the wort. Seal the fermenter with lid, stopper and airlock. Keep the fermenter at room temperature (68 to 72°F/20 to 22°C) during primary fermentation, which typically lasts 1 to 4 days after fermentation begins. (Keep in a dark place or under a lightproof cover if using a glass carboy.)

13. After 1 to 4 days or when the kräusen has fallen, use a sanitized racking cane and siphon to gently rack the beer into the sanitized secondary fermenter. Avoid aerating it, and leave as much of the sediment behind as possible. Seal and keep at room temperature, covered or in a dark place, to allow fermentation to continue.

14. Once the bubbling in the airlock has slowed, confirm completion of fermentation by using the hydrometer to take final gravity readings. (Hydrometer readings should be the same for several days in a row.)

15. Prime and bottle the beer (see page 91) and condition it for 3 to 4 weeks.

Variation

American Wheat: Many brewpubs in North America make a light wheat ale as their entry level beer. To brew in this style switch to a light American hop variety and change the yeast to Wyeast 1056 or 1010, or White Labs WLP01. Estimated OG: 1.048.

**Estimated Original
Gravity: 1.050**

Equipment

- **brew kettle**
- **fermentation gear
  (page 14)**

As you build your brewing skills, switching to liquid yeast products (from Wyeast or White Labs) will give you a brew that is more complex than the ones made with the dry yeast (from Fermentis or Danstar) in the Absolute Beginner recipes. See page 86 for more information about liquid yeasts.

Cream Ale
(Canadian Ale)

Liquid Yeast

1 pack	Wyeast 1056 or White Labs WLP001	1 pack

Grains

8 oz	Carafoam®, Carapils® or dextrin malt	224 g
4 oz	Vienna malt	112 g
5.5 US gal	brewing water (page 89)	21 L

Malt Extract

5.4 lbs	Alexander's Sun Country Pale (or any extra-light), divided 1.4:4 lbs (.625:1.875 kg)	2.5 kg

Bittering Hops

4 to 6 AAUs	hops with alpha acid below 6%	4 to 6 AAUs

Later Additions

1 lb	rice syrup	450 g
8 oz	malto-dextrin powder	224 g
1 tsp	Irish moss	5 mL
1 tsp	yeast nutrient	5 mL

Aroma Hops

.5 oz	hops with alpha acid below 4%	14 g

1. Prepare the liquid yeast in advance, according to the package directions.
2. Coarsely crack the grains and place them in a cheesecloth or nylon grain bag.
3. In a brew kettle, bring at least 3 US gal (11 L) brewing water to steeping temperature (150 to 160°F/65 to 71°C). Turn off the heat, add the grain bag, cover and steep for 30 minutes. (If the temperature drops below steeping temperature, reheat briefly.) Remove grain bag. Place it in a strainer, rinse it over the kettle with steeping water and then discard it.
4. Increase the heat and bring grain tea to a boil. Remove from heat, add 1.4 lbs (.625 kg) of the malt extract and stir until dissolved completely.
5. Return kettle to the burner and increase the heat until the wort begins to boil. Using a spoon, clear any foam to one side. Reduce heat until a rolling boil can be maintained without foam buildup.
6. Add the bittering hops, stirring to combine. Boil for 45 minutes, uncovered. Monitor to prevent boiling over.

7. Meanwhile, prepare the fermentation gear and cooling bath or wort chiller.

8. After 45 minutes, remove the kettle from the heat and add the remaining 4 lbs (1.875 kg) malt extract, rice syrup, malto-dextrin powder, Irish moss and yeast nutrient. Stir to ensure that the extract, syrup, powder and nutrient have dissolved. Return the kettle to the burner and bring back to a rolling boil. Boil for 15 minutes; stir in the aroma hops, turn off the heat and cover.

9. To cool the brew, place the covered kettle in the prepared cooling tub or use a wort chiller according to the manufacturer's directions. Cool to the desired temperature, 75°F (24°C), within 30 to 45 minutes.

10. While the wort is cooling, clean and sanitize the brewing spoon. When the wort has cooled, move the kettle to a counter and stir the wort briskly in one direction for about 5 minutes. After stirring, cover and let rest for 10 to 15 minutes as the hops and trub form a cone.

11. Using sanitized racking cane and siphon, rack as much wort as possible into the sanitized primary fermenter. Using the sanitized funnel and straining screen, strain the rest of the wort into the fermenter. Top off with brewing water to bring the volume to around 5.5 US gal (21 L). Using the hydrometer, take a reading of the specific gravity and record it in your brewing journal.

12. Add the yeast; vigorously stir it with a sanitized spoon to distribute it throughout the wort. Seal the fermenter with lid, stopper and airlock. Keep the fermenter at room temperature (68 to 72°F/20 to 22°C) during primary fermentation, which typically lasts 1 to 4 days after fermentation begins. (Keep in a dark place or under a lightproof cover if using a glass carboy.)

13. After 1 to 4 days or when the kräusen has fallen, use a sanitized racking cane and siphon to gently rack the beer into the sanitized secondary fermenter. Avoid aerating it, and leave as much of the sediment behind as possible. Seal and keep at room temperature, covered or in a dark place, to allow fermentation to continue.

14. Once the bubbling in the airlock has slowed, confirm completion of fermentation by using the hydrometer to take final gravity readings. (Hydrometer readings should be the same for several days in a row.)

15. Prime and bottle the beer (see page 91) and condition it for 3 to 4 weeks.

Variations

Dry Cream Ale: To brew a drier, cheaper version of this ale, substitute dextrose for the rice syrup and eliminate the malto-dextrin powder.

Light Lager: To brew a light lager, follow this recipe but switch to a lager yeast such as Fermentis S-23. Follow the lagering directions with the Fest Bier recipe (see page 245). Since this is not as strong a beer as the Fest Bier, the ferment will likely be shorter.

Honey Cream Ale: To brew a Honey Cream Ale, add 1 lb (450 g) of a light-colored honey as an additional kettle sugar when you add the rice syrup at the end of the 45-minute boil.

Ale-sner

**Estimated Original
Gravity: 1.048**

Equipment

- **brew kettle**
- **fermentation gear
  (page 14)**

As you build your brewing
skills, switching to liquid
yeast products (from
Wyeast or White Labs)
will give you a brew
that is more complex
than the ones made
with the dry yeast (from
Fermentis or Danstar) in
the Absolute Beginner
recipes. See page 86 for
more information about
liquid yeasts.

Liquid Yeast

1 pack	Wyeast 1056 or White Labs WLP001	1 pack

Grains

1 lb	Carafoam® malt	450 g
5.5 US gal	brewing water (page 89)	21 L

Malt Extract

6.6 lbs	any brand extra-light, divided in half	3 kg

Bittering Hops

8 to 10 AAUs	Perle, Premiant or Northern Brewer	8 to 10 AAUs

Later Additions

8 oz	malto-dextrin powder	224 g
1 tsp	Irish moss	5 mL
1 tsp	yeast nutrient	5 mL

Aroma and Dry Hops

3 oz	Saaz (Czech) or Hallertau, Spalt or Tettnang (German), divided in half	85 g

1. Prepare the liquid yeast in advance, according to the package directions.
2. Coarsely crack the grains and place them in a cheesecloth or nylon grain bag.
3. In a brew kettle, bring at least 3 US gal (11 L) brewing water to steeping temperature (150 to 160°F/65 to 71°C). Turn off the heat, add the grain bag, cover and steep for 30 minutes. (If the temperature drops below steeping temperature, reheat briefly.) Remove grain bag. Place it in a strainer, rinse it over the kettle with steeping water and then discard it.
4. Increase the heat and bring grain tea to a boil. Remove from heat, add half the malt extract (3.3 lbs/1.5 kg) and stir until dissolved completely.
5. Return kettle to the burner and increase the heat until the wort begins to boil. Using a spoon, clear any foam to one side. Reduce heat until a rolling boil can be maintained without foam buildup.
6. Add the bittering hops, stirring to combine. Boil for 45 minutes, uncovered. Monitor to prevent boiling over.
7. Meanwhile, prepare the fermentation gear and cooling bath or wort chiller.

8. After 45 minutes, remove the kettle from the heat and add the remaining malt extract (3.3 lbs/1.5 kg), malto-dextrin powder, Irish moss and yeast nutrient. Stir to ensure that the extract, powder and nutrient have dissolved. Return the kettle to the burner and bring back to a rolling boil. Boil for 15 minutes; stir in half the hops (1.5 oz/42 g), turn off the heat and cover.

9. To cool the brew, place the covered kettle in the prepared cooling tub or use a wort chiller according to the manufacturer's directions. Cool to the desired temperature, 75°F (24°C), within 30 to 45 minutes.

10. While the wort is cooling, clean and sanitize the brewing spoon. When the wort has cooled, move the kettle to a counter and stir the wort briskly in one direction for about 5 minutes. After stirring, cover and let rest for 10 to 15 minutes as the hops and trub form a cone.

11. Using sanitized racking cane and siphon, rack as much wort as possible into the sanitized primary fermenter. Using the sanitized funnel and straining screen, strain the rest of the wort into the fermenter. Top off with brewing water to bring the volume to around 5.5 US gal (21 L). Using the hydrometer, take a reading of the specific gravity and record it in your brewing journal.

12. Add the yeast; vigorously stir it with a sanitized spoon to distribute it throughout the wort. Seal the fermenter with lid, stopper and airlock. Keep the fermenter at room temperature (68 to 72°F/20 to 22°C) during primary fermentation, which typically lasts 1 to 4 days after fermentation begins. (Keep in a dark place or under a lightproof cover if using a glass carboy.)

13. After 1 to 4 days or when the kräusen has fallen, use a sanitized racking cane and siphon to gently rack the beer into the sanitized secondary fermenter. Avoid aerating it, and leave as much of the sediment behind as possible. Seal and keep at room temperature, covered or in a dark place, to allow fermentation to continue.

14. Once the bubbling in the airlock has slowed, gently add the remaining hops (1.5 oz/42 g) as a dry hop, reseal the carboy and leave for another week or so. Confirm completion of fermentation by using the hydrometer to take final gravity readings. (Hydrometer readings should be the same for several days in a row.)

15. Prime and bottle the beer (see page 91) and condition it for 3 to 4 weeks.

Part 3

Weird and Extreme Beers and Other Fermentable Beverages

The recipes in this final part of the book are a mix of challenges and fun brewing activities. Now that you have mastered the basic techniques, you should be ready to play with some interesting ingredients and create some more exotic flavors for your beverages.

Weird and Extreme Beers

The recipes for weird and extreme beers include beers made with fruit extracts or whole fruits or vegetables (in this case, peppers). Then come the recipes for spiced beers made with flavors that include cinnamon, cloves, ginger, licorice root, vanilla bean, maple or chocolate, as well as exotic flavors like spruce or juniper. The recipes for smoked beers use smoked malts to add another layer of flavor. The funky beers are sour and get their tart flavor from yeasts added to the secondary fermenter. The final recipes in this category are the gluten-free beers, which are brews that drinkers with celiac disease can enjoy.

You may wish to do some outside research to sample some of these beers before you try to create your own versions using the recipes provided. Once you've mastered these recipes, by all means try your own combinations.

Working with Fruits and Vegetables

Generally speaking, when creating a fruit or vegetable beer, you'll want a light-colored ale, lager or wheat beer that's not too hoppy. That said, I've tasted excellent Cherry Porters and Raspberry Imperial Stouts, but be aware that the fruit flavor will be subdued by the stronger flavor notes of the base beer.

Fruit juice concentrates and purées are the easiest to work with, but you can also use whole fruit (fresh or frozen that is sugar- and preservative-free). Complete instructions for working with all fruit sources, including fresh fruit, are included with each recipe. When working with fresh fruit, be aware that this is not the time to be using fruit that's past its best. Fresh, unblemished fruit at its peak is what you're looking for. (Blemished fruits have oxidized flavors and elevated levels of undesirable funky bugs.)

If you're working with fruit purée or fresh fruit, you'll be doing a three-stage fermentation for these beers. Primary fermentation proceeds as usual. Secondary fermentation of fruit beers is done in an opaque fermenter bucket, and the fruit is added to the secondary fermenter. The beer is later racked to a tertiary fermenter so it can clarify before it's bottled. The details are covered in the recipes.

Other Fermentable Beverages

The final sections of Part 3 deal with other fermentables such as honey and apples or apple cider. Meads (made with honey) have a short boil; ciders have none, although there is some boiling preparation for the yeast nutrient. Meads can be still or sparkling (carbonated) and flavored with fresh fruit or spices. Both meads and ciders generally have a longer fermentation and conditioning time than beers, but the wait is well worth it in terms of flavor.

The recipes for sodas give you a chance to create scratch versions of root beer, birch beer, cream soda and ginger ale. Like the fresh beer you've created, you'll be drinking sodas that taste nothing like the commercial versions. The flavors will amaze you!

Brew Day Process Summary

The following tips and techniques are reference summaries for less-familiar brewing techniques. For a more detailed look at the bottling process, see pages 31 to 33.

❶ Preparing a Yeast Starter

Using a yeast starter requires more advance planning—the starter itself requires at least 24 hours to develop.

1 pack	specified yeast	1 pack	
32 US fl oz	brewing water	950 mL	
3.5 oz	DME	99 g	
½ tsp	yeast nutrient	3 mL	

1. Activate yeast according to package instructions.
2. In a small saucepan, bring the brewing water to a boil. Stir in the DME and nutrient; boil for 20 minutes.
3. Remove from heat and cool to 70°F (21°C).
4. Pour cooled brewing water into a sealable, sanitized jar with lid or bottle with stopper and airlock. Cover loosely and shake well.
5. Add yeast culture and let jar sit, loosely covered to allow gas to escape, at room temperature (below 75°F/24°C) for at least 24 hours. If not using yeast culture immediately, it can be refrigerated for up to one week. Bring the yeast to fermentation temperature before pitching.

How to collect yeast for re-pitching:

- Rack the current brew into the secondary fermenter and set up for secondary fermentation.
- Collect about 1 US quart (1 L) of the slurry from the bottom of the primary fermenter.
- Put the slurry into a sanitized jar with lid or bottle with stopper and airlock, seal it and store it in the refrigerator.
- If not using airlock, "burp" the jar daily.
- Within one week, brew the next batch of beer.
- At the beginning of the next brewing session, remove the sealed jar of slurry from the refrigerator and allow to warm to room temperature.
- To pitch yeast, open jar and pour as much of the top layer of beer as you can down the drain.
- Pour tan yeast layer into new batch of beer in primary fermenter. (Leave trub layer in bottom of the jar.)
- Repeat the yeast collection process at the end of primary fermentation.
- Do not re-pitch a yeast more than five or six times.
- Never re-pitch yeast from a contaminated batch.

❷ Preparing and Using the Cooling Bath

If you're cooling your brew with the ice-and-saltwater bath, prepare it while the boil is on and the fermentation gear is soaking in sanitizer.

1. Fill the tub with enough water to surround your kettle at or above the level of the beer inside it when the kettle is in the tub (in other words, allow for displacement of the water).

2. Add $\frac{1}{2}$ to 1 cup (125 to 250 mL) of salt and stir to dissolve.

3. Add ice to bring the temperature of the saltwater down.

4. At the end of the boil, remove the kettle from the stove, cover it and put it in the saltwater bath, ensuring that the saltwater doesn't get into the brew.

5. Add ice to the bath, and keep the warm water around the kettle on the move to assist in cooling.

6. After 20 minutes, check the wort temperature with the sanitized thermometer. The temperature goal is around 75°F (24°C) or as per yeast instructions. Ideally, you should bring the temperature down within 30 minutes. At that point, the beer can be prepared for racking into the fermenter.

❸ Racking, Priming, Bottling and Conditioning

Once the hydrometer readings confirm that fermentation is complete, your brew is ready to bottle. This step adds some sugar to carbonate the beer as it conditions in the bottle.

1 cup	brewing water	250 mL
5 oz	dextrose (corn sugar) or as directed in recipe for priming	140 g

1. Clean and sanitize the bottles using your standard sanitizing procedure. Sanitize caps, racking cane, siphon hose, spoon, bottle filler and bottling bucket. Run sanitizer through bottling faucet.

2. In a small saucepan, bring brewing water to a boil. Add dextrose. Return mixture to a boil and stir to dissolve dextrose. Remove from heat and cover. Cool to room temperature.

3. Gently rack the beer into the bottling bucket, leaving sediment behind and being careful not to aerate. Gently add priming solution. Using a sanitized spoon, stir the beer gently to ensure even distribution of priming solution.

4. Using bottling faucet or siphon and bottle filler, fill bottles to top; 1 to 1.5 in (2.5 to 3.8 cm) of space remains when filler is removed. Cap bottles securely.

5. Store bottles upright in cool, dark place to allow for carbonation and settling of sediment.

6. After 3 to 4 weeks, hold a bottle to the light to check that sediment is settling. Unless otherwise indicated in the recipe, sample some brew! Note the date, flavor and level of carbonation each time you sample to compare as it ages.

As you play with the new flavors of the brewery, you may want to explore flavors of the kitchen. There are several ways to produce fruit- or vegetable-flavored beers: flavorings, extracts, purées and the actual fruits or vegetables.

Brewing with Fruits and Vegetables

Pepper Beers

Extract Fruit Beer

Fruit flavorings are available for wine and beer. The advantage of this method of flavoring is the flavors are added at bottling time, so you can sample as you build the taste. The amount used varies with the type of fruit flavor so check the package for recommendations. Be conservative! Add a small amount, give a gentle stir and then sample the beer. You can always add more flavor, but you can't remove it.

Estimated Original Gravity: 1.053

Equipment

- **brew kettle**
- **sanitized fermentation gear**

1 pack	Wyeast 1338 or 1187 or White Labs WLP011 or 023 or Fermentis S-04	1 pack
1 lb	Carafoam®, Carapils® or dextrin malt	450 g
5.5 US gal	brewing water	21 L
6.6 lbs	either extra-light malt extract, wheat malt extract or a blend of the two, divided in half	3 kg
2 to 4 AAUs	any variety low-alpha acid hop for bittering	2 to 4 AAUs
1 tsp	Irish moss	5 mL
1 tsp	yeast nutrient	5 mL

No aroma hops in this recipe

Fruit flavoring (any flavor), added to taste at bottling

1. Prepare liquid yeast in advance, according to directions.
2. Coarsely crack the grains and place them in a cheesecloth or nylon grain bag.
3. In a brew kettle, bring at least 3 US gal (11 L) brewing water to steeping temperature (150 to 160°F/65 to 71°C). Turn off the heat, add the grain bag, cover and steep for 30 minutes. (Turn the element back on briefly if the temperature drops below steeping temperature.) Remove grain bag. Place it in a strainer, rinse it over the kettle with steeping water and then discard it.
4. Increase heat and bring grain tea to a boil. Remove from heat, add half of the malt extract (3.3 lbs/1.5 kg) and stir until dissolved.
5. Return kettle to the burner and increase the heat until the wort begins to boil. Using a spoon, clear foam to one side. Reduce heat until a rolling boil is maintained without foam buildup.
6. Add bittering hops, stirring to combine. Boil for 45 minutes, uncovered. Monitor to prevent boiling over.
7. Meanwhile, prepare fermentation gear and cooling bath or wort chiller.
8. After 45 minutes, remove kettle from heat and add remaining half of malt extract (3.3 lbs/1.5 kg), Irish moss and yeast nutrient. Stir to ensure that the extract and nutrient have dissolved. Return kettle to burner and bring back to a rolling boil. Boil for 15 minutes, uncovered; turn off heat and cover.

9. To cool the brew, place covered kettle in prepared cooling bath or use a wort chiller according to manufacturer's directions. Cool to desired temperature of 75°F (24°C) within 30 to 45 minutes.

10. While wort is cooling, clean and sanitize brewing spoon. When wort has cooled, move kettle to counter and stir wort briskly in one direction for about 5 minutes. After stirring, cover and let rest for 10 to 15 minutes while hops and trub form a cone.

11. Using sanitized racking cane and siphon, rack as much wort as possible into sanitized primary fermenter. Then, using a sanitized funnel and straining screen, strain remainder of wort into fermenter. Top off with brewing water to bring volume to around 5.5 US gal (21 L). Using the hydrometer, take a reading of the specific gravity and record it in your brewing journal.

12. Add yeast, vigorously stirring with a sanitized spoon to distribute it throughout wort. Seal fermenter with lid, stopper and airlock. Keep fermenter at room temperature (68 to 72°F/20 to 22°C) during primary fermentation, which typically lasts 1 to 4 days after fermentation begins. (Keep in a dark place or under a lightproof cover if using a glass carboy.)

13. After 1 to 4 days or when the kräusen has fallen, use a sanitized racking cane and siphon to gently rack the beer into the sanitized secondary fermenter. Avoid aerating it, and leave as much of the sediment behind as possible. Seal and keep at room temperature, covered or in a dark place, to allow beer to ferment and condition for 30 days.

14. Once the bubbling in the airlock has slowed, confirm completion of fermentation by using the hydrometer to take final gravity readings. (Hydrometer readings should be the same for several days in a row.)

15. Add fruit flavoring sparingly; stir gently with a sanitized spoon and sample until you achieve the desired taste.

16. Prime and bottle the beer (see page 263). Condition for 3 to 4 weeks.

Brewer's Tip

The baking department of the grocery or gourmet store may carry flavorings not available from winemaking and homebrew suppliers. Feel free to experiment, as long as the flavors are free of preservatives and oils. If the label indicates it contains anything with the suffix "-ite" or "-ate," don't use it. Also avoid "imitation" flavors. They taste fake.

Raspberry Weizen

Fruit purées or juice concentrates are easy to work with. Fresh fruit is more of a challenge, but it can be done. Avoid products with preservatives or added sugar.

Estimated Original Gravity: 1.071

Equipment

- **brew kettle**
- **sanitized fermentation gear**

Brewer's Tip

Beers made with fresh fruit or fruit purées require a three-stage fermentation. Primary fermentation is the same as that for non-fruit beer. Before racking the beer into the secondary fermenter, you will be adding the prepared fruit (or purée) to the secondary fermenter, racking the brew into the fermenter, waiting 30 days and then racking into a tertiary fermenter.

	Raspberries, prepared for brewing, if using (see sidebar)	
1 pack	Wyeast 3056 or White Labs WLP351 or Fermentis WB-06	1 pack
1 lb	Carafoam®, Carapils® or dextrin malt	450 g
5.5 US gal	brewing water	21 L
8 lbs	Alexander's Sun Country Wheat Malt Extract, divided in half	3.6 kg
2 to 4 AAUs	any variety low-alpha acid hops for bittering	2 to 4 AAUs
1 lb	wild raspberry honey	450 g
1 tsp	Irish moss	5 mL
1 tsp	yeast nutrient	5 mL
	No aroma hops in this recipe	
3 to 6 lbs	raspberry purée, in a large straining bag, if using instead of fruit (see Step 13)	1.36 to 2.72 kg

1. Prepare liquid yeast in advance, according to directions.
2. Coarsely crack the grains and place them in a cheesecloth or nylon grain bag.
3. In a brew kettle, bring at least 3 US gal (11 L) brewing water to steeping temperature (150 to 160°F/65 to 71°C). Turn off the heat, add the grain bag, cover and steep for 30 minutes. (Turn the element back on briefly if the temperature drops below steeping temperature.) Remove grain bag. Place it in a strainer, rinse it over the kettle with steeping water and then discard it.
4. Increase heat and bring grain tea to a boil. Remove from heat, add half of the malt extract (4 lbs/1.8 kg) and stir until dissolved.
5. Return kettle to the burner and increase the heat until the wort begins to boil. Using a spoon, clear foam to one side. Reduce heat until a rolling boil is maintained without foam buildup.
6. Add bittering hops, stirring to combine. Boil for 45 minutes, uncovered. Monitor to prevent boiling over.
7. Meanwhile, prepare fermentation gear and cooling bath or wort chiller.

8. After 45 minutes, remove kettle from heat and add remaining half of malt extract (4 lbs/1.8 kg), honey, Irish moss and yeast nutrient. Stir to ensure that the extract, honey and nutrient have dissolved. Return kettle to burner and bring back to a rolling boil. Boil for 15 minutes, uncovered; turn off heat and cover.

9. To cool the brew, place covered kettle in prepared cooling bath or use a wort chiller according to manufacturer's directions. Cool to desired temperature of 75°F (24°C) within 30 to 45 minutes.

10. While wort is cooling, clean and sanitize brewing spoon. When wort has cooled, move kettle to counter and stir wort briskly in one direction for about 5 minutes. After stirring, cover and let rest for 10 to 15 minutes while hops and trub form a cone.

11. Using sanitized racking cane and siphon, rack as much wort as possible into sanitized primary fermenter. Then, using a sanitized funnel and straining screen, strain remainder of wort into fermenter. Top off with brewing water to bring volume to around 5.5 US gal (21 L). Using the hydrometer, take a reading of specific gravity and record it in your brewing journal.

12. Add yeast, vigorously stirring with a sanitized spoon to distribute it throughout wort. Seal fermenter with lid, stopper and airlock. Keep fermenter at room temperature (68 to 72°F/20 to 22°C) during primary fermentation, which typically lasts 1 to 4 days after fermentation begins. (Keep in a dark place or under a lightproof cover if using a glass carboy.)

13. After 1 to 4 days or when the kräusen has fallen, use a sanitized racking cane and siphon to gently rack the beer onto the prepared fruit or purée (see sidebar) in the sanitized secondary fermenter. Avoid aerating it, and leave as much of the sediment behind as possible. Seal and keep at room temperature, covered or in a dark place, to allow beer to ferment and condition for 30 days.

14. Using a sanitized racking cane and siphon, gently rack the beer into a sanitized glass carboy and seal. Store, covered or in a dark place. Once the bubbling in the airlock has slowed, confirm completion of fermentation by using the hydrometer to take final gravity readings. (Hydrometer readings should be the same for several days in a row.)

15. Prime and bottle the beer (see page 263). Condition for 3 to 4 weeks.

Preparing Raspberries

Use 5 to 10 lbs (2.25 to 4.5 kg) fresh or frozen raspberries.

Shortly after brew day, wash and stem (if necessary) fresh fruit and freeze it in resealable bags.

Two days before racking the beer to secondary fermenter, sanitize a fermenter bucket. Transfer frozen fruit (prepared or purchased) to a large, sanitized straining bag (for easier racking and filtering) and thaw fruit in the bucket. Crush the fruit with a sanitized potato masher, if necessary. Dissolve 1 campden tablet for each US gal (3.75 L) of fruit in a small amount of boiling water and, using sanitized spoon, stir the mixture into the fruit in the bag. Seal the fermenter with the lid, stopper and an airlock containing a sterile cotton ball (not the usual water). Leave the fruit for at least 24 hours or until the sulphur smell goes away. This bucket will become your secondary fermenter.

If using purée, put the purée in a sanitized straining bag and place it in the bottom of the sanitized secondary fermenter before racking the beer.

Watermelon Wheat

There's no purée or flavoring for this one so you're going to have to brew it when it's melon season. Experiment with different varieties of melon. This recipe is modeled after the popular brew from the 21st Amendment Brewpub in San Francisco.

Estimated Original Gravity: 1.064

Equipment

- brew kettle
- sanitized fermentation gear

Brewer's Tip

Beers made with fresh fruit or fruit purées require a three-stage fermentation. Primary fermentation is the same as that for non-fruit beer. Before racking the beer into the secondary fermenter, you will be adding the prepared fruit (or purée) to the secondary fermenter, racking the brew into the fermenter, waiting 30 days and then racking into a tertiary fermenter.

	Watermelon, fresh, prepared for brewing (see sidebar)	
1 pack	Wyeast 1010 or White Labs WLP320 or Fermentis S-04	1 pack
1 lb	Carafoam®, Carapils® or dextrin malt	450 g
5.5 US gal	brewing water	21 L
8 lbs	Alexander's Sun Country Wheat Extract, divided in half	3.6 kg
2 to 4 AAUs	any variety low-alpha acid hop for bittering	2 to 4 AAUs
8 oz	malto dextrin powder	224 g
1 tsp	Irish moss	5 mL
1 tsp	yeast nutrient	5 mL

No aroma hops in this recipe

1. Prepare liquid yeast in advance, according to directions.
2. Coarsely crack the grains and place them in a cheesecloth or nylon grain bag.
3. In a brew kettle, bring at least 3 US gal (11 L) brewing water to steeping temperature (150 to 160°F/65 to 71°C). Turn off the heat, add the grain bag, cover and steep for 30 minutes. (Turn the element back on briefly if the temperature drops below steeping temperature.) Remove grain bag. Place it in a strainer, rinse it over the kettle with steeping water and then discard it.
4. Increase heat and bring grain tea to a boil. Remove from heat, add half of the malt extract (4 lbs/1.8 kg) and stir until dissolved.
5. Return kettle to the burner and increase the heat until the wort begins to boil. Using a spoon, clear foam to one side. Reduce heat until a rolling boil is maintained without foam buildup.
6. Add bittering hops, stirring to combine. Boil for 45 minutes, uncovered. Monitor to prevent boiling over.
7. Meanwhile, prepare fermentation gear and cooling bath or wort chiller.

8. After 45 minutes, remove kettle from heat and add remaining half of malt extract (4 lbs/1.8 kg), malto dextrin powder, Irish moss and yeast nutrient. Stir to ensure that the extract, powder and nutrient have dissolved. Return kettle to burner and bring back to a rolling boil. Boil for 15 minutes, uncovered; turn off heat and cover.

9. To cool the brew, place covered kettle in prepared cooling bath or use a wort chiller according to manufacturer's directions. Cool to desired temperature of 75°F (24°C) within 30 to 45 minutes.

10. While wort is cooling, clean and sanitize brewing spoon. When wort has cooled, move kettle to counter and stir wort briskly in one direction for about 5 minutes. After stirring, cover and let rest for 10 to 15 minutes while hops and trub form a cone.

11. Using sanitized racking cane and siphon, rack as much wort as possible into sanitized primary fermenter. Then, using a sanitized funnel and straining screen, strain remainder of wort into fermenter. Top off with brewing water to bring volume to around 5.5 US gal (21 L). Using the hydrometer, take a reading of specific gravity and record it in your brewing journal.

12. Add yeast, vigorously stirring with a sanitized spoon to distribute it throughout wort. Seal fermenter with lid, stopper and airlock. Keep fermenter at room temperature (68 to 72°F/20 to 22°C) during primary fermentation, which typically lasts 1 to 4 days after fermentation begins. (Keep in a dark place or under a lightproof cover if using a glass carboy.)

13. After 1 to 4 days or when the kräusen has fallen, use a sanitized racking cane and siphon to gently rack the beer onto the prepared fruit (see sidebar) in the sanitized secondary fermenter. Avoid aerating it, and leave as much of the sediment behind as possible. Seal and keep at room temperature, covered or in a dark place, to allow beer to ferment and condition for 30 days.

14. Using a sanitized racking cane and siphon, gently rack the beer into a sanitized glass carboy and seal. Store, covered or in a dark place. Once the bubbling in the airlock has slowed, confirm completion of fermentation by using the hydrometer to take final gravity readings. (Hydrometer readings should be the same for several days in a row.)

15. Prime and bottle beer (see page 263). Condition for 3 to 4 weeks.

Preparing Watermelon

Use 10 to 15 lbs (4.5 to 6.8 kg) fresh watermelon pulp.

Shortly after brew day, scoop watermelon pulp, removing as many seeds as possible, and freeze it in resealable bags.

Two days before racking the beer to secondary fermenter, sanitize a fermenter bucket. Transfer frozen fruit to a large, sanitized straining bag (for easier racking and filtering) and thaw pulp in the bucket. Crush the pulp with a sanitized potato masher, if necessary. Dissolve 1 campden tablet for each US gal (3.75 L) of pulp in a small amount of boiling water and, using sanitized spoon, stir the mixture into the pulp in the bag. Seal the fermenter with the lid, stopper and an airlock containing a sterile cotton ball (not the usual water). Leave the pulp for at least 24 hours or until the sulphur smell goes away. This bucket will become your secondary fermenter.

Cranberry Wheat

This brew is the perfect foil for a turkey dinner. Let the wine lovers debate grapes while you enjoy this sweet/tart ale.

Estimated Original Gravity: 1.077

Equipment

- **brew kettle**
- **sanitized fermentation gear**

Brewer's Tip

Beers made with fresh fruit or fruit purées require a three-stage fermentation. Primary fermentation is the same as that for non-fruit beer. Before racking the beer into the secondary fermenter, you will be adding the prepared fruit (or purée) to the secondary fermenter, racking the brew into the fermenter, waiting 30 days and then racking into a tertiary fermenter.

	Cranberries, fresh or frozen, prepared for brewing, if using (see sidebar)	
1 pack	Wyeast 1338 or White Labs WLP011 or Fermentis S-04	1 pack
1 lb	Carafoam®, Carapils® or dextrin malt	450 g
5.5 US gal	brewing water	21 L
8 lbs	Alexander's Sun Country Wheat Malt Extract, divided in half	3.6 kg
2 AAUs	any variety low-alpha acid hops for bittering	2 AAUs
1 lb	cranberry honey	450 g
1 lb	lactose	450 g
1 tsp	Irish moss	5 mL
1 tsp	yeast nutrient	5 mL

No aroma hops in this recipe

8 to 16 US fl oz	100% cranberry juice concentrate, if using instead of fruit (see Step 13)	240 to 475 mL

1. Prepare liquid yeast in advance, according to directions.
2. Coarsely crack the grains and place them in a cheesecloth or nylon grain bag.
3. In a brew kettle, bring at least 3 US gal (11 L) brewing water to steeping temperature (150 to 160°F/65 to 71°C). Turn off the heat, add the grain bag, cover and steep for 30 minutes. (Turn the element back on briefly if the temperature drops below steeping temperature.) Remove grain bag. Place it in a strainer, rinse it over the kettle with steeping water and then discard it.
4. Increase heat and bring grain tea to a boil. Remove from heat, add half of the malt extract (4 lbs/1.8 kg) and stir until dissolved.
5. Return kettle to the burner and increase the heat until the wort begins to boil. Using a spoon, clear foam to one side. Reduce heat until a rolling boil is maintained without foam buildup.
6. Add bittering hops, stirring to combine. Boil for 45 minutes, uncovered. Monitor to prevent boiling over.
7. Meanwhile, prepare fermentation gear and cooling bath or wort chiller.

8. After 45 minutes, remove kettle from heat and add remaining half of malt extract (4 lbs/1.8 kg), honey, lactose, Irish moss and yeast nutrient. Stir to ensure that the extract, sugar and nutrient have dissolved. Return kettle to burner and bring back to a rolling boil. Boil for 15 minutes, uncovered; turn off heat and cover.

9. To cool the brew, place covered kettle in prepared cooling bath or use a wort chiller according to manufacturer's directions. Cool to desired temperature of 75°F (24°C) within 30 to 45 minutes.

10. While wort is cooling, clean and sanitize brewing spoon. When wort has cooled, move kettle to counter and stir wort briskly in one direction for about 5 minutes. After stirring, cover and let rest for 10 to 15 minutes while hops and trub form a cone.

11. Using sanitized racking cane and siphon, rack as much wort as possible into sanitized primary fermenter. Then, using a sanitized funnel and straining screen, strain remainder of wort into fermenter. Top off with brewing water to bring volume to around 5.5 US gal (21 L). Using the hydrometer, take a reading of specific gravity and record it in your brewing journal.

12. Add yeast, vigorously stirring with a sanitized spoon to distribute it throughout wort. Seal fermenter with lid, stopper and airlock. Keep fermenter at room temperature (68 to 72°F/20 to 22°C) during primary fermentation, which typically lasts 7 to 10 days after fermentation begins. (Keep in a dark place or under a lightproof cover if using a glass carboy.)

13. After 7 to 10 days or when the kräusen has fallen, use a sanitized racking cane and siphon to gently rack the beer onto the prepared fruit, if using (see sidebar), in the sanitized secondary fermenter. Avoid aerating it, and leave as much of the sediment behind as possible. (Gently add desired amount of cranberry juice concentrate if using instead of fruit.) Seal and keep at room temperature, covered or in a dark place, to allow beer to ferment and condition for 30 days.

14. Using a sanitized racking cane and siphon, gently rack the beer into a sanitized glass carboy and seal. Store, covered or in a dark place. Once the bubbling in the airlock has slowed, confirm completion of fermentation by using the hydrometer to take final gravity readings. (Hydrometer readings should be the same for several days in a row.)

15. Prime and bottle the beer (see page 263). Condition for 3 to 4 weeks.

Preparing Cranberries

Use 5 to 10 lbs (2.25 to 4.5 kg) fresh or frozen cranberries.

Shortly after brew day, wash and stem (if necessary) fresh fruit and freeze it in resealable bags.

Two days before racking the beer to secondary fermenter, sanitize a fermenter bucket. Transfer frozen fruit (prepared or purchased) to a large, sanitized straining bag (for easier racking and filtering) and thaw fruit in the bucket. Crush the fruit with a sanitized potato masher, if necessary. Dissolve 1 campden tablet for each US gal (3.75 L) of fruit in a small amount of boiling water and, using sanitized spoon, stir the mixture into the fruit in the bag. Seal the fermenter with the lid, stopper and an airlock containing a sterile cotton ball (not the usual water). Leave the fruit for at least 24 hours or until the sulphur smell goes away. This bucket will become your secondary fermenter.

Peachy

Equipment

- **brew kettle**
- **sanitized
  fermentation gear**

Brewer's Tip

Beers made with fresh fruit or fruit purées require a three-stage fermentation. Primary fermentation is the same as that for non-fruit beer. Before racking the beer into the secondary fermenter, you will be adding the prepared fruit (or purée) to the secondary fermenter, racking the brew into the fermenter, waiting 30 days and then racking into a tertiary fermenter.

	Peaches, fresh or frozen, prepared for brewing, if using (see sidebar)	
1 pack	Wyeast 1338 or White Labs WLP011 or Fermentis S-04	1 pack
1 lb	Carafoam®, Carapils® or dextrin malt	450 g
5.5 US gal	brewing water	21 L
8 lbs	Alexander's Sun Country Pale Malt Extract, divided in half	3.6 kg
2 AAUs	any variety low-alpha acid hop for bittering	2 AAUs
1 tsp	Irish moss	5 mL
1 tsp	yeast nutrient	5 mL
	No aroma hops in this recipe	
3 to 6 lbs	peach purée, in a large straining bag, if using instead of fruit (see Step 13)	1.36 to 2.72 kg
4+/- US fl oz	peach flavoring (see Step 15)	118+/- mL

1. Prepare liquid yeast in advance, according to directions.
2. Coarsely crack the grains and place them in a cheesecloth or nylon grain bag.
3. In a brew kettle, bring at least 3 US gal (11 L) brewing water to steeping temperature (150 to 160°F/65 to 71°C). Turn off the heat, add the grain bag, cover and steep for 30 minutes. (Turn the element back on briefly if the temperature drops below steeping temperature.) Remove grain bag. Place it in a strainer, rinse it over the kettle with steeping water and then discard it.
4. Increase heat and bring grain tea to a boil. Remove from heat, add half of the malt extract (4 lbs/1.8 kg) and stir until dissolved.
5. Return kettle to the burner and increase the heat until the wort begins to boil. Using a spoon, clear foam to one side. Reduce heat until a rolling boil is maintained without foam buildup.
6. Add bittering hops, stirring to combine. Boil for 45 minutes, uncovered. Monitor to prevent boiling over.
7. Meanwhile, prepare fermentation gear and cooling bath or wort chiller.

8. After 45 minutes, remove kettle from heat and add remaining half of malt extract (4 lbs/1.8 kg), Irish moss and yeast nutrient. Stir to ensure that the extract and nutrient have dissolved. Return kettle to burner and bring back to a rolling boil. Boil for 15 minutes, uncovered; turn off heat and cover.

9. To cool the brew, place covered kettle in prepared cooling bath or use a wort chiller according to manufacturer's directions. Cool to desired temperature of 75°F (24°C) within 30 to 45 minutes.

10. While wort is cooling, clean and sanitize brewing spoon. When wort has cooled, move kettle to counter and stir wort briskly in one direction for about 5 minutes. After stirring, cover and let rest for 10 to 15 minutes while hops and trub form a cone.

11. Using sanitized racking cane and siphon, rack as much wort as possible into sanitized primary fermenter. Then, using a sanitized funnel and straining screen, strain remainder of wort into fermenter. Top off with brewing water to bring volume to around 5.5 US gal (21 L). Using the hydrometer, take a reading of specific gravity and record it in your brewing journal.

12. Add yeast, vigorously stirring with a sanitized spoon to distribute it throughout wort. Seal fermenter with lid, stopper and airlock. Keep fermenter at room temperature (68 to 72°F/20 to 22°C) during primary fermentation, which typically lasts 1 to 4 days after fermentation begins. (Keep in a dark place or under a lightproof cover if using a glass carboy.)

13. After 1 to 4 days or when the kräusen has fallen, use a sanitized racking cane and siphon to gently rack the beer onto the prepared fruit or purée (see sidebar) in the sanitized secondary fermenter. Avoid aerating it, and leave as much of the sediment behind as possible. Seal and keep at room temperature, covered or in a dark place, to allow beer to ferment and condition for 30 days.

14. Using a sanitized racking cane and siphon, gently rack the beer into a sanitized glass carboy and seal. Store, covered or in a dark place. Once the bubbling in the airlock has slowed, confirm completion of fermentation by using the hydrometer to take final gravity readings. (Hydrometer readings should be the same for several days in a row.)

15. Add fruit flavoring sparingly; stir gently with sanitized spoon. Sample until you achieve desired taste. Prime and bottle the beer (see page 263). Condition for 3 to 4 weeks.

Preparing Peaches

Use 5 to 10 lbs (2.25 to 4.5 kg) fresh or frozen peaches.

Shortly after brew day, peel and pit fresh fruit and freeze it in resealable bags.

Two days before racking the beer to secondary fermenter, sanitize a fermenter bucket. Transfer frozen fruit (prepared or purchased) to a large, sanitized straining bag (for easier racking and filtering) and thaw fruit in the bucket. Crush the fruit with a sanitized potato masher, if necessary. Dissolve 1 campden tablet for each US gal (3.75 L) of fruit in a small amount of boiling water and, using sanitized spoon, stir the mixture into the fruit in the bag. Seal the fermenter with the lid, stopper and an airlock containing a sterile cotton ball (not the usual water). Leave the fruit for at least 24 hours or until the sulphur smell goes away. This bucket will become your secondary fermenter.

If using purée, put the purée in a sanitized straining bag and place it in the bottom of the sanitized secondary fermenter before racking the beer.

Cherry Dubbel

Many brewers of Belgian Abbey-style ales like to add cherries to a beefy Abbey Dubbel. The notes of chocolate and dried fruit play nicely off the fruit addition.

Estimated Original Gravity: 1.083

Equipment

- **brew kettle**
- **sanitized fermentation gear**

Brewer's Tips

Beers made with fresh fruit or fruit purées require a three-stage fermentation. Primary fermentation is the same as that for non-fruit beer. Before racking the beer into the secondary fermenter, you will be adding the prepared fruit (or purée) to the secondary fermenter, racking the brew into the fermenter, waiting 30 days and then racking into a tertiary fermenter.

If the specified brands of grains are not available, use the grains chart on page 77 to find substitutes.

	Cherries, fresh or frozen, prepared for brewing, if using (see sidebar)	
1 pack	Wyeast 1214 or White Labs WLP500 or Fermentis T-58	1 pack
1 lb	Caramunich III® malt	450 g
1 lb	Carabohemian® malt	450 g
1 lb	Caraaroma® or Special B malt	450 g
4 oz	dehusked Carafa I® malt	112 g
5.5 US gal	brewing water	21 L
8 lbs	any brand light malt extract	3.6 kg
4 to 6 AAUs	Northern Brewer or Perle hops for bittering	4 to 6 AAUs
1 lb	Belgian amber or dark candi sugar	450 g
1 tsp	Irish moss	5 mL
1 tsp	yeast nutrient	5 mL
	No aroma hops in this recipe	
3 to 6 lbs	cherry purée, in a large straining bag, if using instead of fruit (see Step 13)	1.36 to 2.72 kg
16 US fl oz	black cherry concentrate, if using instead of fruit	475 mL

1. Prepare liquid yeast in advance, according to directions.
2. Coarsely crack the grains and place them in a cheesecloth or nylon grain bag.
3. In a brew kettle, bring at least 3 US gal (11 L) brewing water to steeping temperature (150 to 160°F/65 to 71°C). Turn off the heat, add the grain bag, cover and steep for 30 minutes. (Turn the element back on briefly if the temperature drops below steeping temperature.) Remove grain bag. Place it in a strainer, rinse it over the kettle with steeping water and then discard it.
4. Increase heat and bring grain tea to a boil. Remove from heat, add malt extract and stir until dissolved.
5. Return kettle to the burner and increase the heat until the wort begins to boil. Using a spoon, clear foam to one side. Reduce heat until a rolling boil is maintained without foam buildup.
6. Add bittering hops, stirring to combine. Boil for 45 minutes, uncovered. Monitor to prevent boiling over.
7. Meanwhile, prepare fermentation gear and cooling bath or wort chiller.

8. After 45 minutes, remove kettle from heat and add sugar, Irish moss and yeast nutrient. Stir to ensure that the sugar and nutrient have dissolved. Return kettle to burner and bring back to a rolling boil. Boil for 15 minutes, uncovered; turn off heat and cover.

9. To cool the brew, place covered kettle in prepared cooling bath or use a wort chiller according to manufacturer's directions. Cool to desired temperature of 75°F (24°C) within 30 to 45 minutes.

10. While wort is cooling, clean and sanitize brewing spoon. When wort has cooled, move kettle to counter and stir wort briskly in one direction for about 5 minutes. After stirring, cover and let rest for 10 to 15 minutes while hops and trub form a cone.

11. Using sanitized racking cane and siphon, rack as much wort as possible into sanitized primary fermenter. Then, using a sanitized funnel and straining screen, strain remainder of wort into fermenter. Top off with brewing water to bring volume to around 5.5 US gal (21 L). Using the hydrometer, take a reading of specific gravity and record it in your brewing journal.

12. Add yeast, vigorously stirring with a sanitized spoon to distribute it throughout wort. Seal fermenter with lid, stopper and airlock. Keep fermenter at room temperature (68 to 72°F/20 to 22°C) during primary fermentation, which typically lasts 7 to 10 days after fermentation begins. (Keep in a dark place or under a lightproof cover if using a glass carboy.)

13. After 7 to 10 days or when the kräusen has fallen, use a sanitized racking cane and siphon to gently rack the beer onto the prepared fruit or purée (see sidebar) in the sanitized secondary fermenter. Avoid aerating it, and leave as much of the sediment behind as possible. (Gently add concentrate if using instead of fruit.) Seal and keep at room temperature, covered or in a dark place, to allow beer to ferment and condition for 30 days.

14. Using a sanitized racking cane and siphon, gently rack the beer into a sanitized glass carboy and seal. Store, covered or in a dark place. Once the bubbling in the airlock has slowed, confirm completion of fermentation by using the hydrometer to take final gravity readings. (Hydrometer readings should be the same for several days in a row.)

15. Prime and bottle beer (see page 263). Condition for 3 to 4 weeks.

Preparing Cherries

Use 5 to 10 lbs (2.25 to 4.5 kg) fresh or frozen cherries.

Shortly after brew day, wash, stem and pit fresh fruit and freeze it in resealable bags.

Two days before racking the beer to secondary fermenter, sanitize a fermenter bucket. Transfer frozen fruit (prepared or purchased) to a large, sanitized straining bag (for easier racking and filtering) and thaw fruit in the bucket. Crush the fruit with a sanitized potato masher, if necessary. Dissolve 1 campden tablet for each US gal (3.75 L) of fruit in a small amount of boiling water and, using sanitized spoon, stir the mixture into the fruit in the bag. Seal the fermenter with the lid, stopper and an airlock containing a sterile cotton ball (not the usual water). Leave the fruit for at least 24 hours or until the sulphur smell goes away. This bucket will become your secondary fermenter.

If using purée, put the purée in a sanitized straining bag and place it in the bottom of the sanitized secondary fermenter before racking the beer.

Apricot IPA

This brew is the exception to the "lightly hopped fruit beer" rule. The notes of apricot play nicely with the fruity notes of the Amarillo hops.

Estimated Original Gravity: 1.058

Equipment

- **brew kettle**
- **sanitized fermentation gear**

Brewer's Tips

Beers made with fresh fruit or fruit purées require a three-stage fermentation. Primary fermentation is the same as that for non-fruit beer. Before racking the beer into the secondary fermenter, you will be adding the prepared fruit (or purée) to the secondary fermenter, racking the brew into the fermenter, waiting 30 days and then racking into a tertiary fermenter.

For information on preparing a yeast starter, see page 262.

If the specified brands of grains are not available, use the grains chart on page 77 to find substitutes.

	Apricots, fresh, prepared for brewing, if using (see sidebar)	
2 packs	Wyeast 1187 or White Labs WLP011 (or 1 pack in starter) or Fermentis S-04	2 packs
1 lb	Caraamber® malt	450 g
1 lb	Caramunich I® malt	450 g
5.5 US gal	brewing water	21 L
6.6 lbs	any brand extra-light malt extract, divided in half	3 kg
8 to 10 AAUs	Amarillo hops for bittering	8 to 10 AAUs
1 tsp	Irish moss	5 mL
1 tsp	yeast nutrient	5 mL
3 oz	Amarillo hops for aroma, divided in thirds	84 g
3 to 6 lbs	apricot purée, in a large straining bag, if using instead of fruit (see Step 13)	1.36 to 2.72 kg
4$^{+/-}$ US fl oz	apricot flavoring (see Step 15)	118$^{+/-}$ mL

1. Prepare liquid yeast in advance, according to directions.
2. Coarsely crack the grains and place them in a cheesecloth or nylon grain bag.
3. In a brew kettle, bring at least 3 US gal (11 L) brewing water to steeping temperature (150 to 160°F/65 to 71°C). Turn off the heat, add the grain bag, cover and steep for 30 minutes. (Turn the element back on briefly if the temperature drops below steeping temperature.) Remove grain bag. Place it in a strainer, rinse it over the kettle with steeping water and then discard it.
4. Increase heat and bring grain tea to a boil. Remove from heat, add half of the malt extract (3.3. lbs/1.5 kg) and stir until dissolved.
5. Return kettle to the burner and increase the heat until the wort begins to boil. Using a spoon, clear foam to one side. Reduce heat until a rolling boil is maintained without foam buildup.
6. Add bittering hops, stirring to combine. Boil for 45 minutes, uncovered. Monitor to prevent boiling over.
7. Meanwhile, prepare fermentation gear and cooling bath or wort chiller.

8. After 45 minutes, remove kettle from heat and add remaining half of malt extract (3.3 lbs/1.5 kg), 1 oz (28 g) aroma hops, Irish moss and yeast nutrient. Stir to ensure that the nutrient has dissolved. Return kettle to burner and bring back to a rolling boil. Boil for 15 minutes, uncovered, then stir in 1 oz (28 g) aroma hops, turn off heat and cover.

9. To cool the brew, place covered kettle in prepared cooling bath or use a wort chiller according to manufacturer's directions. Cool to desired temperature of 75°F (24°C) within 30 to 45 minutes.

10. While wort is cooling, clean and sanitize brewing spoon. When wort has cooled, move kettle to counter and stir wort briskly in one direction for about 5 minutes. After stirring, cover and let rest for 10 to 15 minutes while hops and trub form a cone.

11. Using sanitized racking cane and siphon, rack as much wort as possible into sanitized primary fermenter. Then, using a sanitized funnel and straining screen, strain remainder of wort into fermenter. Top off with brewing water to bring volume to around 5.5 US gal (21 L). Using the hydrometer, take a reading of specific gravity and record it in your brewing journal.

12. Add yeast, vigorously stirring with a sanitized spoon to distribute it throughout wort. Seal fermenter with lid, stopper and airlock. Keep fermenter at room temperature (68 to 72°F/20 to 22°C) during primary fermentation, which typically lasts 1 to 4 days after fermentation begins. (Keep in a dark place or under a lightproof cover if using a glass carboy.)

13. After 1 to 4 days or when the kräusen has fallen, use a sanitized racking cane and siphon to gently rack the beer onto the prepared fruit or purée (see sidebar) in the sanitized secondary fermenter. Avoid aerating it, and leave as much of the sediment behind as possible. Seal and keep at room temperature, covered or in a dark place, to allow beer to ferment and condition for 30 days.

14. Using a sanitized racking cane and siphon, gently rack the beer into a sanitized glass carboy and seal. Store, covered or in a dark place. Once the bubbling in the airlock has slowed, add remaining 1 oz (28 g) of the aroma hops, reseal and leave it for about 2 more weeks. Confirm completion of fermentation by using the hydrometer to take final gravity readings. (Hydrometer readings should be the same for several days in a row.)

15. Add fruit flavoring sparingly; stir gently with sanitized spoon. Sample until you achieve desired taste. Prime and bottle beer (see page 263). Condition for 3 to 4 weeks.

Preparing Apricots

Use 5 to 10 lbs (2.25 to 4.5 kg) fresh apricots.

Shortly after brew day, pit the fruit and freeze it in resealable bags.

Two days before racking the beer to secondary fermenter, sanitize a fermenter bucket. Transfer frozen fruit to a large, sanitized straining bag (for easier racking and filtering) and thaw fruit in the bucket. Crush the fruit with a sanitized potato masher, if necessary. Dissolve 1 campden tablet for each US gal (3.75 L) of fruit in a small amount of boiling water and, using sanitized spoon, stir the mixture into the fruit in the bag. Seal the fermenter with the lid, stopper and an airlock containing a sterile cotton ball (not the usual water). Leave the fruit for at least 24 hours or until the sulphur smell goes away. This bucket will become your secondary fermenter.

If using purée, put the purée in a sanitized straining bag and place it in the bottom of the sanitized secondary fermenter before racking the beer.

Makes 5 US gal (19 L)

Estimated Original Gravity: 1.070

Equipment

- **brew kettle**
- **sanitized fermentation gear**

Brewer's Tip

Beers made with fresh fruit or fruit purées require a three-stage fermentation. Primary fermentation is the same as that for non-fruit beer. Before racking the beer into the secondary fermenter, you will be adding the prepared fruit (or purée) to the secondary fermenter, racking the brew into the fermenter, waiting 30 days and then racking into a tertiary fermenter.

	Strawberries, fresh, prepared for brewing (see sidebar)	
1 pack	Wyeast 1338 or White Labs WLP011 or Fermentis S-05	1 pack
1 lb	Carafoam®, Carapils® or dextrin malt	450 g
1 lb	Vienna malt	450 g
5.5 US gal	brewing water	21 L
8 lbs	Alexander's Sun Country Pale Malt Extract, divided in half	3.6 kg
6 to 8 AAUs	Northern Brewer, Palisades or Perle hops for bitterings	6 to 8 AAU
1 tsp	Irish moss	5 mL
1 tsp	yeast nutrient	5 mL
.5 oz	Liberty or Mt Hood hops for aroma	14 g
4$^{+/-}$ US fl oz	strawberry flavoring (optional; Step 15)	118$^{+/-}$ mL

1. Prepare liquid yeast in advance, according to directions.
2. Coarsely crack the grains and place them in a cheesecloth or nylon grain bag.
3. In a brew kettle, bring at least 3 US gal (11 L) brewing water to steeping temperature (150 to 160°F/65 to 71°C). Turn off the heat, add the grain bag, cover and steep for 30 minutes. (Turn the element back on briefly if the temperature drops below steeping temperature.) Remove grain bag. Place it in a strainer, rinse it over the kettle with steeping water and then discard it.
4. Increase heat and bring grain tea to a boil. Remove from heat, add half of the malt extract (4 lbs/1.8 kg) and stir until dissolved.
5. Return kettle to the burner and increase the heat until the wort begins to boil. Using a spoon, clear foam to one side. Reduce heat until a rolling boil is maintained without foam buildup.
6. Add bittering hops, stirring to combine. Boil for 45 minutes, uncovered. Monitor to prevent boiling over.
7. Meanwhile, prepare fermentation gear and cooling bath or wort chiller.

8. After 45 minutes, remove kettle from heat and add remaining half of the malt extract (4 lbs/1.8 kg), Irish moss and yeast nutrient. Stir to ensure that the extract and nutrient have dissolved. Return kettle to burner and bring back to a rolling boil. Boil for 15 minutes, uncovered, then stir in aroma hops, turn off heat and cover.

9. To cool the brew, place covered kettle in prepared cooling bath or use a wort chiller according to manufacturer's directions. Cool to desired temperature of 75°F (24°C) within 30 to 45 minutes.

10. While wort is cooling, clean and sanitize brewing spoon. When wort has cooled, move kettle to counter and stir wort briskly in one direction for about 5 minutes. After stirring, cover and let rest for 10 to 15 minutes while hops and trub form a cone.

11. Using sanitized racking cane and siphon, rack as much wort as possible into sanitized primary fermenter. Then, using a sanitized funnel and straining screen, strain remainder of wort into fermenter. Top off with brewing water to bring volume to around 5.5 US gal (21 L). Using the hydrometer, take a reading of specific gravity and record it in your brewing journal.

12. Add yeast, vigorously stirring with a sanitized spoon to distribute it throughout wort. Seal fermenter with lid, stopper and airlock. Keep fermenter at room temperature (68 to 72°F/20 to 22°C) during primary fermentation, which typically lasts 7 to 10 days after fermentation begins. (Keep in a dark place or under a lightproof cover if using a glass carboy.)

13. After 7 to 10 days or when the kräusen has fallen, use a sanitized racking cane and siphon to gently rack the beer onto the prepared fruit (see sidebar) in the sanitized secondary fermenter. Avoid aerating it, and leave as much of the sediment behind as possible. Seal and keep at room temperature, covered or in a dark place, to allow beer to ferment and condition for 30 days.

14. Using a sanitized racking cane and siphon, gently rack the beer into a sanitized glass carboy and seal. Store, covered or in a dark place. Once the bubbling in the airlock has slowed, confirm completion of fermentation by using the hydrometer to take final gravity readings. (Hydrometer readings should be the same for several days in a row.)

15. Add fruit flavoring sparingly, stir gently with a sanitized spoon and sample until you achieve the desired taste.

16. Prime and bottle the beer (see page 263). Condition for 3 to 4 weeks.

Preparing Strawberries

Use 10 lbs (4.5 kg) fresh or frozen strawberries.

Shortly after brew day, wash and hull (if necessary) fresh fruit and freeze it in resealable bags.

Two days before racking the beer to secondary fermenter, sanitize a fermenter bucket. Transfer frozen fruit (prepared or purchased) to a large, sanitized straining bag (for easier racking and filtering) and thaw fruit in the bucket. Crush the fruit with a sanitized potato masher, if necessary. Dissolve 1 campden tablet for each US gal (3.75 L) of fruit in a small amount of boiling water and, using sanitized spoon, stir the mixture into the fruit in the bag. Seal the fermenter with the lid, stopper and an airlock containing a sterile cotton ball (not the usual water). Leave the fruit for at least 24 hours or until the sulphur smell goes away. This bucket will become your secondary fermenter.

Kafir Lime Saison

This taste combination goes really well together. I sampled such a beer at a west coast brewpub and have included it in the summer rotation ever since. It's great with southeast Asian food.

Estimated Original Gravity: 1.079

Equipment

- brew kettle
- sanitized fermentation gear

Brewer's Tip

Lime zest is the green part of the lime's rind. Do not include the bitter pith underneath the zest. You should be able to find frozen Kafir lime leaves in Asian grocery stores.

1 pack	Wyeast 3711 or White Labs WLP565 or Fermentis T-58	1 pack
1 lb	Carafoam®, Carapils® or dextrin malt	450 g
1 lb	Carabelge® malt	450 g
5.5 US gal	brewing water	21 L
4 lbs	Alexander's Sun Country Wheat Malt Extract	1.8 kg
4 lbs	Alexander's Sun Country Pale Malt Extract, divided in half	1.8 kg
6 to 8 AAUs	Northern Brewer or Perle hops	6 to 8 AAUs
1 lb	Belgian clear candi sugar	450 g
8 oz	malto dextrin powder	224 g
2 to 3	limes, zest and juice only, to taste	2 to 3
3 to 4	Kafir lime leaves (in a hop bag)	3 to 4
1 tsp	Irish moss	5 mL
1 tsp	yeast nutrient	5 mL

No aroma hops in this recipe

1. Prepare liquid yeast in advance, according to directions.
2. Coarsely crack the grains and place them in a cheesecloth or nylon grain bag.
3. In a brew kettle, bring at least 3 US gal (11 L) brewing water to steeping temperature (150 to 160°F/65 to 71°C). Turn off the heat, add the grain bag, cover and steep for 30 minutes. (Turn the element back on briefly if the temperature drops below steeping temperature.) Remove grain bag. Place it in a strainer, rinse it over the kettle with steeping water and then discard it.
4. Increase heat and bring grain tea to a boil. Remove from heat, and add wheat malt extract and half of the pale malt extract (2 lbs/900 g); stir until dissolved.
5. Return kettle to the burner and increase the heat until the wort begins to boil. Using a spoon, clear foam to one side. Reduce heat until a rolling boil is maintained without foam buildup.
6. Add bittering hops, stirring to combine. Boil for 45 minutes, uncovered. Monitor to prevent boiling over.
7. Meanwhile, prepare fermentation gear and cooling bath or wort chiller.

8. After 45 minutes, remove kettle from heat and add remaining half of pale malt extract (2 lbs/900 g), sugar, malto dextrin powder, lime zest and juice, Kafir leaves, Irish moss and yeast nutrient. Stir to ensure that the extract, sugar, powder and nutrient have dissolved. Return kettle to burner and bring back to a rolling boil. Boil for 15 minutes, uncovered; turn off heat and cover.

9. To cool the brew, place covered kettle in prepared cooling bath or use a wort chiller according to manufacturer's directions. Cool to desired temperature of 75°F (24°C) within 30 to 45 minutes.

10. While wort is cooling, clean and sanitize brewing spoon. When wort has cooled, move kettle to counter and stir wort briskly in one direction for about 5 minutes. After stirring, cover and let rest for 10 to 15 minutes while hops and trub form a cone.

11. Using sanitized racking cane and siphon, rack as much wort as possible into sanitized primary fermenter. Then, using a sanitized funnel and straining screen, strain remainder of wort into fermenter. Top off with brewing water to bring volume to around 5.5 US gal (21 L). Using the hydrometer, take a reading of specific gravity and record it in your brewing journal.

12. Add yeast, vigorously stirring with a sanitized spoon to distribute it throughout wort. Seal fermenter with lid, stopper and airlock. Keep fermenter at room temperature (68 to 72°F/20 to 22°C) during primary fermentation, which typically lasts 7 to 10 days after fermentation begins. (Keep in a dark place or under a lightproof cover if using a glass carboy.)

13. After 7 to 10 days or when the kräusen has fallen, use a sanitized racking cane and siphon to gently rack the beer into the sanitized secondary fermenter. Avoid aerating it, and leave as much of the sediment behind as possible. Seal and keep at room temperature, covered or in a dark place, to allow beer to ferment and condition.

14. Once the bubbling in the airlock has slowed, confirm completion of fermentation by using the hydrometer to take final gravity readings. (Hydrometer readings should be the same for several days in a row.)

15. Prime and bottle the beer (see page 263). Condition for 3 to 4 weeks.

> **Brewer's Tip**
>
> If active fermentation backs up into the airlock, replace airlock with blow-off hose (see page 16). Change water as needed; re-install airlock when fermentation settles down.

Soda Pop Lambics
(Kriek, Framboise or Peche)

The authentic Lambic beers of Belgium are complex sour beers. (Many would call them an acquired taste.) For recipes for these beers read ahead to the funky beer section. Meanwhile many Belgian brewers brew a sweeter, more soda-like, beer for mass consumption. As with other fruit beers, you can use fresh or frozen fruit or purée. Use cherry to produce a Kriek, raspberry to produce Framboise and peach for Peche.

Estimated Original Gravity: will vary according to the type of fruit

Equipment

- **brew kettle**
- **sanitized fermentation gear**

Brewer's Tip

Beers made with fresh fruit or fruit purées require a three-stage fermentation. Primary fermentation is the same as that for non-fruit beer. Before racking the beer into the secondary fermenter, you will be adding the prepared fruit (or purée) to the secondary fermenter, racking the brew into the fermenter, waiting 30 days and then racking into a tertiary fermenter.

	Fresh cherries, raspberries or peaches, if using, prepared for brewing (see sidebar)	
1 pack	Wyeast 1338 or White Labs WLP011 or Fermentis T-58	1 pack
1 lb	Vienna malt	450 g
1 lb	Carabelge® malt	450 g
5.5 US gal	brewing water	21 L
4 lbs	Alexander's Sun Country Wheat Malt Extract	1.8 kg
4 lbs	Alexander's Sun Country Pale Malt Extract, divided in half	1.8 kg
2 to 4 AAUs	Northern Brewer or Perle hops	2 to 4 AAUs
1 lb	lactose	450 g
1 tsp	Irish moss	5 mL
1 tsp	yeast nutrient	5 mL
	No aroma hops in this recipe	
3 to 6 lbs	cherry, raspberry or peach purée, in a large straining bag, if using instead of fruit (see Step 13)	1.36 to 2.72 kg
4$^{+/-}$ US fl oz	cherry, raspberry or peach flavoring, if using (see Step 15)	118$^{+/-}$ mL

1. Prepare liquid yeast in advance, according to directions.
2. Coarsely crack the grains and place them in a cheesecloth or nylon grain bag.
3. In a brew kettle, bring at least 3 US gal (11 L) brewing water to steeping temperature (150 to 160°F/65 to 71°C). Turn off heat, add grain bag, cover and steep for 30 minutes. (Reheat briefly if the temperature drops below steeping temperature.) Remove grain bag. Place it in a strainer, rinse it over kettle with steeping water and discard.
4. Increase heat and bring grain tea to a boil. Remove from heat, add wheat malt extract and half of the pale malt extract (2 lbs/900 g); stir until dissolved.
5. Return kettle to burner and increase heat until wort begins to boil. Using a spoon, clear foam. Reduce heat until a rolling boil is maintained without foam buildup.
6. Add bittering hops, stirring to combine. Boil for 45 minutes, uncovered. Monitor to prevent boiling over.
7. Prepare fermentation gear and cooling bath or wort chiller.

8. After 45 minutes, remove kettle from heat and add remaining pale malt extract (2 lbs/900 g), lactose, Irish moss and yeast nutrient. Stir to ensure that the extract, lactose and nutrient have dissolved. Return kettle to burner and bring back to a rolling boil. Boil for 15 minutes, uncovered; turn off heat and cover.

9. To cool the brew, place covered kettle in prepared cooling bath or use a wort chiller according to manufacturer's directions. Cool to desired temperature of 75°F (24°C) within 30 to 45 minutes.

10. While wort cools, sanitize brewing spoon. When wort has cooled, move kettle to counter and stir wort briskly in one direction for about 5 minutes. After stirring, cover and let rest for 10 to 15 minutes while hops and trub form a cone.

11. Using sanitized racking cane and siphon, rack as much wort as possible into sanitized primary fermenter. Then, using a sanitized funnel and straining screen, strain remainder of wort into fermenter. Top off with brewing water to bring volume to around 5.5 US gal (21 L). Using the hydrometer, take a reading of specific gravity and record it.

12. Add yeast, vigorously stirring with a sanitized spoon to distribute it throughout wort. Seal fermenter with lid, stopper and airlock. Keep fermenter at room temperature (68 to 72°F/20 to 22°C) during primary fermentation, which could last as long as 10 days after fermentation begins, depending on the OG. (Keep in a dark place or under a lightproof cover if using a glass carboy.)

13. When the kräusen has fallen, use a sanitized racking cane and siphon to gently rack the beer onto the prepared fruit or purée (see sidebar) in the sanitized secondary fermenter. Avoid aerating it, and leave as much of the sediment behind as possible. Seal and keep at room temperature, covered or in a dark place, to allow beer to ferment and condition for 30 days.

14. Using a sanitized racking cane and siphon, gently rack the beer into a sanitized glass carboy and seal. Store, covered or in a dark place. Once the bubbling in the airlock has slowed, confirm completion of fermentation by using the hydrometer to take final gravity readings. (Hydrometer readings should be the same for several days in a row.)

15. Add fruit flavoring sparingly; stir gently with sanitized spoon. Sample until you achieve desired taste. Prime and bottle the beer (see page 263). Condition for 3 to 4 weeks.

Preparing Fresh Fruit

Use 5 to 10 lbs (2.25 to 4.5 kg) fresh or frozen fruit.

Shortly after brew day, peel or wash, stem and/ or pit the fresh fruit as appropriate and freeze it in resealable bags.

Two days before racking the beer to secondary fermenter, sanitize a fermenter bucket. Transfer frozen fruit (prepared or purchased) to a large, sanitized straining bag (for easier racking and filtering) and thaw fruit in the bucket. Crush the fruit with a sanitized potato masher, if necessary. Dissolve 1 campden tablet for each US gal (3.75 L) of fruit in a small amount of boiling water and, using sanitized spoon, stir the mixture into the fruit in the bag. Seal the fermenter with the lid, stopper and an airlock containing a sterile cotton ball (not the usual water). Leave the fruit for at least 24 hours or until the sulphur smell goes away. This bucket will become your secondary fermenter.

If using purée, put the purée in a sanitized straining bag and place it in the bottom of the sanitized secondary fermenter before racking the beer.

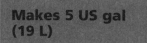
Belgian Raspberry Imperial Stout

Serve this beer with a dessert made with raspberries and chocolate.

Estimated Original Gravity: 1.103

Equipment

- **brew kettle**
- **sanitized fermentation gear**

Brewer's Tips

Beers made with fresh fruit or fruit purées require a three-stage fermentation. Primary fermentation is the same as that for non-fruit beer. Before racking the beer into the secondary fermenter, you will be adding the prepared fruit (or purée) to the secondary fermenter, racking the brew into the fermenter, waiting 30 days and then racking into a tertiary fermenter.

For information on preparing a yeast starter, see page 262.

If the specified brands of grains are not available, use the grains chart on page 77 to find substitutes.

	Raspberries, fresh or frozen, prepared for brewing, if using (see sidebar)	
2 packs	Wyeast 3787 or White Labs WLP545 (or 1 pack in starter) or Fermentis T-58	2 packs
1 lb	Carabohemian® malt	450 g
1 lb	Caraaroma® malt	450 g
8 oz	Dehusked Carafa I® malt	224 g
4 oz	roasted barley	112 g
5.5 US gal	brewing water	21 L
9.9 lbs	any brand light malt extract	4.5 kg
4 to 6 AAUs	Northern Brewer or Perle hops	4 to 6 AAUs
1 lb	lactose	450 g
1 lb	Belgian amber or dark candi sugar	450 g
1 tsp	Irish moss	5 mL
1 tsp	yeast nutrient	5 mL
	No aroma hops in this recipe	
6 lbs	raspberry purée, in a large straining bag, if using instead of fresh fruit (see Step 13)	2.72 kg
4$^{+/-}$ US fl oz	raspberry flavoring, if using (see Step 15)	118$^{+/-}$ mL

1. Prepare liquid yeast in advance, according to directions.
2. Coarsely crack the grains and place in a grain bag.
3. In a brew kettle, bring at least 3 US gal (11 L) brewing water to steeping temperature (150 to 160°F/65 to 71°C). Turn off heat, add grain bag, cover and steep for 30 minutes. (Reheat briefly if temperature drops below steeping temperature.) Remove grain bag. Place in a strainer, rinse over the kettle with steeping water and discard.
4. Increase heat and bring grain tea to a boil. Remove from heat, add malt extract and stir until dissolved.
5. Return kettle to burner and increase heat until wort begins to boil. Using a spoon, clear foam. Reduce heat until a rolling boil is maintained without foam buildup.
6. Add bittering hops, stirring to combine. Boil for 45 minutes, uncovered. Monitor to prevent boiling over.
7. Prepare fermentation gear and cooling bath or wort chiller.

8. After 45 minutes, remove kettle from heat and add lactose, sugar, Irish moss and yeast nutrient. Stir to ensure that the lactose, sugar and nutrient have dissolved. Return kettle to burner and bring back to a rolling boil. Boil for 15 minutes, uncovered; turn off heat and cover.

9. To cool the brew, place covered kettle in prepared cooling bath or use a wort chiller according to manufacturer's directions. Cool to desired temperature of 75°F (24°C) within 30 to 45 minutes.

10. While wort cools, sanitize brewing spoon. When wort has cooled, move kettle to counter and stir wort briskly in one direction for about 5 minutes. After stirring, cover and let rest for 10 to 15 minutes while hops and trub form a cone.

11. Using sanitized racking cane and siphon, rack as much wort as possible into sanitized primary fermenter. Then, using a sanitized funnel and straining screen, strain remainder of wort into fermenter. Top off with brewing water to bring volume to around 5.5 US gal (21 L). Using the hydrometer, take a reading of specific gravity and record it.

12. Add yeast, vigorously stirring with a sanitized spoon to distribute it throughout wort. Seal fermenter with lid, stopper and airlock. Keep fermenter at room temperature (68 to 72°F/20 to 22°C) during primary fermentation, which typically lasts 7 to 10 days after fermentation begins. (Keep in a dark place or under a lightproof cover if using a glass carboy.)

13. After 7 to 10 days or when the kräusen has fallen, use a sanitized racking cane and siphon to gently rack the beer onto the prepared fruit or purée (see sidebar) in the sanitized secondary fermenter. Avoid aerating it, and leave as much of the sediment behind as possible. Seal and keep at room temperature, covered or in a dark place, to allow beer to ferment and condition for 30 days.

14. Using a sanitized racking cane and siphon, gently rack the beer into a sanitized glass carboy and seal. Store, covered or in a dark place. Once the bubbling in the airlock has slowed, confirm completion of fermentation by using the hydrometer to take final gravity readings. (Hydrometer readings should be the same for several days in a row.)

15. Add fruit flavoring sparingly; stir gently with sanitized spoon. Sample until you achieve desired taste. Prime and bottle the beer (see page 263). Condition for 3 to 4 weeks.

Preparing Raspberries

Use 10 lbs (4.5 kg) fresh or frozen raspberries.

Shortly after brew day, wash and stem (if necessary) fresh fruit and freeze it in resealable bags.

Two days before racking the beer to secondary fermenter, sanitize a fermenter bucket. Transfer frozen fruit (prepared or purchased) to a large, sanitized straining bag (for easier racking and filtering) and thaw fruit in the bucket. Crush the fruit with a sanitized potato masher, if necessary. Dissolve 1 campden tablet for each US gal (3.75 L) of fruit in a small amount of boiling water and, using sanitized spoon, stir the mixture into the fruit in the bag. Seal the fermenter with the lid, stopper and an airlock containing a sterile cotton ball (not the usual water). Leave the fruit for at least 24 hours or until the sulphur smell goes away. This bucket will become your secondary fermenter.

If using purée, put the purée in a sanitized straining bag and place it in the bottom of the sanitized secondary fermenter before racking the beer.

Orange Cream Ale

**Estimated Original
Gravity: 1.070**

Equipment

- **brew kettle**
- **sanitized
  fermentation gear**

Brewer's Tips

Grind the orange peel and
coriander. Slit the vanilla
bean open and scrape the
inside with a knife blade.
Add the skin, seeds and
any pulp on the knife to
the brew kettle.

If the specified brands of
grains are not available,
use the grains chart
on page 77 to find
substitutes.

1 pack	Wyeast 1187 or White Labs WLP011 or Fermentis S-04	1 pack
1 lb	Carafoam®, Carapils® or dextrin malt	450 g
1 lb	Vienna malt	450 g
1 lb	Carahell® malt	450 g
5.5 US gal	brewing water	21 L
5.4 lbs	Alexander's Sun Country Pale Malt Extract, divided 1.4:4 lbs/.7:1.8 kg	2.5 kg
2 to 3 AAUs	Liberty or Mt Hood hops for bittering	2 to 3 AAUs
2 lbs	orange blossom honey	900 g
1 lb	rice syrup	450 g
1 lb	lactose	450 g
1 oz	sweet orange peel	28 g
.5 oz	coriander seed	14 g
2	whole vanilla beans	2
1 tsp	Irish moss	5 mL
1 tsp	yeast nutrient	5 mL
	No aroma hops in this recipe	
1$^{+/-}$ tsp	pure vanilla extract, optional, to taste (see Step 15)	5$^{+/-}$ mL

1. Prepare liquid yeast in advance, according to directions.
2. Coarsely crack the grains and place them in a cheesecloth or nylon grain bag.
3. In a brew kettle, bring at least 3 US gal (11 L) brewing water to steeping temperature (150 to 160°F/65 to 71°C). Turn off the heat, add the grain bag, cover and steep for 30 minutes. (Turn the element back on briefly if the temperature drops below steeping temperature.) Remove grain bag. Place it in a strainer, rinse it over the kettle with steeping water and then discard it.
4. Increase heat and bring grain tea to a boil. Remove from heat, add 1.4 lbs (.7 kg) malt extract and stir until dissolved.
5. Return kettle to the burner and increase the heat until the wort begins to boil. Using a spoon, clear foam to one side. Reduce heat until a rolling boil is maintained without foam buildup.
6. Add bittering hops, stirring to combine. Boil for 45 minutes, uncovered. Monitor to prevent boiling over.

7. Meanwhile, prepare fermentation gear and cooling bath or wort chiller.

8. After 45 minutes, remove kettle from heat and add remaining 4 lbs (1.8 kg) malt extract, honey, syrup and lactose. Place peel, coriander, vanilla beans and Irish moss in a hop bag. Add bag and yeast nutrient. Stir to ensure that the extract, honey, syrup, lactose and nutrient have dissolved. Return kettle to burner and bring back to a rolling boil. Boil for 15 minutes, uncovered; turn off heat and cover.

9. To cool the brew, place covered kettle in prepared cooling bath or use a wort chiller according to manufacturer's directions. Cool to desired temperature of 75°F (24°C) within 30 to 45 minutes.

10. While wort is cooling, clean and sanitize brewing spoon. When wort has cooled, move kettle to counter and stir wort briskly in one direction for about 5 minutes. After stirring, cover and let rest for 10 to 15 minutes while hops and trub form a cone.

11. Using sanitized racking cane and siphon, rack as much wort as possible into sanitized primary fermenter. Then, using a sanitized funnel and straining screen, strain remainder of wort into fermenter. Top off with brewing water to bring volume to around 5.5 US gal (21 L). Using the hydrometer, take a reading of specific gravity and record it in your brewing journal.

12. Add yeast, vigorously stirring with a sanitized spoon to distribute it throughout wort. Seal fermenter with lid, stopper and airlock. Keep fermenter at room temperature (68 to 72°F/20 to 22°C) during primary fermentation, which typically lasts 7 to 10 days after fermentation begins. (Keep in a dark place or under a lightproof cover if using a glass carboy.)

13. After 7 to 10 days or when the kräusen has fallen, use a sanitized racking cane and siphon to gently rack the beer into the sanitized secondary fermenter. Avoid aerating it, and leave as much of the sediment behind as possible. Seal and keep at room temperature, covered or in a dark place, to allow beer to ferment and condition for 30 days.

14. Once the bubbling in the airlock has slowed, confirm completion of fermentation by using the hydrometer to take final gravity readings. (Hydrometer readings should be the same for several days in a row.)

15. Add optional vanilla flavoring sparingly, stir gently with a sanitized spoon and sample until you achieve the desired taste. Prime and bottle the beer (see page 263). Condition for 3 to 4 weeks.

Pumpkin Ale

In this recipe, the 6-Row malted barley converts the starch in the pumpkin. Mix the grains, rice hulls and pumpkin well together before wetting in the brew kettle.

Estimated Original Gravity: will depend on the conversion of pumpkin

Equipment

- **brew kettle**
- **sanitized fermentation gear**

1 pack	Wyeast 1187 or White Labs WLP011 or Fermentis S-04	1 pack
2 lbs	6-Row malted barley	900 g
1 lb	Special Roast malt	450 g
1 lb	crystal or caramel malt (60 Lovibond)	450 g
4 oz	dehusked Carafa I® malt	112 g
4 lbs	pumpkin purée	1.8 kg
1 qt	rice hulls	1 L
5.5 US gal	brewing water	21 L
6.6 lbs	any brand light malt extract	3 kg
3 to 4 AAUs	Mt Hood or Liberty hops for bittering	3 to 4 AAUs
1 oz	freshly grated ginger	28 g
2 to 3	whole cinnamon sticks, coarsely ground	2 to 3
2 to 3	whole cloves	2 to 3
¼ tsp	grated nutmeg	1 mL
1 lb	grade B amber maple syrup	450 g
1 tsp	Irish moss	5 mL
1 tsp	yeast nutrient	5 mL

No aroma hops in this recipe

1. Prepare the liquid yeast in advance, according to the package directions.
2. Coarsely crack the grains and mix them thoroughly with the rice hulls and the pumpkin. Place the mixture in a cheesecloth or nylon grain bag.
3. In a brew kettle, bring at least 3 US gal (11 L) brewing water to steeping temperature (150 to 160°F/65 to 71°C). Turn off the heat, add the grain bag, cover and steep for 90 minutes. (If the temperature drops below steeping temperature, turn the element back on briefly to bring it back up.) Remove grain bag. Place it in a strainer, carefully rinse it over the kettle with steeping water and then discard it.
4. Increase the heat and bring grain tea to a boil. Remove from heat, add the malt extract and stir until dissolved completely.
5. Return kettle to the burner and increase the heat until the wort begins to boil. Using a spoon, clear any foam to one side. Reduce heat until a rolling boil can be maintained without foam buildup.

6. Add the bittering hops, stirring to combine. Boil for 45 minutes, uncovered. Monitor to prevent boiling over.

7. Meanwhile, prepare the fermentation gear and cooling bath or wort chiller.

8. After 45 minutes, remove the kettle from the heat. Place the ginger, cinnamon, whole cloves and nutmeg in a cheesecloth bag. Add maple syrup, the bag of spices, Irish moss and yeast nutrient to the kettle. Stir to ensure that the syrup and nutrient have dissolved. Return the kettle to the burner and bring back to a rolling boil. Boil for 15 minutes; turn off the heat and cover.

9. To cool the brew, place the covered kettle in the prepared cooling bath or use a wort chiller according to the manufacturer's directions. Cool to the desired temperature, 75°F (24°C), within 30 to 45 minutes.

10. While the wort is cooling, clean and sanitize the brewing spoon. When the wort has cooled, move the kettle to a counter and stir the wort briskly in one direction for about 5 minutes. After stirring, cover and let rest for 10 to 15 minutes as the hops and trub form a cone.

11. Using sanitized racking cane and siphon, rack as much wort as possible into the sanitized primary fermenter. Then, using a sanitized funnel and straining screen, strain the remainder of the wort into the fermenter. Top off with brewing water to bring the volume to around 5.5 US gal (21 L). Using the hydrometer, take a reading of the specific gravity and record it in your brewing journal.

12. Add the yeast; vigorously stir it with a sanitized spoon to distribute it throughout the wort. Seal the fermenter with lid, stopper and airlock. Keep the fermenter at room temperature (68 to 72°F/20 to 22°C) during primary fermentation, which could last up to 10 days after fermentation begins. (Keep in a dark place or under a lightproof cover if using a glass carboy.)

13. After the kräusen has fallen, use a sanitized racking cane and siphon to gently rack the beer into the sanitized secondary fermenter. Avoid aerating it, and leave as much of the sediment behind as possible. Seal and keep at room temperature, covered or in a dark place, to allow fermentation to continue.

14. Once the bubbling in the airlock has slowed, confirm completion of fermentation by using the hydrometer to take final gravity readings. (Hydrometer readings should be the same for several days in a row.)

15. Prime and bottle the beer (see page 263). Condition for 3 to 4 weeks.

> ## Brewer's Tip
> Be sure to use pumpkin purée, not pumpkin pie filling. Pumpkin must be free of spices and preservatives.

Chipotle Amber

**Estimated Original
Gravity: 1.056**

Equipment

- **brew kettle**
- **sanitized
  fermentation gear**

1 pack	Wyeast 1187 or White Labs WLP011 or Fermentis S-04	1 pack
1 lb	Melanoidin® malt	450 g
1 lb	crystal or caramel malt (60 Lovibond)	450 g
5.5 US gal	brewing water	21 L
6.6 lbs	any brand light malt extract, divided in half	3 kg
4 to 6 AAUs	any variety low- or medium-alpha acid hops for bittering	4 to 6 AAUs
6	whole chipotle peppers, coarsely ground and placed in straining bag	6
1 tsp	Irish moss	5 mL
1 tsp	yeast nutrient	5 mL

No aromas hops in this recipe

1. Prepare the liquid yeast in advance, according to the package directions.
2. Coarsely crack the grains and place them in a cheesecloth or nylon grain bag.
3. In a brew kettle, bring at least 3 US gal (11 L) brewing water to steeping temperature (150 to 160°F/65 to 71°C). Turn off the heat, add the grain bag, cover and steep for 30 minutes. (If the temperature drops below steeping temperature, turn the element back on briefly to bring it back up.) Remove grain bag. Place it in a strainer, rinse it over the kettle with steeping water and then discard it.
4. Increase the heat and bring grain tea to a boil. Remove from heat, add half the malt extract (3.3 lbs/1.5 kg) and stir until dissolved completely.
5. Return kettle to the burner and increase the heat until the wort begins to boil. Using a spoon, clear any foam to one side. Reduce heat until a rolling boil can be maintained without foam buildup.
6. Add the bittering hops, stirring to combine. Boil for 45 minutes, uncovered. Monitor to prevent boiling over.
7. Meanwhile, prepare the fermentation gear and cooling bath or wort chiller.
8. After 45 minutes, remove the kettle from the heat and add remaining half of malt extract (3.3 lbs/1.5 kg), peppers, Irish moss and yeast nutrient. Stir to ensure that the extract and nutrient have dissolved. Return the kettle to the burner and bring back to a rolling boil. Boil for 15 minutes; turn off the heat and cover.

9. To cool the brew, place the covered kettle in the prepared cooling bath or use a wort chiller according to the manufacturer's directions. Cool to the desired temperature, 75°F (24°C), within 30 to 45 minutes.

10. While the wort is cooling, clean and sanitize the brewing spoon. When the wort has cooled, move the kettle to a counter and stir the wort briskly in one direction for about 5 minutes. After stirring, cover and let rest for 10 to 15 minutes as the hops and trub form a cone.

11. Using sanitized racking cane and siphon, rack as much wort as possible into the sanitized primary fermenter. Then, using a sanitized funnel and straining screen, strain the remainder of the wort into the fermenter. Top off with brewing water to bring the volume to around 5.5 US gal (21 L). Using the hydrometer, take a reading of the specific gravity and record it in your brewing journal.

12. Add the yeast; vigorously stir it with a sanitized spoon to distribute it throughout the wort. Seal the fermenter with lid, stopper and airlock. Keep the fermenter at room temperature (68 to 72°F/20 to 22°C) during primary fermentation, which typically lasts 1 to 4 days after fermentation begins. (Keep in a dark place or under a lightproof cover if using a glass carboy.)

13. After 1 to 4 days or when the kräusen has fallen, use a sanitized racking cane and siphon to gently rack the beer into the sanitized secondary fermenter. Avoid aerating it, and leave as much of the sediment behind as possible. Seal and keep at room temperature, covered or in a dark place, to allow fermentation to continue.

14. Once the bubbling in the airlock has slowed, confirm completion of fermentation by using the hydrometer to take final gravity readings. (Hydrometer readings should be the same for several days in a row.)

15. Prime and bottle the beer (see page 263). Condition for 3 to 4 weeks.

Cayenne Weizen

Estimated Original Gravity: 1.070

Equipment

- **brew kettle**
- **sanitized fermentation gear**

1 pack	Wyeast 1010 or White Labs WLP320 or Fermentis S-04	1 pack
1 lb	Carafoam®, Carapils® or dextrin malt	450 g
5.5 US gal	brewing water	21 L
8 lbs	Alexander's Sun Country Wheat Malt Extract, divided in half	3.6 kg
2 to 4 AAUs	any variety low-alpha acid hops for bittering	2 to 4 AAUs
1 lb	lactose	450 g
2 to 3	whole cayenne peppers, chopped, placed in a straining bag	2 to 3
1 tsp	Irish moss	5 mL
1 tsp	yeast nutrient	5 mL

No aroma hops in this recipe

1. Prepare the liquid yeast in advance, according to the package directions.
2. Coarsely crack the grains and place them in a cheesecloth or nylon grain bag.
3. In a brew kettle, bring at least 3 US gal (11 L) brewing water to steeping temperature (150 to 160°F/65 to 71°C). Turn off the heat, add the grain bag, cover and steep for 30 minutes. (If the temperature drops below steeping temperature, turn the element back on briefly to bring it back up.) Remove grain bag. Place it in a strainer, rinse it over the kettle with steeping water and then discard it.
4. Increase the heat and bring grain tea to a boil. Remove from heat, add half of the malt extract (4 lbs/1.8 kg) and stir until dissolved completely.
5. Return kettle to the burner and increase the heat until the wort begins to boil. Using a spoon, clear any foam to one side. Reduce heat until a rolling boil can be maintained without foam buildup.
6. Add the bittering hops, stirring to combine. Boil for 45 minutes, uncovered. Monitor to prevent boiling over.
7. Meanwhile, prepare the fermentation gear and cooling bath or wort chiller.

8. After 45 minutes, remove the kettle from the heat and add remaining half of malt extract (4 lbs/1.8 kg), lactose, peppers, Irish moss and yeast nutrient. Stir to ensure that the extract, lactose and nutrient have dissolved. Return the kettle to the burner and bring back to a rolling boil. Boil for 15 minutes; turn off the heat and cover.

9. To cool the brew, place the covered kettle in the prepared cooling bath or use a wort chiller according to the manufacturer's directions. Cool to the desired temperature, 75°F (24°C), within 30 to 45 minutes.

10. While the wort is cooling, clean and sanitize the brewing spoon. When the wort has cooled, move the kettle to a counter and stir the wort briskly in one direction for about 5 minutes. After stirring, cover and let rest for 10 to 15 minutes as the hops and trub form a cone.

11. Using sanitized racking cane and siphon, rack as much wort as possible into the sanitized primary fermenter. Then, using a sanitized funnel and straining screen, strain the remainder of the wort into the fermenter. Top off with brewing water to bring the volume to around 5.5 US gal (21 L). Using the hydrometer, take a reading of the specific gravity and record it in your brewing journal.

12. Add the yeast; vigorously stir it with a sanitized spoon to distribute it throughout the wort. Seal the fermenter with lid, stopper and airlock. Keep the fermenter at room temperature (68 to 72°F/20 to 22°C) during primary fermentation, which typically lasts 7 to 10 days after fermentation begins. (Keep in a dark place or under a lightproof cover if using a glass carboy.)

13. After 7 to 10 days or when the kräusen has fallen, use a sanitized racking cane and siphon to gently rack the beer into the sanitized secondary fermenter. Avoid aerating it, and leave as much of the sediment behind as possible. Seal and keep at room temperature, covered or in a dark place, to allow fermentation to continue.

14. Once the bubbling in the airlock has slowed, confirm completion of fermentation by using the hydrometer to take final gravity readings. (Hydrometer readings should be the same for several days in a row.)

15. Prime and bottle the beer (see page 263). Condition for 3 to 4 weeks.

Jalapeño Ale

Vary the amount of jalapeño peppers, depending on the size of the peppers you buy, how hot they are and, of course, your personal taste.

Estimated Original Gravity: 1.053

Equipment

- **brew kettle**
- **sanitized fermentation gear**

1 pack	Wyeast 1056 or Fermentis S-05	1 pack
1 lb	Carafoam®, Carapils® or dextrin malt	450 g
5.5 US gal	brewing water	21 L
6.6 lbs	any brand extra-light malt extract, divided in half	3 kg
2 to 4 AAUs	Mt Hood or Liberty hops for bittering	2 to 4 AAUs
4 to 6	fresh whole jalapeños (chopped and placed in straining bag)	4 to 6
1 tsp	Irish moss	5 mL
1 tsp	yeast nutrient	5 mL

No aroma hops in this recipe

1. Prepare the liquid yeast in advance, according to the package directions.
2. Coarsely crack the grains and place them in a cheesecloth or nylon grain bag.
3. In a brew kettle, bring at least 3 US gal (11 L) brewing water to steeping temperature (150 to 160°F/65 to 71°C). Turn off the heat, add the grain bag, cover and steep for 30 minutes. (If the temperature drops below steeping temperature, turn the element back on briefly to bring it back up.) Remove grain bag. Place it in a strainer, rinse it over the kettle with steeping water and then discard it.
4. Increase the heat and bring grain tea to a boil. Remove from heat, add half of the malt extract (3.3 lbs/1.5 kg) and stir until dissolved completely.
5. Return kettle to the burner and increase the heat until the wort begins to boil. Using a spoon, clear any foam to one side. Reduce heat until a rolling boil can be maintained without foam buildup.
6. Add the bittering hops, stirring to combine. Boil for 45 minutes, uncovered. Monitor to prevent boiling over.
7. Meanwhile, prepare the fermentation gear and cooling bath or wort chiller.
8. After 45 minutes, remove the kettle from the heat and add remaining half of malt extract (3.3 lbs/1.5 kg), peppers, Irish moss and yeast nutrient. Stir to ensure that the extract and nutrient have dissolved. Return the kettle to the burner and bring back to a rolling boil. Boil for 15 minutes; turn off the heat and cover.

9. To cool the brew, place the covered kettle in the prepared cooling bath or use a wort chiller according to the manufacturer's directions. Cool to the desired temperature, 75°F (24°C), within 30 to 45 minutes.

10. While the wort is cooling, clean and sanitize the brewing spoon. When the wort has cooled, move the kettle to a counter and stir the wort briskly in one direction for about 5 minutes. After stirring, cover and let rest for 10 to 15 minutes as the hops and trub form a cone.

11. Using sanitized racking cane and siphon, rack as much wort as possible into the sanitized primary fermenter. Then, using a sanitized funnel and straining screen, strain the remainder of the wort into the fermenter. Top off with brewing water to bring the volume to around 5.5 US gal (21 L). Using the hydrometer, take a reading of the specific gravity and record it in your brewing journal.

12. Add the yeast; vigorously stir it with a sanitized spoon to distribute it throughout the wort. Seal the fermenter with lid, stopper and airlock. Keep the fermenter at room temperature (68 to 72°F/20 to 22°C) during primary fermentation, which typically lasts 1 to 4 days after fermentation begins. (Keep in a dark place or under a lightproof cover if using a glass carboy.)

13. After 1 to 4 days or when the kräusen has fallen, use a sanitized racking cane and siphon to gently rack the beer into the sanitized secondary fermenter. Avoid aerating it, and leave as much of the sediment behind as possible. Seal and keep at room temperature, covered or in a dark place, to allow fermentation to continue.

14. Once the bubbling in the airlock has slowed, confirm completion of fermentation by using the hydrometer to take final gravity readings. (Hydrometer readings should be the same for several days in a row.)

15. Prime and bottle the beer (see page 263). Condition for 3 to 4 weeks.

Jalapeño Lager

Vary the amount of jalapeño peppers, depending on the size of the peppers you buy, how hot they are and, of course, your personal taste.

Estimated Original Gravity: 1.053

Equipment

- brew kettle
- sanitized fermentation gear

2 packs	Wyeast 2206 or White Labs WLP838 (or 1 pack in starter) or Fermentis S-23	2 packs
1 lb	Carafoam®, Carapils® or dextrin malt	450 g
5.5 US gal	brewing water	21 L
6.6 lbs	any brand extra-light malt extract, divided in half	3 kg
2 to 4 AAUs	Mt Hood or Liberty hops for bittering	
4 to 6	fresh whole jalapeños (chopped and placed in straining bag)	4 to 6
1 tsp	Irish moss	5 mL
1 tsp	yeast nutrient	5 mL

No aroma hops in this recipe

1. Prepare the liquid yeast in advance, according to the package directions.
2. Coarsely crack the grains and place them in a cheesecloth or nylon grain bag.
3. In a brew kettle, bring at least 3 US gal (11 L) brewing water to steeping temperature (150 to 160°F/65 to 71°C). Turn off the heat, add the grain bag, cover and steep for 30 minutes. (If the temperature drops below steeping temperature, turn the element back on briefly to bring it back up.) Remove grain bag. Place it in a strainer, rinse it over the kettle with steeping water and then discard it.
4. Increase the heat and bring grain tea to a boil. Remove from heat, add half of the malt extract (3.3 lbs/1.5 kg) and stir until dissolved completely.
5. Return kettle to the burner and increase the heat until the wort begins to boil. Using a spoon, clear any foam to one side. Reduce heat until a rolling boil can be maintained without foam buildup.
6. Add the bittering hops, stirring to combine. Boil for 45 minutes, uncovered. Monitor to prevent boiling over.
7. Meanwhile, prepare the fermentation gear and cooling bath or wort chiller.
8. After 45 minutes, remove the kettle from the heat and add the remaining half of the malt extract (3.3 lbs/1.5 kg), peppers, Irish moss and yeast nutrient. Stir to ensure that the extract, sugar and nutrient have dissolved. Return the kettle to the burner and bring back to a rolling boil. Boil for 15 minutes; turn off the heat and cover.

9. To cool the brew, place the covered kettle in the prepared cooling bath or use a wort chiller according to the manufacturer's directions. Cool to the desired temperature, 75°F (24°C), within 30 to 45 minutes.

10. While the wort is cooling, clean and sanitize the brewing spoon. When the wort has cooled, move the kettle to a counter and stir the wort briskly in one direction for about 5 minutes. After stirring, cover and let rest for 10 to 15 minutes as the hops and trub form a cone.

11. Using sanitized racking cane and siphon, rack as much wort as possible into the sanitized primary fermenter. Then, using a sanitized funnel and straining screen, strain the remainder of the wort into the fermenter. Top off with brewing water to bring the volume to around 5.5 US gal (21 L). Using the hydrometer, take a reading of the specific gravity and record it in your brewing journal.

12. Add the yeast; vigorously stirring it with a sanitized spoon to distribute it throughout the wort. Seal the fermenter with lid, stopper and airlock. Keep the fermenter at room temperature (68 to 72°F/20 to 22°C) until fermentation begins (bubbles will be moving through the airlock). Once fermentation begins, drop the temperature to 46 to 55°F (8 to 13°C) for one week of primary fermentation. (Keep fermenter in a dark place or under a lightproof cover if using a glass carboy.)

13. Use a sanitized racking cane and siphon to gently rack the beer into the sanitized secondary fermenter. Avoid aerating it, and leave as much of the sediment behind as possible. Seal and drop the temperature to 35 to 45°F (2 to 7°C); keep it at that temperature, covered or in a dark place, to allow fermentation to continue for 4 weeks.

14. Once the bubbling in the airlock has slowed, confirm completion of fermentation by using the hydrometer to take final gravity readings. (Hydrometer readings should be the same for several days in a row.)

15. Prime and bottle the beer (see page 263). Store it for 1 week at a cool room temperature (around 60°F/15°C or slightly higher); then move the beer to the refrigerator to condition for 3 to 4 weeks.

Brewer's Tip

For information on preparing a yeast starter, see page 262.

The use of spices in the brewing process predates the use of hops. In addition to being a journey into history, the practise of spicing beers brings a whole new level of flavors to the brewer's art. Use the freshest spices and herbs available, and always purchase them whole and grind them yourself. Place spices and herbs in a straining bag before adding them to your brew.

Spiced and Other Flavored Beers

Wassail

Long ago in England, it was a holiday tradition for the town's poorer folks to visit the houses of the wealthy. They'd stand outside singing carols until the squire slipped them some coin. The carolers also came to expect something to drink. They were served a mulled beverage containing ale and/or cider, often with a dash of spirits and spices. The drink was called "wassail," and singing for the drink became known as "wassailing."

Chop the dried fruit and coarsely grind the spices; place both in a hop bag and add during the final 15 minutes of boil. Brew this strong beer in early September so it will be ready for holiday gifts.

Estimated Original Gravity: 1.083

Equipment

- brew kettle
- sanitized fermentation gear

Yeast

1 pack	Wyeast 1187 or White Labs WLP011 or Fermentis S-04	1 pack

Grains

1 lb	UK dark crystal malt (150 Lovibond)	450 g
1 lb	UK amber malt (25 Lovibond)	450 g
4 oz	UK chocolate malt (350 Lovibond)	112 g
5.5 US gal	brewing water	21 L

Malt Extract

8 lbs	any UK brand light	3.6 kg

Bittering Hops

6 to 8 AAUs	any variety medium-alpha acid	6 to 8 AAUs

Later Additions

8 oz	dried apples, coarsely chopped	224 g
4 oz	raisins	112 g
3	cinnamon sticks	3
1 oz	freshly grated ginger	28 g
2 to 3	whole cloves (do not crush)	2 to 3
.25 tsp	grated nutmeg	1 mL
2 lbs	Barbados, baking or amber molasses	900 g
1 tsp	Irish moss	5 mL
1 tsp	yeast nutrient	5 mL

Aroma Hops

None

1. Prepare liquid yeast in advance, according to directions.
2. Coarsely crack the grains and place them in a cheesecloth or nylon grain bag.
3. In a brew kettle, bring at least 3 US gal (11 L) brewing water to steeping temperature (150 to 160°F/65 to 71°C). Turn off heat, add grain bag, cover and steep for 30 minutes. (If temperature drops below steeping temperature, reheat briefly.) Remove grain bag. Place it in a strainer, rinse it over the kettle with steeping water and then discard it.
4. Increase the heat and bring grain tea to a boil. Remove from heat, add the malt extract and stir until dissolved.
5. Return kettle to burner and increase heat until wort begins to boil. Using a spoon, clear any foam. Reduce heat until a rolling boil is maintained without foam buildup.

6. Add the bittering hops, stirring to combine. Boil for 45 minutes, uncovered. Monitor to prevent boiling over.

7. Meanwhile, prepare the fermentation gear and cooling bath or wort chiller.

8. After 45 minutes, remove the kettle from the heat and add hop bag containing apples, raisins, cinnamon sticks, ginger, cloves and nutmeg. Add molasses, Irish moss and yeast nutrient. Stir to ensure that molasses and nutrient are dissolved. Return the kettle to the burner and bring back to a rolling boil. Boil for 15 minutes; turn off the heat and cover.

9. To cool the brew, place the covered kettle in the prepared cooling bath or use a wort chiller according to the manufacturer's directions. Cool to the desired temperature, 75°F (24°C), within 30 to 45 minutes.

10. While the wort is cooling, clean and sanitize the brewing spoon. When the wort has cooled, move the kettle to a counter and stir the wort briskly in one direction for about 5 minutes. After stirring, cover and let rest for 10 to 15 minutes as the hops and trub form a cone.

11. Using sanitized racking cane and siphon, rack as much wort as possible into the sanitized primary fermenter. Then, using a sanitized funnel and straining screen, strain the remainder of the wort into the fermenter. Top off with brewing water to bring the volume to around 5.5 US gal (21 L). Using the hydrometer, take a reading of the specific gravity and record it in your brewing journal.

12. Add the yeast; vigorously stir it with a sanitized spoon to distribute it throughout the wort. Seal the fermenter with lid, stopper and airlock. Keep the fermenter at room temperature (68 to 72°F/20 to 22°C) during primary fermentation, which typically lasts 7 to 10 days after fermentation begins. (Keep in a dark place or under a lightproof cover if using a glass carboy.)

13. After 7 to 10 days or when the kräusen has fallen, use a sanitized racking cane and siphon to gently rack the beer into the sanitized secondary fermenter. Avoid aerating it, and leave as much of the sediment behind as possible. Seal and keep at room temperature, covered or in a dark place, to allow fermentation to continue.

14. Once the bubbling in the airlock has slowed, confirm completion of fermentation by using the hydrometer to take final gravity readings. (Hydrometer readings should be the same for several days in a row.)

15. Prime and bottle the beer (see page 263). Condition for 3 to 4 weeks.

Brewer's Tip

If active fermentation backs up into the airlock, replace airlock with blow-off hose (see page 16). Change water as needed; re-install airlock when fermentation settles down.

Gingered Ale

This predecessor to modern sodas is a light alcoholic drink laced with ginger. This drink is not for the kiddies. Refer to the soda section at the back of the book for a family-friendly ginger ale recipe.

Estimated Original Gravity: 1.058

Equipment

- **brew kettle**
- **sanitized fermentation gear**

Brewer's Tips

If the specified brands of grains are not available, use the grains chart on page 77 to find substitutes.

Yeast

1 pack	Wyeast 1187 or White Labs WLP011 or Fermentis S-04	1 pack

Grains

1 lb	Melanoidin® malt	450 g
1 lb	Caramunich I® malt	450 g
5.5 US gal	brewing water	21 L

Malt Extract

5.4 lbs	Alexander's Sun Country Pale Malt Extract	2.5 kg

Bittering Hops

2 AAUs	any variety low-alpha acid	2 AAUs

Later Additions

4$^{+/-}$ oz	grated fresh ginger	112$^{+/-}$ g
1 lb	clover honey	450 g
8 oz	malto dextrin powder	224 g
1 tsp	Irish moss	5 mL
1 tsp	yeast nutrient	5 mL

Aroma Hops

None

1. Prepare the liquid yeast in advance, according to the package directions.
2. Coarsely crack the grains and place them in a cheesecloth or nylon grain bag.
3. In a brew kettle, bring at least 3 US gal (11 L) brewing water to steeping temperature (150 to 160°F/65 to 71°C). Turn off the heat, add the grain bag, cover and steep for 30 minutes. (If the temperature drops below steeping temperature, turn the element back on briefly to bring it back up.) Remove grain bag. Place it in a strainer, rinse it over the kettle with steeping water and then discard it.
4. Increase the heat and bring grain tea to a boil. Remove from heat, add the malt extract and stir until dissolved completely.
5. Return kettle to the burner and increase the heat until the wort begins to boil. Using a spoon, clear any foam to one side. Reduce heat until a rolling boil can be maintained without foam buildup.
6. Add the bittering hops, stirring to combine. Boil for 45 minutes, uncovered. Monitor to prevent boiling over.

7. Meanwhile, prepare the fermentation gear and cooling bath or wort chiller.

8. After 45 minutes, remove the kettle from the heat. Place the ginger in a hop bag. Add honey, malto dextrin powder, ginger, Irish moss and yeast nutrient. Stir to ensure that the honey, powder and nutrient are dissolved. Return the kettle to the burner and bring back to a rolling boil. Boil for 15 minutes; turn off the heat and cover.

9. To cool the brew, place the covered kettle in the prepared cooling bath or use a wort chiller according to the manufacturer's directions. Cool to the desired temperature, 75°F (24°C), within 30 to 45 minutes.

10. While the wort is cooling, clean and sanitize the brewing spoon. When the wort has cooled, move the kettle to a counter and stir the wort briskly in one direction for about 5 minutes. After stirring, cover and let rest for 10 to 15 minutes as the hops and trub form a cone.

11. Using sanitized racking cane and siphon, rack as much wort as possible into the sanitized primary fermenter. Then, using a sanitized funnel and straining screen, strain the remainder of the wort into the fermenter. Top off with brewing water to bring the volume to around 5.5 US gal (21 L). Using the hydrometer, take a reading of the specific gravity and record it in your brewing journal.

12. Add the yeast; vigorously stir it with a sanitized spoon to distribute it throughout the wort. Seal the fermenter with lid, stopper and airlock. Keep the fermenter at room temperature (68 to 72°F/20 to 22°C) during primary fermentation, which typically lasts 1 to 4 days after fermentation begins. (Keep in a dark place or under a lightproof cover if using a glass carboy.)

13. After 1 to 4 days or when the kräusen has fallen, use a sanitized racking cane and siphon to gently rack the beer into the sanitized secondary fermenter. Avoid aerating it, and leave as much of the sediment behind as possible. Seal and keep at room temperature, covered or in a dark place, to allow fermentation to continue.

14. Once the bubbling in the airlock has slowed, confirm completion of fermentation by using the hydrometer to take final gravity readings. (Hydrometer readings should be the same for several days in a row.)

15. Prime and bottle the beer (see page 263). Condition for 3 to 4 weeks.

Variation

Gingered Lager: To brew a gingered lager, substitute any lager yeast and ferment according to lager technique described on page 88.

Gruit

This ancient brew goes back to the days when hops weren't used in the brewing process. Instead, brewers used various herbs and spices to produce gruits (rhymes with fruits.) Half of the spices are added for the full boil, and the remainder are added for the final 15 minutes.

Estimated Original Gravity: 1.056

Equipment

- **brew kettle**
- **sanitized fermentation gear**

Yeast

1 pack	Wyeast 1028 or White Labs WLP013 or Fermentis S-04	1 pack

Grains

1 lb	Special Roast malt	450 g
1 lb	any brand crystal malt (60 Lovibond)	450 g
5.5 US gal	brewing water	21 L

Malt Extract

6.6 lbs	any brand light	3 kg
1 oz	yarrow, divided in half	28 g
1 oz	sweet gale, divided in half	28 g
1 oz	rosemary, divided in half	28 g

Later Additions

1 tsp	Irish moss	5 mL
1 tsp	yeast nutrient	5 mL

1. Prepare the liquid yeast in advance, according to the package directions.
2. Coarsely crack the grains and place them in a cheesecloth or nylon grain bag.
3. In a brew kettle, bring at least 3 US gal (11 L) brewing water to steeping temperature (150 to 160°F/65 to 71°C). Turn off the heat, add the grain bag, cover and steep for 30 minutes. (If the temperature drops below steeping temperature, turn the element back on briefly to bring it back up.) Remove grain bag. Place it in a strainer, rinse it over the kettle with steeping water and then discard it.
4. Increase the heat and bring grain tea to a boil. Remove from heat, add the malt extract and stir until dissolved completely. Place .5 oz (14 g) each of the yarrow, sweet gale and rosemary into a hop bag and add the bag to the kettle.
5. Return kettle to the burner and increase the heat until the wort begins to boil. Using a spoon, clear any foam to one side. Reduce heat until a rolling boil can be maintained without foam buildup. Boil for 45 minutes, uncovered. Monitor to prevent boiling over.
6. Meanwhile, prepare the fermentation gear and cooling bath or wort chiller.

7. Place the remaining .5 oz (14 g) each of the yarrow, sweet gale and rosemary into a hop bag. After 45 minutes, remove the kettle from the heat and add the second hop bag, the Irish moss and yeast nutrient. Stir to ensure that the nutrient has dissolved. Return the kettle to the burner and bring back to a rolling boil. Boil for 15 minutes; turn off the heat and cover.

8. To cool the brew, place the covered kettle in the prepared cooling bath or use a wort chiller according to the manufacturer's directions. Cool to the desired temperature, 75°F (24°C), within 30 to 45 minutes.

9. While the wort is cooling, clean and sanitize the brewing spoon. When the wort has cooled, move the kettle to a counter and stir the wort briskly in one direction for about 5 minutes. After stirring, cover and let rest for 10 to 15 minutes as the hops and trub form a cone.

10. Using sanitized racking cane and siphon, rack as much wort as possible into the sanitized primary fermenter. Then, using a sanitized funnel and straining screen, strain the remainder of the wort into the fermenter. Top off with brewing water to bring the volume to around 5.5 US gal (21 L). Using the hydrometer, take a reading of the specific gravity and record it in your brewing journal.

11. Add the yeast; vigorously stir it with a sanitized spoon to distribute it throughout the wort. Seal the fermenter with lid, stopper and airlock. Keep the fermenter at room temperature (68 to 72°F/20 to 22°C) during primary fermentation, which typically lasts 1 to 4 days after fermentation begins. (Keep in a dark place or under a lightproof cover if using a glass carboy.)

12. After 1 to 4 days or when the kräusen has fallen, use a sanitized racking cane and siphon to gently rack the beer into the sanitized secondary fermenter. Avoid aerating it, and leave as much of the sediment behind as possible. Seal and keep at room temperature, covered or in a dark place, to allow fermentation to continue.

13. Once the bubbling in the airlock has slowed, confirm completion of fermentation by using the hydrometer to take final gravity readings. (Hydrometer readings should be the same for several days in a row.)

14. Prime and bottle the beer (see page 263). Condition for 3 to 4 weeks.

Bourbon Barrel Porter

Many craft brewers age their beer in old bourbon barrels to get new depths of flavor. Homebrewers are now asking if they can get a barrel. The good news: probably, yes; the bad news: a barrel holds 50 US gallons! (This is perhaps a tad more than you were planning on making!)

We've come up with an answer for those of you who are less ambitious: you can steep oak chips in bourbon for a month before you brew. (See the sidebar for details.)

Estimated Original Gravity: 1.073

Equipment

- brew kettle
- sanitized fermentation gear

4 oz	oak chips or cubes (see sidebar to prepare Bourbon-soaked chips)	112 g

Yeast

1 pack	Wyeast 1187 or White Labs WLP011 or Fermentis S-04	1 pack

Grains

1 lb	UK amber malt	450 g
8 oz	UK brown malt	224 g
1 lb	Caraboheme® malt	450 g
1 lb	Caraaroma® malt	450 g
8 oz	dehusked Carafa I® malt	224 g
5.5 US gal	brewing water	21 L

Malt Extract

8 lbs	any UK brand	3.6 kg

Bittering Hops

4 to 6 AAUs	any variety light- to medium-alpha acid	4 to 6 AAUs

Later Additions

1 tsp	Irish moss	5 mL
1 tsp	yeast nutrient	5 mL

Aroma Hops

None

1. Prepare the oak chips one month in advance, according to the sidebar instructions.
2. Prepare liquid yeast in advance, according to directions.
3. Coarsely crack the grains and place them in a cheesecloth or nylon grain bag.
4. In a brew kettle, bring at least 3 US gal (11 L) brewing water to steeping temperature (150 to 160°F/65 to 71°C). Turn off the heat, add the grain bag, cover and steep for 30 minutes. (If the temperature drops below steeping temperature, turn the element back on briefly to bring it back up.) Remove grain bag. Place it in a strainer, rinse it over the kettle with steeping water and then discard it.
5. Increase the heat and bring grain tea to a boil. Remove from heat, add the malt extract and stir until dissolved completely.
6. Return kettle to the burner and increase the heat until the wort begins to boil. Using a spoon, clear any foam to one side. Reduce heat until a rolling boil can be maintained without foam buildup.

7. Add the bittering hops, stirring to combine. Boil for 45 minutes, uncovered. Monitor to prevent boiling over.

8. Meanwhile, prepare the fermentation gear and cooling bath or wort chiller.

9. After 45 minutes, remove the kettle from the heat and add Irish moss and yeast nutrient. Stir to ensure that the nutrient has dissolved. Return the kettle to the burner and bring back to a rolling boil. Boil for 15 minutes; turn off the heat and cover.

10. To cool the brew, place the covered kettle in the prepared cooling bath or use a wort chiller according to the manufacturer's directions. Cool to the desired temperature, 75°F (24°C), within 30 to 45 minutes.

11. While the wort is cooling, clean and sanitize the brewing spoon. When the wort has cooled, move the kettle to a counter and stir the wort briskly in one direction for about 5 minutes. After stirring, cover and let rest for 10 to 15 minutes as the hops and trub form a cone.

12. Using sanitized racking cane and siphon, rack as much wort as possible into the sanitized primary fermenter. Then, using a sanitized funnel and straining screen, strain the remainder of the wort into the fermenter. Top off with brewing water to bring the volume to around 5.5 US gal (21 L). Using the hydrometer, take a reading of the specific gravity and record it in your brewing journal.

13. Add the yeast; vigorously stir it with a sanitized spoon to distribute it throughout the wort. Seal the fermenter with lid, stopper and airlock. Keep the fermenter at room temperature (68 to 72°F/20 to 22°C) during primary fermentation, which typically lasts 7 to 10 days after fermentation begins. (Keep in a dark place or under a lightproof cover if using a glass carboy.)

14. After 7 to 10 days or when the kräusen has fallen, use a sanitized racking cane and siphon to gently rack the beer into the sanitized secondary fermenter. Avoid aerating it, and leave as much of the sediment behind as possible. Seal and keep at room temperature, covered or in a dark place, to allow fermentation to continue.

15. Once the bubbling in the airlock has slowed, add the bourbon chips and reseal. Taste the beer about every two days to check on the development of the flavor. Confirm completion of fermentation by using the hydrometer to take final gravity readings. (Hydrometer readings should be the same for several days in a row.)

16. Prime and bottle the beer (see page 263). Condition for 3 to 4 weeks.

Preparing "Bourbon" Chips

Get 4 oz (112 g) dark-toasted (or light or medium, if you prefer) oak chips or cubes from the homebrew supplier and put them in a hop bag. Put the chips in a jar, and cover them with bourbon. Allow the chips to steep in the bourbon for 30 days before adding them to the secondary fermenter.

Brewer's Tip

If active fermentation backs up into the airlock, replace airlock with blow-off hose (see page 16). Change water as needed; re-install airlock when fermentation settles down.

Vanilla Cream Stout

If we can make a milk stout and a chocolate stout, can we make a vanilla stout? Yes!

Estimated Original Gravity: 1.064

Equipment

- **brew kettle**
- **sanitized fermentation gear**

Yeast

1 pack	Wyeast 1028 or White Labs WLP013 or Fermentis S-04	1 pack

Grains

1 lb	UK crystal malt (60 Lovibond)	450 g
8 oz	UK brown malt	224 g
4 oz	UK chocolate malt	112 g
4 oz	UK black patent malt	112 g
4 oz	UK roast barley	112 g
5.5 US gal	brewing water	21 L

Malt Extract

6.6 lbs	any UK brand light	3 kg

Bittering Hops

4 to 6 AAUs	any variety medium-alpha acid	4 to 6 AAUs

Later Additions

1 lb	lactose	450 g
1	vanilla bean (2 if small)	1
1 tsp	Irish moss	5 mL
1 tsp	yeast nutrient	5 mL

Aroma Hops

	None	
1+ tsp	vanilla extract (optional at bottling time)	5+ mL

1. Prepare the liquid yeast in advance, according to the package directions.
2. Coarsely crack the grains and place them in a cheesecloth or nylon grain bag.
3. In a brew kettle, bring at least 3 US gal (11 L) brewing water to steeping temperature (150 to 160°F/65 to 71°C). Turn off the heat, add the grain bag, cover and steep for 30 minutes. (If the temperature drops below steeping temperature, turn the element back on briefly to bring it back up.) Remove grain bag. Place it in a strainer, rinse it over the kettle with steeping water and then discard it.
4. Increase the heat and bring grain tea to a boil. Remove from heat, add the malt extract and stir until dissolved completely.
5. Return kettle to the burner and increase the heat until the wort begins to boil. Using a spoon, clear any foam to one side. Reduce heat until a rolling boil can be maintained without foam buildup.

6. Add the bittering hops, stirring to combine. Boil for 45 minutes, uncovered. Monitor to prevent boiling over.

7. Meanwhile, prepare the fermentation gear and cooling bath or wort chiller.

8. After 45 minutes, remove the kettle from the heat and add lactose, vanilla bean (see sidebar), Irish moss and yeast nutrient. Stir to ensure that the lactose and nutrient are dissolved. Return the kettle to the burner and bring back to a rolling boil. Boil for 15 minutes; turn off the heat and cover.

9. To cool the brew, place the covered kettle in the prepared cooling bath or use a wort chiller according to the manufacturer's directions. Cool to the desired temperature, 75°F (24°C), within 30 to 45 minutes.

10. While the wort is cooling, clean and sanitize the brewing spoon. When the wort has cooled, move the kettle to a counter and stir the wort briskly in one direction for about 5 minutes. After stirring, cover and let rest for 10 to 15 minutes as the hops and trub form a cone.

11. Using sanitized racking cane and siphon, rack as much wort as possible into the sanitized primary fermenter. Then, using a sanitized funnel and straining screen, strain the remainder of the wort into the fermenter. Top off with brewing water to bring the volume to around 5.5 US gal (21 L). Using the hydrometer, take a reading of the specific gravity and record it in your brewing journal.

12. Add the yeast; vigorously stir it with a sanitized spoon to distribute it throughout the wort. Seal the fermenter with lid, stopper and airlock. Keep the fermenter at room temperature (68 to 72°F/20 to 22°C) during primary fermentation, which typically lasts 7 to 10 days after fermentation begins. (Keep in a dark place or under a lightproof cover if using a glass carboy.)

13. After 7 to 10 days or when the kräusen has fallen, use a sanitized racking cane and siphon to gently rack the beer into the sanitized secondary fermenter. Avoid aerating it, and leave as much of the sediment behind as possible. Seal and keep at room temperature, covered or in a dark place, to allow fermentation to continue.

14. Once the bubbling in the airlock has slowed, confirm completion of fermentation by using the hydrometer to take final gravity readings. (Hydrometer readings should be the same for several days in a row.) Test the flavor and add more vanilla flavor, if desired.

15. Prime and bottle the beer (see page 263). Condition for 3 to 4 weeks.

Vanilla in Your Beer

During the early boil, slit the vanilla bean open and scrape the inside with a knife blade. Add the skin, seeds and any pulp on the knife to the brew kettle as a later addition.

At bottling time, tweak the flavor with a quality (not imitation!) vanilla flavoring. As always, be careful with the quantity!

Brown Ale with Nuts

The classic brew "Samuel Smith's Nut Brown Ale" has inspired many brewers to take the nuttiness to the next level and include actual nuts.

Original Gravity will depend on the starch conversion of the nuts.

Equipment

- brew kettle
- sanitized fermentation gear

Yeast

1 pack	Wyeast 1187 or White Labs WLP001 or Fermentis S-04	1 pack

Grains and Nuts

2 lbs	6-Row brewer's malt	900 g
1 lb	Caraaroma® or other crystal malt (over 100 Lovibond)	450 g
1 lb	UK brown malt	450 g
4 oz	dehusked Carafa I® malt	112 g
1 lb	hazelnuts or almonds, shelled	450 g
5.5 US gal	brewing water	21 L

Malt Extract

6.6 lbs	any brand light	3 kg

Bittering Hops

2 to 4 AAUs	any variety low-alpha acid	2 to 4 AAUs

Later Additions

1 lb	Demerara or other dark raw sugar	450 g
8 oz	malto dextrin powder	224 g
1 tsp	Irish moss	5 mL
1 tsp	yeast nutrient	5 mL

Aroma Hops

	None	
1+ tsp	hazelnut or almond flavor extract (add to taste at bottling)	5+ mL

1. Prepare liquid yeast in advance, according to directions.
2. Coarsely crack the grains and chop the nuts. Place both in a cheesecloth or nylon grain bag.
3. In a brew kettle, bring at least 3 US gal (11 L) brewing water to steeping temperature (150 to 160°F/65 to 71°C). Turn off heat, add grain bag, cover and steep for 90 minutes. (If temperature drops below steeping temperature, reheat briefly.) Remove grain bag. Place it in a strainer, rinse it over the kettle with steeping water and then discard it.
4. Increase the heat and bring grain and nut tea to a boil. Remove from heat, add the malt extract and stir until dissolved completely.
5. Return kettle to burner and increase heat until wort begins to boil. Using a spoon, clear any foam. Reduce heat until a rolling boil is maintained without foam buildup.

6. Add the bittering hops, stirring to combine. Boil for 45 minutes, uncovered. Monitor to prevent boiling over.

7. Meanwhile, prepare the fermentation gear and cooling bath or wort chiller.

8. After 45 minutes, remove the kettle from the heat and add sugar, malto dextrin powder, Irish moss and yeast nutrient. Stir to ensure that the sugar, powder and nutrient are dissolved. Return the kettle to the burner and bring back to a rolling boil. Boil for 15 minutes; turn off the heat and cover.

9. To cool the brew, place the covered kettle in the prepared cooling bath or use a wort chiller according to the manufacturer's directions. Cool to the desired temperature, 75°F (24°C), within 30 to 45 minutes.

10. While the wort is cooling, clean and sanitize the brewing spoon. When the wort has cooled, move the kettle to a counter and stir the wort briskly in one direction for about 5 minutes. After stirring, cover and let rest for 10 to 15 minutes as the hops and trub form a cone.

11. Using sanitized racking cane and siphon, rack as much wort as possible into the sanitized primary fermenter. Then, using a sanitized funnel and straining screen, strain the remainder of the wort into the fermenter. Top off with brewing water to bring the volume to around 5.5 US gal (21 L). Using the hydrometer, take a reading of the specific gravity and record it in your brewing journal.

12. Add the yeast; vigorously stir it with a sanitized spoon to distribute it throughout the wort. Seal the fermenter with lid, stopper and airlock. Keep the fermenter at room temperature (68 to 72°F/20 to 22°C) during primary fermentation, which could last up to 10 days after fermentation begins, depending on the original gravity reading. (Keep in a dark place or under a lightproof cover if using a glass carboy.)

13. When the kräusen has fallen, use a sanitized racking cane and siphon to gently rack the beer into the sanitized secondary fermenter. Avoid aerating it, and leave as much of the sediment behind as possible. Seal and keep at room temperature, covered or in a dark place, to allow fermentation to continue.

14. Once the bubbling in the airlock has slowed, confirm completion of fermentation by using the hydrometer to take final gravity readings. (Hydrometer readings should be the same for several days in a row.) Test the flavor and add more nut flavor, if desired.

15. Prime and bottle the beer (see page 263). Condition for 3 to 4 weeks.

Using Nuts in Brewing

Chop the nuts and add them to the grain bag with the grains. To get all the nutty goodness, steep the grain bag for 90 minutes rather than the usual 30.

As with other flavorings, the nut extract is added at bottling. Buy a good nut extract from the grocery store or look at nut liqueur kits at your homebrew store.

Chocolate Stout

Nothing complements the flavor of stout and porter like chocolate does. Many drinkers have observed that dark grains already possess chocolate-like notes.

Estimated Original Gravity: 1.064

Equipment

- brew kettle
- sanitized fermentation gear

Yeast

1 pack	Wyeast 1187 or White Labs WLP011 or Fermentis S-04	1 pack

Grains

1 lb	UK crystal malt (60 Lovibond)	450 g
8 oz	UK brown malt	224 g
4 oz	UK chocolate malt	112 g
4 oz	UK black patent malt	112 g
4 oz	UK roast barley	112 g
5.5 US gal	brewing water	21 L

Malt Extract

6.6 lbs	any UK brand dark	3 kg

Bittering Hops

4 to 6 AAUs	medium-alpha acid (such as Northern Brewer)	4 to 6 AAUs

Later Additions

1 lb	lactose	450 g
8 oz	high-quality unsweetened cocoa powder	224 g
1 tsp	Irish moss	5 mL
1 tsp	yeast nutrient	5 mL

Aroma Hops

None

1. Prepare the liquid yeast in advance, according to the package directions.
2. Coarsely crack the grains and place them in a cheesecloth or nylon grain bag.
3. In a brew kettle, bring at least 3 US gal (11 L) brewing water to steeping temperature (150 to 160°F/65 to 71°C). Turn off the heat, add the grain bag, cover and steep for 30 minutes. (If the temperature drops below steeping temperature, turn the element back on briefly to bring it back up.) Remove grain bag. Place it in a strainer, rinse it over the kettle with steeping water and then discard it.
4. Increase the heat and bring grain tea to a boil. Remove from heat, add the malt extract and stir until dissolved completely.
5. Return kettle to the burner and increase the heat until the wort begins to boil. Using a spoon, clear any foam to one side. Reduce heat until a rolling boil can be maintained without foam buildup.

6. Add the bittering hops, stirring to combine. Boil for 45 minutes, uncovered. Monitor to prevent boiling over.

7. Meanwhile, prepare the fermentation gear and cooling bath or wort chiller.

8. After 45 minutes, remove the kettle from the heat and add lactose, cocoa powder, Irish moss and yeast nutrient. Stir to ensure that the lactose, cocoa and nutrient are evenly distributed. Return the kettle to the burner and bring back to a rolling boil. Boil for 15 minutes; turn off the heat and cover.

9. To cool the brew, place the covered kettle in the prepared cooling bath or use a wort chiller according to the manufacturer's directions. Cool to the desired temperature, 75°F (24°C), within 30 to 45 minutes.

10. While the wort is cooling, clean and sanitize the brewing spoon. When the wort has cooled, move the kettle to a counter and stir the wort briskly in one direction for about 5 minutes. After stirring, cover and let rest for 10 to 15 minutes as the hops and trub form a cone.

11. Using sanitized racking cane and siphon, rack as much wort as possible into the sanitized primary fermenter. Then, using a sanitized funnel and straining screen, strain the remainder of the wort into the fermenter. Top off with brewing water to bring the volume to around 5.5 US gal (21 L). Using the hydrometer, take a reading of the specific gravity and record it in your brewing journal.

12. Add the yeast; vigorously stir it with a sanitized spoon to distribute it throughout the wort. Seal the fermenter with lid, stopper and airlock. Keep the fermenter at room temperature (68 to 72°F/20 to 22°C) during primary fermentation, which typically lasts 1 to 4 days after fermentation begins. (Keep in a dark place or under a lightproof cover if using a glass carboy.)

13. After 1 to 4 days or when the kräusen has fallen, use a sanitized racking cane and siphon to gently rack the beer into the sanitized secondary fermenter. Avoid aerating it, and leave as much of the sediment behind as possible. Seal and keep at room temperature, covered or in a dark place, to allow fermentation to continue.

14. Once the bubbling in the airlock has slowed, confirm completion of fermentation by using the hydrometer to take final gravity readings. (Hydrometer readings should be the same for several days in a row.)

15. Prime and bottle the beer (see page 263). Condition for 3 to 4 weeks.

Variations

Coffee Stout: Coffee flavor and dark beer also go well together. To brew a Coffee Stout, follow the Chocolate Stout recipe but eliminate the cocoa powder. At the beginning of the bottling session, brew a double-strong pot of coffee, using twice as much coffee as usual. Allow the coffee to cool to room temperature. Mix into beer prior to priming and bottling.

Chocolate Coffee Stout: If you want to brew Chocolate Coffee Stout, follow the Chocolate Stout recipe (keeping the cocoa powder). At the beginning of the bottling session, brew a double-strong pot of coffee, using twice as much coffee as usual. Allow the coffee to cool to room temperature. Mix into beer prior to priming and bottling.

Chocolate Weizenbock

I was skeptical when a friend of ours brewed a beer like this one. Tasting it, however, made me a believer.

Estimated Original Gravity: 1.093

Equipment

- **brew kettle**
- **sanitized fermentation gear**
- **blow-off hose (page 16)**

Brewer's Tips

If the specified brands of grains are not available, use the grains chart on page 77 to find substitutes.

Yeast

2 packs	Wyeast 3056 or White Labs WLP300 (or 1 pack in starter) or Fermentis WB-06	2 packs

Grains

1 lb	Melanoidin® malt	450 g
1 lb	Carabohemian® malt	450 g
1 lb	Caramunich III® malt	450 g
8 oz	dehusked Carafa I® malt	224 g
5.5 US gal	brewing water	21 L

Malt Extract

9.9 lbs	wheat or weizen	4.5 kg

Bittering Hops

4 to 6 AAUs	Tettnang, Spalt or other German Noble Hops	4 to 6 AAUs

Later Additions

1 lb	lactose	450 g
8 oz	high-quality unsweetened cocoa powder	224 g
1 tsp	Irish moss	5 mL
1 tsp	yeast nutrient	5 mL

Aroma Hops

None

1. Prepare the liquid yeast in advance, according to the package directions.
2. Coarsely crack the grains and place them in a cheesecloth or nylon grain bag.
3. In a brew kettle, bring at least 3 US gal (11 L) brewing water to steeping temperature (150 to 160°F/65 to 71°C). Turn off the heat, add the grain bag, cover and steep for 30 minutes. (If the temperature drops below steeping temperature, turn the element back on briefly to bring it back up.) Remove grain bag. Place it in a strainer, rinse it over the kettle with steeping water and then discard it.
4. Increase the heat and bring grain tea to a boil. Remove from heat, add the malt extract and stir until dissolved completely.
5. Return kettle to the burner and increase the heat until the wort begins to boil. Using a spoon, clear any foam to one side. Reduce heat until a rolling boil can be maintained without foam buildup.

6. Add the bittering hops, stirring to combine. Boil for 45 minutes, uncovered. Monitor to prevent boiling over.

7. Meanwhile, prepare the fermentation gear and cooling bath or wort chiller.

8. After 45 minutes, remove the kettle from the heat and add lactose, cocoa powder, Irish moss and yeast nutrient. Stir to ensure that the lactose, cocoa powder and nutrient are evenly distributed. Return the kettle to the burner and bring back to a rolling boil. Boil for 15 minutes; turn off the heat and cover.

9. To cool the brew, place the covered kettle in the prepared cooling bath or use a wort chiller according to the manufacturer's directions. Cool to the desired temperature, 75°F (24°C), within 30 to 45 minutes.

10. While the wort is cooling, clean and sanitize the brewing spoon. When the wort has cooled, move the kettle to a counter and stir the wort briskly in one direction for about 5 minutes. After stirring, cover and let rest for 10 to 15 minutes as the hops and trub form a cone.

11. Using sanitized racking cane and siphon, rack as much wort as possible into the sanitized primary fermenter. Then, using a sanitized funnel and straining screen, strain the remainder of the wort into the fermenter. Top off with brewing water to bring the volume to around 5.5 US gal (21 L). Using the hydrometer, take a reading of the specific gravity and record it in your brewing journal.

12. Add the yeast; vigorously stir it with a sanitized spoon to distribute it throughout the wort. Seal the fermenter with lid, stopper and airlock or blow-off hose. Keep the fermenter at room temperature (68 to 72°F/20 to 22°C) during primary fermentation, which typically lasts 7 to 10 days after fermentation begins. (Keep in a dark place or under a lightproof cover if using a glass carboy.)

13. After 7 to 10 days or when the kräusen has fallen, use a sanitized racking cane and siphon to gently rack the beer into the sanitized secondary fermenter. Avoid aerating it, and leave as much of the sediment behind as possible. Seal and keep at room temperature, covered or in a dark place, to allow fermentation to continue.

14. Once the bubbling in the airlock has slowed, confirm completion of fermentation by using the hydrometer to take final gravity readings. (Hydrometer readings should be the same for several days in a row.)

15. Prime and bottle the beer (see page 263). Condition for 3 to 4 weeks.

Brewer's Tips

If active fermentation backs up into the airlock, replace airlock with blow-off hose (see page 16). Change water as needed; re-install airlock when fermentation settles down.

For information on preparing a yeast starter, see page 262.

Valentine Imperial Porter

Estimated Original Gravity: 1.084

Equipment

- **brew kettle**
- **sanitized fermentation gear**
- **blow-off hose (page 16)**

Brewer's Tip

Beers made with fresh fruit or fruit purées require a three-stage fermentation. Before racking the beer into the secondary fermenter, you will be adding the prepared fruit (or purée) to the secondary fermenter, racking the brew into the fermenter, waiting 30 days and then racking into a tertiary fermenter.

If you choose to work with cherry concentrate instead, you will need only the primary and secondary fermentation. The flavoring will be added and taste-tested just before bottling.

Cherries, prepared for brewing, if using (see sidebar)

Yeast

1 pack	Wyeast 1187 or White Labs WLP011 or Fermentis S-04	1 pack

Grains

1 lb	UK crystal malt (60 Lovibond)	450 g
8 oz	UK brown malt	224 g
8 oz	UK chocolate malt	224 g
5.5 US gal	brewing water	21 L

Malt Extract

8 lbs	any UK brand dark	3.6 kg

Bittering Hops

4 to 6 AAUs	medium-alpha acid (such as Northern Brewer)	4 to 6 AAUs

Later Additions

1 lb	lactose	450 g
1 lb	Demerara sugar	450 g
8 oz	high-quality unsweetened cocoa powder	224 g
1 tsp	Irish moss	5 mL
1 tsp	yeast nutrient	5 mL
16 US fl oz	black cherry concentrate (option if not using fruit)	475 mL
4$^{+/-}$ US fl oz	cherry flavoring or extract (to taste at bottling)	118$^{+/-}$ mL

1. Prepare liquid yeast in advance, according to directions.
2. Coarsely crack the grains and place them in a cheesecloth or nylon grain bag.
3. In a brew kettle, bring at least 3 US gal (11 L) brewing water to steeping temperature (150 to 160°F/65 to 71°C). Turn off heat, add grain bag, cover and steep for 30 minutes. (If temperature drops below steeping temperature, reheat briefly.) Remove grain bag. Place it in a strainer, rinse it over the kettle with steeping water and then discard it.
4. Increase the heat and bring grain tea to a boil. Remove from heat, add the malt extract and stir until dissolved.
5. Return kettle to burner and increase heat until wort begins to boil. Using a spoon, clear any foam. Reduce heat until a rolling boil is maintained without foam buildup.

6. Add the bittering hops, stirring to combine. Boil for 45 minutes, uncovered. Monitor to prevent boiling over.

7. Meanwhile, prepare the fermentation gear and cooling bath or wort chiller.

8. After 45 minutes, remove the kettle from the heat and add lactose, sugar, cocoa powder, Irish moss and yeast nutrient. Stir to ensure that the lactose, sugar and nutrient are dissolved. Return the kettle to the burner and bring back to a rolling boil. Boil for 15 minutes; turn off the heat and cover.

9. To cool the brew, place the covered kettle in the prepared cooling bath or use a wort chiller according to the manufacturer's directions. Cool to the desired temperature, 75°F (24°C), within 30 to 45 minutes.

10. While the wort is cooling, clean and sanitize the brewing spoon. When the wort has cooled, move the kettle to a counter and stir the wort briskly in one direction for about 5 minutes. After stirring, cover and let rest for 10 to 15 minutes as the hops and trub form a cone.

11. Using sanitized racking cane and siphon, rack as much wort as possible into the sanitized primary fermenter. Then, using a funnel and straining screen, strain the remainder of the wort into the fermenter. Top off with brewing water to bring the volume to around 5.5 US gal (21 L). Using the hydrometer, take a reading of the specific gravity and record it in your brewing journal.

12. Add the yeast; vigorously stir it with a sanitized spoon to distribute it throughout the wort. Seal the fermenter with lid, stopper and airlock or blow-off hose. Keep the fermenter at room temperature (68 to 72°F/20 to 22°C) during primary fermentation, which typically lasts 7 to 10 days after fermentation begins. (Keep in a dark place or under a lightproof cover if using a glass carboy.)

13. After 7 to 10 days or when the kräusen has fallen, use a sanitized racking cane and siphon to gently rack the beer onto the cherries, if using (see sidebar) in the sanitized secondary fermenter. (Or gently add concentrate.) Avoid aerating it, and leave as much of the sediment behind as possible. Seal and keep at room temperature, covered or in a dark place, to allow fermentation to continue.

14. Using a sanitized racking cane and siphon, gently rack the beer into a sanitized glass carboy and seal. Store, covered or in a dark place, until the beer has cleared. Once the bubbling in the airlock has slowed, confirm completion of fermentation by taking several final gravity readings.

15. If using cherry flavoring or extract, add it sparingly until you achieve the desired taste. Prime and bottle the beer (see page 263). Condition for 3 to 4 weeks.

Choosing and Preparing Cherries

You can use 5 to 10 lbs (2.25 to 4.5 kg) fresh or frozen cherries or 3 to 6 lbs (1.36 to 2.72 kg) of cherry purée. As yet another alternative, you can use 2.5 to 5 lbs (1.13 to 2.25 kg) dried cherries.

Shortly after brew day, wash the fruit and pit it and freeze it in resealable bags.

Two days before racking the beer to secondary fermenter, sanitize a primary fermenter bucket. Thaw the fruit in the bucket and crush it with a sanitized potato masher, if necessary. Dissolve 1 campden tablet for each US gal (3.75 L) of fruit in a small amount of boiling water and stir the mixture into the fruit. Seal the fermenter with the lid, stopper and an airlock containing a sterile cotton ball (not the usual water). Leave the fruit for at least 24 hours or until the sulphur smell goes away. This bucket will become your secondary fermenter.

Licorice Porter

The flavor of licorice goes really well with this rich sweet porter. The brew is a throwback to an old Pennsylvania style called Swanky.

For a fun way to serve Licorice Porter, put a brownie in a glass and pour the beer over it. Float vanilla ice cream on top and garnish it with candy licorice bits—you will amaze your friends!

Estimated Original Gravity: 1.076

Equipment

- **brew kettle**
- **sanitized fermentation gear**

Yeast

1 pack	Wyeast 1187 or White Labs WLP002 or Fermentis S-04	1 pack

Grains

1 lb	UK brown malt	450 g
1 lb	Caraboheme® malt	450 g
1 lb	Caraaroma® malt	450 g
8 oz	dehusked Carafa I® malt	224 g
5.5 US gal	brewing water	21 L

Malt Extract

8 lbs	any brand light	3.6 kg

Bittering Hops

4 to 6 AAUs	any variety light- to medium-alpha acid	4 to 6 AAUs

Later Additions

1 oz	licorice root	28 g
1 oz	star anise	28 g
1 oz	fennel seed	28 g
8 oz	malto dextrin powder	224 g
1 tsp	Irish moss	5 mL
1 tsp	yeast nutrient	5 mL

Aroma Hops

None

1. Prepare the liquid yeast in advance, according to the package directions.
2. Coarsely crack the grains and place them in a cheesecloth or nylon grain bag.
3. In a brew kettle, bring at least 3 US gal (11 L) brewing water to steeping temperature (150 to 160°F/65 to 71°C). Turn off the heat, add the grain bag, cover and steep for 30 minutes. (If the temperature drops below steeping temperature, turn the element back on briefly to bring it back up.) Remove grain bag. Place it in a strainer, rinse it over the kettle with steeping water and then discard it.
4. Increase the heat and bring grain tea to a boil. Remove from heat, add the malt extract and stir until dissolved completely.
5. Return kettle to the burner and increase the heat until the wort begins to boil. Using a spoon, clear any foam to one side. Reduce heat until a rolling boil can be maintained without foam buildup.

6. Add the bittering hops, stirring to combine. Boil for 45 minutes, uncovered. Monitor to prevent boiling over.

7. Meanwhile, prepare the fermentation gear and cooling bath or wort chiller.

8. After 45 minutes, remove the kettle from the heat. Place the licorice root, star anise and fennel seed in a hop bag. Add bag, malto dextrin powder, Irish moss and yeast nutrient to the kettle. Stir to ensure that the powder and nutrient have dissolved. Return the kettle to the burner and bring back to a rolling boil. Boil for 15 minutes; turn off the heat and cover.

9. To cool the brew, place the covered kettle in the prepared cooling bath or use a wort chiller according to the manufacturer's directions. Cool to the desired temperature, 75°F (24°C), within 30 to 45 minutes.

10. While the wort is cooling, clean and sanitize the brewing spoon. When the wort has cooled, move the kettle to a counter and stir the wort briskly in one direction for about 5 minutes. After stirring, cover and let rest for 10 to 15 minutes as the hops and trub form a cone.

11. Using sanitized racking cane and siphon, rack as much wort as possible into the sanitized primary fermenter. Then, using a sanitized funnel and straining screen, strain the remainder of the wort into the fermenter. Top off with brewing water to bring the volume to around 5.5 US gal (21 L). Using the hydrometer, take a reading of the specific gravity and record it in your brewing journal.

12. Add the yeast; vigorously stir it with a sanitized spoon to distribute it throughout the wort. Seal the fermenter with lid, stopper and airlock. Keep the fermenter at room temperature (68 to 72°F/20 to 22°C) during primary fermentation, which typically lasts 7 to 10 days after fermentation begins. (Keep in a dark place or under a lightproof cover if using a glass carboy.)

13. After 7 to 10 days or when the kräusen has fallen, use a sanitized racking cane and siphon to gently rack the beer into the sanitized secondary fermenter. Avoid aerating it, and leave as much of the sediment behind as possible. Seal and keep at room temperature, covered or in a dark place, to allow fermentation to continue.

14. Once the bubbling in the airlock has slowed, confirm completion of fermentation by using the hydrometer to take final gravity readings. (Hydrometer readings should be the same for several days in a row.)

15. Prime and bottle the beer (see page 263). Condition for 3 to 4 weeks.

Sahti (Juniper)

This brew is based on the classic juniper-spiced rye beer of Finland. If you like juniper flavor (think "gin"), then you'll enjoy this traditional brew. If you don't like juniper flavor, choose a different recipe!

Estimated Original Gravity: 1.057

Equipment

- **brew kettle**
- **sanitized fermentation gear**

Yeast

1 pack	Wyeast 3056 or White Labs WLP300 or Fermentis WB-06	1 pack

Grains

2 lbs	6-Row malted barley	900 g
2 lbs	rye malt	900 g
1 lb	light Munich malt	450 g
1 lb	Cararye® malt	450 g
1 qt	rice hulls	1 L
5.5 US gal	brewing water	21 L

Malt Extract

4 lbs	Alexander's Sun Country Wheat	1.8 kg

Bittering Hops

3 to 4 AAUs	Tettnang or Spalt	3 to 4 AAUs

Later Additions

1 tsp	Irish moss	5 mL
1 tsp	yeast nutrient	5 mL
.5 oz	juniper berries, crushed, in hop bag	14 g

Aroma Hops

None

1. Prepare the liquid yeast in advance, according to the package directions.
2. Coarsely crack the grains, mix them thoroughly and place them in a cheesecloth or nylon grain bag. Add rice hulls and mix thoroughly.
3. In a brew kettle, bring at least 3 US gal (11 L) brewing water to steeping temperature (150 to 160°F/65 to 71°C). Turn off the heat, add the grain bag, cover and steep for 90 minutes. (If the temperature drops below steeping temperature, turn the element back on briefly to bring it back up.) Remove grain bag. Place it in a strainer, carefully rinse it over the kettle with steeping water and then discard it.
4. Increase the heat and bring grain tea to a boil. Remove from heat, add the malt extract and stir until dissolved completely.
5. Return kettle to the burner and increase the heat until the wort begins to boil. Using a spoon, clear any foam to one side. Reduce heat until a rolling boil can be maintained without foam buildup.

6. Add the bittering hops, stirring to combine. Boil for 45 minutes, uncovered. Monitor to prevent boiling over.

7. Meanwhile, prepare the fermentation gear and cooling bath or wort chiller.

8. After 45 minutes, remove the kettle from the heat and add Irish moss, yeast nutrient and juniper berries. Stir to ensure that the nutrient has dissolved. Return the kettle to the burner and bring back to a rolling boil. Boil for 15 minutes; turn off the heat and cover.

9. To cool the brew, place the covered kettle in the prepared cooling bath or use a wort chiller according to the manufacturer's directions. Cool to the desired temperature, 75°F (24°C), within 30 to 45 minutes.

10. While the wort is cooling, clean and sanitize the brewing spoon. When the wort has cooled, move the kettle to a counter and stir the wort briskly in one direction for about 5 minutes. After stirring, cover and let rest for 10 to 15 minutes as the hops and trub form a cone.

11. Using sanitized racking cane and siphon, rack as much wort as possible into the sanitized primary fermenter. Then, using a sanitized funnel and straining screen, strain the remainder of the wort into the fermenter. Top off with brewing water to bring the volume to around 5.5 US gal (21 L). Using the hydrometer, take a reading of the specific gravity and record it in your brewing journal.

12. Add the yeast; vigorously stir it with a sanitized spoon to distribute it throughout the wort. Seal the fermenter with lid, stopper and airlock. Keep the fermenter at room temperature (68 to 72°F/20 to 22°C) during primary fermentation, which typically lasts 1 to 4 days after fermentation begins. (Keep in a dark place or under a lightproof cover if using a glass carboy.)

13. After 1 to 4 days or when the kräusen has fallen, use a sanitized racking cane and siphon to gently rack the beer into the sanitized secondary fermenter. Avoid aerating it, and leave as much of the sediment behind as possible. Seal and keep at room temperature, covered or in a dark place, to allow fermentation to continue.

14. Once the bubbling in the airlock has slowed, confirm completion of fermentation by using the hydrometer to take final gravity readings. (Hydrometer readings should be the same for several days in a row.)

15. Prime and bottle the beer (see page 263). Condition for 3 to 4 weeks.

Spruce Beer

When the hop supply dwindled in colonial times, brewers looked for other botanicals to flavor their beers. You can do the same, especially if you have a spruce tree in the yard.

Brew this in spring, using the fresh green tips of a spruce tree, but only if trees have not been sprayed with pesticides.

Estimated Original Gravity: 1.060

Equipment

- **brew kettle**
- **sanitized fermentation gear**

Yeast

1 pack	Wyeast 1028 or White Labs WLP013 or Fermentis S-04	1 pack

Grains

1 lb	UK crystal malt (60 Lovibond)	450 g
1 lb	UK brown malt	450 g
4 oz	UK dark crystal malt (150 Lovibond)	112 g
4 oz	UK chocolate malt	112 g
5.5 US gal	brewing water	21 L

Malt Extract

6.6 lbs	any UK brand light	3 kg

Bittering Hops

6 to 8 AAUs	medium-alpha acid (such as Northern Brewer)	6 to 8 AAUs

Later Additions

2 oz	fresh spruce tips (if available)	56 g
1 tsp	Irish moss	5 mL
1 tsp	yeast nutrient	5 mL

Aroma Hops

	None	
1+ tsp	spruce flavor extract (for bottling, in place of fresh spruce tips)	5+ mL

1. Prepare the liquid yeast in advance, according to the package directions.
2. Coarsely crack the grains and place them in a cheesecloth or nylon grain bag.
3. In a brew kettle, bring at least 3 US gal (11 L) brewing water to steeping temperature (150 to 160°F/65 to 71°C). Turn off the heat, add the grain bag, cover and steep for 30 minutes. (If the temperature drops below steeping temperature, turn the element back on briefly to bring it back up.) Remove grain bag. Place it in a strainer, rinse it over the kettle with steeping water and then discard it.
4. Increase the heat and bring grain tea to a boil. Remove from heat, add the malt extract and stir until dissolved completely.
5. Return kettle to the burner and increase the heat until the wort begins to boil. Using a spoon, clear any foam to one side. Reduce heat until a rolling boil can be maintained without foam buildup.

6. Add the bittering hops, stirring to combine. Boil for 45 minutes, uncovered. Monitor to prevent boiling over.

7. Meanwhile, prepare the fermentation gear and cooling bath or wort chiller.

8. After 45 minutes, remove the kettle from the heat. If using fresh spruce tips, put them in a hop bag. Add the bag, Irish moss and yeast nutrient. Stir to ensure that the nutrient has dissolved. Return the kettle to the burner and bring back to a rolling boil. Boil for 15 minutes; turn off the heat and cover.

9. To cool the brew, place the covered kettle in the prepared cooling bath or use a wort chiller according to the manufacturer's directions. Cool to the desired temperature, 75°F (24°C), within 30 to 45 minutes.

10. While the wort is cooling, clean and sanitize the brewing spoon. When the wort has cooled, move the kettle to a counter and stir the wort briskly in one direction for about 5 minutes. After stirring, cover and let rest for 10 to 15 minutes as the hops and trub form a cone.

11. Using sanitized racking cane and siphon, rack as much wort as possible into the sanitized primary fermenter. Then, using a sanitized funnel and straining screen, strain the remainder of the wort into the fermenter. Top off with brewing water to bring the volume to around 5.5 US gal (21 L). Using the hydrometer, take a reading of the specific gravity and record it in your brewing journal.

12. Add the yeast; vigorously stir it with a sanitized spoon to distribute it throughout the wort. Seal the fermenter with lid, stopper and airlock. Keep the fermenter at room temperature (68 to 72°F/20 to 22°C) during primary fermentation, which typically lasts 1 to 4 days after fermentation begins. (Keep in a dark place or under a lightproof cover if using a glass carboy.)

13. After 1 to 4 days or when the kräusen has fallen, use a sanitized racking cane and siphon to gently rack the beer into the sanitized secondary fermenter. Avoid aerating it, and leave as much of the sediment behind as possible. Seal and keep at room temperature, covered or in a dark place, to allow fermentation to continue.

14. Once the bubbling in the airlock has slowed, confirm completion of fermentation by using the hydrometer to take final gravity readings. (Hydrometer readings should be the same for several days in a row.) If using spruce flavor extract *instead of* fresh spruce tips, add it sparingly until you achieve the desired taste.

15. Prime and bottle the beer (see page 263). Condition for 3 to 4 weeks.

Maple Beer

Maple beer is a New England tradition from the "ferment what you've got" school of colonial brewing.

Estimated Original Gravity: 1.059

Equipment

- **brew kettle**
- **sanitized fermentation gear**

Yeast

1 pack	Wyeast 1098 or White Labs WLP002 or Fermentis S-04 or Danstar Nottingham ale yeast	1 pack

Grains

8 oz	UK brown malt	224 g
8 oz	UK dark crystal malt	224 g
4 oz	UK chocolate malt	112 g
5.5 US gal	brewing water	21 L

Malt Extract

4 lbs	any UK brand light	1.8 kg

Bittering Hops

4 to 6 AAUs	East Kent Golding or Fuggle	4 to 6 AAUs

Later Additions

4 lbs	grade B maple syrup	1.8 kg
1 tsp	Irish moss	5 mL
1 tsp	yeast nutrient	5 mL

Aroma Hops

None

1. Prepare the liquid yeast in advance, according to the package directions.
2. Coarsely crack the grains and place them in a cheesecloth or nylon grain bag.
3. In a brew kettle, bring at least 3 US gal (11 L) brewing water to steeping temperature (150 to 160°F/65 to 71°C). Turn off the heat, add the grain bag, cover and steep for 30 minutes. (If the temperature drops below steeping temperature, turn the element back on briefly to bring it back up.) Remove grain bag. Place it in a strainer, rinse it over the kettle with steeping water and then discard it.
4. Increase the heat and bring grain tea to a boil. Remove from heat, add the malt extract and stir until dissolved completely.
5. Return kettle to the burner and increase the heat until the wort begins to boil. Using a spoon, clear any foam to one side. Reduce heat until a rolling boil can be maintained without foam buildup.
6. Add the bittering hops, stirring to combine. Boil for 45 minutes, uncovered. Monitor to prevent boiling over.

7. Meanwhile, prepare the fermentation gear and cooling bath or wort chiller.

8. After 45 minutes, remove the kettle from the heat and add maple syrup, Irish moss and yeast nutrient. Stir to ensure that the syrup and nutrient are dissolved. Return the kettle to the burner and bring back to a rolling boil. Boil for 15 minutes; turn off the heat and cover.

9. To cool the brew, place the covered kettle in the prepared cooling bath or use a wort chiller according to the manufacturer's directions. Cool to the desired temperature, 75°F (24°C), within 30 to 45 minutes.

10. While the wort is cooling, clean and sanitize the brewing spoon. When the wort has cooled, move the kettle to a counter and stir the wort briskly in one direction for about 5 minutes. After stirring, cover and let rest for 10 to 15 minutes as the hops and trub form a cone.

11. Using sanitized racking cane and siphon, rack as much wort as possible into the sanitized primary fermenter. Then, using a sanitized funnel and straining screen, strain the remainder of the wort into the fermenter. Top off with brewing water to bring the volume to around 5.5 US gal (21 L). Using the hydrometer, take a reading of the specific gravity and record it in your brewing journal.

12. Add the yeast; vigorously stir it with a sanitized spoon to distribute it throughout the wort. Seal the fermenter with lid, stopper and airlock. Keep the fermenter at room temperature (68 to 72°F/20 to 22°C) during primary fermentation, which typically lasts 1 to 4 days after fermentation begins. (Keep in a dark place or under a lightproof cover if using a glass carboy.)

13. After 1 to 4 days or when the kräusen has fallen, use a sanitized racking cane and siphon to gently rack the beer into the sanitized secondary fermenter. Avoid aerating it, and leave as much of the sediment behind as possible. Seal and keep at room temperature, covered or in a dark place, to allow fermentation to continue.

14. Once the bubbling in the airlock has slowed, confirm completion of fermentation by using the hydrometer to take final gravity readings. (Hydrometer readings should be the same for several days in a row.)

15. Prime and bottle the beer (see page 263). Condition for 3 to 4 weeks.

This recipe was developed by my wife Nancy. It's a great beverage to pair with Thai food. The lemongrass and Thai ginger (galanga) are available in Asian grocery stores.

Estimated Original Gravity: 1.064

Equipment

- **brew kettle**
- **sanitized fermentation gear**

Thai Lemongrass and Galanga

Yeast

1 pack	Wyeast 1010 or White Labs WLP320 or Fermentis S-04	1 pack

Grains

1 lb	Carafoam®, Carapils® or dextrin malt	450 g
5.5 US gal	brewing water	21 L

Malt Extract

8 lbs	Alexander's Sun Country Wheat, divided in half	3.6 kg

Bittering Hops

2 to 4 AAUs	any variety low-alpha acid	2 to 4 AAUs

Later Additions

2 oz	galanga (Thai ginger, substitute regular fresh ginger if unavailable), chopped	56 g
4 to 6	stalks of fresh (or frozen, thawed) lemongrass, chopped, white part only	4 to 6
1 tsp	Irish moss	5 mL
1 tsp	yeast nutrient	5 mL

Aroma Hops

None

1. Prepare the liquid yeast in advance, according to the package directions.
2. Coarsely crack the grains and place them in a cheesecloth or nylon grain bag.
3. In a brew kettle, bring at least 3 US gal (11 L) brewing water to steeping temperature (150 to 160°F/65 to 71°C). Turn off the heat, add the grain bag, cover and steep for 30 minutes. (If the temperature drops below steeping temperature, turn the element back on briefly to bring it back up.) Remove grain bag. Place it in a strainer, rinse it over the kettle with steeping water and then discard it.
4. Increase the heat and bring grain tea to a boil. Remove from heat, add half of the malt extract (4 lbs/1.8 kg) and stir until dissolved completely.
5. Return kettle to the burner and increase the heat until the wort begins to boil. Using a spoon, clear any foam to one side. Reduce heat until a rolling boil can be maintained without foam buildup.
6. Add the bittering hops, stirring to combine. Boil for 45 minutes, uncovered. Monitor to prevent boiling over.

7. Meanwhile, prepare the fermentation gear and cooling bath or wort chiller.

8. After 45 minutes, remove the kettle from the heat and add remaining half of the malt extract (4 lbs/1.8 kg), ginger, lemongrass, Irish moss and yeast nutrient. Stir to ensure that the extract and nutrient are dissolved. Return the kettle to the burner and bring back to a rolling boil. Boil for 15 minutes; turn off the heat and cover.

9. To cool the brew, place the covered kettle in the prepared cooling bath or use a wort chiller according to the manufacturer's directions. Cool to the desired temperature, 75°F (24°C), within 30 to 45 minutes.

10. While the wort is cooling, clean and sanitize the brewing spoon. When the wort has cooled, move the kettle to a counter and stir the wort briskly in one direction for about 5 minutes. After stirring, cover and let rest for 10 to 15 minutes as the hops and trub form a cone.

11. Using sanitized racking cane and siphon, rack as much wort as possible into the sanitized primary fermenter. Then, using a sanitized funnel and straining screen, strain the remainder of the wort into the fermenter. Top off with brewing water to bring the volume to around 5.5 US gal (21 L). Using the hydrometer, take a reading of the specific gravity and record it in your brewing journal.

12. Add the yeast; vigorously stir it with a sanitized spoon to distribute it throughout the wort. Seal the fermenter with lid, stopper and airlock. Keep the fermenter at room temperature (68 to 72°F/20 to 22°C) during primary fermentation, which typically lasts 1 to 4 days after fermentation begins. (Keep in a dark place or under a lightproof cover if using a glass carboy.)

13. After 1 to 4 days or when the kräusen has fallen, use a sanitized racking cane and siphon to gently rack the beer into the sanitized secondary fermenter. Avoid aerating it, and leave as much of the sediment behind as possible. Seal and keep at room temperature, covered or in a dark place, to allow fermentation to continue.

14. Once the bubbling in the airlock has slowed, confirm completion of fermentation by using the hydrometer to take final gravity readings. (Hydrometer readings should be the same for several days in a row.)

15. Prime and bottle the beer (see page 263). Condition for 3 to 4 weeks.

Once upon a time, all malt was roasted over wood fires, which gave all beers a smoky flavor. Only two styles of smoked beers remain to this day.

Smoked Beers

Bamberg Rauchbier

The classic smoked beer of Germany is brewed in the town of Bamberg. Brewers smoke their malt over beechwood fires. Try this smoky treat with some smoked sausages.

Estimated Original Gravity: 1.051

Equipment

- brew kettle
- sanitized fermentation gear

Yeast

| 2 packs | Wyeast 2308 or White Labs WLP830 (or 1 pack in starter) or Fermentis S-23 | 2 packs |

Grains

3 lbs	German rauchmaltz	1.36 kg
1 lb	dark Munich malt	450 g
5.5 US gal	brewing water	21 L

Malt Extract

| 4 lbs | Alexander's Sun Country Pale | 1.8 kg |

Bittering Hops

| 6 to 8 AAUs | Perle | 6 to 8 AAUs |

Later Additions

| 1 tsp | Irish moss | 5 mL |
| 1 tsp | yeast nutrient | 5 mL |

Aroma Hops

None

1. Prepare the liquid yeast in advance, according to the package directions.
2. Coarsely crack the grains and place them in a cheesecloth or nylon grain bag.
3. In a brew kettle, bring at least 3 US gal (11 L) brewing water to steeping temperature (150 to 160°F/65 to 71°C). Turn off the heat, add the grain bag, cover and steep for 90 minutes. (If the temperature drops below steeping temperature, reheat briefly to bring it back up.) Remove grain bag. Place it in a strainer, rinse it carefully over the kettle with steeping water and then discard it.
4. Increase the heat and bring grain tea to a boil. Remove from heat, add the malt extract and stir until dissolved completely.
5. Return kettle to the burner and increase the heat until the wort begins to boil. Using a spoon, clear any foam to one side. Reduce heat until a rolling boil can be maintained without foam buildup.
6. Add the bittering hops, stirring to combine. Boil for 45 minutes, uncovered. Monitor to prevent boiling over.
7. Meanwhile, prepare the fermentation gear and cooling bath or wort chiller.

8. After 45 minutes, remove the kettle from the heat and add Irish moss and yeast nutrient. Stir to ensure that the nutrient has dissolved. Return the kettle to the burner and bring back to a rolling boil. Boil for 15 minutes; turn off the heat and cover.

9. To cool the brew, place the covered kettle in the prepared cooling bath or use a wort chiller according to the manufacturer's directions. Cool to the desired temperature, 75°F (24°C), within 30 to 45 minutes.

10. While the wort is cooling, clean and sanitize the brewing spoon. When the wort has cooled, move the kettle to a counter and stir the wort briskly in one direction for about 5 minutes. After stirring, cover and let rest for 10 to 15 minutes as the hops and trub form a cone.

11. Using sanitized racking cane and siphon, rack as much wort as possible into the sanitized primary fermenter. Then, using a sanitized funnel and straining screen, strain the remainder of the wort into the fermenter. Top off with brewing water to bring the volume to around 5.5 US gal (21 L). Using the hydrometer, take a reading of the specific gravity and record it in your brewing journal.

12. Add the yeast; vigorously stir it with a sanitized spoon to distribute it throughout the wort. Seal the fermenter with lid, stopper and airlock. Keep the fermenter at room temperature (68 to 72°F/20 to 22°C) until fermentation begins (bubbles will be moving through the airlock). (Keep it in a dark place or under a lightproof cover if using a glass carboy.) Once fermentation begins, drop the temperature to 46 to 55°F (8 to 13°C) for one week of primary fermentation.

13. Gently rack the beer into the secondary fermenter to avoid aerating it, leaving as much of the sediment behind as possible. Seal and drop the temperature to 35 to 45°F (2 to 7°C); keep it at that temperature, covered or in a dark place, to allow fermentation to continue for 4 weeks.

14. Once the bubbling in the airlock has slowed, confirm completion of fermentation by using the hydrometer to take final gravity readings. (Hydrometer readings should be the same for several days in a row.)

15. Prime and bottle the beer (see page 263). Condition it in the refrigerator for 3 to 4 weeks.

Brewer's Tip

For information on preparing a yeast starter, see page 262.

Rauch Dopplebok

The brew is Rauchbier's big brother!

Estimated Original Gravity: 1.096

Equipment

- brew kettle
- sanitized fermentation gear
- blow-off hose

Yeast

| 2 packs | Wyeast 2206 or White Labs WLP833 (or 1 pack in starter) or Fermentis S-23 | 2 packs |

Grains

3 lbs	German rauchmaltz	1.36 kg
1 lb	Carabohemian® malt	450 g
1 lb	Caraaroma® malt	450 g
5.5 US gal	brewing water	21 L

Malt Extract

| 9.9 lbs | any brand light | 4.5 kg |

Bittering Hops

| 6 to 8 AAUs | Northern Brewer or Perle | 6 to 8 AAUs |

Flavor and Aroma Hops

| 1 oz | Tettnang, Spalt or other German Noble Hops, divided in half | 28 g |

Later Additions

| 1 tsp | Irish moss | 5 mL |
| 1 tsp | yeast nutrient | 5 mL |

1. Prepare the liquid yeast in advance, according to the package directions.
2. Coarsely crack the grains and place them in a cheesecloth or nylon grain bag.
3. In a brew kettle, bring at least 3 US gal (11 L) brewing water to steeping temperature (150 to 160°F/65 to 71°C). Turn off the heat, add the grain bag, cover and steep for 90 minutes. (If the temperature drops below steeping temperature, reheat briefly to bring it back up.) Remove grain bag. Place it in a strainer, rinse it carefully over the kettle with steeping water and then discard it.
4. Increase the heat and bring grain tea to a boil. Remove from heat, add the malt extract and stir until dissolved completely.
5. Return kettle to the burner and increase the heat until the wort begins to boil. Using a spoon, clear any foam to one side. Reduce heat until a rolling boil can be maintained without foam buildup.
6. Add the bittering hops, stirring to combine. Boil for 45 minutes, uncovered. Monitor to prevent boiling over.
7. Meanwhile, prepare the fermentation gear and cooling bath or wort chiller.

8. After 45 minutes, remove the kettle from the heat and add .5 oz (14 g) hops for flavor, Irish moss and yeast nutrient. Stir to ensure that the nutrient has dissolved. Return the kettle to the burner and bring back to a rolling boil. Boil for 15 minutes, stir in the remaining .5 oz (14) of hops for aroma, turn off the heat and cover.

9. To cool the brew, place the covered kettle in the prepared cooling bath or use a wort chiller according to the manufacturer's directions. Cool to the desired temperature, 75°F (24°C), within 30 to 45 minutes.

10. While the wort is cooling, clean and sanitize the brewing spoon. When the wort has cooled, move the kettle to a counter and stir the wort briskly in one direction for about 5 minutes. After stirring, cover and let rest for 10 to 15 minutes as the hops and trub form a cone.

11. Using sanitized racking cane and siphon, rack as much wort as possible into the sanitized primary fermenter. Then, using a sanitized funnel and straining screen, strain the remainder of the wort into the fermenter. Top off with brewing water to bring the volume to around 5.5 US gal (21 L). Using the hydrometer, take a reading of the specific gravity and record it in your brewing journal.

12. Add the yeast; vigorously stir it with a sanitized spoon to distribute it throughout the wort. Seal the fermenter with lid, stopper and airlock or blow-off hose. Keep the fermenter at room temperature (68 to 72°F/20 to 22°C) until fermentation begins (bubbles will be moving through the airlock). (Keep it in a dark place or under a lightproof cover if using a glass carboy.) Once fermentation begins, drop the temperature to 46 to 55°F (8 to 13°C) for one week of primary fermentation.

13. Gently rack the beer into the secondary fermenter to avoid aerating it, leaving as much of the sediment behind as possible. Seal and drop the temperature to 35 to 45°F (2 to 7°C); keep it at that temperature, covered or in a dark place, to allow fermentation to continue for 4 to 6 weeks.

14. Once the bubbling in the airlock has slowed, confirm completion of fermentation by using the hydrometer to take final gravity readings. (Hydrometer readings should be the same for several days in a row.)

15. Prime and bottle the beer (see page 263). Condition it in the refrigerator for 3 to 4 weeks.

Brewer's Tips

For information on preparing a yeast starter, see page 262.

If active fermentation backs up into the airlock, replace airlock with blow-off hose (see page 16). Change water as needed; re-install airlock when fermentation settles down.

Grodzinsky

This is the traditional smoked wheat beer of Poland. It's the perfect companion for grilled smoked kielbasa.

Estimated Original Gravity: 1.056

Equipment

- **brew kettle**
- **sanitized fermentation gear**

Brewer's Tips

If the specified brands of grains are not available, use the grains chart on page 77 to find substitutes.

Yeast

1 pack	Wyeast 1338 or White Labs WLP011 or Fermentis S-33	1 pack

Grains

1 lb	Briess Smoked malt (cherry wood)	450 g
1 lb	Carared® malt	450 g
5.5 US gal	brewing water	21 L

Malt Extract

6.6 lbs	any brand wheat	3 kg

Bittering Hops

4 to 6 AAUs	Spalt or Tettnang hops	4 to 6 AAUs

Later Additions

1 tsp	Irish moss	5 mL
1 tsp	yeast nutrient	5 mL

Aroma Hops

None

1. Prepare the liquid yeast in advance, according to the package directions.
2. Coarsely crack the grains and place them in a cheesecloth or nylon grain bag.
3. In a brew kettle, bring at least 3 US gal (11 L) brewing water to steeping temperature (150 to 160°F/65 to 71°C). Turn off the heat, add the grain bag, cover and steep for 30 minutes. (If the temperature drops below steeping temperature, turn the element back on briefly to bring it back up.) Remove grain bag. Place it in a strainer, rinse it over the kettle with steeping water and then discard it.
4. Increase the heat and bring grain tea to a boil. Remove from heat, add the malt extract and stir until dissolved completely.
5. Return kettle to the burner and increase the heat until the wort begins to boil. Using a spoon, clear any foam to one side. Reduce heat until a rolling boil can be maintained without foam buildup.
6. Add the bittering hops, stirring to combine. Boil for 45 minutes, uncovered. Monitor to prevent boiling over.
7. Meanwhile, prepare the fermentation gear and cooling bath or wort chiller.

8. After 45 minutes, remove the kettle from the heat and add Irish moss and yeast nutrient. Stir to ensure that the nutrient has dissolved. Return the kettle to the burner and bring back to a rolling boil. Boil for 15 minutes; turn off the heat and cover.

9. To cool the brew, place the covered kettle in the prepared cooling bath or use a wort chiller according to the manufacturer's directions. Cool to the desired temperature, 75°F (24°C), within 30 to 45 minutes.

10. While the wort is cooling, clean and sanitize the brewing spoon. When the wort has cooled, move the kettle to a counter and stir the wort briskly in one direction for about 5 minutes. After stirring, cover and let rest for 10 to 15 minutes as the hops and trub form a cone.

11. Using sanitized racking cane and siphon, rack as much wort as possible into the sanitized primary fermenter. Then, using a sanitized funnel and straining screen, strain the remainder of the wort into the fermenter. Top off with brewing water to bring the volume to around 5.5 US gal (21 L). Using the hydrometer, take a reading of the specific gravity and record it in your brewing journal.

12. Add the yeast; vigorously stir it with a sanitized spoon to distribute it throughout the wort. Seal the fermenter with lid, stopper and airlock. Keep the fermenter at room temperature (68 to 72°F/20 to 22°C) during primary fermentation, which typically lasts 1 to 4 days after fermentation begins. (Keep in a dark place or under a lightproof cover if using a glass carboy.)

13. After 1 to 4 days or when the kräusen has fallen, use a sanitized racking cane and siphon to gently rack the beer into the sanitized secondary fermenter. Avoid aerating it, and leave as much of the sediment behind as possible. Seal and keep at room temperature, covered or in a dark place, to allow fermentation to continue.

14. Once the bubbling in the airlock has slowed, confirm completion of fermentation by using the hydrometer to take final gravity readings. (Hydrometer readings should be the same for several days in a row.)

15. Prime and bottle the beer (see page 263). Condition for 3 to 4 weeks.

Peated Scottish Ale

Many modern brewers have decided to add peat-smoked malt to their brews. This is the same malt used to produce Scotch whisky. If you like smoky Scotches, this is your brew. If you don't like them, move on, laddie (or lassie).

Estimated Original Gravity: 1.098

Equipment

- **brew kettle**
- **sanitized fermentation gear**

Liquid Yeast

2 packs	Wyeast 1728 or White Labs WLP028 (or 1 pack in a starter)	2 packs

Grains

1 lb	UK crystal malt (60 Lovibond)	450 g
1 lb	UK peat-smoked malt	450 g
8 oz	UK brown malt	224 g
8 oz	UK dark crystal malt	224 g
5.5 US gal	brewing water	21 L

Malt Extract

8 lbs	any UK brand amber DME	3.6 kg

Bittering Hops

8 to 10 AAUs	Challenger, Northern Brewer or Target	8 to 10 AAUs

Later Additions

1 lb	Demerara sugar or other dark raw sugar	450 g
1 tsp	Irish moss	5 mL
1 tsp	yeast nutrient	5 mL

Aroma Hops

.5 oz	Fuggle or Willamette	14 g

1. Prepare the liquid yeast in advance, according to the package directions.
2. Coarsely crack the grains and place them in a cheesecloth or nylon grain bag.
3. In a brew kettle, bring at least 3 US gal (11 L) brewing water to steeping temperature (150 to 160°F/65 to 71°C). Turn off the heat, add the grain bag, cover and steep for 30 minutes. (If the temperature drops below steeping temperature, turn the element back on briefly to bring it back up.) Remove grain bag. Place it in a strainer, rinse it over the kettle with steeping water and then discard it.
4. Increase the heat and bring grain tea to a boil. Remove from heat, add the malt extract and stir until dissolved completely.
5. Return kettle to the burner and increase the heat until the wort begins to boil. Using a spoon, clear any foam to one side. Reduce heat until a rolling boil can be maintained without foam buildup.
6. Add the bittering hops, stirring to combine. Boil for 45 minutes, uncovered. Monitor to prevent boiling over.

7. Meanwhile, prepare the fermentation gear and cooling bath or wort chiller.

8. After 45 minutes, remove the kettle from the heat and add sugar, Irish moss and yeast nutrient. Stir to ensure that the sugar and nutrient are dissolved. Return the kettle to the burner and bring back to a rolling boil. Boil for 15 minutes, then stir in the aroma hops, turn off the heat and cover.

9. To cool the brew, place the covered kettle in the prepared cooling bath or use a wort chiller according to the manufacturer's directions. Cool to the desired temperature, 75°F (24°C), within 30 to 45 minutes.

10. While the wort is cooling, clean and sanitize the brewing spoon. When the wort has cooled, move the kettle to a counter and stir the wort briskly in one direction for about 5 minutes. After stirring, cover and let rest for 10 to 15 minutes as the hops and trub form a cone.

11. Using sanitized racking cane and siphon, rack as much wort as possible into the sanitized primary fermenter. Then, using a sanitized funnel and straining screen, strain the remainder of the wort into the fermenter. Top off with brewing water to bring the volume to around 5.5 US gal (21 L). Using the hydrometer, take a reading of the specific gravity and record it.

12. Add the yeast; vigorously stir it with a sanitized spoon to distribute it throughout the wort. Seal the fermenter with lid, stopper and airlock. Keep the fermenter at room temperature (68 to 72°F/20 to 22°C) during primary fermentation, which typically lasts 7 to 10 days after fermentation begins. (Keep in a dark place or under a lightproof cover if using a glass carboy.)

13. After 7 to 10 days or when the kräusen has fallen, use a sanitized racking cane and siphon to gently rack the beer into the sanitized secondary fermenter. Avoid aerating it, and leave as much of the sediment behind as possible. Seal and keep at room temperature, covered or in a dark place, to allow fermentation to continue.

14. Once the bubbling in the airlock has slowed, confirm completion of fermentation by using the hydrometer to take final gravity readings. (Hydrometer readings should be the same for several days in a row.)

15. Prime and bottle the beer (see page 263). Condition for 3 to 4 weeks.

Brewer's Tip

For information on preparing a yeast starter, see page 262.

Soak the oak chips in vodka to sanitize them.

Estimated Original Gravity: 1.064

Equipment

- **brew kettle**
- **sanitized fermentation gear**

Brewer's Tip

Before brewing, place the oak chips in a hop bag, tie the bag and soak the chips for a few days in vodka to sanitize them.

Oak and Smoke Brown Ale

Yeast

1 pack	Wyeast 1028 or White Labs WLP013 or Fermentis S-04	1 pack

Grains

1 lb	UK crystal malt (60 Lovibond)	450 g
1 lb	UK brown malt	450 g
1 lb	Briess Smoked malt (cherry wood)	450 g
5.5 US gal	brewing water	21 L

Malt Extract

6.6 lbs	any UK brand light	3 kg

Bittering Hops

6 to 8 AAUs	medium-alpha acid (such as Northern Brewer)	6 to 8 AAUs

Later Additions

1 tsp	Irish moss	5 mL
1 tsp	yeast nutrient	5 mL

Aroma Hops

.5 oz	Fuggle or Kent Golding	14 g
4 oz	heavy toast oak chips or cubes, soaked in vodka	112 g

1. Prepare liquid yeast in advance, according to directions.
2. Coarsely crack grains and place them in a grain bag.
3. In a brew kettle, bring at least 3 US gal (11 L) brewing water to steeping temperature (150 to 160°F/65 to 71°C). Turn off heat, add grain bag, cover and steep for 30 minutes. (If temperature drops below steeping temperature, reheat briefly to bring it back up.) Remove grain bag. Place in a strainer, rinse over the kettle with steeping water and discard.
4. Increase the heat and bring grain tea to a boil. Remove from heat, add malt extract and stir until dissolved.
5. Return kettle to burner and increase heat until wort begins to boil. Using a spoon, clear any foam to one side. Reduce heat until a rolling boil is maintained without foam buildup.
6. Add the bittering hops, stirring to combine. Boil for 45 minutes, uncovered. Monitor to prevent boiling over.
7. Meanwhile, prepare the fermentation gear and cooling bath or wort chiller.

8. After 45 minutes, remove kettle from heat and add Irish moss and yeast nutrient. Stir to ensure that nutrient has dissolved. Return the kettle to the burner and bring back to a rolling boil. Boil for 15 minutes, then stir in the aroma hops, turn off heat and cover.

9. To cool the brew, place the covered kettle in the prepared cooling bath or use a wort chiller according to the manufacturer's directions. Cool to the desired temperature, 75°F (24°C), within 30 to 45 minutes.

10. While wort is cools, sanitize brewing spoon. When wort has cooled, move kettle to a counter and stir wort briskly in one direction for about 5 minutes. After stirring, cover and let rest for 10 to 15 minutes as hops and trub form a cone.

11. Using sanitized racking cane and siphon, rack as much wort as possible into sanitized primary fermenter. Then, using a sanitized funnel and straining screen, strain remainder of wort into fermenter. Top off with brewing water to bring volume to around 5.5 US gal (21 L). Using hydrometer, take a reading of specific gravity and record it.

12. Add the yeast; vigorously stir it with a sanitized spoon to distribute it throughout the wort. Seal the fermenter with lid, stopper and airlock. Keep the fermenter at room temperature (68 to 72°F/20 to 22°C) during primary fermentation, which typically lasts 1 to 4 days after fermentation begins. (Keep in a dark place or under a lightproof cover if using a glass carboy.)

13. After 1 to 4 days or when the kräusen has fallen, use a sanitized racking cane and siphon to gently rack the beer into the sanitized secondary fermenter. Avoid aerating it, and leave as much of the sediment behind as possible. Seal and keep at room temperature, covered or in a dark place, to allow fermentation to continue.

14. Once the bubbling in the airlock has slowed, add the oak chips (in a sanitized hop bag) and reseal. Sample developing flavor every two days; if desired oakiness is reached before fermentation is complete, use sanitized racking cane and siphon to rack into a sanitized tertiary fermenter. Confirm completion of fermentation by using the hydrometer to take final gravity readings. (Hydrometer readings should be the same for several days in a row.)

15. Prime and bottle the beer (see page 263). Condition for 3 to 4 weeks.

There are many examples of modern smoked porters. The most famous is from Alaskan Brewing Co., which uses alder smoke. You can experiment with different smoked malts as well.

Estimated Original Gravity: 1.066

Equipment

- **brew kettle**
- **sanitized fermentation gear**

Cherry Wood Smoked Porter

Yeast

1 pack	Wyeast 1028 or White Labs WLP013 or Fermentis S-04	1 pack

Grains

1 lb	UK crystal malt (60 Lovibond)	450 g
1 lb	UK brown malt	450 g
1 lb	Briess Smoked malt (cherry wood)	450 g
4 oz	UK dark crystal malt (150 Lovibond)	112 g
4 oz	UK chocolate malt	112 g
2 oz	UK black patent malt	56 g
5.5 US gal	brewing water	21 L

Malt Extract

6.6 lbs	any UK brand light	3 kg

Bittering Hops

6 to 8 AAUs	medium-alpha acid (such as Northern Brewer)	6 to 8 AAUs

Later Additions

1 tsp	Irish moss	5 mL
1 tsp	yeast nutrient	5 mL

Aroma Hops

	None	

1. Prepare liquid yeast in advance, according to directions.
2. Coarsely crack grains and place them in a grain bag.
3. In a brew kettle, bring at least 3 US gal (11 L) brewing water to steeping temperature (150 to 160°F/65 to 71°C). Turn off the heat, add the grain bag, cover and steep for 30 minutes. (If the temperature drops below steeping temperature, turn the element back on briefly to bring it back up.) Remove grain bag. Place it in a strainer, rinse it over the kettle with steeping water and then discard.
4. Increase the heat and bring grain tea to a boil. Remove from heat, add the malt extract and stir until dissolved.
5. Return kettle to burner and increase heat until wort begins to boil. Using a spoon, clear foam to one side. Reduce heat until a rolling boil is maintained without foam buildup.
6. Add the bittering hops, stirring to combine. Boil for 45 minutes, uncovered. Monitor to prevent boiling over.

7. Meanwhile, prepare the fermentation gear and cooling bath or wort chiller.

8. After 45 minutes, remove the kettle from the heat and add Irish moss and yeast nutrient. Stir to ensure that the extract, sugar and nutrient are dissolved. Return the kettle to the burner and bring back to a rolling boil. Boil for 15 minutes; turn off the heat and cover.

9. To cool the brew, place the covered kettle in the prepared cooling bath or use a wort chiller according to the manufacturer's directions. Cool to the desired temperature, 75°F (24°C), within 30 to 45 minutes.

10. While the wort is cooling, clean and sanitize the brewing spoon. When the wort has cooled, move the kettle to a counter and stir the wort briskly in one direction for about 5 minutes. After stirring, cover and let rest for 10 to 15 minutes as the hops and trub form a cone.

11. Using sanitized racking cane and siphon, rack as much wort as possible into the sanitized primary fermenter. Then, using a sanitized funnel and straining screen, strain the remainder of the wort into the fermenter. Top off with brewing water to bring the volume to around 5.5 US gal (21 L). Using the hydrometer, take a reading of the specific gravity and record it in your brewing journal.

12. Add the yeast; vigorously stir it with a sanitized spoon to distribute it throughout the wort. Seal the fermenter with lid, stopper and airlock. Keep the fermenter at room temperature (68 to 72°F/20 to 22°C) during primary fermentation, which typically lasts 7 to 10 days after fermentation begins. (Keep in a dark place or under a lightproof cover if using a glass carboy.)

13. After 7 to 10 days or when the kräusen has fallen, use a sanitized racking cane and siphon to gently rack the beer into the sanitized secondary fermenter. Avoid aerating it, and leave as much of the sediment behind as possible. Seal and keep at room temperature, covered or in a dark place, to allow fermentation to continue.

14. Once the bubbling in the airlock has slowed, confirm completion of fermentation by using the hydrometer to take final gravity readings. (Hydrometer readings should be the same for several days in a row.)

15. Prime and bottle the beer (see page 263). Condition for 3 to 4 weeks.

This is a wonderful brew to enjoy on a crisp fall evening. The combination of smoke, maple and malt will tickle your taste buds.

Estimated Original Gravity: 1.070

Equipment

- **brew kettle**
- **sanitized fermentation gear**

Smoked Amber Ale with Maple

Yeast

| 1 pack | Wyeast 1084 or White Labs WLP004 or Fermentis S-33 | 1 pack |

Grains

1 lb	Melanoidin® malt or other toasted malt (25 to 40 Lovibond)	450 g
1 lb	any brand crystal or caramel malt (40 to 60 Lovibond)	450 g
1 lb	Briess Smoked malt (cherry wood)	450 g
1 oz	any dark roasted malt (such as chocolate, black patent, Carafa® or Roast Barley)	28 g
5.5 US gal	brewing water	21 L

Malt Extract

| 6.6 lbs | Briess, Coopers or Northwestern (or any brand) light or gold, divided in half | 3 kg |

Bittering Hops

| 6 to 8 AAUs | any variety low- or medium-alpha acid | 6 to 8 AAUs |

Later Additions

1 lb	amber grade B maple syrup	450 g
1 tsp	Irish moss	5 mL
1 tsp	yeast nutrient	5 mL

Aroma Hops

None

1. Prepare liquid yeast in advance, according to directions.
2. Coarsely crack grains and place them in a grain bag.
3. In a brew kettle, bring at least 3 US gal (11 L) brewing water to steeping temperature (150 to 160°F/65 to 71°C). Turn off heat, add grain bag, cover and steep for 30 minutes. (If temperature drops below steeping temperature, reheat briefly to bring it back up.) Remove grain bag. Place in a strainer, rinse over kettle with steeping water and discard.
4. Increase the heat and bring grain tea to a boil. Remove from heat, add half of the malt extract (3.3 lbs/1.5 kg) and stir until dissolved completely.
5. Return kettle to burner and increase heat until wort begins to boil. Using a spoon, clear foam. Reduce heat until a rolling boil is maintained without foam buildup.

6. Add the bittering hops, stirring to combine. Boil for 45 minutes, uncovered. Monitor to prevent boiling over.

7. Meanwhile, prepare the fermentation gear and cooling bath or wort chiller.

8. After 45 minutes, remove the kettle from the heat and add the remaining half of the malt extract (3.3 lbs/1.5 kg), maple syrup, Irish moss and yeast nutrient. Stir to ensure that the extract, syrup and nutrient have dissolved. Return the kettle to the burner and bring back to a rolling boil. Boil for 15 minutes; turn off the heat and cover.

9. To cool the brew, place the covered kettle in the prepared cooling bath or use a wort chiller according to the manufacturer's directions. Cool to the desired temperature, 75°F (24°C), within 30 to 45 minutes.

10. While wort cools, sanitize the brewing spoon. When wort has cooled, move kettle to a counter and stir wort briskly in one direction for about 5 minutes. After stirring, cover and let rest for 10 to 15 minutes as the trub forms a cone.

11. Using sanitized racking cane and siphon, rack as much wort as possible into sanitized primary fermenter. Using a sanitized funnel and straining screen, strain remainder of wort into fermenter. Top off with brewing water to bring the volume to around 5.5 US gal (21 L). Using hydrometer, take a reading of specific gravity and record it.

12. Add the yeast; vigorously stir it with a sanitized spoon to distribute it throughout the wort. Seal the fermenter with lid, stopper and airlock. Keep the fermenter at room temperature (68 to 72°F/20 to 22°C) during primary fermentation, which typically lasts 7 to 10 days after fermentation begins. (Keep in a dark place or under a lightproof cover if using a glass carboy.)

13. After 7 to 10 days or when the kräusen has fallen, use a sanitized racking cane and siphon to gently rack the beer into the sanitized secondary fermenter. Avoid aerating it, and leave as much of the sediment behind as possible. Seal and keep at room temperature, covered or in a dark place, to allow fermentation to continue.

14. Once the bubbling in the airlock has slowed, confirm completion of fermentation by using the hydrometer to take final gravity readings. (Hydrometer readings should be the same for several days in a row.)

15. Prime and bottle the beer (see page 263). Condition for 3 to 4 weeks.

Smoked Pumpkin Ale

Why brew one style of extreme beer when you can combine them and brew two?

Estimated Original Gravity: varies according to starch conversion in pumpkin

---

Equipment

- **brew kettle**
- **sanitized fermentation gear**

Brewer's Tips

For easier brewing, place the spices in a hop bag and add the bag to the kettle. If you add these ingredients directly to the liquid, you will need to be much more careful about straining the brew as it moves through fermentation.

For information on preparing a yeast starter, see page 262.

5 lbs	pumpkin, home-smoked (see sidebar)	2.25 kg

Yeast

2 packs	Wyeast 1187 or White Labs WLP004 (or 1 pack in starter) or Fermentis S-04	2 packs

Grains

2 lbs	6-Row malted barley	900 g
1 lb	Special Roast malt	450 g
1 lb	crystal or caramel malt (60 Lovibond)	450 g
1 lb	Briess Smoked malt (cherry wood)	450 g
4 oz	dehusked Carafa I® malt	112 g
1 qt	rice hulls	1 L
5.5 US gal	brewing water	21 L

Malt Extract

6.6 lbs	any brand light	3 kg

Bittering Hops

3 to 4 AAUs	Mt Hood or Liberty	3 to 4 AAUs

Later Additions

1 lb	grade B amber maple syrup	450 g
1 oz	freshly grated ginger	28 g
2 to 3	whole cinnamon sticks, coarsely ground	2 to 3
2 to 3	whole cloves, leave whole	2 to 3
.25 tsp	grated nutmeg	1 mL
1 tsp	Irish moss	5 mL
1 tsp	yeast nutrient	5 mL

Aroma Hops

None

1. Prepare liquid yeast in advance, according to directions.
2. Coarsely crack the grains and combine them thoroughly with smoked pumpkin and rice hulls before placing the mixture in a cheesecloth or nylon grain bag.
3. In a brew kettle, bring at least 3 US gal (11 L) brewing water to steeping temperature (150 to 160°F/65 to 71°C). Turn off heat, add grain bag, cover and steep for 90 minutes. (If temperature drops below steeping temperature, reheat briefly.) Remove grain bag. Place in a strainer, carefully rinse over kettle with steeping water and discard.
4. Increase the heat and bring grain tea to a boil. Remove from heat, add the malt extract and stir until dissolved.

5. Return kettle to burner and increase heat until wort begins to boil. Using a spoon, clear foam. Reduce heat until a rolling boil is maintained without foam buildup.

6. Add the bittering hops, stirring to combine. Boil for 45 minutes, uncovered. Monitor to prevent boiling over.

7. Meanwhile, prepare the fermentation gear and cooling bath or wort chiller.

8. After 45 minutes, remove the kettle from the heat and add maple syrup, ginger, cinnamon sticks, cloves, nutmeg, Irish moss and yeast nutrient. Stir to ensure that the syrup and nutrient have dissolved. Return the kettle to the burner and bring back to a rolling boil. Boil for 15 minutes; turn off the heat and cover.

9. To cool the brew, place the covered kettle in the prepared cooling bath or use a wort chiller according to the manufacturer's directions. Cool to the desired temperature, 75°F (24°C), within 30 to 45 minutes.

10. While wort cools, sanitize brewing spoon. When wort has cooled, move the kettle to a counter and stir wort briskly in one direction for about 5 minutes. After stirring, cover and let rest for 10 to 15 minutes as the trub forms a cone.

11. Using sanitized racking cane and siphon, rack as much wort as possible into sanitized primary fermenter. Then, using a sanitized funnel and straining screen, strain remainder of wort into fermenter. Top off with brewing water to bring volume to around 5.5 US gal (21 L). Using hydrometer, take a reading of specific gravity and record it.

12. Add yeast; vigorously stir it with a sanitized spoon to distribute it. Seal fermenter with lid, stopper and airlock. Keep fermenter at room temperature (68 to 72°F/20 to 22°C) during primary fermentation, which could last up to 10 days after fermentation begins, depending on the OG of brew. (If OG is higher than 1.065 it should last 7 to 10 days.) (Keep in a dark place or under a lightproof cover if using a glass carboy.)

13. When the kräusen has fallen, use a sanitized racking cane and siphon to gently rack the beer into the sanitized secondary fermenter. Avoid aerating it, and leave as much of the sediment behind as possible. Seal and keep at room temperature, covered or in a dark place, to allow fermentation to continue.

14. Once the bubbling in the airlock has slowed, confirm completion of fermentation by using the hydrometer to take final gravity readings. (Hydrometer readings should be the same for several days in a row.)

15. Prime and bottle the beer (see page 263). Condition for 3 to 4 weeks.

Preparing Smoked Pumpkin

Cut a whole pumpkin into chunks and place them, skin side down, in a barbeque, over your favorite smoking wood. Allow the pumpkin to smoke for several hours or until the flesh is softened, caramelized and nice and smoky. Scoop out the flesh; yield should be about 5 lbs (2.25 kg). Set pumpkin aside to be thoroughly combined with the grains and rice hulls in the grain bag before steeping.

Some of the most intriguing styles of beer are the funky or sour beers of the world. These are an acquired taste, so you may want to "research" commercial examples before brewing an entire batch.

Making sour beers is a commitment—you will need to devote any plastic brewing components to the production of sour beer. Otherwise, the persistent microbes you use in these recipes could turn all your beers into sour ones if they're allowed to roam freely! The secondary yeasts are the wild yeasts (Brettanomyces aka Brett) that you've been warned about (and sanitizing to prevent) in the previous recipes. (Another potential addition is lactobacillus culture.) Don't panic if these beers exhibit symptoms that would normally mean contamination (such as an oily film on the surface or a pellicle in the fermenter or bottles).

You'll find most of these sour beers require longer ferment times and storage of three months or longer at room temperature to develop their sour flavor. Your reward is that you're duplicating beers that can be quite pricey.

Funky Beers

Gueuze or Lambic
(Kriek, Framboise or Peche)

The classic, spontaneously fermented ales of Belgium can be approximated using the cultured yeast available to the homebrewer. A Gueuze is the sour base ale. Lambics are the base beer with fruit added.

Estimated Original Gravity: 1.070

Equipment

- **brew kettle**
- **sanitized fermentation gear**

Brewer's Tip

Use cherries to produce a Kriek, raspberries to produce Framboise and peaches for Peche.

Beers made with fresh fruit or fruit purées require a three-stage fermentation. Before racking the beer into the secondary fermenter, you will be adding prepared fruit (or purée) to the secondary fermenter, racking the brew into the fermenter, waiting 30 days and then racking into a tertiary fermenter.

Liquid Yeast

1 pack	Wyeast 3278 or White Labs WLP655	1 pack

Grains

1 lb	Carafoam®, Carapils® or dextrin malt	450 g
1 lb	Carabelge® malt	450 g
5.5 US gal	brewing water	21 L

Malt Extracts

4 lbs	Alexander's Sun Country Wheat	1.8 kg
4 lbs	Alexander's Sun Country Pale (late addition)	1.8 kg

Bittering Hops

2 to 4 AAUs	Northern Brewer or Perle	2 to 4 AAUs

Later Additions

1 tsp	Irish moss	5 mL
1 tsp	yeast nutrient	5 mL
5 to 10 lbs	appropriate fruit (if making a Lambic, see sidebar notes)	2.25 to 4.5 kg

Aroma Hops

None

1. Prepare liquid yeast in advance, according to directions.
2. Coarsely crack the grains and place them in a grain bag.
3. In a brew kettle, bring at least 3 US gal (11 L) brewing water to steeping temperature (150 to 160°F/65 to 71°C). Turn off the heat, add the grain bag, cover and steep for 30 minutes. (If the temperature drops below steeping temperature, reheat briefly.) Remove grain bag. Place it in a strainer, rinse it over the kettle with steeping water and discard.
4. Increase heat and bring grain tea to a boil. Remove from heat, add wheat malt extract only and stir until dissolved.
5. Return kettle to burner and increase the heat until wort begins to boil. Clear any foam to one side. Reduce heat until a rolling boil can be maintained without foam buildup.
6. Add the bittering hops, stirring to combine. Boil for 45 minutes, uncovered. Monitor to prevent boiling over.
7. Meanwhile, prepare the fermentation and cooling equipment.

8. After 45 minutes, remove the kettle from the heat and add the pale malt extract, Irish moss and yeast nutrient. Stir to ensure that the extract and nutrient have dissolved. Return the kettle to the burner and bring back to a rolling boil. Boil for 15 minutes; turn off the heat and cover.

9. To cool the brew, place the covered kettle in the prepared cooling bath or use a wort chiller according to the manufacturer's directions. Cool to the desired temperature, 75°F (24°C), within 30 to 45 minutes.

10. While the wort is cooling, clean and sanitize the brewing spoon. When the wort has cooled, move the kettle to a counter and stir the wort briskly in one direction for about 5 minutes. After stirring, cover and let rest for 10 to 15 minutes as the hops and trub form a cone.

11. Using a sanitized racking cane and siphon, rack as much wort as possible into the primary fermenter. Then, using a sanitized funnel and screen, strain the remainder of the wort into the fermenter. Top off with brewing water to bring the volume to around 5.5 US gal (21 L). Using the hydrometer, take a reading of the specific gravity and record it in your brewing journal.

12. Add the yeast; vigorously stir it with a sanitized spoon to distribute it throughout the wort. Seal the fermenter with lid, stopper and airlock. Keep the fermenter at room temperature (68 to 72°F/20 to 22°C) during primary fermentation, which typically lasts 3 to 5 days after fermentation begins. (Keep in a dark place or under a lightproof cover if using a glass carboy.)

13. After 7 to 10 days or when the kräusen has fallen, use a sanitized racking cane and siphon to gently rack the beer into the sanitized secondary fermenter. (If brewing a Lambic, see right sidebar on preparing fruit for brewing and left sidebar for the procedure for 3-stage fermentation.) Avoid aerating the brew, and leave as much of the sediment behind as possible. Seal and keep at room temperature, covered or in a dark place, to allow fermentation to continue.

14. Once the bubbling in the airlock has slowed, confirm completion of fermentation by using the hydrometer to take final gravity readings. (Hydrometer readings should be the same for several days in a row.)

15. Prime and bottle the beer (see page 263). Condition for a minimum of 3 months.

Preparing Fruit for Brewing

Shortly after brew day, wash and stem (if necessary) fresh fruit and freeze it in resealable bags.

Two days before racking the beer to secondary fermenter, sanitize a fermenter bucket. Transfer frozen fruit (prepared or purchased) to a large, sanitized straining bag (for easier racking and filtering) and thaw fruit in the bucket. Crush the fruit with a sanitized potato masher, if necessary. Dissolve 1 campden tablet for each US gal (3.75 L) of fruit in a small amount of boiling water and, using sanitized spoon, stir the mixture into the fruit in the straining bag. Seal the fermenter with the lid, stopper and an airlock containing a sterile cotton ball (not the usual water). Leave the fruit for at least 24 hours or until the sulphur smell goes away. This bucket will become your secondary fermenter.

If using purée, put the purée in a sanitized straining bag and place it in the bottom of the sanitized secondary fermenter before racking the beer.

The classic sour wheat ale of Berlin is different than the Bavarian Weizens brewed in the south. While this is often served with a dash of raspberry or woodruff syrup, it is tart and refreshing when served plain.

Estimated Original Gravity: 1.057

Equipment

- **brew kettle**
- **sanitized fermentation gear**

Brewer's Tip

Wyeast 3191 is only seasonally available. If it is not available when you want to brew, use a neutral ale yeast such as Wyeast 1007 in the primary fermenter and Wyeast 5335 in the secondary fermenter.

Berliner Weisse

Liquid Yeast

1 pack	Wyeast 3191 or any neutral German or European ale yeast	1 pack

Grains

1 lb	Pilsner malt	450 g
1 lb	wheat malt	450 g
1 lb	acidulated (sauer) malt	450 g
5.5 US gal	brewing water	21 L

Malt Extracts

1.4 lbs	Alexander's Sun Country Pale	635 g
4 lbs	Alexander's Sun Country Wheat (late addition)	1.8 kg

Bittering Hops

2 to 3 AAUs	Hallertau, Tettnang or Spaltz	2 to 3 AAUs

Later Additions

1 tsp	Irish moss	5 mL
1 tsp	yeast nutrient	5 mL

Aroma Hops

None

1. Prepare the liquid yeast in advance, according to the package directions.
2. Coarsely crack the grains and place them in a cheesecloth or nylon grain bag.
3. In a brew kettle, bring at least 3 US gal (11 L) brewing water to steeping temperature (150 to 160°F/65 to 71°C). Turn off the heat, add the grain bag, cover and steep for 60 minutes. (If the temperature drops below steeping temperature, reheat briefly to bring it back up.) Remove grain bag. Place it in a strainer, rinse it over the kettle with steeping water and then discard it.
4. Increase the heat and bring grain tea to a boil. Remove from heat, add the pale malt extract only and stir until dissolved completely.
5. Return kettle to the burner and increase the heat until the wort begins to boil. Using a spoon, clear any foam to one side. Reduce heat until a rolling boil can be maintained without foam buildup.
6. Add the bittering hops, stirring to combine. Boil for 45 minutes, uncovered. Monitor to prevent boiling over.
7. Meanwhile, prepare the fermentation gear and cooling bath or wort chiller.

8. After 45 minutes, remove the kettle from the heat and add wheat malt extract, Irish moss and yeast nutrient. Stir to ensure that the extract and nutrient have dissolved. Return the kettle to the burner and bring back to a rolling boil. Boil for 15 minutes; turn off the heat and cover.

9. To cool the brew, place the covered kettle in the prepared cooling bath or use a wort chiller according to the manufacturer's directions. Cool to the desired temperature, 75°F (24°C), within 30 to 45 minutes.

10. While the wort is cooling, clean and sanitize the brewing spoon. When the wort has cooled, move the kettle to a counter and stir the wort briskly in one direction for about 5 minutes. After stirring, cover and let rest for 10 to 15 minutes as the hops and trub form a cone.

11. Using a sanitized racking cane and siphon, rack as much wort as possible into the sanitized primary fermenter. Then, using a sanitized funnel and screen, strain the remainder of the wort into the fermenter. Top off with brewing water to bring the volume to around 5.5 US gal (21 L). Using the hydrometer, take a reading of the specific gravity and record it in your brewing journal.

12. Add the yeast; vigorously stir it with a sanitized spoon to distribute it throughout the wort. Seal the fermenter with lid, stopper and airlock. Keep the fermenter at room temperature (68 to 72°F/20 to 22°C) during primary fermentation, which typically lasts 1 to 4 days after fermentation begins. (Keep in a dark place or under a lightproof cover if using a glass carboy.)

13. After 1 to 4 days or when the kräusen has fallen, use a sanitized racking cane and siphon to gently rack the beer into the sanitized secondary fermenter. Avoid aerating it, and leave as much of the sediment behind as possible. Seal and keep at room temperature, covered or in a dark place, to allow fermentation to continue.

14. Once the bubbling in the airlock has slowed, confirm completion of fermentation by using the hydrometer to take final gravity readings. (Hydrometer readings should be the same for several days in a row.)

15. Prime and bottle the beer (see page 263). Condition for a minimum of 3 months.

Variation

Gosser: This is a revived German beer style that's certainly not for everyone. Brew the Berliner Weisse recipe and add these two items during the final 15 minutes of the boil: .5 oz (14 g) coriander seed (crushed) and .5 oz (14 g) of kosher or other non-iodized salt.

The sour ales of Flanders are some of the most unusual and food-friendly beers found anywhere in the world. This recipe is for the classic example, Rodenbach (Flemish Red), brewed in the town of Roselare.

Estimated Original Gravity: 1.056

Equipment

- **brew kettle**
- **sanitized fermentation gear**

Brewer's Tips

If the specified brands of grains are not available, use the grains chart on page 77 to find substitutes.

Before brewing, place the oak chips in a hop bag, tie the bag and soak the chips for a few days in vodka to sanitize them. The chips will be added to the primary fermenter.

Flemish Red

Liquid Yeast

1 pack	Wyeast 3763 or White Labs WLP655	1 pack

Grains

1 lb	Caramunich III® malt	450 g
8 oz	Caraboheme® malt	224 g
4 oz	Caraaroma® malt	112 g
5.5 US gal	brewing water	21 L

Malt Extracts

3.3 lbs	UK light	1.5 kg
3.3 lbs	UK wheat	1.5 kg

Bittering Hops

4 to 6 AAUs	Styrian Golding	4 to 6 AAUs

Later Additions

1 tsp	Irish moss	5 mL
1 tsp	yeast nutrient	5 mL

Aroma Hops

.5 oz	Saaz hops	14 g
2 oz	light toast oak chips, soaked in vodka (see Brewer's Tip)	56 g

1. Prepare the liquid yeast in advance, according to the package directions.
2. Coarsely crack the grains and place them in a cheesecloth or nylon grain bag.
3. In a brew kettle, bring at least 3 US gal (11 L) brewing water to steeping temperature (150 to 160°F/65 to 71°C). Turn off the heat, add the grain bag, cover and steep for 30 minutes. (If the temperature drops below steeping temperature, reheat briefly to bring it back up.) Remove grain bag. Place it in a strainer, rinse it over the kettle with steeping water and then discard it.
4. Increase the heat and bring grain tea to a boil. Remove from heat, add both malt extracts and stir until dissolved completely.
5. Return kettle to the burner and increase the heat until the wort begins to boil. Using a spoon, clear any foam to one side. Reduce heat until a rolling boil can be maintained without foam buildup.
6. Add the bittering hops, stirring to combine. Boil for 45 minutes, uncovered. Monitor to prevent boiling over.

7. Meanwhile, prepare the fermentation gear and cooling bath or wort chiller.

8. After 45 minutes, remove the kettle from the heat and add the Irish moss and yeast nutrient. Stir to ensure that the nutrient has dissolved. Return the kettle to the burner and bring back to a rolling boil. Boil for 15 minutes; stir in the aroma hops, turn off the heat and cover.

9. To cool the brew, place the covered kettle in the prepared cooling bath or use a wort chiller according to the manufacturer's directions. Cool to the desired temperature, 75°F (24°C), within 30 to 45 minutes.

10. While the wort is cooling, clean and sanitize the brewing spoon. When the wort has cooled, move the kettle to a counter and stir the wort briskly in one direction for about 5 minutes. After stirring, cover and let rest for 10 to 15 minutes as the hops and trub form a cone.

11. Remove hop bag containing oak chips from vodka and add to sanitized primary fermenter. Using sanitized racking cane and siphon, rack as much wort as possible into the primary fermenter. Then, using a sanitized funnel and straining screen, strain the remainder of the wort into the fermenter. Top off with brewing water to bring the volume to around 5.5 US gal (21 L). Using the hydrometer, take a reading of the specific gravity and record it in your brewing journal.

12. Add the yeast; vigorously stir it with a sanitized spoon to distribute it throughout the wort. Seal the fermenter with lid, stopper and airlock. Keep the fermenter at room temperature (68 to 72°F/20 to 22°C) during primary fermentation, which typically lasts 1 to 4 days after fermentation begins. (Keep in a dark place or under a lightproof cover if using a glass carboy.)

13. After 1 to 4 days or when the kräusen has fallen, use a sanitized racking cane and siphon to gently rack the beer into the sanitized secondary fermenter. Avoid aerating it, and leave as much of the sediment behind as possible. Seal and keep at room temperature, covered or in a dark place, to allow fermentation to continue.

14. Once the bubbling in the airlock has slowed, confirm completion of fermentation by using the hydrometer to take final gravity readings. (Hydrometer readings should be the same for several days in a row.)

15. Prime and bottle the beer (see page 263). Condition for a minimum of 3 months.

Variation

Flemish Brown: To brew a Flemish Brown, add 4 oz (112 g) dehusked Carafa I® malt to the grain bill for the Flemish Red.

Trappist-Style Ale with Brettanomyces

The brews from the Orval Trappist monastery stand out from the other monastery offerings because their brews feature a distinctive note from a sour fermentation. The beer is moderate in color and alcohol.

Estimated Original Gravity: 1.085

Equipment

- brew kettle
- sanitized fermentation gear

Yeast

1 pack	Wyeast 3522 or White Labs WLP550 or Fermentis T-58	1 pack
1 pack	Wyeast 5151 or White Labs WLP645 (secondary yeast)	1 pack

Grains

1 lb	Vienna malt	450 g
1 lb	aromatic malt	450 g
1 lb	Caravienne® malt	450 g
5.5 US gal	brewing water	21 L

Malt Extract

8 lbs	Alexander's Sun Country Pale, divided in half	3.6 kg

Bittering Hops

6 to 8 AAUs	AAU Perle or Styrian Golding	6 to 8 AAUs

Later Additions

1 lb	Belgian clear candi sugar	450 g
1 tsp	Irish moss	5 mL
1 tsp	yeast nutrient	5 mL

Aroma and Dry Hops

1 oz	Styrian Golding	28 g
.5 oz	Saaz hops (dry hop)	14 g

1. Prepare first liquid yeast in advance, according to directions.
2. Coarsely crack the grains and place in a grain bag.
3. In brew kettle, bring at least 3 US gal (11 L) brewing water to steeping temperature (150 to 160°F/65 to 71°C). Turn off heat, add grain bag, cover and steep for 30 minutes. (If temperature drops below steeping temperature, reheat briefly.) Remove grain bag. Place in a strainer, rinse over the kettle with steeping water and discard.
4. Bring grain tea to a boil. Remove from heat, add half the malt extract (4 lbs/1.8 kg) and stir until dissolved.
5. Return kettle to burner and increase heat until wort begins to boil. Clear any foam to one side. Reduce heat until a rolling boil can be maintained without foam buildup.
6. Add the bittering hops, stirring to combine. Boil for 45 minutes, uncovered. Monitor to prevent boiling over.
7. Meanwhile, prepare the fermentation gear and cooling bath or wort chiller.

8. After 45 minutes, remove kettle from heat and add remaining malt extract (4 lbs/1.8 kg), candi sugar, Irish moss and yeast nutrient. Stir to ensure that extract, sugar and nutrient have dissolved. Return kettle to burner and bring back to a rolling boil. Boil for 15 minutes; stir in the aroma hops (Styrian Golding), turn off heat and cover.

9. To cool the brew, place the covered kettle in the prepared cooling bath or use a wort chiller according to the manufacturer's directions. Cool to the desired temperature, 75°F (24°C), within 30 to 45 minutes.

10. While the wort is cooling, clean and sanitize the brewing spoon. When the wort has cooled, move the kettle to a counter and stir the wort briskly in one direction for about 5 minutes. After stirring, cover and let rest for 10 to 15 minutes as the hops and trub form a cone.

11. Using sanitized racking cane and siphon, rack as much wort as possible into the sanitized primary fermenter. Then, using a sanitized funnel and screen, strain the remainder of the wort into the fermenter. Top off with brewing water to bring the volume to around 5.5 US gal (21 L). Using the hydrometer, take a reading of the specific gravity and record it in your brewing journal.

12. Add the yeast; vigorously stir it with a sanitized spoon to distribute it throughout the wort. Seal the fermenter with lid, stopper and airlock. Keep the fermenter at room temperature (68 to 72°F/20 to 22°C) during primary fermentation, which typically lasts 7 to 10 days after fermentation begins. (Keep in a dark place or under a lightproof cover if using a glass carboy.)

13. After 7 to 10 days or when the kräusen has fallen, use a sanitized racking cane and siphon to gently rack the beer into the sanitized secondary fermenter. Avoid aerating it, and leave as much of the sediment behind as possible. Seal and keep at room temperature, covered or in a dark place, to allow fermentation to continue.

14. Once bubbling in airlock has slowed, sanitize remaining yeast pack and pour yeast into the beer; add dry hops (.5 oz/14 g Saaz), reseal and leave brew for 2 to 4 more weeks. Confirm completion of fermentation by using hydrometer to take final gravity readings. (Hydrometer readings should be the same for several days in a row.)

15. Prime and bottle the beer (see page 263). Condition for a minimum of 3 months.

A modern blending of styles has craft brewers mixing the IPA style with funk cultures. Since original IPAs most likely picked up some funk from aging in oak barrels, once again what's old is new again.

Estimated Original Gravity: 1.084

Equipment

- **brew kettle**
- **sanitized fermentation gear**

IPA with Brettanomyces

Yeast

1 pack	Wyeast 1275 or White Labs WLP051 or Fermentis US-05	1 pack
1 pack	Wyeast 5112 or White Labs WLP650 (secondary yeast)	1 pack

Grains

1 lb	Vienna malt	450 g
1 lb	dark Munich malt	450 g
1 lb	Carahell® malt	450 g
5.5 US gal	brewing water	21 L

Malt Extract

8 lbs	any brand light, divided in half	3.6 kg

Bittering Hops

10 to 12 AAUs	Centennial, Chinook or Columbus	10 to 12 AAUs

Later Additions

1 lb	turbinado or other light raw sugar	450 g
1 tsp	Irish moss	5 mL
1 tsp	yeast nutrient	5 mL

Aroma and Dry Hops

4 oz	Ahtanum, Cascade or Willamette, divided in half	112 g

1. Prepare first liquid yeast in advance, according to directions.
2. Coarsely crack grains and place in a grain bag.
3. In a brew kettle, bring at least 3 US gal (11 L) brewing water to steeping temperature (150 to 160°F/65 to 71°C). Turn off heat, add grain bag, cover and steep for 30 minutes. (If temperature drops below steeping temperature, reheat briefly.) Remove grain bag. Place it in a strainer, rinse it over kettle with steeping water and discard.
4. Increase heat and bring grain tea to a boil. Remove from heat, add half the malt extract (4 lbs/1.8 kg) and stir until dissolved.
5. Return kettle to burner and increase heat until wort begins to boil. Clear any foam to one side. Reduce heat until a rolling boil can be maintained without foam buildup.
6. Add the bittering hops, stirring to combine. Boil for 45 minutes, uncovered. Monitor to prevent boiling over.

7. Prepare fermentation and cooling equipment.

8. After 45 minutes, remove kettle from heat and add remaining malt extract (4 lbs/1.8 kg), turbinado sugar, Irish moss and yeast nutrient. Stir to ensure extract, sugar and nutrient have dissolved. Return kettle to burner and bring back to a rolling boil. Boil for 15 minutes; stir in half the aroma hops (2 oz/56 g), turn off heat and cover.

9. To cool the brew, place the covered kettle in the prepared cooling bath or use a wort chiller according to the manufacturer's directions. Cool to the desired temperature, 75°F (24°C), within 30 to 45 minutes.

10. While the wort is cooling, clean and sanitize the brewing spoon. When the wort has cooled, move the kettle to a counter and stir the wort briskly in one direction for about 5 minutes. After stirring, cover and let rest for 10 to 15 minutes as the hops and trub form a cone.

11. Using sanitized racking cane and siphon, rack as much wort as possible into the sanitized primary fermenter. Then, using a sanitized funnel and screen, strain the remainder of the wort into the fermenter. Top off with brewing water to bring the volume to around 5.5 US gal (21 L). Using the hydrometer, take a reading of the specific gravity and record it in your brewing journal.

12. Add the yeast; vigorously stir it with a sanitized spoon to distribute it throughout the wort. Seal the fermenter with lid, stopper and airlock. Keep the fermenter at room temperature (68 to 72°F/20 to 22°C) during primary fermentation, which typically lasts 7 to 10 days after fermentation begins. (Keep in a dark place or under a lightproof cover if using a glass carboy.)

13. After 7 to 10 days or when kräusen has fallen, use sanitized racking cane and siphon to gently rack beer into secondary fermenter. Avoid aerating, and leave sediment behind. Seal and keep at room temperature, covered or in a dark place, to allow fermentation to continue.

14. Once bubbling in airlock has slowed, sanitize remaining yeast pack and pour yeast into beer. Add remaining dry hops (2 oz/56 g), reseal carboy and leave brew for 2 to 4 more weeks. Confirm completion of fermentation by using hydrometer to take final gravity readings. (Hydrometer readings should be the same for several days in a row.)

15. Prime and bottle the beer (see page 263). Condition for a minimum of 3 months.

Old Ale with Lactobacillus

Equipment

- brew kettle
- sanitized fermentation gear

Brewer's Tip

Before brewing, place the oak chips in a hop bag, tie the bag and soak the chips for a few days in vodka to sanitize them.

Yeast

1 pack	Wyeast 1098 or White Labs WLP005 or Fermentis S-04 or Danstar Nottingham ale	1 pack
1 pack	Wyeast 5335 or White Labs WLP677 (secondary yeast)	1 pack

Grains

8 oz	UK brown malt	224 g
8 oz	UK dark crystal malt	224 g
4 oz	UK chocolate malt	112 g
5.5 US gal	brewing water	21 L

Malt Extract

8 lbs	any UK brand light	3.6 kg

Bittering Hops

6 to 7 AAUs	UK hops (such as Bramling Cross, East Kent Golding, Fuggle or other)	6 to 7 AAUs

Later Additions

2 lbs	amber, Barbados or baking molasses	900 g
1 tsp	Irish moss	5 mL
1 tsp	yeast nutrient	5 mL

Aroma Hops

.5 oz	UK hops (such as Bramling Cross, Fuggle or East Kent Golding)	14 g
2 oz	light toast oak chips, soaked in vodka (see Brewer's Tip)	56 g

1. Prepare first liquid yeast in advance, according to directions.
2. Coarsely crack grains and place them in a grain bag.
3. In brew kettle, bring at least 3 US gal (11 L) brewing water to steeping temperature (150 to 160°F/65 to 71°C). Turn off heat, add grain bag, cover and steep for 30 minutes. (If temperature drops below steeping temperature, turn element back on briefly.) Remove grain bag. Place in a strainer, rinse over kettle with steeping water and discard.
4. Increase heat and bring grain tea to a boil. Remove from heat, add malt extract and stir until dissolved.
5. Return kettle to burner and increase heat until wort begins to boil. Clear any foam to one side. Reduce heat until a rolling boil can be maintained without foam buildup.

6. Add the bittering hops, stirring to combine. Boil for 45 minutes, uncovered. Monitor to prevent boiling over.

7. Prepare fermentation and cooling equipment.

8. After 45 minutes, remove kettle from heat and add molasses, Irish moss and yeast nutrient. Stir to ensure that molasses and nutrient have dissolved. Return kettle to burner and bring back to a rolling boil. Boil for 15 minutes; stir in aroma hops, turn off heat and cover.

9. Use cooling bath or wort chiller to cool wort to the desired temperature, 75°F (24°C), within 30 to 45 minutes.

10. While the wort is cooling, clean and sanitize the brewing spoon. When the wort has cooled, move the kettle to a counter and stir the wort briskly in one direction for about 5 minutes. After stirring, cover and let rest for 10 to 15 minutes as the hops and trub form a cone.

11. Using sanitized racking cane and siphon, rack as much wort as possible into the sanitized primary fermenter. Then, using a sanitized funnel and screen, strain the remainder of the wort into the fermenter. Top off with brewing water to bring the volume to around 5.5 US gal (21 L). Using the hydrometer, take a reading of the specific gravity and record it in your brewing journal.

12. Add the yeast; vigorously stir it with a sanitized spoon to distribute it throughout the wort. Seal the fermenter with lid, stopper and airlock. Keep the fermenter at room temperature (68 to 72°F/20 to 22°C) during primary fermentation, which typically lasts 7 to 10 days after fermentation begins. (Keep in a dark place or under a lightproof cover if using a glass carboy.)

13. When kräusen has fallen, use a sanitized racking cane and siphon to gently rack the beer into the sanitized secondary fermenter. Avoid aerating it, and leave as much of the sediment behind as possible. Seal and keep at room temperature, covered or in a dark place.

14. Once bubbling in airlock has slowed, sanitize remaining yeast pack and pour yeast into beer; add sanitized oak chips, reseal carboy and leave it for 1 week. Rack to sanitized tertiary fermenter. Discard oak. Leave for 2 to 3 weeks. Confirm completion of fermentation by checking final gravity readings.

15. Prime and bottle the beer (see page 263). Condition for a minimum of 3 months.

Historic Porter

Original porters had a lactic character from wood barrel aging. You can recreate this taste by adding lactic culture and oak chips to the secondary fermenter.

Estimated Original Gravity: 1.061

Equipment

- **brew kettle**
- **sanitized fermentation gear**

Brewer's Tip

Before brewing, place the oak chips in a hop bag, tie the bag and soak the chips for a few days in vodka to sanitize them.

Yeast

1 pack	Wyeast 1028 or White Labs WLP013 or Fermentis S-04	1 pack
1 pack each	Wyeast 5335 or White Labs WLP677 AND Wyeast 5112 or White Labs WLP67 (secondary yeasts)	1 pack each

Grains

1 lb	UK crystal malt (60 Lovibond)	450 g
1 lb	UK brown malt	450 g
4 oz	UK dark crystal malt (150 Lovibond)	114 g
4 oz	UK chocolate malt	114 g
2 oz	UK black patent malt	56 g
5.5 US gal	brewing water	21 L

Malt Extract

6.6 lbs	any UK brand light	3 kg

Bittering Hops

8 to 10 AAUs	medium-alpha acid (such as Northern Brewer)	8 to 10 AAUs

Later Additions

1 tsp	Irish moss	5 mL
1 tsp	yeast nutrient	5 mL

Aroma Hops

.5 oz	Fuggle or Kent Golding	14 g
2 oz	light toast oak chips, soaked in vodka (see Brewer's Tip)	56 g

1. Prepare first liquid yeast in advance, according to directions.
2. Coarsely crack grains and place in a grain bag.
3. In a brew kettle, bring at least 3 US gal (11 L) brewing water to steeping temperature (150 to 160°F/65 to 71°C). Turn off the heat, add the grain bag, cover and steep for 30 minutes. (If the temperature drops below steeping temperature, reheat briefly to bring it back up.) Remove grain bag. Place it in a strainer, rinse it over the kettle with steeping water and then discard it.
4. Increase heat and bring grain tea to a boil. Remove from heat, add malt extract and stir until dissolved.
5. Return kettle to burner and increase heat until wort begins to boil. Clear any foam to one side. Reduce heat until a rolling boil can be maintained without foam buildup.

6. Add the bittering hops, stirring to combine. Boil for 45 minutes, uncovered. Monitor to prevent boiling over.

7. Meanwhile, prepare the fermentation gear and cooling bath or wort chiller.

8. After 45 minutes, remove the kettle from the heat and add Irish moss and yeast nutrient. Stir to ensure that the nutrient has dissolved. Return the kettle to the burner and bring back to a rolling boil. Boil for 15 minutes; stir in the aroma hops, turn off the heat and cover.

9. To cool the brew, place the covered kettle in the prepared cooling bath or use a wort chiller according to the manufacturer's directions. Cool to the desired temperature, 75°F (24°C), within 30 to 45 minutes.

10. While the wort is cooling, clean and sanitize the brewing spoon. When the wort has cooled, move the kettle to a counter and stir the wort briskly in one direction for about 5 minutes. After stirring, cover and let rest for 10 to 15 minutes as the hops and trub form a cone.

11. Using sanitized racking cane and siphon, rack as much wort as possible into the sanitized primary fermenter. Then, using a sanitized funnel and screen, strain the remainder of the wort into the fermenter. Top off with brewing water to bring the volume to around 5.5 US gal (21 L). Using the hydrometer, take a reading of the specific gravity and record it in your brewing journal.

12. Add the yeast; vigorously stir it with a sanitized spoon to distribute it throughout the wort. Seal the fermenter with lid, stopper and airlock. Keep the fermenter at room temperature (68 to 72°F/20 to 22°C) during primary fermentation, which typically lasts 1 to 4 days after fermentation begins. (Keep in a dark place or under a lightproof cover if using a glass carboy.)

13. After 1 to 4 days or when the kräusen has fallen, use a sanitized racking cane and siphon to gently rack the beer into the sanitized secondary fermenter. Avoid aerating it, and leave as much of the sediment behind as possible. Seal and keep at room temperature, covered or in a dark place, to allow fermentation to continue.

14. Once the bubbling in the airlock has slowed, sanitize two remaining yeast packs and pour yeasts into beer; add sanitized oak chips, reseal carboy and leave the brew for 1 week. Rack to sanitized tertiary fermenter. Discard oak. Leave for 2 to 3 weeks. Confirm completion of fermentation by using the hydrometer to take final gravity readings.

15. Prime and bottle the beer (see page 263). Condition for a minimum of 3 months.

Those with celiac disease cannot drink beverages made from barley. The recipes in this section will supply them with delightful alternative beverages. Since there are no grains in these recipes, the brewing instructions are almost the same as the ones followed in the recipes for Absolute Beginners. The yeasts specified are gluten-free dry yeasts. Check the availability of gluten-free liquid yeast cultures with your supplier.

Beyond the gluten-free recipes here, recipes in the following sections are devoted to mead and cider, which are all free of gluten (with two exceptions: Braggot and Bertha).

Gluten-Free Beers

**Estimated Original
Gravity: 1.047**

Equipment

- brew kettle
- sanitized
  fermentation gear

Gluten-Free Pale Ale (APA)

5.5 US gal	brewing water	21 L
6.6 lbs	white sorghum syrup	3 kg

Bittering Hops

30 AAUs	Chinook, Columbus or Warrior	30 AAUs

Later Additions

1 tsp	Irish moss	5 mL
1 tsp	yeast nutrient	5 mL

Aroma and Dry Hops

2 oz	Cascade or Willamette, divided $\frac{3}{4}$:$\frac{1}{4}$	56 g

Yeast

1 pack	Fermentis S-05	1 pack

1. In a brew kettle, bring at least 3 US gal (11 L) brewing water to a boil. Remove from the heat, add the sorghum syrup and stir until dissolved completely. Do not allow the syrup to settle and scorch.

2. Return kettle to the burner and increase the heat until the wort begins to boil. Using a spoon, clear any foam to one side. Reduce the heat until a rolling boil can be maintained without foam buildup.

3. Add the bittering hops, stirring to combine. Boil for 45 minutes, uncovered. Monitor to prevent boiling over.

4. Meanwhile, prepare the fermentation gear and cooling bath or wort chiller.

5. After 45 minutes, remove the kettle from the heat and add Irish moss and yeast nutrient. Stir to ensure that the nutrient has dissolved. Return the kettle to the burner and bring wort back to a rolling boil. Boil for 15 minutes, uncovered; stir in 1.5 oz (42 g) of the aroma hops, turn off the heat and cover.

6. To cool the brew, place the covered kettle in the prepared cooling bath or use a wort chiller according to the manufacturer's directions. Cool to yeast-pitching temperature, 75°F (24°C), within 30 to 45 minutes (see page 263).

7. While the wort is cooling, clean and sanitize the brewing spoon. When the wort has cooled, move the kettle to a counter and stir wort briskly in one direction for about 5 minutes. After stirring, cover and let rest for 10 to 15 minutes; the hops and trub should form a cone in the bottom of the kettle.

8. Using a sanitized racking cane and siphon, rack as much wort as possible into the sanitized primary fermenter. Then, using a sanitized funnel and straining screen, strain the remainder of the wort into the fermenter. Top off with brewing water to bring the volume to around 5.5 US gal (21 L). Using the hydrometer, take a reading of the specific gravity and record it in your brewing journal.

9. Sprinkle the yeast over the surface; vigorously stir it with a sanitized spoon until evenly distributed. Seal the fermenter with lid, stopper and airlock. Keep the fermenter at room temperature (68 to 72°F/20 to 22°C) during primary fermentation, which typically lasts 1 to 4 days after fermentation begins. (If using a glass carboy, keep in a dark place or under a lightproof cover.)

10. After 1 to 4 days or when the kräusen has peaked and begun to fall, sanitize the equipment and gently rack the beer into the secondary fermenter to avoid aerating it, leaving most of the sediment behind. Seal and keep at room temperature, covered or in a dark place, to allow fermentation to continue.

11. Once the bubbling in the airlock has slowed, add the remaining .5 oz (14 g) of the aroma hops as a dry hop and leave the brew for about 2 more weeks. Confirm completion of fermentation by using the hydrometer to take final gravity readings. (Hydrometer readings should be the same for several days in a row.)

12. Prime, bottle and condition the beer (see page 263).

Estimated Original Gravity: 1.048

Equipment

- **brew kettle**
- **sanitized fermentation gear**

Gluten-Free British Pale Ale

5.5 US gal	brewing water	21 L
6.6 lbs	white sorghum syrup	3 kg

Bittering Hops

25 AAUs	Chinook, Columbus or Warrior	25 AAUs

Later Additions

1 tsp	Irish moss	5 mL
1 tsp	yeast nutrient	5 mL

Aroma and Dry Hops

2 oz	East Kent Golding or Fuggle, divided $\frac{3}{4}:\frac{1}{4}$	56 g

Yeast

1 pack	Fermentis S-04	1 pack

1. In a brew kettle, bring at least 3 US gal (11 L) brewing water to a boil. Remove from the heat, add the sorghum syrup and stir until dissolved completely. Do not allow the syrup to settle and scorch.

2. Return kettle to the burner and increase the heat until the wort begins to boil. Using a spoon, clear any foam to one side. Reduce the heat until a rolling boil can be maintained without foam buildup.

3. Add the bittering hops, stirring to combine. Boil for 45 minutes, uncovered. Monitor to prevent boiling over.

4. Meanwhile, prepare the fermentation gear and cooling bath or wort chiller.

5. After 45 minutes, remove the kettle from the heat and add Irish moss and yeast nutrient. Stir to ensure that the nutrient has dissolved. Return the kettle to the burner and bring wort back to a rolling boil. Boil for 15 minutes; stir in 1.5 oz (42 g) of the aroma hops, turn off the heat and cover.

6. To cool the brew, place the covered kettle in the prepared cooling bath or use a wort chiller according to the manufacturer's directions. Cool to yeast-pitching temperature, 75°F (24°C), within 30 to 45 minutes (see page 263).

7. While the wort is cooling, clean and sanitize the brewing spoon. When the wort has cooled, move the kettle to a counter and stir wort briskly in one direction for about 5 minutes. After stirring, cover and let rest for 10 to 15 minutes; the hops and trub should form a cone in the bottom of the kettle.

8. Using a sanitized racking cane and siphon, rack as much wort as possible into the sanitized primary fermenter. Then, using a sanitized funnel and straining screen, strain the remainder of the wort into the fermenter. Top off with brewing water to bring the volume to around 5.5 US gal (21 L). Using the hydrometer, take a reading of the specific gravity and record it in your brewing journal.

9. Sprinkle the yeast over the surface; vigorously stir it with a sanitized spoon until evenly distributed. Seal the fermenter with lid, stopper and airlock. Keep the fermenter at room temperature (68 to 72°F/20 to 22°C) during primary fermentation, which typically lasts 1 to 4 days after fermentation begins. (If using a glass carboy, keep in a dark place or under a lightproof cover.)

10. After 1 to 4 days or when the kräusen has peaked and begun to fall, sanitize the equipment and gently rack the beer into the secondary fermenter to avoid aerating it, leaving most of the sediment behind. Seal and keep at room temperature, covered or in a dark place, to allow fermentation to continue.

11. Once the bubbling in the airlock has slowed, add the remaining .5 oz (14 g) of the aroma hops as a dry hop and leave the brew for about 2 more weeks. Confirm completion of fermentation by using the hydrometer to take final gravity readings. (Hydrometer readings should be the same for several days in a row.)

12. Prime, bottle and condition the beer (see page 263).

Light Gluten-Free Ale

Estimated Original Gravity: 1.042

Equipment

- brew kettle
- sanitized fermentation gear

5.5 US gal	brewing water	21 L
3.3 lbs	white sorghum syrup	1.5 kg

Bittering Hops
14 AAUs	Chinook, Columbus or Warrior	14 AAUs

Later Additions
1 lb	rice syrup	450 g
1 lb	dextrose	450 g
1 tsp	Irish moss	5 mL
1 tsp	yeast nutrient	5 mL

Aroma Hops
1 oz	Liberty or Mt Hood	28 g

Yeast
1 pack	Fermentis S-05	1 pack

1. In a brew kettle, bring at least 3 US gal (11 L) brewing water to a boil. Remove from the heat, add the sorghum syrup and stir until dissolved completely. Do not allow the syrup to settle and scorch.

2. Return kettle to the burner and increase the heat until the wort begins to boil. Using a spoon, clear any foam to one side. Reduce the heat until a rolling boil can be maintained without foam buildup.

3. Add the bittering hops, stirring to combine. Boil for 45 minutes, uncovered. Monitor to prevent boiling over.

4. Meanwhile, prepare the fermentation gear and cooling bath or wort chiller.

5. After 45 minutes, remove the kettle from the heat and add syrup, dextrose, Irish moss and yeast nutrient. Stir to ensure that the kettle sugars and nutrient have dissolved. Return the kettle to the burner and bring wort back to a rolling boil. Boil for 15 minutes; stir in the aroma hops, turn off the heat and cover.

6. To cool the brew, place the covered kettle in the prepared cooling bath or use a wort chiller according to the manufacturer's directions. Cool to yeast-pitching temperature, 75°F (24°C), within 30 to 45 minutes (see page 263).

7. While the wort is cooling, clean and sanitize the brewing spoon. When the wort has cooled, move the kettle to a counter and stir wort briskly in one direction for about 5 minutes. After stirring, cover and let rest for 10 to 15 minutes; the hops and trub should form a cone in the bottom of the kettle.

8. Using a sanitized racking cane and siphon, rack as much wort as possible into the sanitized primary fermenter. Then, using a sanitized funnel and straining screen, strain the remainder of the wort into the fermenter. Top off with brewing water to bring the volume to around 5.5 US gal (21 L). Using the hydrometer, take a reading of the specific gravity and record it in your brewing journal.

9. Sprinkle the yeast over the surface; vigorously stir it with a sanitized spoon until evenly distributed. Seal the fermenter with lid, stopper and airlock. Keep the fermenter at room temperature (68 to 72°F/20 to 22°C) during primary fermentation, which typically lasts 1 to 4 days after fermentation begins. (If using a glass carboy, keep in a dark place or under a lightproof cover.)

10. After 1 to 4 days or when the kräusen has peaked and begun to fall, sanitize the equipment and gently rack the beer into the secondary fermenter to avoid aerating it, leaving most of the sediment behind. Seal and keep at room temperature, covered or in a dark place, to allow fermentation to continue.

11. Once the bubbling in the airlock has slowed, confirm completion of fermentation by using the hydrometer to take final gravity readings. (Hydrometer readings should be the same for several days in a row.)

12. Prime, bottle and condition the beer (see page 263).

Estimated Original Gravity:

Equipment

- brew kettle
- sanitized fermentation gear

Light Gluten-Free Lager

5.5 US gal	brewing water	21 L
3.3 lbs	white sorghum syrup	1.5 kg

Bittering Hops

14 AAUs	Chinook, Columbus or Warrior	14 AAUs

Later Additions

1 lb	rice syrup	450 g
1 lb	dextrose	450 g
1 tsp	Irish moss	5 mL
1 tsp	yeast nutrient	5 mL

Aroma Hops

1 oz	Liberty or Mt Hood	28 g

Yeast

1 pack	Fermentis S-23	1 pack

1. In a brew kettle, bring at least 3 US gal (11 L) brewing water to a boil. Remove from the heat, add the sorghum syrup and stir until dissolved completely. Do not allow the syrup to settle and scorch.

2. Return kettle to the burner and increase the heat until the wort begins to boil. Using a spoon, clear any foam to one side. Reduce the heat until a rolling boil can be maintained without foam buildup.

3. Add the bittering hops, stirring to combine. Boil for 45 minutes, uncovered. Monitor to prevent boiling over.

4. Meanwhile, prepare the fermentation gear and cooling bath or wort chiller.

5. After 45 minutes, remove the kettle from the heat and add syrup, dextrose, Irish moss and yeast nutrient. Stir to ensure that the kettle sugars and nutrient have dissolved. Return the kettle to the burner and bring wort back to a rolling boil. Boil for 15 minutes; stir in the aroma hops, turn off the heat and cover.

6. To cool the brew, place the covered kettle in the prepared cooling bath or use a wort chiller according to the manufacturer's directions. Cool to yeast-pitching temperature, 75°F (24°C), within 30 to 45 minutes (see page 263).

7. While the wort is cooling, clean and sanitize the brewing spoon. When the wort has cooled, move the kettle to a counter and stir wort briskly in one direction for about 5 minutes. After stirring, cover and let rest for 10 to 15 minutes; the hops and trub should form a cone in the bottom of the kettle.

8. Using a sanitized racking cane and siphon, rack as much wort as possible into the sanitized primary fermenter. Then, using a sanitized funnel and straining screen, strain the remainder of the wort into the fermenter. Top off with brewing water to bring the volume to around 5.5 US gal (21 L). Using the hydrometer, take a reading of the specific gravity and record it in your brewing journal.

9. Sprinkle the yeast over the surface; vigorously stir it with a sanitized spoon until evenly distributed. Seal the fermenter with lid, stopper and airlock. Keep the fermenter at room temperature (68 to 72°F/20 to 22°C) until fermentation begins—bubbles will be moving through the airlock. (Keep it in a dark place or under a lightproof cover if using a glass carboy.) Once fermentation begins, drop the temperature to 46 to 55°F (8 to 13°C) for one week of primary fermentation.

10. Using sanitized racking cane and siphon, gently rack the beer into the sanitized secondary fermenter to avoid aerating it, leaving as much of the sediment behind as possible. Seal and drop the temperature to 35 to 45°F (2 to 7°C); keep it at that temperature, covered or in a dark place, to allow fermentation to continue for 4 weeks.

11. Once the bubbling in the airlock has slowed, confirm completion of fermentation by using the hydrometer to take final gravity readings. (Hydrometer readings should be the same for several days in a row.)

12. Prime, bottle and condition the beer (see page 263).

Estimated Original Gravity: 1.061

Equipment

- brew kettle
- sanitized fermentation gear

Gluten-Free Winter Warmer

5.5 US gal	brewing water	21 L
6.6 lbs	white sorghum syrup	3 kg

Bittering Hops

25 AAUs	Chinook, Columbus or Warrior	25 AAUs

Later Additions

2 lbs	Barbados, amber or baking molasses	900 g
1 tsp	Irish moss	5 mL
1 tsp	yeast nutrient	5 mL

Aroma and Dry Hops

2 oz	East Kent Golding or Fuggle, divided $\frac{3}{4}:\frac{1}{4}$	56 g

Yeast

1 pack	Fermentis S-33	1 pack

1. In a brew kettle, bring at least 3 US gal (11 L) brewing water to a boil. Remove from the heat, add the sorghum syrup and stir until dissolved completely. Do not allow the syrup to settle and scorch.

2. Return kettle to the burner and increase the heat until the wort begins to boil. Using a spoon, clear any foam to one side. Reduce the heat until a rolling boil can be maintained without foam buildup.

3. Add the bittering hops, stirring to combine. Boil for 45 minutes, uncovered. Monitor to prevent boiling over.

4. Meanwhile, prepare the fermentation gear and cooling bath or wort chiller.

5. After 45 minutes, remove the kettle from the heat and add molasses, Irish moss and yeast nutrient. Stir to ensure that the molasses and nutrient have dissolved. Return the kettle to the burner and bring wort back to a rolling boil. Boil for 15 minutes; stir in 1.5 oz (42 g) of the aroma hops, turn off the heat and cover.

6. To cool the brew, place the covered kettle in the prepared cooling bath or use a wort chiller according to the manufacturer's directions. Cool to yeast-pitching temperature, 75°F (24°C), within 30 to 45 minutes (see page 263).

7. While the wort is cooling, clean and sanitize the brewing spoon. When the wort has cooled, move the kettle to a counter and stir wort briskly in one direction for about 5 minutes. After stirring, cover and let rest for 10 to 15 minutes; the hops and trub should form a cone in the bottom of the kettle.

8. Using a sanitized racking cane and siphon, rack as much wort as possible into the sanitized primary fermenter. Then, using a sanitized funnel and straining screen, strain the remainder of the wort into the fermenter. Top off with brewing water to bring the volume to around 5.5 US gal (21 L). Using the hydrometer, take a reading of the specific gravity and record it in your brewing journal.

9. Sprinkle the yeast over the surface; vigorously stir it with a sanitized spoon until evenly distributed. Seal the fermenter with lid, stopper and airlock. Keep the fermenter at room temperature (68 to 72°F/20 to 22°C) during primary fermentation, which typically lasts 5 to 7 days after fermentation begins. (If using a glass carboy, keep in a dark place or under a lightproof cover.)

10. After 5 to 7 days or when the kräusen has peaked and begun to fall, sanitize the equipment and gently rack the beer into the secondary fermenter to avoid aerating it, leaving most of the sediment behind. Seal and keep at room temperature, covered or in a dark place, to allow fermentation to continue.

11. Once the bubbling in the airlock has slowed, add the remaining .5 oz (14 g) of the aroma hops as a dry hop and leave the brew for about 2 more weeks. Confirm completion of fermentation by using the hydrometer to take final gravity readings. (Hydrometer readings should be the same for several days in a row.)

12. Prime, bottle and condition the beer (see page 263).

Variation

Spiced Winter Warmer: To brew a spiced version, place the following in a hop bag: 8 oz (224 g) dried apples, 4 oz (112 g) raisins, 3 cinnamon sticks, 1 oz (28 g) freshly grated ginger, 2 to 3 whole cloves (not crushed) and .25 tsp (1 mL) grated nutmeg. Add the bag in Step 5, with the other later additions.

Gluten-Free Porter

Equipment

- **brew kettle**
- **sanitized
  fermentation gear**

5.5 US gal	brewing water	21 L
6.6 lbs	white sorghum syrup	3 kg

Bittering Hops

25 AAUs	Chinook, Columbus or Warrior	25 AAUs

Later Additions

1 lb	blackstrap molasses	450 g
1 tsp	Irish moss	5 mL
1 tsp	yeast nutrient	5 mL

Aroma and Dry Hops

2 oz	East Kent Golding or Fuggle, divided $\frac{3}{4}$:$\frac{1}{4}$	56 g

Yeast

1 pack	Fermentis S-04	1 pack

1. In a brew kettle, bring at least 3 US gal (11 L) brewing water to a boil. Remove from the heat, add the sorghum syrup and stir until dissolved completely. Do not allow the syrup to settle and scorch.

2. Return kettle to the burner and increase the heat until the wort begins to boil. Using a spoon, clear any foam to one side. Reduce the heat until a rolling boil can be maintained without foam buildup.

3. Add the bittering hops, stirring to combine. Boil for 45 minutes, uncovered. Monitor to prevent boiling over.

4. Meanwhile, prepare the fermentation gear and cooling bath or wort chiller.

5. After 45 minutes, remove the kettle from the heat and add molasses, Irish moss and yeast nutrient. Stir to ensure that the molasses and nutrient have dissolved. Return the kettle to the burner and bring wort back to a rolling boil. Boil for 15 minutes; stir in 1.5 oz (42 g) of the aroma hops, turn off the heat and cover.

6. To cool the brew, place the covered kettle in the prepared cooling bath or use a wort chiller according to the manufacturer's directions. Cool to yeast-pitching temperature, 75°F (24°C), within 30 to 45 minutes (see page 263).

7. While the wort is cooling, clean and sanitize the brewing spoon. When the wort has cooled, move the kettle to a counter and stir wort briskly in one direction for about 5 minutes. After stirring, cover and let rest for 10 to 15 minutes; the hops and trub should form a cone in the bottom of the kettle.

8. Using a sanitized racking cane and siphon, rack as much wort as possible into the sanitized primary fermenter. Then, using a sanitized funnel and straining screen, strain the remainder of the wort into the fermenter. Top off with brewing water to bring the volume to around 5.5 US gal (21 L). Using the hydrometer, take a reading of the specific gravity and record it in your brewing journal.

9. Sprinkle the yeast over the surface; vigorously stir it with a sanitized spoon until evenly distributed. Seal the fermenter with lid, stopper and airlock. Keep the fermenter at room temperature (68 to 72°F/20 to 22°C) during primary fermentation, which typically lasts 1 to 4 days after fermentation begins. (If using a glass carboy, keep in a dark place or under a lightproof cover.)

10. After 1 to 4 days or when the kräusen has peaked and begun to fall, sanitize the equipment and gently rack the beer into the secondary fermenter to avoid aerating it, leaving most of the sediment behind. Seal and keep at room temperature, covered or in a dark place, to allow fermentation to continue.

11. Once the bubbling in the airlock has slowed, add the remaining .5 oz (14 g) of the aroma hops as a dry hop and leave the brew for about 2 more weeks. Confirm completion of fermentation by using the hydrometer to take final gravity readings. (Hydrometer readings should be the same for several days in a row.)

12. Prime, bottle and condition the beer (see page 263).

Abbey de Gluten-Free

5.5 US gal	brewing water	21 L
6.6 lbs	white sorghum syrup	3 kg

Bittering Hops

25 AAUs	Chinook, Columbus or Warrior	25 AAUs

Later Additions

2 lbs	Belgian amber or dark candi sugar	900 g
1 tsp	Irish moss	5 mL
1 tsp	yeast nutrient	5 mL

Aroma and Dry Hops

2 oz	East Kent Golding or Fuggle, divided $^3/_4$:$^1/_4$	56 g

Yeast

1 pack	Fermentis T-58	1 pack

Estimated Original Gravity: 1.065

Equipment

- brew kettle
- sanitized fermentation gear

1. In a brew kettle, bring at least 3 US gal (11 L) brewing water to a boil. Remove from the heat, add the sorghum syrup and stir until dissolved completely. Do not allow the syrup to settle and scorch.

2. Return kettle to the burner and increase the heat until the wort begins to boil. Using a spoon, clear any foam to one side. Reduce the heat until a rolling boil can be maintained without foam buildup.

3. Add the bittering hops, stirring to combine. Boil for 45 minutes, uncovered. Monitor to prevent boiling over.

4. Meanwhile, prepare the fermentation gear and cooling bath or wort chiller.

5. After 45 minutes, remove the kettle from the heat and add candi sugar, Irish moss and yeast nutrient. Stir to ensure that the sugar and nutrient have dissolved. Return the kettle to the burner and bring wort back to a rolling boil. Boil for 15 minutes; stir in 1.5 oz (42 g) of the aroma hops, turn off the heat and cover.

6. To cool the brew, place the covered kettle in the prepared cooling bath or use a wort chiller according to the manufacturer's directions. Cool to yeast-pitching temperature, 75°F (24°C), within 30 to 45 minutes (see page 263).

7. While the wort is cooling, clean and sanitize the brewing spoon. When the wort has cooled, move the kettle to a counter and stir wort briskly in one direction for about 5 minutes. After stirring, cover and let rest for 10 to 15 minutes; the hops and trub should form a cone in the bottom of the kettle.

8. Using a sanitized racking cane and siphon, rack as much wort as possible into the sanitized primary fermenter. Then, using a sanitized funnel and strainer, strain the remainder of the wort into the fermenter. Top off with brewing water to bring the volume to around 5.5 US gal (21 L). Using the hydrometer, take a reading of the specific gravity and record it in your brewing journal.

9. Sprinkle the yeast over the surface; vigorously stir it with a sanitized spoon until evenly distributed. Seal the fermenter with lid, stopper and airlock. Keep the fermenter at room temperature (68 to 72°F/20 to 22°C) during primary fermentation, which typically lasts 7 to 10 days after fermentation begins. (If using a glass carboy, keep in a dark place or under a lightproof cover.)

10. After 7 to 10 days or when the kräusen has peaked and begun to fall, sanitize the equipment and gently rack the beer into the secondary fermenter to avoid aerating it, leaving most of the sediment behind. Seal and keep at room temperature, covered or in a dark place, to allow fermentation to continue.

11. Once the bubbling in the airlock has slowed, add the remaining .5 oz (14 g) of the aroma hops as a dry hop and leave the brew for about 2 more weeks. Confirm completion of fermentation by using the hydrometer to take final gravity readings. (Hydrometer readings should be the same for several days in a row.)

12. Prime, bottle and condition the beer (see page 263).

Making mead is another fun home-fermentation project. Dating from ancient times, meads are fermented honey beverages, often with added spices or fruits. There are several types of mead—still or sparkling, sweet or dry. Sparkling mead is primed with dextrose prior to bottling to ensure carbonation; potassium sorbate is added to still meads before bottling.

If a mead has spice in it, it is called hippocras. If it contains fruit, it is called a melomel mead—unless the fruit is grape (pyment) or apple (cyser). The procedure for making meads is a simplified version of the basic brewing procedure. Except where indicated, these mead recipes are gluten-free.

Brewing Meads and Flavored Meads

Still Mead

Equipment

- **brew kettle**
- **sanitized
  fermentation gear**

Brewer's Tip

For information on
preparing a yeast starter,
see page 262.

Yeast

2	packs Wyeast 4632 or White Labs WLP715 (or 1 pack in starter) or Lalvin EC-1118	2 packs
5.5 US gal	brewing water	21 L
10 to 15 lbs	clover, orange-blossom or wildflower honey	4.5 to 6.8 kg
5 tsp	diammonium phosphate (DAP)	25 mL
2 tsp	yeast nutrient	10 mL
1 tsp	Irish moss	5 mL

For bottling

2 tsp	potassium sorbate	10 mL

1. Prepare the liquid yeast in advance, according to the package directions (if using).
2. In brew kettle, bring 1 US gal (3.75 L) of the brewing water to a boil. Remove from heat. Stir in honey, diammonium phosphate, yeast nutrient and Irish moss until honey, diammonium phosphate and nutrient have dissolved.
3. Return kettle to heat and bring mead mixture to a simmer. Simmer, uncovered, for 15 minutes. Monitor the liquid, using a spoon or strainer to remove and discard as much of the waxy meringue from the surface as possible.
4. Meanwhile, prepare the cooling bath or wort chiller.
5. At the end of 15 minutes, turn off the heat, cover kettle and transfer it into the prepared cooling bath (or use a wort chiller, according to the manufacturer's directions). Cool mead to the desired temperature, 75°F (24°C), within 30 to 45 minutes while you prepare the fermentation gear.
6. Clean and sanitize the spoon. Using sanitized racking cane and siphon, rack as much of the mead as possible into the sanitized primary fermenter. Then, using a sanitized funnel and straining screen, strain remaining mead into the fermenter. Add enough brewing water to bring volume to about 5.5 US gal (21 L). Using the hydrometer, take a reading of the specific gravity and record it in your brewing journal.

7. Add yeast to mead, stirring vigorously with sanitized spoon until evenly distributed. Seal fermenter with lid, stopper and airlock. Keep at room temperature (68 to 72°F/20 to 22°C) during primary fermentation, which typically lasts for 7 to 10 days after fermentation begins. (Keep fermenter in a dark place or under a lightproof cover if using a glass carboy.)

8. After 7 to 10 days or when the bubbling in airlock slows, gently rack the mead into secondary fermenter to avoid aerating it. Seal and keep at room temperature, covered or in a dark place, to allow fermentation to continue.

9. Once the bubbling in the airlock has slowed further, confirm completion of fermentation by using the hydrometer to take final gravity readings. (Hydrometer readings should be the same for several days in a row.)

10. Prime and bottle the mead using potassium sorbate (see page 263 for method) and condition for at least 3 months before sampling it.

To Hydrate Lalvin Yeast

In a sanitized bowl or measuring cup, dissolve Lalvin yeast in 1.5 US fl oz (50 mL) of boiled water cooled to 104 to 109°F (40 to 43°C). Let stand for 15 minutes without stirring; then stir with a sanitized spoon to distribute yeast in water.

Sparkling Quick Mead

This quick mead should take about as long as a normal-strength beer to ferment and condition.

Estimated Original Gravity: 1.049

Equipment

- **brew kettle**
- **sanitized fermentation gear**

Yeast

1 pack	Wyeast 1099 or White Labs WLP005 or Fermentis S-33	1 pack
5.5 US gal	brewing water	21 L
7 lbs	clover, orange-blossom or wildflower honey	3.2 kg
5 tsp	diammonium phosphate (DAP)	25 mL
2 tsp	yeast nutrient	10 mL
1 tsp	Irish moss	5 mL

For bottling

5 oz	dextrose (corn sugar)	140 g

1. Prepare the liquid yeast in advance, according to the package directions (if using).
2. In brew kettle, bring 1 US gal (3.75 L) of the brewing water to a boil. Remove from heat. Stir in honey, diammonium phosphate, yeast nutrient and Irish moss until honey, diammonium phosphate and nutrient have dissolved.
3. Return kettle to heat and bring mead mixture to a simmer. Simmer, uncovered, for 15 minutes. Monitor the liquid, using a spoon or strainer to remove and discard as much of the waxy meringue from the surface as possible.
4. Meanwhile, prepare the cooling bath or wort chiller.
5. At the end of 15 minutes, turn off the heat, cover kettle and transfer it into the prepared cooling bath (or use a wort chiller, according to the manufacturer's directions). Cool mead to the desired temperature, 75°F (24°C), within 30 to 45 minutes while you prepare the fermentation gear.
6. Clean and sanitize the spoon. Using sanitized racking cane and siphon, rack as much of the mead as possible into the sanitized primary fermenter. Then, using a sanitized funnel and straining screen, strain remaining mead into the fermenter. Add enough brewing water to bring volume to about 5.5 US gal (21 L). Using the hydrometer, take a reading of the specific gravity and record it in your brewing journal.
7. Add yeast to mead, stirring vigorously with sanitized spoon until evenly distributed. Seal fermenter with lid, stopper and airlock. Keep at room temperature (68 to 72°F/20 to 22°C) during primary fermentation, which typically lasts for 7 to 10 days after fermentation begins. (Keep fermenter in a dark place or under a lightproof cover if using a glass carboy.)

8. After 7 to 10 days or when the bubbling in airlock slows, gently rack the mead into secondary fermenter to avoid aerating it. Seal and keep at room temperature, covered or in a dark place, to allow fermentation to continue.

9. Once the bubbling in the airlock has slowed further, confirm completion of fermentation by using the hydrometer to take final gravity readings. (Hydrometer readings should be the same for several days in a row.)

10. Prime and bottle the mead using dextrose (see page 263 for method) and condition for 6 to 8 weeks before sampling it.

Sweet Mead

Equipment

- **brew kettle**
- **sanitized
  fermentation gear**

Brewer's Tip

For information on
preparing a yeast starter,
see page 262.

Yeast

2	packs Wyeast 4184 or White Labs WLP720 (or 1 pack in starter) or Lalvin D-47	2 packs
5.5 US gal	brewing water	21 L
16 to 20 lbs	clover, orange-blossom or wildflower honey	7.25 to 9 kg
5 tsp	diammonium phosphate (DAP)	25 mL
2 tsp	yeast nutrient	10 mL
1 tsp	Irish moss	5 mL

For bottling

2 tsp	potassium sorbate	10 mL

1. Prepare the liquid yeast in advance, according to the package directions (if using).
2. In brew kettle, bring 1 US gal (3.75 L) of the brewing water to a boil. Remove from heat. Stir in honey, diammonium phosphate, yeast nutrient and Irish moss until honey, diammonium phosphate and nutrient have dissolved.
3. Return kettle to heat and bring mead mixture to a simmer. Simmer, uncovered, for 15 minutes. Monitor the liquid, using a spoon or strainer to remove and discard as much of the waxy meringue from the surface as possible.
4. Meanwhile, prepare the cooling bath or wort chiller.
5. At the end of 15 minutes, turn off the heat, cover kettle and transfer it into the prepared cooling bath (or use a wort chiller, according to the manufacturer's directions). Cool mead to the desired temperature, 75°F (24°C), within 30 to 45 minutes while you prepare the fermentation gear.
6. Clean and sanitize the spoon. Using sanitized racking cane and siphon, rack as much of the mead as possible into the sanitized primary fermenter. Then, using a sanitized funnel and straining screen, strain remaining mead into the fermenter. Add enough brewing water to bring volume to about 5.5 US gal (21 L). Using the hydrometer, take a reading of the specific gravity and record it in your brewing journal.
7. Add yeast to mead, stirring vigorously with sanitized spoon until evenly distributed. Seal fermenter with lid, stopper and airlock. Keep at room temperature (68 to 72°F/20 to 22°C) during primary fermentation, which typically lasts for 7 to 10 days after fermentation begins. (Keep fermenter in a dark place or under a lightproof cover if using a glass carboy.)

8. After 7 to 10 days or when the bubbling in airlock slows, gently rack the mead into secondary fermenter to avoid aerating it. Seal and keep at room temperature, covered or in a dark place, to allow fermentation to continue.

9. Once the bubbling in the airlock has slowed further, confirm completion of fermentation by using the hydrometer to take final gravity readings. (Hydrometer readings should be the same for several days in a row.)

10. Prime and bottle the mead using potassium sorbate (see page 263 for method) and condition for at least 3 months before sampling it.

To Hydrate Lalvin Yeast

In a sanitized bowl or measuring cup, dissolve Lalvin yeast in 1.5 US fl oz (50 mL) of boiled water cooled to 104 to 109°F (40 to 43°C). Let stand for 15 minutes without stirring; then stir with a sanitized spoon to distribute yeast in water.

Dry Mead (Still)

Equipment

- **brew kettle**
- **sanitized
  fermentation gear**

Acid Blend

Winemakers' acid blend
is equal parts citric, malic
and tartaric acids. It is
added to compensate for
low acidity and sharpen
up the taste.

Brewer's Tip

For information on
preparing a yeast starter,
see page 262.

Yeast

2 packs	Wyeast 4632 or White Labs WLP715 (or 1 pack in starter) or Lalvin EC-1118	2 packs
5.5 US gal	brewing water	21 L
10 to 15 lbs	clover, orange-blossom or wildflower honey	4.5 to 6.8 kg
5 tsp	diammonium phosphate (DAP)	25 mL
2 tsp	yeast nutrient	10 mL
1 tsp	Irish moss	5 mL
5 tsp	acid blend	25 mL

For bottling

2 tsp	potassium sorbate	10 mL

1. Prepare the liquid yeast in advance, according to the package directions (if using).
2. In brew kettle, bring 1 US gal (3.75 L) of the brewing water to a boil. Remove from heat. Stir in honey, diammonium phosphate, yeast nutrient, Irish moss and acid blend until honey, diammonium phosphate and nutrient have dissolved.
3. Return kettle to heat and bring mead mixture to a simmer. Simmer, uncovered, for 15 minutes. Monitor the liquid, using a spoon or strainer to remove and discard as much of the waxy meringue from the surface as possible.
4. Meanwhile, prepare the cooling bath or wort chiller.
5. At the end of 15 minutes, turn off the heat, cover kettle and transfer it into the prepared cooling bath (or use a wort chiller, according to the manufacturer's directions). Cool mead to the desired temperature, 75°F (24°C), within 30 to 45 minutes. Prepare the fermentation gear.
6. Clean and sanitize the spoon. Using sanitized racking cane and siphon, rack as much of the mead as possible into the sanitized primary fermenter. Then, using a sanitized funnel and straining screen, strain remaining mead into the fermenter. Add enough brewing water to bring volume to about 5.5 US gal (21 L). Using the hydrometer, take a reading of the specific gravity and record it in your brewing journal.
7. Add yeast to mead, stirring vigorously with sanitized spoon until evenly distributed. Seal fermenter with lid, stopper and airlock. Keep at room temperature (68 to 72°F/20 to 22°C) during primary fermentation, which typically lasts for 7 to 10 days after fermentation begins. (Keep fermenter in a dark place or under a lightproof cover if using a glass carboy.)

8. After 7 to 10 days or when the bubbling in airlock slows, gently rack the mead into secondary fermenter to avoid aerating it. Seal and keep at room temperature, covered or in a dark place, to allow fermentation to continue.

9. Once the bubbling in the airlock has slowed further, confirm completion of fermentation by using the hydrometer to take final gravity readings. (Hydrometer readings should be the same for several days in a row.)

10. Prime and bottle the mead using potassium sorbate (see page 263 for method) and condition for at least 3 months before sampling it.

Variation

Standard Dry Mead (Sparkling): To produce a dry sparkling mead, follow the Dry Mead (still) recipe, above, but omit the potassium sorbate and prime with 5 oz (140 g) dextrose at bottling.

To Hydrate Lalvin Yeast

In a sanitized bowl or measuring cup, dissolve Lalvin yeast in 1.5 US fl oz (50 mL) of boiled water cooled to 104 to 109°F (40 to 43°C). Let stand for 15 minutes without stirring; then stir with a sanitized spoon to distribute yeast in water.

Sack Mead (Still)

Equipment

- **brew kettle**
- **sanitized
  fermentation gear**

Brewer's Tip

For information on
preparing a yeast starter,
see page 262.

Yeast

2 packs	Wyeast 4184 or White Labs WLP720 (or 1 pack in starter) or Lalvin D-47	2 packs
5.5 US gal	brewing water	21 L
20 to 22 lbs	clover, orange-blossom or wildflower honey	9 to 10 kg
5 tsp	diammonium phosphate (DAP)	25 mL
2 tsp	yeast nutrient	10 mL
1 tsp	Irish moss	5 mL

For bottling

2 tsp	potassium sorbate	10 mL

1. Prepare the liquid yeast in advance, according to the package directions (if using).
2. In brew kettle, bring 1 US gal (3.75 L) of the brewing water to a boil. Remove from heat. Stir in honey, diammonium phosphate, yeast nutrient and Irish moss until honey, diammonium phosphate and nutrient have dissolved.
3. Return kettle to heat and bring mead mixture to a simmer. Simmer, uncovered, for 15 minutes. Monitor the liquid, using a spoon or strainer to remove and discard as much of the waxy meringue from the surface as possible.
4. Meanwhile, prepare the cooling bath or wort chiller.
5. At the end of 15 minutes, turn off the heat, cover kettle and transfer it into the prepared cooling bath (or use a wort chiller, according to the manufacturer's directions). Cool mead to the desired temperature, 75°F (24°C), within 30 to 45 minutes while you prepare the fermentation gear.
6. Clean and sanitize the spoon. Using sanitized racking cane and siphon, rack as much of the mead as possible into the sanitized primary fermenter. Then, using a sanitized funnel and straining screen, strain remaining mead into the fermenter. Add enough brewing water to bring volume to about 5.5 US gal (21 L). Using the hydrometer, take a reading of the specific gravity and record it in your brewing journal.
7. Add yeast to mead, stirring vigorously with sanitized spoon until evenly distributed. Seal fermenter with lid, stopper and airlock. Keep at room temperature (68 to 72°F/20 to 22°C) during primary fermentation, which can last up to two weeks after fermentation begins. (Keep fermenter in a dark place or under a lightproof cover if using a glass carboy.)

8. When the bubbling in airlock slows, gently rack the mead into secondary fermenter to avoid aerating it. Seal and keep at room temperature, covered or in a dark place, to allow fermentation to continue.

9. Once the bubbling in the airlock has slowed further, confirm completion of fermentation by using the hydrometer to take final gravity readings. (Hydrometer readings should be the same for several days in a row.)

10. Prime and bottle the mead using potassium sorbate (see page 263 for method) and condition for at least 6 months before sampling it.

To Hydrate Lalvin Yeast

In a sanitized bowl or measuring cup, dissolve Lalvin yeast in 1.5 US fl oz (50 mL) of boiled water cooled to 104 to 109°F (40 to 43°C). Let stand for 15 minutes without stirring; then stir with a sanitized spoon to distribute yeast in water.

<table>
<tr><td>Makes 5 US gal (19 L)</td></tr>
</table>

Estimated Original Gravity: 1.070 to 1.105

Equipment

- **brew kettle**
- **sanitized fermentation gear**

Brewer's Tips

For easier brewing, place the peel and spices in a hop bag and add the bag to the kettle. If you prefer to add these ingredients directly to the liquid, you will need to be much more careful about straining the mead as it moves through fermentation.

For information on preparing a yeast starter, see page 262.

Orange-Blossom Special Mead (Sparkling)

Yeast

2 packs	Wyeast 4632 or White Labs WLP715 (or 1 pack in starter) or Lalvin D-47	2 packs
5.5 US gal	brewing water	21 L
10 to 15 lbs	orange-blossom honey	4.5 to 6.8 kg
5 tsp	diammonium phosphate (DAP)	25 mL
2 tsp	yeast nutrient	10 mL
1 tsp	Irish moss	5 mL
2 oz	sweet orange peel	56 g
1 oz	coriander seed, crushed	28 g
1 oz	dried orange blossoms, optional* *Alternatively, add orange flower water (available in Middle Eastern or Asian grocery stores) to taste, when bottling.	28 g
3$^{+/-}$ tbsp	orange flower water	45$^{+/-}$ mL

For bottling

5 oz	dextrose (corn sugar)	140 g

1. Prepare the liquid yeast in advance, according to the package directions (if using).
2. In brew kettle, bring 1 US gal (3.75 L) of the brewing water to a boil. Remove from heat. Stir in honey, diammonium phosphate, yeast nutrient and Irish moss until honey, diammonium phosphate and nutrient have dissolved. Place orange peel, coriander seed and orange blossoms in a hop bag; add bag to kettle.
3. Return kettle to heat and bring mead mixture to a simmer. Simmer, uncovered, for 15 minutes. Monitor the liquid, using a spoon or strainer to remove and discard as much of the waxy meringue from the surface as possible.
4. Meanwhile, prepare the cooling bath or wort chiller.
5. At the end of 15 minutes, turn off the heat, remove hop bag, cover kettle and transfer it into the prepared cooling bath (or use a wort chiller, according to the manufacturer's directions). Cool mead to the desired temperature, 75°F (24°C), within 30 to 45 minutes while you prepare the fermentation gear.

392 BREWING MEADS AND FLAVORED MEADS

6. Clean and sanitize the spoon. Using sanitized racking cane and siphon, rack as much of the mead as possible into the sanitized primary fermenter. Then, using a sanitized funnel and straining screen, strain remaining mead into the fermenter. Add enough brewing water to bring volume to about 5.5 US gal (21 L). Using the hydrometer, take a reading of the specific gravity and record it in your brewing journal.

7. Add yeast to mead, stirring vigorously with sanitized spoon until evenly distributed. Seal fermenter with lid, stopper and airlock. Keep at room temperature (68 to 72°F/20 to 22°C) during primary fermentation, which typically lasts for 7 to 10 days after fermentation begins. (Keep fermenter in a dark place or under a lightproof cover if using a glass carboy.)

8. After 7 to 10 days or when the bubbling in airlock slows, gently rack the mead into secondary fermenter to avoid aerating it. Seal and keep at room temperature, covered or in a dark place, to allow fermentation to continue.

9. Once the bubbling in the airlock has slowed further, confirm completion of fermentation by using the hydrometer to take final gravity readings. (Hydrometer readings should be the same for several days in a row.)

10. Using sanitized racking cane and siphon, gently rack mead into sanitized bottling bucket. Add up to 3 tablespoons (45 mL) of orange flower water to taste.

11. Prime and bottle the mead using dextrose (see page 263 for method) and condition for at least 3 months before sampling it.

To Hydrate Lalvin Yeast

In a sanitized bowl or measuring cup, dissolve Lalvin yeast in 1.5 US fl oz (50 mL) of boiled water cooled to 104 to 109°F (40 to 43°C). Let stand for 15 minutes without stirring; then stir with a sanitized spoon to distribute yeast in water.

Blueberry Bliss Mead (Still)

Estimated Original Gravity: 1.105

Equipment

- brew kettle
- sanitized fermentation gear

Brewer's Tip

For information on preparing a yeast starter, see page 262.

To Hydrate Lalvin Yeast

In a sanitized bowl or measuring cup, dissolve Lalvin yeast in 1.5 US fl oz (50 mL) of boiled water cooled to 104 to 109°F (40 to 43°C). Let stand for 15 minutes without stirring; then stir with a sanitized spoon to distribute yeast in water.

	Blueberries, fresh or frozen, prepared for brewing, if using (see sidebar)	
Yeast		
2 packs	Wyeast 4632 or White Labs WLP720 (or 1 pack in starter) or Lalvin D-47	2 packs
5.5 US gal	brewing water	21 L
15 lbs	blueberry honey	6.8 kg
5 tsp	diammonium phosphate (DAP)	25 mL
2 tsp	yeast nutrient	10 mL
1 tsp	Irish moss	5 mL
6 to 9 lbs	blueberry purée, in large, sanitized straining bag, if using instead of fruit (see Step 8)	2.72 to 4 kg
8 to 16 US fl oz	blueberry juice concentrate, if using instead of fruit or purée (see Step 8)	240 to 475 mL
3$^{+/-}$ tbsp	blueberry flavoring	45 mL
For bottling		
2 tsp	potassium sorbate	10 mL

1. Prepare the liquid yeast in advance, according to the package directions (if using).
2. In brew kettle, bring 1 US gal (3.75 L) of the brewing water to a boil. Remove from heat. Stir in honey, diammonium phosphate, yeast nutrient and Irish moss until honey, diammonium phosphate and nutrient have dissolved.
3. Return kettle to heat and bring mead mixture to a simmer. Simmer, uncovered, for 15 minutes. Monitor the liquid, using a spoon or strainer to remove and discard as much of the waxy meringue from the surface as possible.
4. Meanwhile, prepare the cooling bath or wort chiller.
5. At the end of 15 minutes, turn off the heat, cover kettle and transfer it into the prepared cooling bath (or use a wort chiller, according to the manufacturer's directions). Cool mead to the desired temperature, 75°F (24°C), within 30 to 45 minutes while you prepare the fermentation gear.

6. Clean and sanitize the spoon. Using sanitized racking cane and siphon, rack as much of the mead as possible into the sanitized primary fermenter. Then, using a sanitized funnel and straining screen, strain remaining mead into the fermenter. Add enough brewing water to bring volume to about 5.5 US gal (21 L). Using the hydrometer, take a reading of the specific gravity and record it in your brewing journal.

7. Add yeast to mead, stirring vigorously with sanitized spoon until evenly distributed. Seal fermenter with lid, stopper and airlock. Keep at room temperature (68 to 72°F/20 to 22°C) during primary fermentation, which typically lasts for 7 to 10 days after fermentation begins. (Keep fermenter in a dark place or under a lightproof cover if using a glass carboy.)

8. After 7 to 10 days or when the bubbling in airlock slows, rack the mead into secondary fermenter on top of the fruit or purée (if using). (Gently add desired amount of blueberry juice concentrate if using instead of fruit.) Avoid aerating the mead. Seal and keep at room temperature, covered or in a dark place, to allow fermentation to continue.

9. Once the bubbling in the airlock has slowed further, confirm completion of fermentation by using the hydrometer to take final gravity readings. (Hydrometer readings should be the same for several days in a row.)

10. Using sanitized racking cane and siphon, gently rack mead into sanitized bottling bucket. Add up to 3 tablespoons (45 mL) of blueberry flavoring to taste.

11. Prime and bottle the mead using potassium sorbate (see page 263 for method) and condition for at least 3 months before sampling it.

Preparing Blueberries

Use 10 to 15 lbs (4.5 to 6.8 kg) fresh or frozen (preservative-free) blueberries.

If you are using fresh blueberries, wash and stem the fruit and freeze it in resealable bags shortly after brew day.

Two days before racking the mead to the secondary fermenter, sanitize a primary fermenter bucket. Transfer frozen fruit to a large, sanitized straining bag (for easier racking and filtering) and thaw it in the bucket. Crush the fruit with a sanitized potato masher, if necessary. Dissolve 1 campden tablet for each US gal (3.75 L) of fruit in a small amount of boiling water and, using a sanitized spoon, stir the mixture into the fruit in the bag. Seal the fermenter with the lid, stopper and an airlock containing a sterile cotton ball (not the usual water). Leave the fruit for at least 24 hours or until the sulphur smell goes away. This bucket will become your secondary fermenter.

If using purée, put the purée in a sanitized straining bag and place it in the bottom of the sanitized secondary fermenter before racking the beer.

Raspberry Melomel Mead (Sparkling)

Equipment

- **brew kettle**
- **sanitized fermentation gear**

Brewer's Tip

For information on preparing a yeast starter, see page 262.

To Hydrate Lalvin Yeast

In a sanitized bowl or measuring cup, dissolve Lalvin yeast in 1.5 US fl oz (50 mL) of boiled water cooled to 104 to 109°F (40 to 43°C). Let stand for 15 minutes without stirring; then stir with a sanitized spoon to distribute yeast in water.

	Raspberries, fresh or frozen, prepared for brewing, if using (see sidebar)	
Yeast		
2 packs	Wyeast 4632 or White Labs WLP720 (or 1 pack in starter) or Lalvin D-47	2 packs
5.5 US gal	brewing water	21 L
15 lbs	raspberry honey	6.8 kg
5 tsp	diammonium phosphate (DAP)	25 mL
2 tsp	yeast nutrient	10 mL
1 tsp	Irish moss	5 mL
3 to 6 lbs	raspberry purée, in a large, sanitized straining bag, if using instead of fruit (see Step 8)	1.36 to 2.72 kg

For bottling

5 oz	dextrose (corn sugar)	140 g

1. Prepare the liquid yeast in advance, according to the package directions (if using).
2. In brew kettle, bring 1 US gal (3.75 L) of the brewing water to a boil. Remove from heat. Stir in honey, diammonium phosphate, yeast nutrient and Irish moss until honey, diammonium phosphate and nutrient have dissolved.
3. Return kettle to heat and bring mead mixture to a simmer. Simmer, uncovered, for 15 minutes. Monitor the liquid, using a spoon or strainer to remove and discard as much of the waxy meringue from the surface as possible.
4. Meanwhile, prepare the cooling bath or wort chiller.
5. At the end of 15 minutes, turn off the heat, cover kettle and transfer it into the prepared cooling bath (or use a wort chiller, according to the manufacturer's directions). Cool mead to the desired temperature, 75°F (24°C), within 30 to 45 minutes while you prepare the fermentation gear.
6. Clean and sanitize the spoon. Using sanitized racking cane and siphon, rack as much of the mead as possible into the sanitized primary fermenter. Then, using a sanitized funnel and straining screen, strain remaining mead into the fermenter. Add enough brewing water to bring volume to about 5.5 US gal (21 L). Using the hydrometer, take a reading of the specific gravity and record it in your brewing journal.

7. Add yeast to mead, stirring vigorously with sanitized spoon until evenly distributed. Seal fermenter with lid, stopper and airlock. Keep at room temperature (68 to 72°F/20 to 22°C) during primary fermentation, which typically lasts for 7 to 10 days after fermentation begins. (Keep fermenter in a dark place or under a lightproof cover if using a glass carboy.)

8. After 7 to 10 days or when the bubbling in airlock slows, gently rack the mead into secondary fermenter on top of the fruit or purée. Avoid aerating the mead. Seal and keep at room temperature, covered or in a dark place, to allow fermentation to continue.

9. Once the bubbling in the airlock has slowed further, confirm completion of fermentation by using the hydrometer to take final gravity readings. (Hydrometer readings should be the same for several days in a row.)

10. Prime and bottle the mead using dextrose (see page 263 for method) and condition for at least 3 months before sampling it.

Preparing Raspberries

Use 5 to 10 lbs (2.25 to 4.5 kg) fresh or frozen (preservative-free) raspberries.

If you are using fresh raspberries, shortly after brew day, wash and stem the fruit and freeze it in resealable bags.

Two days before racking the mead to the secondary fermenter, sanitize a primary fermenter bucket. Transfer frozen fruit to a large, sanitized straining bag (for easier racking and filtering) and thaw it in the bucket. Crush the fruit with a sanitized potato masher, if necessary. Dissolve 1 campden tablet for each US gal (3.75 L) of fruit in a small amount of boiling water and, using a sanitized spoon, stir the mixture into the fruit in the bag. Seal the fermenter with the lid, stopper and an airlock containing a sterile cotton ball (not the usual water). Leave the fruit for at least 24 hours or until the sulphur smell goes away. This bucket will become your secondary fermenter.

If using purée, put the purée in a sanitized straining bag and place it in the bottom of the sanitized secondary fermenter before racking the beer.

Pyment Mead (Grape, Still)

Equipment

- **brew kettle**
- **sanitized fermentation gear**

Brewer's Tip

For information on preparing a yeast starter, see page 262.

To Hydrate Lalvin Yeast

In a sanitized bowl or measuring cup, dissolve Lalvin yeast in 1.5 US fl oz (50 mL) of boiled water cooled to 104 to 109°F (40 to 43°C). Let stand for 15 minutes without stirring; then stir with a sanitized spoon to distribute yeast in water.

	Grapes, fresh, prepared for brewing, if using (see sidebar)	
Yeast		
2 packs	Wyeast 4632 or White Labs WLP720 (or 1 pack in starter) or Lalvin D-47	2 packs
5.5 US gal	brewing water	21 L
15 lbs	clover, orange-blossom or wildflower honey	6.8 kg
5 tsp	diammonium phosphate (DAP)	25 mL
2 tsp	yeast nutrient	10 mL
1 tsp	Irish moss	5 mL
8 to 16 US fl oz	grape juice concentrate, if using instead of fruit (see Step 8)	240 mL to 475 mL
For bottling		
2 tsp	potassium sorbate	10 mL

1. Prepare the liquid yeast in advance, according to the package directions (if using).
2. In brew kettle, bring 1 US gal (3.75 L) of the brewing water to a boil. Remove from heat. Stir in honey, diammonium phosphate, yeast nutrient and Irish moss until honey, diammonium phosphate and nutrient have dissolved.
3. Return kettle to heat and bring mead mixture to a simmer. Simmer, uncovered, for 15 minutes. Monitor the liquid, using a spoon or strainer to remove and discard as much of the waxy meringue from the surface as possible.
4. Meanwhile, prepare the cooling bath or wort chiller.
5. At the end of 15 minutes, turn off the heat, cover kettle and transfer it into the prepared cooling bath (or use a wort chiller, according to the manufacturer's directions). Cool mead to the desired temperature, 75°F (24°C), within 30 to 45 minutes while you prepare the fermentation gear.
6. Clean and sanitize the spoon. Using sanitized racking cane and siphon, rack as much of the mead as possible into the sanitized primary fermenter. Then, using a sanitized funnel and straining screen, strain remaining mead into the fermenter. Add enough brewing water to bring volume to about 5.5 US gal (21 L). Using the hydrometer, take a reading of the specific gravity and record it in your brewing journal.

7. Add yeast to mead, stirring vigorously with sanitized spoon until evenly distributed. Seal fermenter with lid, stopper and airlock. Keep at room temperature (68 to 72°F/20 to 22°C) during primary fermentation, which typically lasts for 7 to 10 days after fermentation begins. (Keep fermenter in a dark place or under a lightproof cover if using a glass carboy.)

8. After 7 to 10 days or when the bubbling in airlock slows, gently rack the mead into secondary fermenter on top of the fruit, if using. Avoid aerating the mead. (Gently add desired amount of grape juice concentrate if using instead of fruit.) Seal and keep at room temperature, covered or in a dark place, to allow fermentation to continue.

9. Once the bubbling in the airlock has slowed further, confirm completion of fermentation by using the hydrometer to take final gravity readings. (Hydrometer readings should be the same for several days in a row.)

10. Prime and bottle the mead using potassium sorbate (see page 263 for method) and condition for at least 3 months before sampling it.

Preparing Grapes

Use 10 to 15 lbs (4.5 to 6.8 kg) fresh grapes.

Shortly after brew day, wash and stem the fruit; freeze it in resealable bags.

Two days before racking the mead to the secondary fermenter, sanitize a primary fermenter bucket. Transfer frozen fruit to a large, sanitized straining bag (for easier racking and filtering) and thaw fruit in the bucket. Crush the fruit with a sanitized potato masher, if necessary. Dissolve 1 campden tablet for each US gal (3.75 L) of fruit in a small amount of boiling water and, using sanitized spoon, stir the mixture into the fruit in the bag. Seal the fermenter with the lid, stopper and an airlock containing a sterile cotton ball (not the usual water). Leave the fruit for at least 24 hours or until the sulphur smell goes away. This bucket will become your secondary fermenter.

Equipment

- **brew kettle**
- **sanitized fermentation gear**

Brewer's Tip

For information on preparing a yeast starter, see page 262.

To Hydrate Lalvin Yeast

In a sanitized bowl or measuring cup, dissolve Lalvin yeast in 1.5 US fl oz (50 mL) of boiled water cooled to 104 to 109°F (40 to 43°C). Let stand for 15 minutes without stirring; then stir with a sanitized spoon to distribute yeast in water.

Cranberry Mead (Sparkling)

	Cranberries, fresh or frozen, prepared for brewing, if using (see sidebar)	
Yeast		
2 packs	Wyeast 4632 or White Labs WLP720 (or 1 pack in starter) or Lalvin D-47	2 packs
5.5 US gal	brewing water	21 L
15 lbs	cranberry honey	6.9 kg
5 tsp	diammonium phosphate (DAP)	25 mL
2 tsp	yeast nutrient	10 mL
1 tsp	Irish moss	5 mL
8 to 16 US fl oz	cranberry juice concentrate, if using instead of fruit (see Step 8)	240 to 475 mL
For bottling		
5 oz	dextrose (corn sugar)	140 g

1. Prepare the liquid yeast in advance, according to the package directions (if using).
2. In brew kettle, bring 1 US gal (3.75 L) of the brewing water to a boil. Remove from heat. Stir in honey, diammonium phosphate, yeast nutrient and Irish moss until honey, diammonium phosphate and nutrient have dissolved.
3. Return kettle to heat and bring mead mixture to a simmer. Simmer, uncovered, for 15 minutes. Monitor the liquid, using a spoon or strainer to remove and discard as much of the waxy meringue from the surface as possible.
4. Meanwhile, prepare the cooling bath or wort chiller.
5. At the end of 15 minutes, turn off the heat, cover kettle and transfer it into the prepared cooling bath (or use a wort chiller, according to the manufacturer's directions). Cool mead to the desired temperature, 75°F (24°C), within 30 to 45 minutes while you prepare the fermentation gear.

6. Clean and sanitize the spoon. Using sanitized racking cane and siphon, rack as much of the mead as possible into the sanitized primary fermenter. Then, using a sanitized funnel and straining screen, strain remaining mead into the fermenter. Add enough brewing water to bring volume to about 5.5 US gal (21 L). Using the hydrometer, take a reading of the specific gravity and record it in your brewing journal.

7. Add yeast to mead, stirring vigorously with sanitized spoon until evenly distributed. Seal fermenter with lid, stopper and airlock. Keep at room temperature (68 to 72°F/20 to 22°C) during primary fermentation, which typically lasts for 7 to 10 days after fermentation begins. (Keep fermenter in a dark place or under a lightproof cover if using a glass carboy.)

8. After 7 to 10 days or when the bubbling in airlock slows, gently rack the mead into secondary fermenter on top of the fruit. Avoid aerating the mead. (Gently add desired amount of cranberry juice concentrate if using instead of fruit.) Seal and keep at room temperature, covered or in a dark place, to allow fermentation to continue.

9. Once the bubbling in the airlock has slowed further, confirm completion of fermentation by using the hydrometer to take final gravity readings. (Hydrometer readings should be the same for several days in a row.)

10. Prime and bottle the mead using dextrose (see page 263 for method) and condition for at least 3 months before sampling it.

Preparing Cranberries

Use 5 to 10 lbs (2.25 to 4.5 kg) fresh or frozen (preservative-free) cranberries.

If using fresh cranberries, wash and stem the fruit and freeze it in resealable bags shortly after brew day.

Two days before racking the mead to the secondary fermenter, sanitize a primary fermenter bucket. Transfer frozen fruit to a large, sanitized straining bag (for easier racking and filtering) and thaw fruit in the bucket. Crush the fruit with a sanitized potato masher, if necessary. Dissolve 1 campden tablet for each US gal (3.75 L) of fruit in a small amount of boiling water and, using sanitized spoon, stir the mixture into the fruit in the bag. Seal the fermenter with the lid, stopper and an airlock containing a sterile cotton ball (not the usual water). Leave the fruit for at least 24 hours or until the sulphur smell goes away. This bucket will become your secondary fermenter.

Mango Mead (Sparkling)

Equipment

- **brew kettle**
- **sanitized fermentation gear**

Brewer's Tip

For information on preparing a yeast starter, see page 262.

To Hydrate Lalvin Yeast

In a sanitized bowl or measuring cup, dissolve Lalvin yeast in 1.5 US fl oz (50 mL) of boiled water cooled to 104 to 109°F (40 to 43°C). Let stand for 15 minutes without stirring; then stir with a sanitized spoon to distribute yeast in water.

	Mango, fresh or frozen, prepared for brewing (see sidebar)	
Yeast		
2 packs	Wyeast 4632 or White Labs WLP720 (or 1 pack in starter) or Lalvin D-47	2 packs
5.5 US gal	brewing water	21 L
12 lbs	clover, orange-blossom or wildflower honey	5.4 kg
5 tsp	diammonium phosphate (DAP)	25 mL
2 tsp	yeast nutrient	10 mL
1 tsp	Irish moss	5 mL
For bottling		
5 oz	dextrose (corn sugar)	140 g

1. Prepare the liquid yeast in advance, according to the package directions (if using).
2. In brew kettle, bring 1 US gal (3.75 L) of the brewing water to a boil. Remove from heat. Stir in honey, diammonium phosphate, yeast nutrient and Irish moss until honey, diammonium phosphate and nutrient have dissolved.
3. Return kettle to heat and bring mead mixture to a simmer. Simmer, uncovered, for 15 minutes. Monitor the liquid, using a spoon or strainer to remove and discard as much of the waxy meringue from the surface as possible.
4. Meanwhile, prepare the cooling bath or wort chiller.
5. At the end of 15 minutes, turn off the heat, cover kettle and transfer it into the prepared cooling bath (or use a wort chiller, according to the manufacturer's directions). Cool mead to the desired temperature, 75°F (24°C), within 30 to 45 minutes while you prepare the fermentation gear.
6. Clean and sanitize the spoon. Using sanitized racking cane and siphon, rack as much of the mead as possible into the sanitized primary fermenter. Then, using a sanitized funnel and straining screen, strain remaining mead into the fermenter. Add enough brewing water to bring volume to about 5.5 US gal (21 L). Using the hydrometer, take a reading of the specific gravity and record it in your brewing journal.

7. Add yeast to mead, stirring vigorously with sanitized spoon until evenly distributed. Seal fermenter with lid, stopper and airlock. Keep at room temperature (68 to 72°F/20 to 22°C) during primary fermentation, which typically lasts for 7 to 10 days after fermentation begins. (Keep fermenter in a dark place or under a lightproof cover if using a glass carboy.)

8. After 7 to 10 days or when the bubbling in airlock slows, gently rack the mead into secondary fermenter on top of the fruit. Avoid aerating the mead. Seal and keep at room temperature, covered or in a dark place, to allow fermentation to continue.

9. Once the bubbling in the airlock has slowed further, confirm completion of fermentation by using the hydrometer to take final gravity readings. (Hydrometer readings should be the same for several days in a row.)

10. Prime and bottle the mead using dextrose (see page 263 for method) and condition for at least 3 months before sampling it.

Preparing Mangos

Use 10 to 15 lbs (4.5 to 6.8 kg) fresh or frozen (preservative-free) mangos.

If using fresh mangos, peel and pit the fruit; chop it coarsely and freeze it in resealable bags shortly after brew day.

Two days before racking the mead to the secondary fermenter, sanitize a primary fermenter bucket. Transfer frozen fruit to a large, sanitized straining bag (for easier racking and filtering) and thaw fruit in the bucket. Crush the fruit with a sanitized potato masher, if necessary. Dissolve 1 campden tablet for each US gal (3.75 L) of fruit in a small amount of boiling water and, using sanitized spoon, stir the mixture into the fruit in the bag. Seal the fermenter with the lid, stopper and an airlock containing a sterile cotton ball (not the usual water). Leave the fruit for at least 24 hours or until the sulphur smell goes away. This bucket will become your secondary fermenter.

Fig Mead (Sparkling)

Estimated Original Gravity: 1.084

Equipment

- **brew kettle**
- **sanitized fermentation gear**

Brewer's Tip

For information on preparing a yeast starter, see page 262.

To Hydrate Lalvin Yeast

In a sanitized bowl or measuring cup, dissolve Lalvin yeast in 1.5 US fl oz (50 mL) of boiled water cooled to 104 to 109°F (40 to 43°C). Let stand for 15 minutes without stirring; then stir with a sanitized spoon to distribute yeast in water.

	Figs, fresh, prepared for brewing, if using (see sidebar)	
Yeast		
2 packs	Wyeast 4632 or White Labs WLP720 (or 1 pack in starter) or Lalvin D-47	2 packs
5.5 US gal	brewing water	21 L
12 lbs	wildflower honey	5.4 kg
5 tsp	diammonium phosphate (DAP)	25 mL
2 tsp	yeast nutrient	10 mL
1 tsp	Irish moss	5 mL
10 to 15 lbs	fig purée, in a large, sanitized straining bag, if using instead of fruit (see Step 8)	4.5 to 6.8 kg
For bottling		
5 oz	dextrose (corn sugar)	140 g

1. Prepare the liquid yeast in advance, according to the package directions (if using).
2. In brew kettle, bring 1 US gal (3.75 L) of the brewing water to a boil. Remove from heat. Stir in honey, diammonium phosphate, yeast nutrient and Irish moss until honey, diammonium phosphate and nutrient have dissolved.
3. Return kettle to heat and bring mead mixture to a simmer. Simmer, uncovered, for 15 minutes. Monitor the liquid, using a spoon or strainer to remove and discard as much of the waxy meringue from the surface as possible.
4. Meanwhile, prepare the cooling bath or wort chiller.
5. At the end of 15 minutes, turn off the heat, cover kettle and transfer it into the prepared cooling bath (or use a wort chiller, according to the manufacturer's directions). Cool mead to the desired temperature, 75°F (24°C), within 30 to 45 minutes while you prepare the fermentation gear.
6. Clean and sanitize the spoon. Using sanitized racking cane and siphon, rack as much of the mead as possible into the sanitized primary fermenter. Then, using a sanitized funnel and straining screen, strain remaining mead into the fermenter. Add enough brewing water to bring volume to about 5.5 US gal (21 L). Using the hydrometer, take a reading of the specific gravity and record it in your brewing journal.

7. Add yeast to mead, stirring vigorously with sanitized spoon until evenly distributed. Seal fermenter with lid, stopper and airlock. Keep at room temperature (68 to 72°F/20 to 22°C) during primary fermentation, which typically lasts for 7 to 10 days after fermentation begins. (Keep fermenter in a dark place or under a lightproof cover if using a glass carboy.)

8. After 7 to 10 days or when the bubbling in airlock slows, gently rack the mead on top of the fruit or purée. Avoid aerating the mead. Seal and keep at room temperature, covered or in a dark place, to allow fermentation to continue.

9. Once the bubbling in the airlock has slowed further, confirm completion of fermentation by using the hydrometer to take final gravity readings. (Hydrometer readings should be the same for several days in a row.)

10. Prime and bottle the mead using dextrose (see page 263 for method) and condition for at least 3 months before sampling it.

Preparing Figs

Use 10 to 15 lbs (4.5 to 6.8 kg) fresh figs.

Shortly after brew day, freeze the fruit in resealable bags.

Two days before racking the mead to the secondary fermenter, sanitize a primary fermenter bucket. Transfer frozen fruit to a large, sanitized straining bag (for easier racking and filtering) and thaw fruit in the bucket. Crush the fruit with a sanitized potato masher, if necessary. Dissolve 1 campden tablet for each US gal (3.75 L) of fruit in a small amount of boiling water and, using sanitized spoon, stir the mixture into the fruit in the bag. Seal the fermenter with the lid, stopper and an airlock containing a sterile cotton ball (not the usual water). Leave the fruit for at least 24 hours or until the sulphur smell goes away. This bucket will become your secondary fermenter.

If using purée, put the purée in a sanitized straining bag and place it in the bottom of the sanitized secondary fermenter before racking the beer.

Pomegranate Mead (Sparkling)

Equipment

- **brew kettle**
- **sanitized fermentation gear**

Brewer's Tip

For information on preparing a yeast starter, see page 262.

Yeast

2 packs	Wyeast 4632 or White Labs WLP720 (or 1 pack in starter) or Lalvin D-47	2 packs
5.5 US gal	brewing water	21 L
15 lbs	clover, orange-blossom or wildflower honey	6.8 kg
5 tsp	diammonium phosphate (DAP)	25 mL
2 tsp	yeast nutrient	10 mL
1 tsp	Irish moss	5 mL
8 to 16 US fl oz	pomegranate juice concentrate (see Step 8)	240 to 275 mL

For bottling

5 oz	dextrose (corn sugar)	140 g

1. Prepare the liquid yeast in advance, according to the package directions (if using).
2. In brew kettle, bring 1 US gal (3.75 L) of the brewing water to a boil. Remove from heat. Stir in honey, diammonium phosphate, yeast nutrient and Irish moss until honey, diammonium phosphate and nutrient have dissolved.
3. Return kettle to heat and bring mead mixture to a simmer. Simmer, uncovered, for 15 minutes. Monitor the liquid, using a spoon or strainer to remove and discard as much of the waxy meringue from the surface as possible.
4. Meanwhile, prepare the cooling bath or wort chiller.
5. At the end of 15 minutes, turn off the heat, cover kettle and transfer it into prepared cooling bath (or use a wort chiller, according to the manufacturer's directions). Cool mead to the desired temperature, 75°F (24°C), within 30 to 45 minutes while you prepare the fermentation gear.
6. Clean and sanitize the spoon. Using sanitized racking cane and siphon, rack as much of the mead as possible into the sanitized primary fermenter. Then, using a sanitized funnel and straining screen, strain remaining mead into the fermenter. Add enough brewing water to bring volume to about 5.5 US gal (21 L). Using the hydrometer, take a reading of the specific gravity and record it in your brewing journal.

7. Add yeast to mead, stirring vigorously with sanitized spoon until evenly distributed. Seal fermenter with lid, stopper and airlock. Keep at room temperature (68 to 72°F/20 to 22°C) during primary fermentation, which typically lasts for 7 to 10 days after fermentation begins. (Keep fermenter in a dark place or under a lightproof cover if using a glass carboy.)

8. After 7 to 10 days or when the bubbling in airlock slows, gently rack the mead into secondary fermenter to avoid aerating it. Gently add pomegranate juice concentrate. Seal and keep at room temperature, covered or in a dark place, to allow fermentation to continue.

9. Once the bubbling in the airlock has slowed further, confirm completion of fermentation by using the hydrometer to take final gravity readings. (Hydrometer readings should be the same for several days in a row.)

10. Prime and bottle the mead using dextrose (see page 263 for method) and condition for at least 3 months before sampling it.

To Hydrate Lalvin Yeast

In a sanitized bowl or measuring cup, dissolve Lalvin yeast in 1.5 US fl oz (50 mL) of boiled water cooled to 104 to 109°F (40 to 43°C). Let stand for 15 minutes without stirring; then stir with a sanitized spoon to distribute yeast in water.

Pandanus (Bai Toey) Mead (Still)

Equipment

- **brew kettle**
- **sanitized fermentation gear**

Brewer's Tips

For easier brewing, place the coconut in a hop bag and add the bag to the kettle. If you prefer to add these ingredients directly to the liquid, you will need to be much more careful about straining the mead as it moves through fermentation.

For information on preparing a yeast starter, see page 262.

Yeast

2 packs	Wyeast 4632 or White Labs WLP720 (or 1 pack in starter) or Lalvin D-47	2 packs
5.5 US gal	brewing water	21 L
15 lbs	clover, orange-blossom or wildflower honey	6.8 kg
1 lb	dried, flaked coconut (in grain bag)	450 g
5 tsp	diammonium phosphate (DAP)	25 mL
2 tsp	yeast nutrient	10 mL
1 tsp	Irish moss	5 mL
	Pandanus (bai toey) flavor extract (available in Asian markets), to taste (see Step 10)	

For bottling

2 tsp	potassium sorbate	10 mL

1. Prepare the liquid yeast in advance, according to the package directions (if using).
2. In brew kettle, bring 1 US gal (3.75 L) of the brewing water to a boil. Remove from heat. Stir in honey, coconut, diammonium phosphate, yeast nutrient and Irish moss until honey, diammonium phosphate and nutrient have dissolved.
3. Return kettle to heat and bring mead mixture to a simmer. Simmer, uncovered, for 15 minutes. Monitor the liquid, using a spoon or strainer to remove and discard as much of the waxy meringue from the surface as possible.
4. Meanwhile, prepare the cooling bath or wort chiller.
5. At the end of 15 minutes, turn off the heat, cover kettle and transfer it into the prepared cooling bath (or use a wort chiller, according to the manufacturer's directions). Cool mead to the desired temperature, 75°F (24°C), within 30 to 45 minutes while you prepare the fermentation gear.
6. Clean and sanitize the spoon. Using sanitized racking cane and siphon, rack as much of the mead as possible into the sanitized primary fermenter. Then, using a sanitized funnel and straining screen, strain remaining mead into the fermenter. Add enough brewing water to bring volume to about 5.5 US gal (21 L). Using the hydrometer, take a reading of the specific gravity and record it in your brewing journal.

7. Add yeast to mead, stirring vigorously with sanitized spoon until evenly distributed. Seal fermenter with lid, stopper and airlock. Keep at room temperature (68 to 72°F/20 to 22°C) during primary fermentation, which typically lasts for 7 to 10 days after fermentation begins. (Keep fermenter in a dark place or under a lightproof cover if using a glass carboy.)

8. After 7 to 10 days or when the bubbling in airlock slows, gently rack the mead into secondary fermenter to avoid aerating it. Seal and keep at room temperature, covered or in a dark place, to allow fermentation to continue.

9. Once the bubbling in the airlock has slowed further, confirm completion of fermentation by using the hydrometer to take final gravity readings. (Hydrometer readings should be the same for several days in a row.)

10. Add pandanus flavor extract sparingly until you reach the desired taste.

11. Prime and bottle the mead using potassium sorbate (see page 263 for method) and condition for at least 3 months before sampling it.

To Hydrate Lalvin Yeast

In a sanitized bowl or measuring cup, dissolve Lalvin yeast in 1.5 US fl oz (50 mL) of boiled water cooled to 104 to 109°F (40 to 43°C). Let stand for 15 minutes without stirring; then stir with a sanitized spoon to distribute yeast in water.

Strawberry Mead (Still)

Equipment

- **brew kettle**
- **sanitized fermentation gear**

Brewer's Tip

For information on preparing a yeast starter, see page 262.

To Hydrate Lalvin Yeast

In a sanitized bowl or measuring cup, dissolve Lalvin yeast in 1.5 US fl oz (50 mL) of boiled water cooled to 104 to 109°F (40 to 43°C). Let stand for 15 minutes without stirring; then stir with a sanitized spoon to distribute yeast in water.

	Strawberries, fresh or frozen, prepared for brewing, if using (see sidebar)	
Yeast		
2 packs	Wyeast 4632 or White Labs WLP720 (or 1 pack in starter) or Lalvin D-47	2 packs
5.5 US gal	brewing water	21 L
15 lbs	wildflower honey	6.8 kg
5 tsp	diammonium phosphate (DAP)	25 mL
2 tsp	yeast nutrient	10 mL
1 tsp	Irish moss	5 mL
6 to 9 lbs	strawberry purée in a large straining bag, if using instead of fruit (see Step 8)	2.72 to 4 kg
For bottling		
2 tsp	potassium sorbate	10 mL

1. Prepare the liquid yeast in advance, according to the package directions (if using).
2. In brew kettle, bring 1 US gal (3.75 L) of the brewing water to a boil. Remove from heat. Stir in honey, diammonium phosphate, yeast nutrient and Irish moss until honey, diammonium phosphate and nutrient have dissolved.
3. Return kettle to heat and bring mead mixture to a simmer. Simmer, uncovered, for 15 minutes. Monitor the liquid, using a spoon or strainer to remove and discard as much of the waxy meringue from the surface as possible.
4. Meanwhile, prepare the cooling bath or wort chiller.
5. At the end of 15 minutes, turn off the heat, cover kettle and transfer it into the prepared cooling bath (or use a wort chiller, according to the manufacturer's directions). Cool mead to the desired temperature, 75°F (24°C), within 30 to 45 minutes while you prepare the fermentation gear.
6. Clean and sanitize the spoon. Using sanitized racking cane and siphon, rack as much of the mead as possible into the sanitized primary fermenter. Then, using a sanitized funnel and straining screen, strain remaining mead into the fermenter. Add enough brewing water to bring volume to about 5.5 US gal (21 L). Using the hydrometer, take a reading of the specific gravity and record it in your brewing journal.

7. Add yeast to mead, stirring vigorously with sanitized spoon until evenly distributed. Seal fermenter with lid, stopper and airlock. Keep at room temperature (68 to 72°F/20 to 22°C) during primary fermentation, which typically lasts for 7 to 10 days after fermentation begins. (Keep fermenter in a dark place or under a lightproof cover if using a glass carboy.)

8. After 7 to 10 days or when the bubbling in airlock slows, add strawberry purée, if using, to sanitized secondary fermenter and gently rack the mead on top of the fruit or purée. Avoid aerating the mead. Seal and keep at room temperature, covered or in a dark place, to allow fermentation to continue.

9. Once the bubbling in the airlock has slowed further, confirm completion of fermentation by using the hydrometer to take final gravity readings. (Hydrometer readings should be the same for several days in a row.)

10. Prime and bottle the mead using potassium sorbate (see page 263 for method) and condition for at least 3 months before sampling it.

Preparing Strawberries

Use 10 to 15 lbs (4.5 to 6.8 kg) fresh or frozen (preservative-free) strawberries.

If using fresh strawberries, wash and stem the fruit and freeze it in resealable bags shortly after brew day.

Two days before racking the mead to the secondary fermenter, sanitize a primary fermenter bucket. Transfer frozen fruit to a large, sanitized straining bag (for easier racking and filtering) and thaw fruit in the bucket. Crush the fruit with a sanitized potato masher, if necessary. Dissolve 1 campden tablet for each US gal (3.75 L) of fruit in a small amount of boiling water and, using sanitized spoon, stir the mixture into the fruit in the bag. Seal the fermenter with the lid, stopper and an airlock containing a sterile cotton ball (not the usual water). Leave the fruit for at least 24 hours or until the sulphur smell goes away. This bucket will become your secondary fermenter.

If using purée, put the purée in a sanitized straining bag and place it in the bottom of the sanitized secondary fermenter before racking the beer.

Winter Spice Mead (Sparkling)

Estimated Original Gravity: 1.084

Equipment

- **brew kettle**
- **sanitized fermentation gear**

Brewer's Tips

For easier brewing, place the peel and spices in a hop bag and add the bag to the kettle. If you prefer to add these ingredients directly to the liquid, you will need to be much more careful about straining the mead as it moves through fermentation.

For information on preparing a yeast starter, see page 262.

Yeast

2 packs	Wyeast 4632 or White Labs WLP 720 (or 1 pack in starter) or Lalvin D-47	2 packs
5.5 US gal	brewing water	21 L
12 lbs	orange-blossom honey	5.4 kg
5 tsp	diammonium phosphate (DAP)	25 mL
2 tsp	yeast nutrient	10 mL
1 tsp	Irish moss	5 mL
1 oz	sweet orange peel	28 g
1 oz	freshly grated gingerroot	28 g
2 to 3	whole cloves (do not crush)	2 to 3
3	cinnamon sticks	3
1/4 tsp	freshly grated nutmeg	1 mL

For bottling

5 oz	dextrose (corn sugar)	140 g

1. Prepare the liquid yeast in advance, according to the package directions (if using).
2. In brew kettle, bring 1 US gal (3.75 L) of the brewing water to a boil. Remove from heat. Stir in honey, diammonium phosphate, yeast nutrient, Irish moss and spices until honey, diammonium phosphate and nutrient have dissolved.
3. Return kettle to heat and bring mead mixture to a simmer. Simmer, uncovered, for 15 minutes. Monitor the liquid, using a spoon or strainer to remove and discard as much of the waxy meringue from the surface as possible.
4. Meanwhile, prepare the cooling bath or wort chiller.
5. At the end of 15 minutes, turn off the heat, cover kettle and transfer it into the prepared cooling bath (or use a wort chiller, according to the manufacturer's directions). Cool mead to the desired temperature, 75°F (24°C), within 30 to 45 minutes while you prepare the fermentation gear.
6. Clean and sanitize the spoon. Using sanitized racking cane and siphon, rack as much of the mead as possible into the sanitized primary fermenter. Then, using a sanitized funnel and straining screen, strain remaining mead into the fermenter. Add enough brewing water to bring volume to about 5.5 US gal (21 L). Using the hydrometer, take a reading of the specific gravity and record it in your brewing journal.

7. Add yeast to mead, stirring vigorously with sanitized spoon until evenly distributed. Seal fermenter with lid, stopper and airlock. Keep at room temperature (68 to 72°F/20 to 22°C) during primary fermentation, which typically lasts for 7 to 10 days after fermentation begins. (Keep fermenter in a dark place or under a lightproof cover if using a glass carboy.)

8. After 7 to 10 days or when the bubbling in airlock slows, gently rack the mead into secondary fermenter to avoid aerating it. Seal and keep at room temperature, covered or in a dark place, to allow fermentation to continue.

9. Once the bubbling in the airlock has slowed further, confirm completion of fermentation by using the hydrometer to take final gravity readings. (Hydrometer readings should be the same for several days in a row.)

10. Prime and bottle the mead using dextrose (see page 263 for method) and condition for at least 3 months before sampling it.

To Hydrate Lalvin Yeast

In a sanitized bowl or measuring cup, dissolve Lalvin yeast in 1.5 US fl oz (50 mL) of boiled water cooled to 104 to 109°F (40 to 43°C). Let stand for 15 minutes without stirring; then stir with a sanitized spoon to distribute yeast in water.

Tej (Sparkling)

This quick mead is the traditional mead of Ethiopia. Gesho is a bitter herb available in African markets.

If gesho is not available in your area, substitute 1 oz (28 g) of a medium-alpha acid hop.

Estimated Original Gravity: 1.049

Equipment

- **brew kettle**
- **sanitized fermentation gear**

Yeast

1 pack	Wyeast 1099 or White Labs WLP005 or Fermentis S-33	1 pack
5.5 US gal	brewing water	21 L
7 lbs	wildflower honey	3.2 kg
5 tsp	diammonium phosphate (DAP)	25 mL
2 tsp	yeast nutrient	10 mL
1 tsp	Irish moss	5 mL
1 oz	gesho (found in Ethiopian markets)	28 g

For bottling

5 oz	dextrose (corn sugar)	140 g

1. Prepare the liquid yeast in advance, according to the package directions (if using).
2. In brew kettle, bring 1 US gal (3.75 L) of the brewing water to a boil. Remove from heat. Stir in honey, diammonium phosphate, yeast nutrient, Irish moss and gesho until honey, diammonium phosphate and nutrient have dissolved.
3. Return kettle to heat and bring mead mixture to a simmer. Simmer, uncovered, for 15 minutes. Monitor the liquid, using a spoon or strainer to remove and discard as much of the waxy meringue from the surface as possible.
4. Meanwhile, prepare the cooling bath or wort chiller.
5. At the end of 15 minutes, turn off the heat, cover kettle and transfer it into the prepared cooling bath (or use a wort chiller, according to the manufacturer's directions). Cool mead to the desired temperature, 75°F (24°C), within 30 to 45 minutes while you prepare the fermentation gear.
6. Clean and sanitize the spoon. Using sanitized racking cane and siphon, rack as much of the mead as possible into the sanitized primary fermenter. Then, using a sanitized funnel and straining screen, strain remaining mead into the fermenter. Add enough brewing water to bring volume to about 5.5 US gal (21 L). Using the hydrometer, take a reading of the specific gravity and record it in your brewing journal.
7. Add yeast to mead, stirring vigorously with sanitized spoon until evenly distributed. Seal fermenter with lid, stopper and airlock. Keep at room temperature (68 to 72°F/20 to 22°C) during primary fermentation, which typically lasts for 7 to 10 days after fermentation begins. (Keep fermenter in a dark place or under a lightproof cover if using a glass carboy.)

8. After 7 to 10 days or when the bubbling in airlock slows, gently rack the mead into secondary fermenter to avoid aerating it. Seal and keep at room temperature, covered or in a dark place, to allow fermentation to continue.

9. Once the bubbling in the airlock has slowed further, confirm completion of fermentation by using the hydrometer to take final gravity readings. (Hydrometer readings should be the same for several days in a row.)

10. Prime and bottle the mead using dextrose (see page 263 for method) and condition for at least 3 months before sampling it.

Estimated Original Gravity: 1.105

Equipment

- **brew kettle**
- **sanitized fermentation gear**

Brewer's Tip

For easier brewing, place the peppers and spices in a hop bag and add the bag to the kettle. If you prefer to add these ingredients directly to the liquid, you will need to be much more careful about straining the mead as it moves through fermentation.

Cinnamon Fire Mead (Still)

Yeast

2 packs	Wyeast 4184 or White Labs WLP720 (or 1 pack in starter) or Lalvin D-47	2 packs
5.5 US gal	brewing water	21 L
15 lbs	wildflower honey	6.8 kg
5 tsp	diammonium phosphate (DAP)	25 mL
2 tsp	yeast nutrient	10 mL
1 tsp	Irish moss	5 mL
5	cayenne peppers (fresh or dried), chopped	5
5	cinnamon sticks, coarsely ground	5

For bottling

2 tsp	potassium sorbate	10 mL

1. Prepare the liquid yeast in advance, according to the package directions (if using).
2. In brew kettle, bring 1 US gal (3.75 L) of the brewing water to a boil. Remove from heat. Stir in honey, diammonium phosphate, yeast nutrient and Irish moss until honey, diammonium phosphate and nutrient have dissolved. Place peppers and cinnamon sticks in a hop bag; add bag to kettle.
3. Return kettle to heat and bring mead mixture to a simmer. Simmer, uncovered, for 15 minutes. Monitor the liquid, using a spoon or strainer to remove and discard as much of the waxy meringue from the surface as possible.
4. Meanwhile, prepare the cooling bath or wort chiller.
5. At the end of 15 minutes, turn off the heat, remove hop bag, cover kettle and transfer it into the prepared cooling bath (or use a wort chiller, according to the manufacturer's directions). Cool mead to the desired temperature, 75°F (24°C), within 30 to 45 minutes while you prepare the fermentation gear.
6. Clean and sanitize the spoon. Using sanitized racking cane and siphon, rack as much of the mead as possible into the sanitized primary fermenter. Then, using a sanitized funnel and straining screen, strain remaining mead into the fermenter. Add enough brewing water to bring volume to about 5.5 US gal (21 L). Using the hydrometer, take a reading of the specific gravity and record it in your brewing journal.

7. Add yeast to mead, stirring vigorously with sanitized spoon until evenly distributed. Seal fermenter with lid, stopper and airlock. Keep at room temperature (68 to 72°F/20 to 22°C) during primary fermentation, which typically lasts for 7 to 10 days after fermentation begins. (Keep fermenter in a dark place or under a lightproof cover if using a glass carboy.)

8. After 7 to 10 days or when the bubbling in airlock slows, gently rack the mead into secondary fermenter to avoid aerating it. Seal and keep at room temperature, covered or in a dark place, to allow fermentation to continue.

9. Once the bubbling in the airlock has slowed further, confirm completion of fermentation by using the hydrometer to take final gravity readings. (Hydrometer readings should be the same for several days in a row.)

10. Prime and bottle the mead using potassium sorbate (see page 263 for method) and condition for at least 3 months before sampling it.

In this beverage, mead and cider meet. Simply use the apple juice in place of the top-off brewing water. If the apple juice is not pasteurized, use campden tablets according to the package directions.

Estimated Original Gravity: Varies depending on sugar content of apple juice

Equipment

- **brew kettle**
- **sanitized fermentation gear**

Acid Blend

Winemakers' acid blend is equal parts citric, malic and tartaric acids. It is added to compensate for low acidity and sharpen up the taste.

Brewer's Tip

For information on preparing a yeast starter, see page 262.

Cyser Mead (Apple, Sparkling)

Yeast

2 packs	Wyeast 4632 or White Labs WLP720 (or 1 pack in starter) or Lalvin D-47	2 packs
1 US gal	brewing water	3.8 L
10 to 12 lbs	clover, orange-blossom or wildflower honey	4.5 to 5.4 kg
5 tsp	diammonium phosphate (DAP)	25 mL
2 tsp	yeast nutrient	10 mL
1 tsp	Irish moss	5 mL
5 tsp	acid blend	25 mL
	Pectic enzyme (use according to package instructions; add to primary fermenter)	
4 US gal	preservative-free apple juice, pasteurized or treated with campden tablets	15 L

For bottling

5 oz	dextrose (corn sugar)	140 g

1. Prepare the liquid yeast in advance, according to the package directions (if using).
2. In brew kettle, bring 1 US gal (3.75 L) of the brewing water to a boil. Remove from heat. Stir in honey, diammonium phosphate, yeast nutrient, Irish moss and acid blend until honey, diammonium phosphate and nutrient have dissolved.
3. Return kettle to heat and bring mead mixture to a simmer. Simmer, uncovered, for 15 minutes. Monitor the liquid, using a spoon or strainer to remove and discard as much of the waxy meringue from the surface as possible.
4. Meanwhile, prepare the cooling bath or wort chiller.
5. At the end of 15 minutes, turn off the heat, cover kettle and transfer it into the prepared cooling bath (or use a wort chiller, according to the manufacturer's directions). Cool mead to the desired temperature, 75°F (24°C), within 30 to 45 minutes while you prepare the fermentation gear.

6. Clean and sanitize the spoon. Using sanitized racking cane and siphon, rack as much of the mead as possible into the sanitized primary fermenter. Then, using a sanitized funnel and straining screen, strain remaining mead into the fermenter. Add pectic enzyme and enough apple juice to bring volume to about 5 US gal (19 L). Using the hydrometer, take a reading of the specific gravity and record it in your brewing journal.

7. Add yeast to mead, stirring vigorously with sanitized spoon until evenly distributed. Seal fermenter with lid, stopper and airlock. Keep at room temperature (68 to 72°F/20 to 22°C) during primary fermentation, which typically lasts for 7 to 10 days after fermentation begins. (Keep fermenter in a dark place or under a lightproof cover if using a glass carboy.)

8. After 7 to 10 days or when the bubbling in airlock slows, gently rack the mead into secondary fermenter to avoid aerating it. Seal and keep at room temperature, covered or in a dark place, to allow fermentation to continue.

9. Once the bubbling in the airlock has slowed further, confirm completion of fermentation by using the hydrometer to take final gravity readings. (Hydrometer readings should be the same for several days in a row.)

10. Prime and bottle the mead using dextrose (see page 263 for method) and condition for at least 3 months before sampling it.

To Hydrate Lalvin Yeast

In a sanitized bowl or measuring cup, dissolve Lalvin yeast in 1.5 US fl oz (50 mL) of boiled water cooled to 104 to 109°F (40 to 43°C). Let stand for 15 minutes without stirring; then stir with a sanitized spoon to distribute yeast in water.

Brewer's Tip

If using unpasteurized apple juice, add 1 crushed campden tablet to each jug of apple juice 24 to 48 hours before brew day (or leave until sulphur smell goes away). Replace jug cap with a cotton ball to allow gas to escape but keep contaminants out.

Mint Mead (Still)

Equipment

- **brew kettle**
- **sanitized
  fermentation gear**

Brewer's Tip

For easier brewing, place
the mint in a hop bag
and add the bag to the
kettle. If you prefer to add
these ingredients directly
to the liquid, you will
need to be much more
careful about straining
the mead as it moves
through fermentation.

Yeast

2 packs	Wyeast 4184 or White Labs WLP720 (or 1 pack in starter) or Lalvin D-47	2 packs
5.5 US gal	brewing water	21 L
16 to 20 lbs	clover, orange-blossom or wildflower honey	7.25 to 9 kg
5 tsp	diammonium phosphate (DAP)	25 mL
2 tsp	yeast nutrient	10 mL
1 tsp	Irish moss	5 mL
4 oz	dried mint (your favorite type or a blend)	112 g

For bottling

2 tsp	potassium sorbate	10 mL

1. Prepare the liquid yeast in advance, according to the package directions (if using).
2. In brew kettle, bring 1 US gal (3.75 L) of the brewing water to a boil. Remove from heat. Stir in honey, diammonium phosphate, yeast nutrient, Irish moss and mint until honey, diammonium phosphate and nutrient have dissolved.
3. Return kettle to heat and bring mead mixture to a simmer. Simmer, uncovered, for 15 minutes. Monitor the liquid, using a spoon or strainer to remove and discard as much of the waxy meringue from the surface as possible.
4. Meanwhile, prepare the cooling bath or wort chiller.
5. At the end of 15 minutes, turn off the heat, cover kettle and transfer it into the prepared cooling bath (or use a wort chiller, according to the manufacturer's directions). Cool mead to the desired temperature, 75°F (24°C), within 30 to 45 minutes while you prepare the fermentation gear.
6. Clean and sanitize the spoon. Using sanitized racking cane and siphon, rack as much of the mead as possible into the sanitized primary fermenter. Then, using a sanitized funnel and straining screen, strain remaining mead into the fermenter. Add enough brewing water to bring volume to about 5.5 US gal (21 L). Using the hydrometer, take a reading of the specific gravity and record it in your brewing journal.
7. Add yeast to mead, stirring vigorously with sanitized spoon until evenly distributed. Seal fermenter with lid, stopper and airlock. Keep at room temperature (68 to 72°F/20 to 22°C) during primary fermentation, which typically lasts for 7 to 10 days after fermentation begins. (Keep fermenter in a dark place or under a lightproof cover if using a glass carboy.)

8. After 7 to 10 days or when the bubbling in airlock slows, gently rack the mead into secondary fermenter to avoid aerating it. Seal and keep at room temperature, covered or in a dark place, to allow fermentation to continue.

9. Once the bubbling in the airlock has slowed further, confirm completion of fermentation by using the hydrometer to take final gravity readings. (Hydrometer readings should be the same for several days in a row.)

10. Prime and bottle the mead using potassium sorbate (see page 263 for method) and condition for at least 3 months before sampling it.

To Hydrate Lalvin Yeast

In a sanitized bowl or measuring cup, dissolve Lalvin yeast in 1.5 US fl oz (50 mL) of boiled water cooled to 104 to 109°F (40 to 43°C). Let stand for 15 minutes without stirring; then stir with a sanitized spoon to distribute yeast in water.

The inclusion of dry malt extract means that this is one of the two recipes in this section that is not gluten-free.

Estimated Original Gravity: 1.081

Equipment

- **brew kettle**
- **sanitized fermentation gear**

Braggot (Sparkling)

Yeast

2 packs	Wyeast 4632 or White Labs WLP720 (or 1 pack in starter) or Lalvin D-47	2 packs
5.5 US gal	brewing water	21 L
5 lbs	any brand amber DME	2.25 kg
3 to 5 AAUs	Hallertau, Liberty or Mt Hood hops for bittering	3 to 5 AAUs
5 lbs	clover, orange-blossom or wildflower honey	2.25 kg
5 tsp	diammonium phosphate (DAP)	25 mL
2 tsp	yeast nutrient	10 mL
1 tsp	Irish moss	5 mL
.5 oz	Hallertau, Liberty or Mt Hood hops for aroma	14 g

For bottling

5 oz	dextrose (corn sugar)	140 g

1. Prepare the liquid yeast in advance, according to the package directions (if using).
2. In brew kettle, bring 1 US gal (3.75 L) of the brewing water to a boil. Remove from heat. Stir in bittering hops and malt, until malt has dissolved.
3. Return kettle to heat and bring to a rolling boil. Boil, uncovered, for 45 minutes. Monitor the liquid, using a spoon or strainer to keep any foam from sealing the top of the liquid.
4. Meanwhile, prepare the cooling bath or wort chiller.
5. After 45 minutes, remove kettle from heat and add honey, DAP, yeast nutrient and Irish moss. Stir to ensure that honey, DAP and nutrient have dissolved. Return kettle to burner and bring back to a rolling boil. Monitor the boil and remove and discard as much of the waxy meringue from the surface as possible. Boil for 15 minutes, uncovered, stir in the aroma hops, turn off heat and cover.
6. At the end of 15 minutes, turn off the heat, cover kettle and transfer it into the prepared cooling bath (or use a wort chiller, according to the manufacturer's directions). Cool mead to the desired temperature, 75°F (24°C), within 30 to 45 minutes while you prepare the fermentation gear.

7. While the wort is cooling, clean and sanitize the brewing spoon. When the wort has cooled, move the kettle to a counter and stir the wort briskly in one direction for about 5 minutes. After stirring, cover and let rest for 10 to 15 minutes as the hops and trub form a cone.

8. Using sanitized racking cane and siphon, rack as much of the mead as possible into the sanitized primary fermenter. Then, using a sanitized funnel and straining screen, strain remaining mead into the fermenter. Add enough brewing water to bring volume to about 5.5 US gal (21 L). Using the hydrometer, take a reading of the specific gravity and record it in your brewing journal.

9. Add yeast to mead, stirring vigorously with sanitized spoon until evenly distributed. Seal fermenter with lid, stopper and airlock. Keep at room temperature (68 to 72°F/20 to 22°C) during primary fermentation, which typically lasts for 7 to 10 days after fermentation begins. (Keep fermenter in a dark place or under a lightproof cover if using a glass carboy.)

10. After 7 to 10 days or when the kräusen has fallen, use sanitized racking cane and siphon to gently rack the mead into secondary fermenter. Avoid aerating it. Seal and keep at room temperature, covered or in a dark place, to allow fermentation to continue.

11. Once the bubbling in the airlock has slowed further, confirm completion of fermentation by using the hydrometer to take final gravity readings. (Hydrometer readings should be the same for several days in a row.)

12. Prime and bottle the mead using dextrose (see page 263 for method) and condition for at least 3 months before sampling it.

To Hydrate Lalvin Yeast

In a sanitized bowl or measuring cup, dissolve Lalvin yeast in 1.5 US fl oz (50 mL) of boiled water cooled to 104 to 109°F (40 to 43°C). Let stand for 15 minutes without stirring; then stir with a sanitized spoon to distribute yeast in water.

Bertha (Sparkling)

This is the second of the two recipes in this section that are not gluten-free. You need patience with this one—my version of this über braggot took five years to carbonate!

Estimated Original Gravity: 1.185

Equipment

- **large brew kettle**
- **sanitized fermentation gear (including blow-off hose)**

Brewer's Tips

For easier brewing, place the peel and spices in a hop bag and add the bag to the kettle. If you prefer to add these ingredients directly to the liquid, you will need to be much more careful about straining the mead as it moves through fermentation.

If active fermentation backs up into the airlock, replace airlock with blow-off hose (see page 16). Change water as needed; re-install airlock when fermentation settles down.

Yeast

2 packs	Wyeast 4632 or White Labs WLP099 (or 1 pack in starter) or Lalvin EC-1118	2 packs
1	pack Turbo Yeast 48-hour (secondary)	1
1 lb	any brand crystal malt grains (40 to 60 Lovibond)	450 g
1 lb	any brand toasted malt grains (50 to 70 Lovibond)	450 g
5.5 US gal	brewing water	21 L
12.2 lbs	any brand light malt extract	5.4 kg
25 to 30 AAUs	Columbus or Warrior hops for bittering	25 to 30 AAUs
12 lbs	orange-blossom honey	5.4 kg
5 tsp	diammonium phosphate (DAP)	25 mL
2 tsp	yeast nutrient	10 mL
1 tsp	Irish moss	5 mL
2 oz	sweet orange peel	56 g
1 oz	coriander seed, crushed	28 g
1 oz	Fuggle hops for aroma	28 g
5 tsp	yeast energizer	25 mL

For bottling

5 oz	dextrose (corn sugar)	140 g

1. Prepare liquid yeast in advance, according to directions (if using).
2. Coarsely crack the grains and place them in a grain bag.
3. In a brew kettle, bring at least 3 US gal (11 L) brewing water to steeping temperature (150 to 160°F/65 to 71°C). Turn off heat, add grain bag, cover and steep for 30 minutes. (If temperature drops below steeping temperature, reheat briefly.) Remove grain bag. Place in a strainer, rinse it over the kettle with steeping water and discard.
4. Increase the heat and bring grain tea to a boil. Remove from heat, add the malt extract and stir until dissolved.
5. Return kettle to burner and increase heat until wort begins to boil. Using a spoon, clear any foam. Reduce heat until rolling boil is maintained without foam buildup.
6. Add the bittering hops, stirring to combine. Boil for 45 minutes, uncovered. Monitor to prevent boiling over.
7. Meanwhile, prepare the fermentation gear and cooling bath or wort chiller.

8. After 45 minutes, remove kettle from heat and add honey, diammonium phosphate, yeast nutrient, Irish moss, orange peel and coriander seed. Stir to ensure that honey, diammonium phosphate and nutrient have dissolved. Return kettle to burner and bring back to a rolling boil. Boil for 15 minutes; stir in aroma hops, turn off heat and cover.

9. To cool, place the covered kettle in the prepared cooling bath or use a wort chiller according to the manufacturer's directions. Cool to the desired temperature, 75°F (24°C), within 30 to 45 minutes.

10. While the wort is cooling, clean and sanitize the brewing spoon. When the wort has cooled, move the kettle to a counter and stir the wort briskly in one direction for about 5 minutes. After stirring, cover and let rest for 10 to 15 minutes as the hops and trub form a cone.

11. Using sanitized racking cane and siphon, rack as much wort as possible into the sanitized primary fermenter. Then, using a sanitized funnel and straining screen, strain the remainder of the wort into the fermenter. Top off with brewing water to bring the volume to around 5.5 US gal (21 L). Using the hydrometer, take a reading of the specific gravity and record it in your brewing journal.

12. Add the yeast; vigorously stir it with a sanitized spoon to distribute it throughout. Seal the fermenter with lid, stopper and airlock. Keep the fermenter at room temperature (68 to 72°F/20 to 22°C) during primary fermentation, which will be lengthy. (Keep in a dark place or under a lightproof cover if using a glass carboy.)

13. When the kräusen has fallen, use a sanitized racking cane and siphon to gently rack mead into sanitized secondary fermenter. Avoid aerating it. Add Turbo Yeast and yeast energizer. Seal and keep at room temperature, covered or in a dark place, to allow fermentation to continue.

14. Once bubbling in airlock has slowed, use a sanitized racking cane and siphon to gently rack mead into sanitized tertiary fermenter. Seal and keep at room temperature, covered or in a dark place, to allow fermentation to finish. Confirm completion of fermentation by using hydrometer to take final gravity readings. (Hydrometer readings should be the same for several days in a row.)

15. Prime and bottle the mead using dextrose (see page 263 for method) and condition.

To Hydrate Lalvin Yeast

In a sanitized bowl or measuring cup, dissolve Lalvin yeast in 1.5 US fl oz (50 mL) of boiled water cooled to 104 to 109°F (40 to 43°C). Let stand for 15 minutes without stirring; then stir with a sanitized spoon to distribute yeast in water.

Making ciders is another fun activity to try with your brewing gear.

If you can obtain a variety of apples, as well as a juicer or a press, you can select your own mix of apples and make your own apple juice. If that's the case, you'll want about 20% of the mix to be high-acid apples such as Granny Smiths or even crabapples. If you're a bit more urban, you can ferment juice or cider you buy at the farmers' market or grocery store. Just remember that the juice or cider you start with must be free of preservatives.

There is limited cooking required—you don't cook the juice—you just boil a small quantity of water in which the dextrose (or other sugar), acid blend and yeast nutrient are dissolved. Once again, unless you decide to experiment with malt as an adjunct sugar, these ciders are gluten-free.

Ciders

Hard Cider

Preparing Juice or Cider

If the juice or cider is not pasteurized, add 5 campden tablets to each 5 US gal (19 L) of juice or cider to inhibit any wild yeast, just as you did for the fruit beers.

You will also need to add winemakers' acid blend (equal parts citric, malic and tartaric acids) to all juice or cider to compensate for the low acidity, adding more as needed to sharpen up the taste.

Add pectic enzyme (pectinase) to the primary fermenter to remove the haze in the cider, particularly if the juice has been pasteurized. Pectic enzyme is sold in several different forms and its use varies with the form, so use according to package instructions.

Equipment

- **large pot**
- **sanitized fermentation gear**

Yeast

2 packs	Wyeast 4776 or White Labs WLP775 (or 1 pack in starter)	2 packs
	OR	
2 packs	Lalvin D-47	2 packs
2 US qt	brewing water	1.9 L
3 to 4 lbs	dextrose or other sugar (see Brewer's Tip)	1.36 to 1.8 kg
+/-5 tsp	acid blend	+/-25 mL
5 tsp	yeast nutrient	25 mL
5 US gal	preservative-free apple juice or cider	19 L
5	campden tablets (if juice is unpasteurized), crushed	5
	Pectic enzyme, according to package directions	

For bottling

5 oz	dextrose (corn sugar), for priming	140 g

1. Prepare the liquid yeast in advance, according to package directions (if using).
2. In a large pot, bring water to a boil. Remove from heat. Stir in dextrose, acid blend and yeast nutrient until dextrose, acid blend and nutrient have dissolved.
3. Return the pot to heat and bring dextrose mixture to a boil. Remove from heat, cover and cool to the desired temperature, 75°F (24°C). (Use a cooling bath, if desired.)
4. Meanwhile, prepare the fermentation bucket.
5. Clean and sanitize brewing spoon. Add juice or cider to sanitized primary fermenter. Add the dextrose mixture, campden tablets (if using), pectic enzyme and yeast, stirring vigorously with sanitized spoon until evenly distributed. Use sanitized hydrometer to take a reading of original gravity, and record it in your brewing journal.
6. Seal fermenter with lid, stopper and airlock. Keep at room temperature (68 to 72°F/20 to 22°C) during primary fermentation of 1 to 2 weeks. (Keep fermenter in a dark place or under a lightproof cover if using a glass carboy.)
7. Using sanitized racking cane and siphon, gently rack the cider into sanitized secondary fermenter to avoid aerating it. Seal with stopper and airlock and keep at room temperature, in a dark place or covered, to allow fermentation to continue.

8. Once the bubbling in the airlock has slowed, confirm completion of fermentation by using the hydrometer to take final gravity readings. (Hydrometer readings should be the same for several days in a row.)

9. Prime and bottle the cider using dextrose, according to the instructions on page 263, and condition for at least 6 months before sampling it.

Variation

Berry or Stone Fruit Cider: To add flavor from fruits such as blueberries, cherries or cranberries, add 8 to 16 US fl oz (240 to 475 mL) 100% pure juice concentrate to the secondary fermenter in Step 7.

Brewer's Tips

Dextrose is the most neutral sugar (that is, it contributes the least flavor) but feel free to experiment with portions of different sugars such as raw sugar, maple syrup or honey.

For information on preparing a yeast starter, see page 262.

To Hydrate Lalvin Yeast

In a sanitized bowl or measuring cup, dissolve Lalvin yeast in 1.5 US fl oz (50 mL) of boiled water cooled to 104 to 109°F (40 to 43°C). Let stand for 15 minutes without stirring; then stir with a sanitized spoon to distribute yeast in water.

This cider will have the classic barnyard character of Normandy cider.

Estimated Original Gravity: will vary according to the sugar content of the apple juice. Final gravity is usually below 1.000.

Preparing Juice or Cider

If the juice or cider is not pasteurized, add 5 campden tablets to each 5 US gal (19 L) of juice or cider to inhibit any wild yeast, just as you did for the fruit beers.

You will also need to add winemakers' acid blend (equal parts citric, malic and tartaric acids) to all juice or cider to compensate for the low acidity, adding more as needed to sharpen up the taste.

Add pectic enzyme (pectinase) to the primary fermenter to remove the haze in the cider, particularly if the juice has been pasteurized. Pectic enzyme is sold in several different forms and its use varies with the form, so use according to package instructions.

Equipment

- **large pot**
- **sanitized fermentation gear**

Cider with Brettanomyces

Yeast

2 packs	Wyeast 4776 or White Labs WLP775 (or 1 pack in starter)	2 packs
	OR	
2 packs	Lalvin D-47	2 packs
	AND	
1 pack	Wyeast 5112 or White Labs WLP650 (secondary yeast)	1 pack
2 US qt	brewing water	1.9 L
3 to 4 lbs	dextrose or other sugar (see Brewer's Tip)	1.36 to 1.8 kg
+/-5 tsp	acid blend	+/-25 mL
5 tsp	yeast nutrient	25 mL
5 US gal	preservative-free apple juice or cider	19 L
5	campden tablets (if juice is unpasteurized), crushed	5
	Pectic enzyme, according to package directions	

For bottling

5 oz	dextrose (corn sugar), for priming	140 g

1. Prepare the liquid yeast in advance, according to package directions (if using).
2. In a large pot, bring water to a boil. Remove from heat. Stir in dextrose, acid blend and yeast nutrient until dextrose, acid blend and nutrient have dissolved.
3. Return the pot to heat and bring dextrose mixture to a boil. Remove from heat, cover and cool to the desired temperature, 75°F (24°C). (Use a cooling bath, if desired.)
4. Meanwhile, prepare the fermentation bucket.
5. Clean and sanitize brewing spoon. Add juice or cider to sanitized primary fermenter. Add the dextrose mixture, campden tablets (if using), pectic enzyme and yeast, stirring vigorously with sanitized spoon until evenly distributed. Use sanitized hydrometer to take a reading of original gravity, and record it in your brewing journal.
6. Seal fermenter with lid, stopper and airlock. Keep at room temperature (68 to 72°F/20 to 22°C) during primary fermentation of 1 to 2 weeks. (Keep fermenter in a dark place or under a lightproof cover if using a glass carboy.)

7. Using sanitized racking cane and siphon, gently rack the cider into sanitized secondary fermenter to avoid aerating it. Seal with stopper and airlock and keep at room temperature, in a dark place or covered, to allow fermentation to continue.

8. Once the bubbling in the airlock has slowed, sanitize the two remaining yeast packs. Pour yeast into the cider, reseal the fermenter and leave for 2 to 4 more weeks. Confirm completion of fermentation by using the hydrometer to take final gravity readings. (Hydrometer readings should be the same for several days in a row.)

9. Prime and bottle the cider using dextrose, according to the instructions on page 263, and condition for at least 6 months before sampling it.

Brewer's Tips

Dextrose is the most neutral sugar (that is, it contributes the least flavor) but feel free to experiment with portions of different sugars such as raw sugar, maple syrup or honey.

For information on preparing a yeast starter, see page 262.

For information on working with wild secondary yeasts, see page 348.

To Hydrate Lalvin Yeast

In a sanitized bowl or measuring cup, dissolve Lalvin yeast in 1.5 US fl oz (50 mL) of boiled water cooled to 104 to 109°F (40 to 43°C). Let stand for 15 minutes without stirring; then stir with a sanitized spoon to distribute yeast in water.

Sweet Cider

Estimated Original
Gravity: will vary
according to the sugar
content of the apple
juice. Final gravity is
usually below 1.000.

Preparing Juice or Cider

If the juice or cider is
not pasteurized, add
1 campden tablet for each
1 US gal (3.75 L) of juice
or cider to inhibit any wild
yeast, just as you did for
the fruit beers.

You will also need to
add winemakers' acid
blend (equal parts citric,
malic and tartaric acids)
to all juice or cider to
compensate for the low
acidity, adding more as
needed to sharpen up
the taste.

Add pectic enzyme
(pectinase) to the primary
fermenter to remove
the haze in the cider,
particularly if the juice
has been pasteurized.
Pectic enzyme is sold in
several different forms
and its use varies with the
form, so use according to
package instructions.

Equipment

- **large pot**
- **sanitized
  fermentation gear**

Yeast

2 packs	Wyeast 1099 or White Labs WLP005 (or 1 pack in starter)	2 packs
	OR	
2 packs	Fermentis S-33	2 packs
2 US qt	brewing water	1.9 L
3 to 4 lbs	dextrose or other sugar (see Brewer's Tip)	1.36 to 1.8 kg
1 lb	lactose	450 g
+/-5 tsp	acid blend	+/-25 mL
5 tsp	yeast nutrient	25 mL
5 US gal	preservative-free apple juice or cider	19 L
5	campden tablets (if juice is unpasteurized), crushed	5
	Pectic enzyme, according to package directions	

For bottling

5 oz	dextrose (corn sugar), for priming	140 g

1. Prepare the liquid yeast in advance, according to package directions (if using).
2. In a large pot, bring water to a boil. Remove from heat. Stir in dextrose, lactose, acid blend and yeast nutrient until dextrose, lactose, acid blend and nutrient have dissolved.
3. Return the pot to heat and bring dextrose mixture to a boil. Remove from heat, cover and cool to the desired temperature, 75°F (24°C). (Use a cooling bath, if desired.)
4. Meanwhile, prepare the fermentation bucket.
5. Clean and sanitize brewing spoon. Add juice or cider to sanitized primary fermenter. Add the dextrose mixture, campden tablets (if using), pectic enzyme and yeast, stirring vigorously with sanitized spoon until evenly distributed. Use sanitized hydrometer to take a reading of original gravity, and record it in your brewing journal.
6. Seal fermenter with lid, stopper and airlock. Keep at room temperature (68 to 72°F/20 to 22°C) during primary fermentation of 1 to 2 weeks. (Keep fermenter in a dark place or under a lightproof cover if using a glass carboy.)
7. Using sanitized racking cane and siphon, gently rack the cider into sanitized secondary fermenter to avoid aerating it. Seal with stopper and airlock and keep at room temperature, in a dark place or covered, to allow fermentation to continue.

8. Once the bubbling in the airlock has slowed, confirm completion of fermentation by using the hydrometer to take final gravity readings. (Hydrometer readings should be the same for several days in a row.)

9. Prime and bottle the cider using dextrose, according to the instructions on page 263, and condition for at least 6 months before sampling it.

Brewer's Tips

Dextrose is the most neutral sugar (that is, it contributes the least flavor) but feel free to experiment with portions of different sugars such as raw sugar, maple syrup or honey.

For information on preparing a yeast starter, see page 262.

Perry (Pear Cider)

Preparing Juice or Cider

If the juice or cider is not pasteurized, add 1 campden tablet for each 1 US gal (3.75 L) of juice or cider to inhibit any wild yeast, just as you did for the fruit beers.

You will also need to add winemakers' acid blend (equal parts citric, malic and tartaric acids) to all juice or cider to compensate for the low acidity, adding more as needed to sharpen up the taste.

Add pectic enzyme (pectinase) to the primary fermenter to remove the haze in the cider, particularly if the juice has been pasteurized. Pectic enzyme is sold in several different forms and its use varies with the form, so use according to package instructions.

Equipment

- **large pot**
- **sanitized fermentation gear**

Yeast

2 packs	Wyeast 4776 or White Labs WLP775 (or 1 pack in starter)	2 packs
	OR	
2 packs	Lalvin D-47	2 packs
2 US qt	brewing water	1.9 L
3 to 4 lbs	dextrose or other sugar (see Brewer's Tip)	1.36 to 1.8 kg
+/-5 tsp	acid blend	+/-25 mL
5 tsp	yeast nutrient	25 mL
5 US gal	preservative-free pear juice	19 L
5	campden tablets (if juice is unpasteurized), crushed	5
	Pectic enzyme, according to package directions	

For bottling

5 oz	dextrose (corn sugar), for priming	140 g

1. Prepare the liquid yeast in advance, according to package directions (if using).
2. In a large pot, bring water to a boil. Remove from heat. Stir in dextrose, acid blend and yeast nutrient until dextrose, acid blend and nutrient have dissolved.
3. Return the pot to heat and bring dextrose mixture to a boil. Remove from heat, cover and cool to the desired temperature, 75°F (24°C). (Use a cooling bath, if desired.)
4. Meanwhile, prepare the fermentation bucket.
5. Clean and sanitize brewing spoon. Add juice or cider to sanitized primary fermenter. Add the dextrose mixture, campden tablets (if using), pectic enzyme and yeast, stirring vigorously with sanitized spoon until evenly distributed. Use sanitized hydrometer to take a reading of original gravity, and record it in your brewing journal.
6. Seal fermenter with lid, stopper and airlock. Keep at room temperature (68 to 72°F/20 to 22°C) during primary fermentation of 1 to 2 weeks. (Keep fermenter in a dark place or under a lightproof cover if using a glass carboy.)
7. Using sanitized racking cane and siphon, gently rack the cider into sanitized secondary fermenter to avoid aerating it. Seal with stopper and airlock and keep at room temperature, in a dark place or covered, to allow fermentation to continue.

8. Once the bubbling in the airlock has slowed, confirm completion of fermentation by using the hydrometer to take final gravity readings. (Hydrometer readings should be the same for several days in a row.)

9. Prime and bottle the cider using dextrose, according to the instructions on page 263, and condition for at least 6 months before sampling it.

Brewer's Tips

Dextrose is the most neutral sugar (that is, it contributes the least flavor) but feel free to experiment with portions of different sugars such as raw sugar, maple syrup or honey.

For information on preparing a yeast starter, see page 262.

Asian Pear Cider

Preparing Juice or Cider

If the juice or cider is not pasteurized, add 1 campden tablet for each 1 US gal (3.75 L) of juice or cider to inhibit any wild yeast, just as you did for the fruit beers.

You will also need to add winemakers' acid blend (equal parts citric, malic and tartaric acids) to all juice or cider to compensate for the low acidity, adding more as needed to sharpen up the taste.

Add pectic enzyme (pectinase) to the primary fermenter to remove the haze in the cider, particularly if the juice has been pasteurized. Pectic enzyme is sold in several different forms and its use varies with the form, so use according to package instructions.

Equipment

- **large pot**
- **sanitized fermentation gear**

Yeast

2 packs	Lalvin D-47	2 packs
2 US qt	brewing water	1.9 L
3 to 4 lbs	dextrose or other sugar (see Brewer's Tip)	1.36 to 1.8 kg
+/-5 tsp	acid blend	+/-25 mL
5 tsp	yeast nutrient	25 mL
5 US gal	preservative-free Asian pear juice	19 L
5	campden tablets (if juice is unpasteurized), crushed	5
	Pectic enzyme, according to package directions	

For bottling

5 oz	dextrose (corn sugar), for priming	140 g

1. Rehydrate yeast according to package directions.
2. In a large pot, bring water to a boil. Remove from heat. Stir in dextrose, acid blend and yeast nutrient until dextrose, acid blend and nutrient have dissolved.
3. Return the pot to heat and bring dextrose mixture to a boil. Remove from heat, cover and cool to the desired temperature, 75°F (24°C). (Use a cooling bath, if desired.)
4. Meanwhile, prepare the fermentation bucket.
5. Clean and sanitize brewing spoon. Add juice to sanitized primary fermenter. Add the dextrose mixture, campden tablets (if using), pectic enzyme and yeast, stirring vigorously with sanitized spoon until evenly distributed. Use sanitized hydrometer to take a reading of original gravity, and record it in your brewing journal.
6. Seal fermenter with lid, stopper and airlock. Keep at room temperature (68 to 72°F/20 to 22°C) during primary fermentation of 1 to 2 weeks. (Keep fermenter in a dark place or under a lightproof cover if using a glass carboy.)
7. Using sanitized racking cane and siphon, gently rack the cider into sanitized secondary fermenter to avoid aerating it. Seal with stopper and airlock and keep at room temperature, in a dark place or covered, to allow fermentation to continue.

8. Once the bubbling in the airlock has slowed, confirm completion of fermentation by using the hydrometer to take final gravity readings. (Hydrometer readings should be the same for several days in a row.)

9. Prime and bottle the cider using dextrose, according to the instructions on page 263, and condition for at least 6 months before sampling it.

Brewer's Tip

Dextrose is the most neutral sugar (that is, it contributes the least flavor) but feel free to experiment with portions of different sweeteners such as raw sugar, maple syrup, honey or Demerara sugar. Include these to help make up the total amount of sweetener.

The easiest sodas to make at home are the ones made from concentrates. If you're making sodas for or with kids, the products made from concentrates will taste the most like store-bought sodas. The concentrates come in all the classic soda flavors and make about 4 US gallons (15 L) of soda. All you need is a concentrate, some sugar, champagne yeast and plastic soda bottles. The concentrate package will tell you the step-by-step process.

The recipes in this section are for sodas made from scratch, using herbs and spices. Mix and bottle the soda on the same day; the only fermentation required is for carbonating the drink.

The shelf life of homemade soda is much shorter than that of homemade beer or ciders, so don't make more than you can fit into your refrigerator or drink within three months!

Scratch Sodas

Root Beer

Preparing Vanilla Beans

Slit the bean open and scrape the inside with a knife blade. Add the skin, seeds and any pulp on the knife to the hop bag.

Brewer's Tips

Since sodas carbonate in their bottles, PET bottles are recommended because the plastic best withstands the pressure and the bottle itself makes it easy to judge the progress of carbonation.

When uncapping your cold soda, do so slowly in order to slowly release the pressure inside.

Flavorings

2 oz	wintergreen, dried	56 g
2 oz	birch bark, shredded	56 g
2 oz	sarsaparilla, shredded	56 g
2 oz	licorice root or bark	56 g
2 oz	sassafras root	56 g
2 to 3	star anise	2 to 3
1	vanilla bean (see sidebar)	1
1	cinnamon stick, coarsely chopped	1
5 US gal	brewing water	19 L

Sugars

3 US qts	amber, Barbados or baking molasses	2.8 L
1 lb	Demerara or other raw sugar	450 g
8 oz	malto-dextrin powder	224 g

Yeast

1 pack	Lalvin EC1118 dry yeast	1 pack

1. Put the wintergreen, birch bark, sarsaparilla, licorice root, sassafras root, star anise, vanilla bean and cinnamon stick in a hop bag.
2. In a medium pot, bring about 1 US gal (3.75 L) brewing water to a boil and add molasses, sugar and malto-dextrin powder, stirring to dissolve. Add hop bag and bring back to a boil.
3. Turn off the heat, cover and steep for 2 hours. Remove hop bag and discard.
4. Meanwhile, sanitize bottles and bottling bucket.
5. In a sanitized bowl or measuring cup, dissolve the yeast in 1.5 US fl oz (50 mL) of boiled water cooled to 104 to 109°F (40 to 43°C). Let stand for 15 minutes without stirring, then stir well with a sanitized spoon to distribute yeast in water, creating a yeast slurry.
6. Add remaining 4 US gal (15.2 L) brewing water to sanitized bottling bucket. Pour in steeping mixture and yeast slurry and stir vigorously with a sanitized spoon.
7. Fill sanitized bottles, leaving 1 inch (2.5 cm) of headroom, and cap.
8. Store bottles at cool room temperature for 2 to 7 days or until bottle begins to feel hard from the buildup of carbonation pressure. Bottles can safely sit at cool room temperature for up to 2 weeks. Move bottles to the refrigerator and store for no longer than 3 months.

Birch Beer

Equipment

- **hop bag**
- **medium pot**
- **sanitized small bowl**
- **sanitized bottling bucket**
- **sanitized PET (polyethylene terephthalate) bottles and caps**

Brewer's Tips

Since sodas carbonate in their bottles, PET bottles are recommended because the plastic best withstands the pressure and the bottle itself makes it easy to judge the progress of carbonation.

When uncapping your cold soda, do so slowly in order to slowly release the pressure inside.

To Hydrate Lalvin Yeast

In a sanitized bowl or measuring cup, dissolve Lalvin yeast in 1.5 US fl oz (50 mL) of boiled water cooled to 104 to 109°F (40 to 43°C). Let stand for 15 minutes without stirring; then stir with a sanitized spoon to distribute yeast in water.

Flavorings

4 oz	birch root, shredded	112 g
1 oz	wintergreen, dried	28 g
2 to 3	cinnamon sticks, coarsely chopped	2 to 3
5 US gal	brewing water	19 L

Sugars

4 lbs	turbinado sugar	1.8 kg
1 cup	blackstrap molasses	250 mL
8 oz	malto-dextrin powder	224 g

Yeast

1 pack	Lalvin EC1118 dry yeast	1 pack

1. Put the birch root, wintergreen and cinnamon sticks in a hop bag.
2. In a medium pot, bring about 1 US gal (3.75 L) brewing water to a boil and add sugar, molasses and malto-dextrin powder, stirring to dissolve. Add hop bag and bring back to a boil.
3. Turn off the heat, cover and steep for 2 hours. Remove hop bag and discard.
4. Meanwhile, sanitize bottles and bottling bucket.
5. In a sanitized bowl or measuring cup, dissolve the yeast in 1.5 US fl oz (50 mL) of boiled water cooled to 104 to 109°F (40 to 43°C). Let stand for 15 minutes without stirring, then stir well with a sanitized spoon to distribute yeast in water, creating a yeast slurry.
6. Add remaining 4 US gal (15.2 L) brewing water to sanitized bottling bucket. Pour in steeping mixture; and yeast slurry and stir vigorously with a sanitized spoon.
7. Fill sanitized bottles, leaving 1 inch (2.5 cm) of headroom, and cap.
8. Store bottles at cool room temperature for 2 to 7 days or until bottle begins to feel hard from the buildup of carbonation pressure. Bottles can safely sit at cool room temperature for up to 2 weeks. Move bottles to the refrigerator and store for no longer than 3 months.

Cream Soda

This soda contains dry malt extract and therefore is not gluten-free.

Equipment

- **hop bag**
- **medium pot**
- **sanitized small bowl**
- **sanitized bottling bucket**
- **sanitized PET (polyethylene terephthalate) bottles and caps**

Preparing Vanilla Beans

Slit the bean open and scrape the inside with a knife blade. Add the skin, seeds and any pulp on the knife to the hop bag.

Brewer's Tips

Since sodas carbonate in their bottles, PET bottles are recommended because the plastic best withstands the pressure and the bottle itself makes it easy to judge the progress of carbonation.

When uncapping your cold soda, do so slowly in order to slowly release the pressure inside.

Flavorings

4 to 6	vanilla beans, each about 6 inches (15 cm) long	4 to 6
1	cinnamon stick, coarsely chopped	1
1 tsp	cream of tartar	5 mL
5 US gal	brewing water	19 L

Sugars

1 cup	amber dry malt extract (DME)	250 mL
4 lbs	turbinado sugar	1.8 kg

Yeast

1 pack	Lalvin EC1118 dry yeast	1 pack

1. Put the vanilla beans and cinnamon sticks only in a hop bag.
2. In a medium pot, bring about 1 US gal (3.75 L) brewing water to a boil and add DME and sugar, stirring to dissolve. Add hop bag and bring back to a boil.
3. Turn off the heat, add the cream of tartar, cover and steep for 2 hours. Remove hop bag and discard.
4. Meanwhile, sanitize bottles and bottling bucket.
5. In a sanitized bowl or measuring cup, dissolve the yeast in 1.5 US fl oz (50 mL) of boiled water cooled to 104 to 109°F (40 to 43°C). Let stand for 15 minutes without stirring, then stir well with a sanitized spoon to distribute yeast in water, creating a yeast slurry.
6. Add remaining 4 US gal (15.2 L) brewing water to sanitized bottling bucket. Pour in steeping mixture; add yeast slurry and stir vigorously with a sanitized spoon.
7. Fill sanitized bottles, leaving 1 inch (2.5 cm) of headroom, and cap.
8. Store bottles at cool room temperature for 2 to 7 days or until bottle begins to feel hard from the buildup of carbonation pressure. Bottles can safely sit at cool room temperature for up to 2 weeks. Move bottles to the refrigerator and store for no longer than 3 months.

Ginger Ale

This soda contains malt extract and therefore is not gluten-free.

Equipment

- **hop bag**
- **medium pot**
- **sanitized small bowl**
- **sanitized bottling bucket**
- **sanitized PET (polyethylene terephthalate) bottles and caps**

Brewer's Tips

Since sodas carbonate in their bottles, PET bottles are recommended because the plastic best withstands the pressure and the bottle itself makes it easy to judge the progress of carbonation.

When uncapping your cold soda, do so slowly in order to slowly release the pressure inside.

To Hydrate Lalvin Yeast

In a sanitized bowl or measuring cup, dissolve Lalvin yeast in 1.5 US fl oz (50 mL) of boiled water cooled to 104 to 109°F (40 to 43°C). Let stand for 15 minutes without stirring; then stir with a sanitized spoon to distribute yeast in water.

Flavoring

10 oz	fresh gingerroot, peeled and coarsely grated or chopped	284 g
2 tsp	citric acid	10 mL
5 US gal	brewing water	19 L

Sugars

4 lbs	any brand light malt extract	1.8 kg
8 oz	malto-dextrin powder	224 g

Yeast

1 pack	Lalvin EC1118 dry yeast	1 pack

1. Put the gingerroot in a hop bag.
2. In a medium pot, bring about 1 US gal (3.75 L) brewing water to a boil and add malt extract and malto-dextrin powder, stirring to dissolve. Add hop bag and bring back to a boil.
3. Turn off the heat, add citric acid, cover and steep for 2 hours. Remove hop bag and discard.
4. Meanwhile, sanitize bottles and bottling bucket.
5. In a sanitized bowl or measuring cup, dissolve the yeast in 1.5 US fl oz (50 mL) of boiled water cooled to 104 to 109°F (40 to 43°C). Let stand for 15 minutes without stirring, then stir well with a sanitized spoon to distribute yeast in water, creating a yeast slurry.
6. Add remaining 4 US gal (15.2 L) brewing water to sanitized bottling bucket. Pour in steeping mixture; add yeast slurry and stir vigorously with a sanitized spoon.
7. Fill sanitized bottles, leaving 1 inch (2.5 cm) of headroom, and cap.
8. Store bottles at cool room temperature for 2 to 7 days or until bottle begins to feel hard from the buildup of carbonation pressure. Bottles can safely sit at cool room temperature for up to 2 weeks. Move bottles to the refrigerator and store for no longer than 3 months.

Glassware and The "Beer Clean Glass" (BCG)

An important part of enjoying a homebrew (or any other beer) is seeing it in a proper glass that is properly clean. (Drinking from said glass also adds to the enjoyment.) The correct glass showcases the beer's qualities and is designed to maximize the enjoyment of a particular style of beer. The chart below will help you select the correct glass for your beer.

Glass Type	Beer Type
• straight-sided pint glass	• most ale styles
• bulbous-top pint glass	• porters and stouts
• Pilsner glass	• Pilsner, blonde ale and cream ale
• mug	• Oktoberfest beer and dark lagers
• snifter	• old ales, imperial stout and barley wine
• tulip glass	• most Belgian ales
• chalice	• Belgian abbey styles
• chunky tumbler	• Belgian wit
• wheat beer glass (tall glass, similar to Pilsner with a fatter bottom)	• Bavarian weizen
• champagne flute	• fruit beers and lambics

The "Beer Clean Glass" (BCG)

A properly clean glass is as important to your enjoyment of the brew as the correct glass is. Commercial beers include "heading agents" in their formulation to compensate for less-than-ideal serving situations. Rather than add chemicals to your beer, just be sure that your glassware is "beer clean."

Never use soap or detergent on beer glasses (or on any of your beer gear, for that matter). Use the homebrew cleanser that you use to clean your brewing gear to clean your glassware. Refer to the recommended cleansers in the list of gear (see page 14) for cleaners. (Hint: B-Brite really makes glass shine.)

Glossary

adhesive strip thermometer: a flexible thermometer that can be permanently affixed to the outside of a clean, dry fermenter; used to monitor temperature during fermentation

airlock: a one-way trap valve filled with sanitizing solution; allows the pressure built up during fermentation to escape without allowing air or microorganisms to enter the fermenter

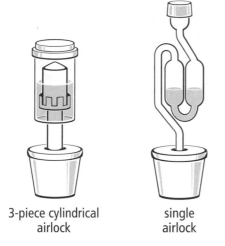

3-piece cylindrical airlock   single airlock

ale: beer fermented at temperatures above 60°F (15°C)

ale yeast: yeast that works at the top of the fermenter; used for making ales

alpha acid: The component in hops that provides bitterness to the beer. Different hops have different amounts of bitterness (and different alpha acid numbers) that may vary from crop to crop.

auto-siphon: a racking cane with a pump fitted around it

avinator: used to pump sanitizer into bottles

blow-off hose: a piece of plastic that temporarily replaces the airlock. When fermentation becomes particularly active, installation of a blow-off hose allows excess foam to escape from the fermenter.

blow-off hose

bottle capper: a crimping tool used to attach caps to bottles; avoid the old hammer-style capper

bottle conditioning: the storage of beer after bottling and prior to consumption; the process used by homebrewers to naturally carbonate their beer and allow flavors to mellow with time

bottle filler/bottle filler wand: a rigid plastic rod with a valve tip that attaches to the siphon hose or bottling bucket to fill bottles

bottling bucket: bucket made of food-grade plastic, usually with a faucet; can double as primary fermenter if fitted with a lid

brettanomyces (pronounced breht-tan-uh-MI-sees): naturally occurring yeast (fungus) that lives in the wild on the skins of fruit; often associated with contamination, it can be used to create a funky brew

campden tablets: potassium metabisulphite in convenient tablet form; used by brewers to de-chlorinate water or to inhibit the growth of wild yeast on fruit when making fruit beers

carboy: a large, narrow-necked glass bottle, usually used as a secondary (or tertiary) fermenter; if used as a primary fermenter, must be at least 25% larger than the size of the batch

cold break: as wort chills, proteins and tannins in solution coagulate and settle out; this is called cold break

condition: leaving beer to mellow, mature and carbonate

dextrose: corn sugar, also sometimes called brewing sugar; used as a priming sugar to carbonate beer. May be used as a kettle sugar in some beers.

final gravity (FG): the specific gravity of beer at the end of fermentation

food-grade plastic: Plastic that has been deemed safe for contact with food (especially alcohol!). All plastic components used in brewing should be food-grade plastic.

grain bag: a small bag made of either cheesecloth or nylon; used to hold grains and make their removal from the brew kettle easy

hop bag: a small bag made of either cheesecloth or nylon; used to hold hops and make their removal from the brew kettle or fermenter easy

hops: the bitter flower of the plant *humulus lupus*; used in the brewing process for its preservative, bitter and aromatic properties

hot break: thick foam that forms in the brew kettle on the surface of nearly boiling wort; composed mostly of protein and tannins

hydrometer: A device that measures the specific gravity (density) of wort or beer in relationship to that of water. It is used to determine the strength of beer and the conclusion of fermentation. (See page 26 for instructions on how to take a hydrometer reading.)

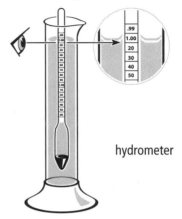

hydrometer

Irish moss: neither Irish nor moss; it's actually seaweed also known as carrageenan; used to clarify beer

kettle sugars: sugars that are added to the kettle during the brewing process; could be in the form of granular sugar, molasses or syrup; provide food for the yeast during fermentation as well as adding color, aroma and flavor to the brew

kräusen (pronounced KROY-zen): from German, literally meaning "crown"; refers to the crown of foam that appears on fermenting beer

lactose: non-fermentable sugar derived from milk

lager: beer fermented at temperatures below 60°F(15°C)

lager yeast: yeast that works at the bottom of the fermenter; used for making lagers

late extract addition: addition of the bulk (or at least half) of a brew's malt extract to the kettle during the boil's final 15 minutes to cut down on caramelization and darkening; method used in lighter or stronger malt-heavy beers

Lovibond: the darkness of a malt's roast is measured in degrees Lovibond; scale ranges from 1 to 3 for Pils and pale malts to as high as 500 or more for dark-roasted grains

malt extract: sugar derived from malted grains; comes in two forms: dry (DME) or liquid (syrup)

malted grains: Grains with enzymes that had activated and started to convert starch to sugar but were then roasted to arrest the process. Usually barley; can also be wheat, rye or oats.

original gravity (OG): the specific gravity of wort at the beginning of fermentation; the benchmark for evaluating fermentation of the batch

primary fermenter: oversized (by 25 to 30%) sealable container used for the initial stage of fermentation; usually opaque and made from food-grade plastic or glass

priming sugar: sugar (often dextrose) added at the time of bottling to carbonate the beer

racking: the process of siphoning beer from one container to another while leaving waste products (sediments) behind

racking cane: a clear plastic tube, usually curved at the top, with a cup-like filter on the tip; attaches to the siphoning tube and

used to assist siphoning of beer into another container while leaving the waste products behind

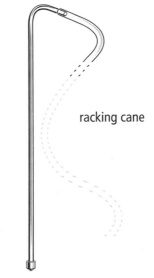

racking cane

sanitize: to take a clean object (usually a piece of gear) and soak it in sanitizing solution for the prescribed time; goal is to eliminate potential contaminants after the boil

secondary fermenter: sealable vessel, usually glass, the same size as the batch; used for the secondary (or tertiary) fermentation; if glass, must be covered to prevent light from oxidizing the brew during fermentation

siphon hose: length of flexible, clear vinyl tubing fitted with a flow-regulating clamp; used in conjunction with racking cane, bottle filler (during bottling) and containers such as fermenters or bottling bucket

specific gravity: the weight (density) of a liquid compared to that of water

straining bag: reusable bag for holding fruit pulp but allowing juice to flow out; bags come in a variety of sizes and degrees of filtering (e.g., coarse or fine)

The Thief: a combination of hydrometer and sample tube that simplifies the task of taking a sample and measuring the specific gravity; if sanitized, sample can be returned to the container

trub: waste products of cooking and fermentation

yeast: The organism that converts sugar to alcohol and CO_2; only use brewing yeast (or occasionally wine yeast). Never substitute baking yeast for brewing yeasts. (Brewing yeast can be used for baking.)

yeast energizer: a mixture of nutrients and minerals designed to restart stuck fermentations or coax along stronger beers

yeast nutrient: a mixture of nutrients and trace minerals designed to get yeast working as quickly as possible

wort: unfermented beer; sometimes called "sweet wort" before the addition of hops

wort aerator: a small diffuser that attaches to the end of the siphon tube going into the new container; it is only used to add air to the brew before primary fermentation

wort chiller: a heat exchanger used to rapidly drop the temperature of boiled wort

wort chiller

Library and Archives Canada Cataloguing in Publication

Hummel, George, 1954–
    The complete homebrew beer book : 200 easy recipes from ales & lagers to extreme beers & international favorites / George Hummel.

Includes index.
ISBN 978-0-7788-0268-6

    1. Beer. 2. Brewing—Amateurs' manuals. I. Title.

TP570.H86 2011   641.8'73   C2010-907386-X

Index